I want B facing forward in frame 2... But B talks first... And...
1
2
1
2
2
1

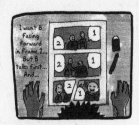

岸本斉史

I've recently been feeling the limits of expression in manga. With manga's particular style of reading from top right to bottom left, the order of dialogue severely limits the angle of the camera... Isn't there another way...?

—Masashi Kishimoto, 2003

Author/artist Masashi Kishimoto was born in 1974 in rural Okayama Prefecture, Japan. After spending time in art college, he won the Hop Step Award for new manga artists with his manga **Karakuri** (Mechanism). Kishimoto decided to base his next story on traditional Japanese culture. His first version of **Naruto**, drawn in 1997, was a one-shot story about fox spirits; his final version, which debuted in **Weekly Shonen Jump** in 1999, quickly became the most popular ninja manga in Japan.

ラーメン一楽
一楽

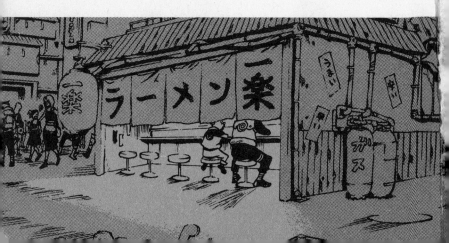

NARUTO VOL. 20
SHONEN JUMP Manga Edition

STORY AND ART BY MASASHI KISHIMOTO

Translation & English Adaptation/Joe Yamazaki
Touch-Up Art & Lettering/Annaliese Christman
Design/Yvonne Cai
Editor/Joel Enos

Printed in the U.S.A.

Published by VIZ Media, LLC
P.O. Box 77010
San Francisco, CA 94107

10 9 8
First printing, October 2007
Eighth printing, December 2017

www.viz.com

RATED T FOR TEEN

PARENTAL ADVISORY
NARUTO is rated T for Teen and is recommended for ages 13 and up. This volume contains realistic and fantasy violence.

ratings.viz.com

SHONEN JUMP MANGA EDITION

NARUTO

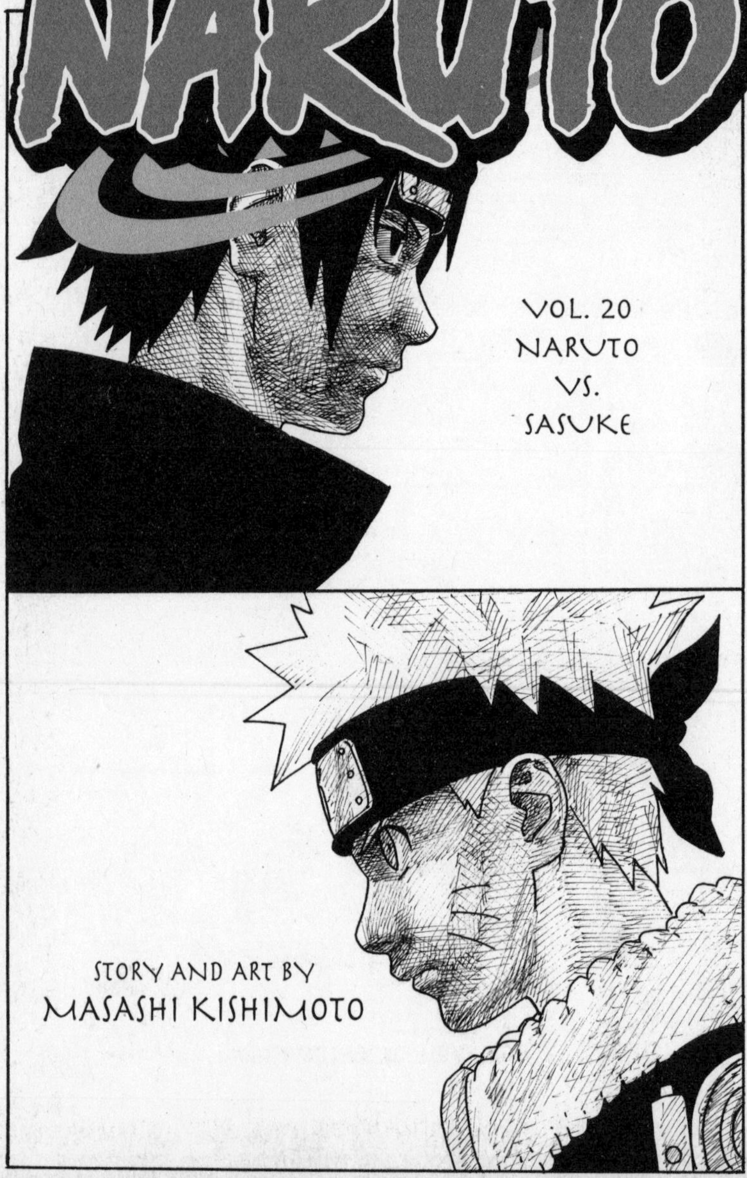

VOL. 20
NARUTO
VS.
SASUKE

STORY AND ART BY
MASASHI KISHIMOTO

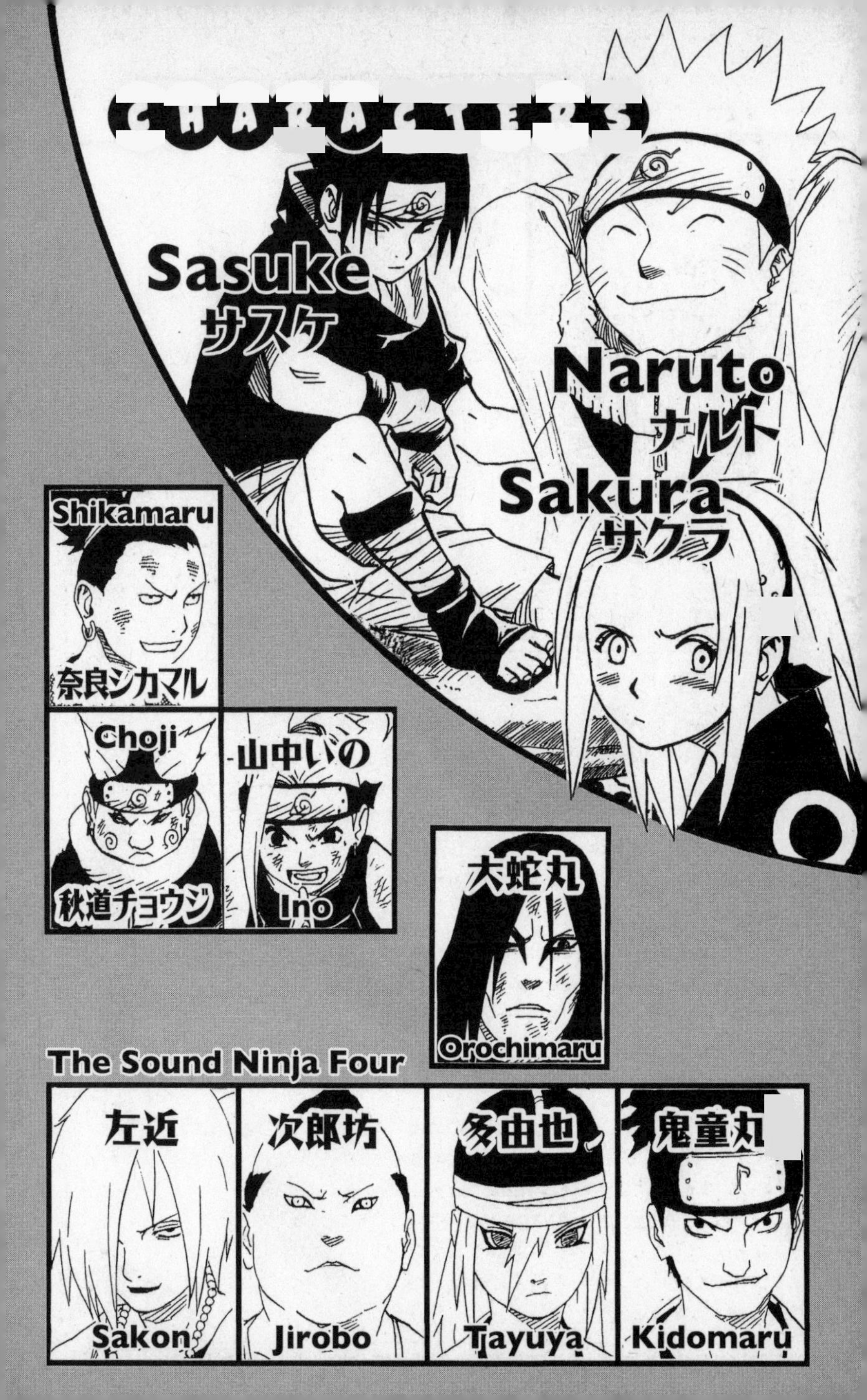
CHARACTERS
Sasuke
サスケ
Naruto
ナルト
Sakura
サクラ
Shikamaru
奈良シカマル
Choji
秋道チョウジ
山中いの
Ino
大蛇丸
Orochimaru
The Sound Ninja Four
左近
Sakon
次郎坊
Jirobo
多由也
Tayuya
鬼童丸
Kidomaru

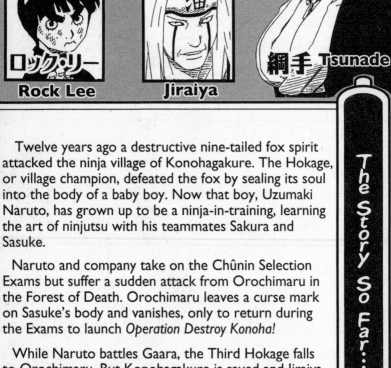

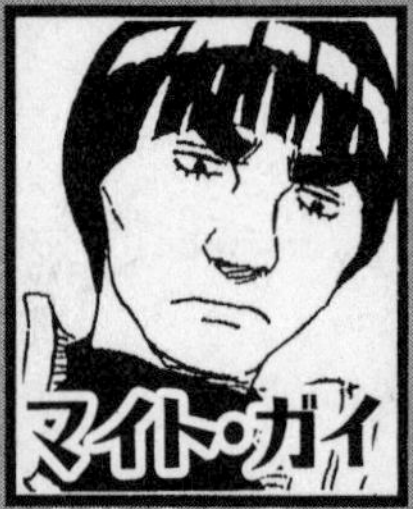
マイト・ガイ
Might Guy

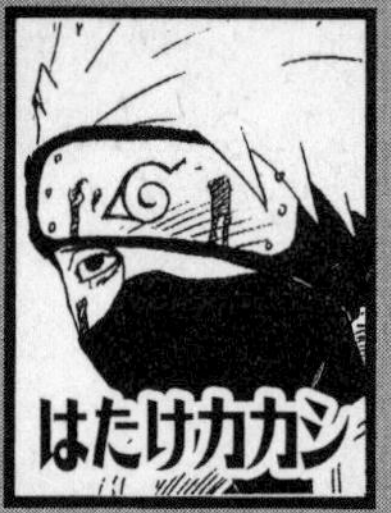
はたけカカシ
Kakashi

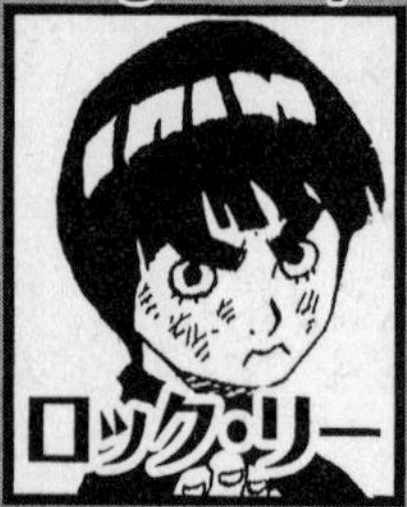
ロック・リー
Rock Lee

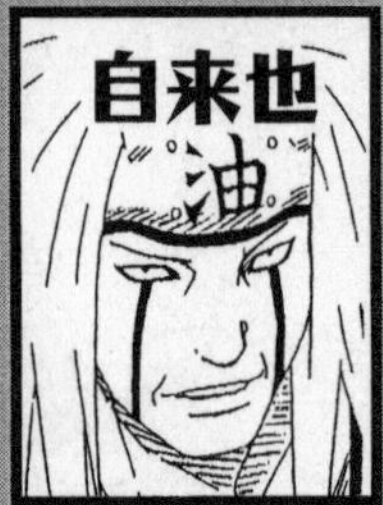
自来也
油
Jiraiya

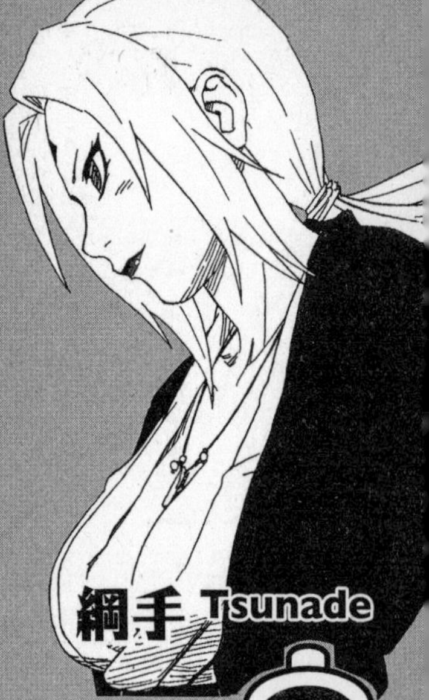
綱手
Tsunade

The Story So Far...

Twelve years ago a destructive nine-tailed fox spirit attacked the ninja village of Konohagakure. The Hokage, or village champion, defeated the fox by sealing its soul into the body of a baby boy. Now that boy, Uzumaki Naruto, has grown up to be a ninja-in-training, learning the art of ninjutsu with his teammates Sakura and Sasuke.

Naruto and company take on the Chûnin Selection Exams but suffer a sudden attack from Orochimaru in the Forest of Death. Orochimaru leaves a curse mark on Sasuke's body and vanishes, only to return during the Exams to launch *Operation Destroy Konoha!*

While Naruto battles Gaara, the Third Hokage falls to Orochimaru. But Konohagakure is saved and Jiraiya and Naruto set out to hunt down the future Fifth Hokage, Tsunade. On the way, they encounter Itachi, Sasuke's demented older brother. And Tsunade has a strange encounter with Orochimaru, resulting in a battle that ends in deadlock!

NARUTO

VOL. 20
NARUTO VS. SASUKE

CONTENTS

Number 172: The Return

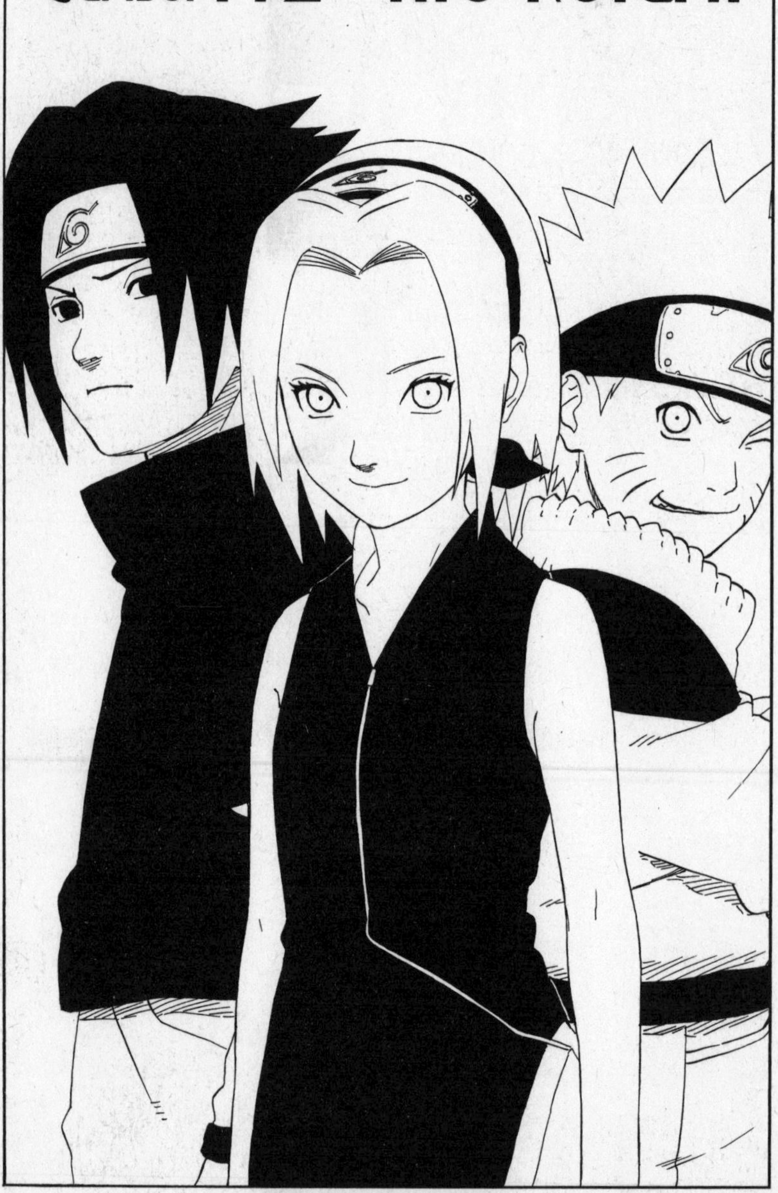

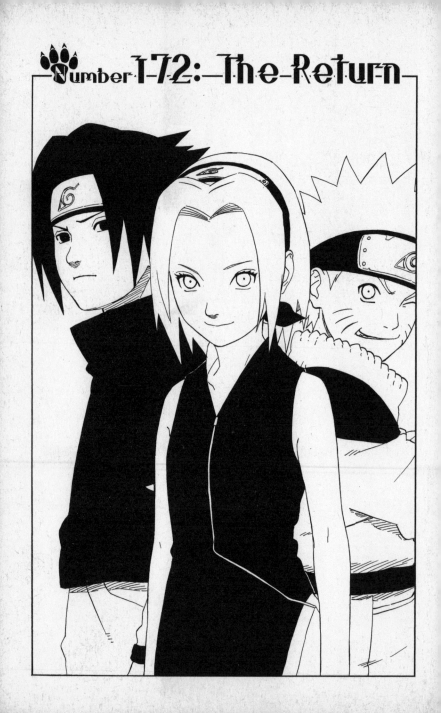

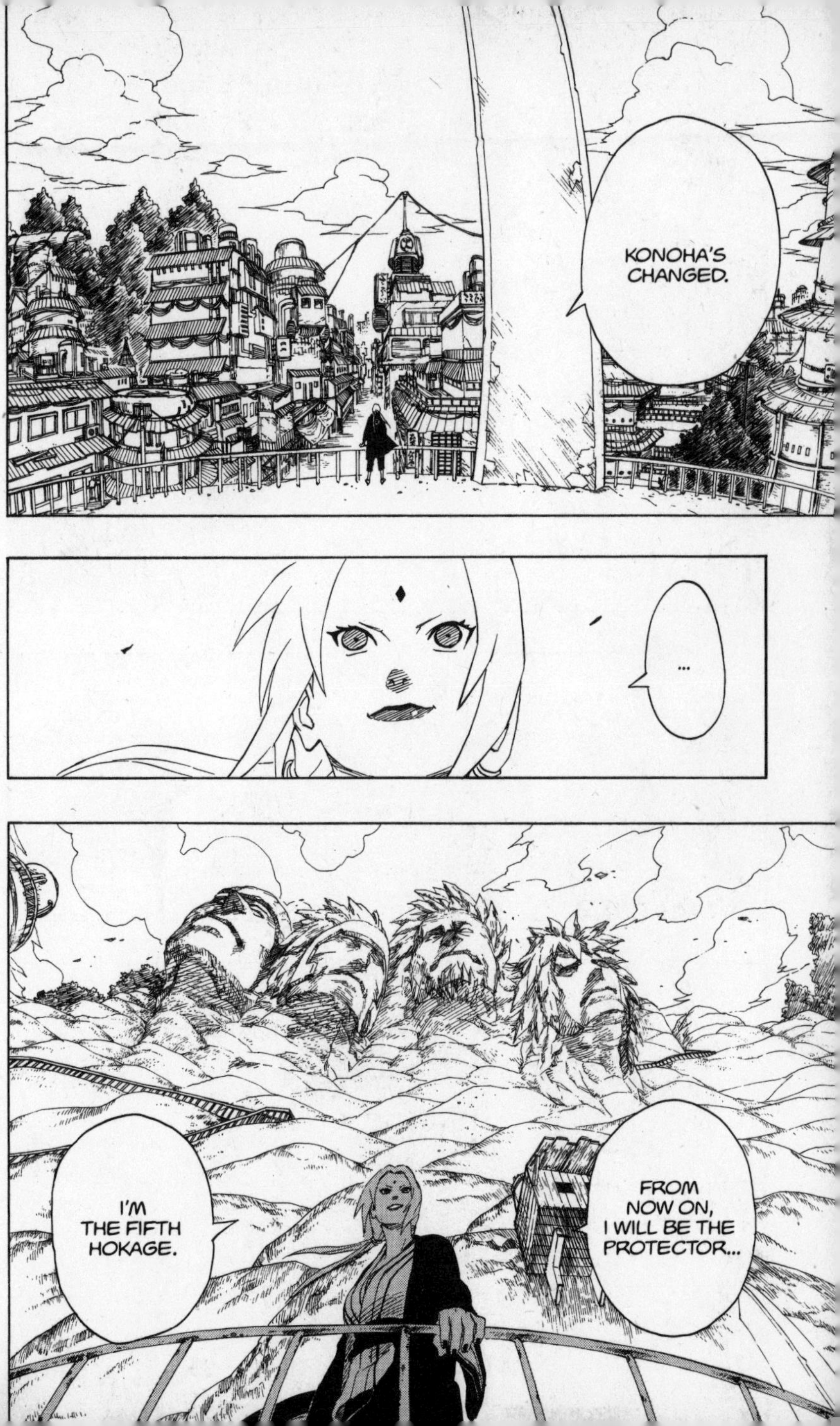
KONOHA'S CHANGED.
...
FROM NOW ON, I WILL BE THE PROTECTOR...
I'M THE FIFTH HOKAGE.

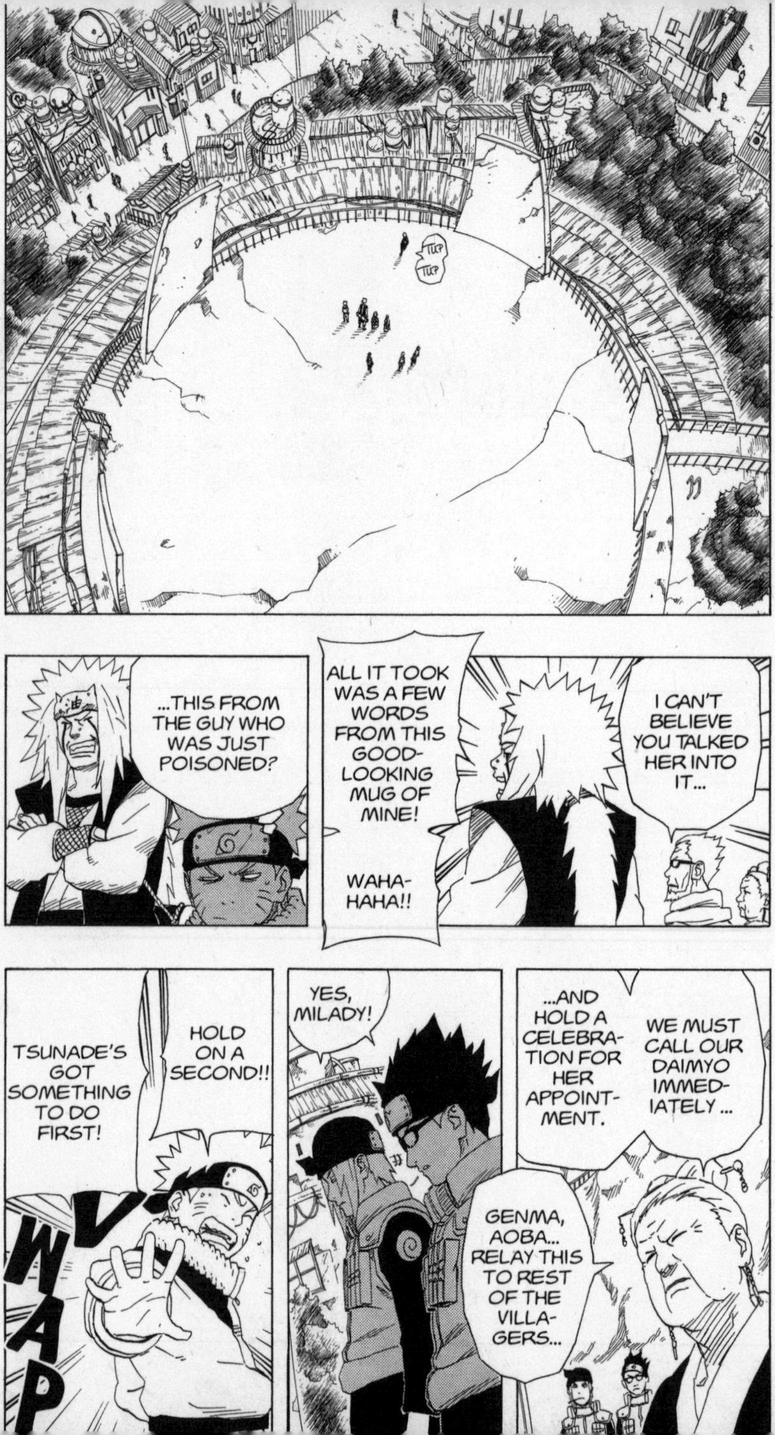
TUP
TUP
I CAN'T BELIEVE YOU TALKED HER INTO IT...
ALL IT TOOK WAS A FEW WORDS FROM THIS GOOD-LOOKING MUG OF MINE!
WAHA-HAHA!!
...THIS FROM THE GUY WHO WAS JUST POISONED?
WE MUST CALL OUR DAIMYO IMMEDIATELY...
...AND HOLD A CELEBRATION FOR HER APPOINTMENT.
GENMA, AOBA... RELAY THIS TO REST OF THE VILLAGERS...
YES, MILADY!
HOLD ON A SECOND!!
TSUNADE'S GOT SOMETHING TO DO FIRST!
VWAP

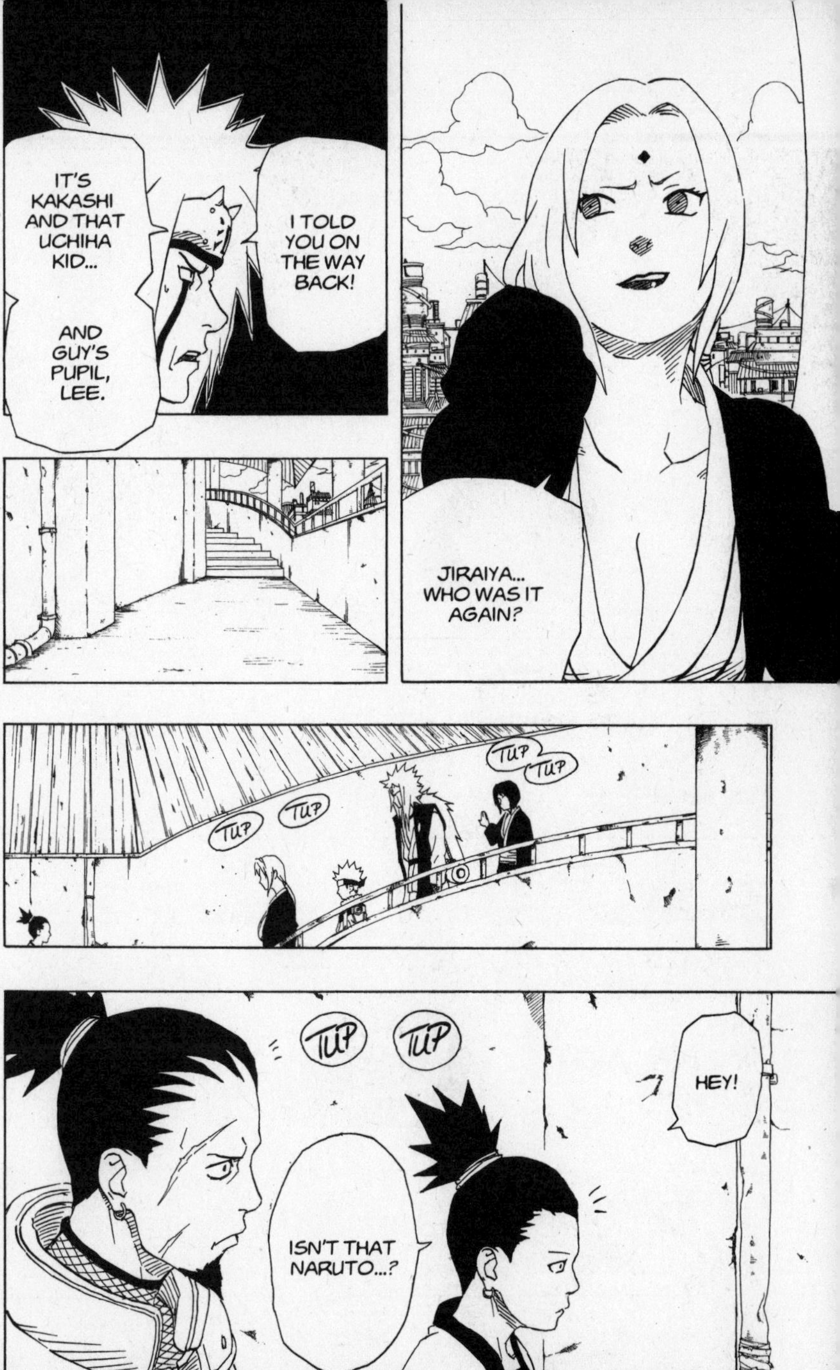
JIRAIYA... WHO WAS IT AGAIN?
I TOLD YOU ON THE WAY BACK!
IT'S KAKASHI AND THAT UCHIHA KID...
AND GUY'S PUPIL, LEE.
TUP
TUP
TUP
TUP
HEY!
TUP
TUP
ISN'T THAT NARUTO...?

READ THIS WAY

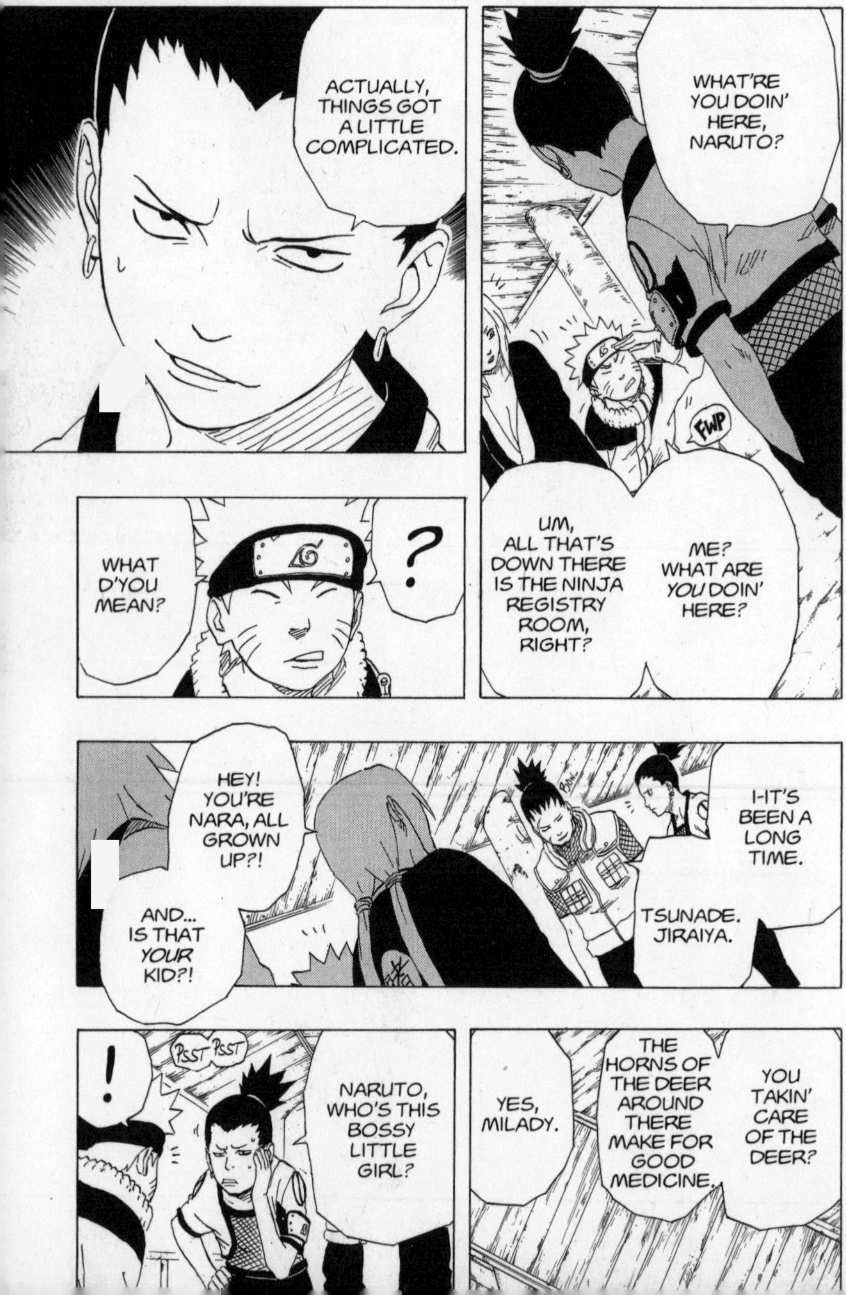
WHAT'RE YOU DOIN' HERE, NARUTO?
FWP
ME? WHAT ARE YOU DOIN' HERE?
UM, ALL THAT'S DOWN THERE IS THE NINJA REGISTRY ROOM, RIGHT?
ACTUALLY, THINGS GOT A LITTLE COMPLICATED.
?
WHAT D'YOU MEAN?
I-IT'S BEEN A LONG TIME.
TSUNADE. JIRAIYA.
BOW
HEY! YOU'RE NARA, ALL GROWN UP?!
AND... IS THAT YOUR KID?!
YOU TAKIN' CARE OF THE DEER?
THE HORNS OF THE DEER AROUND THERE MAKE FOR GOOD MEDICINE.
YES, MILADY.
NARUTO, WHO'S THIS BOSSY LITTLE GIRL?
PSST PSST
!

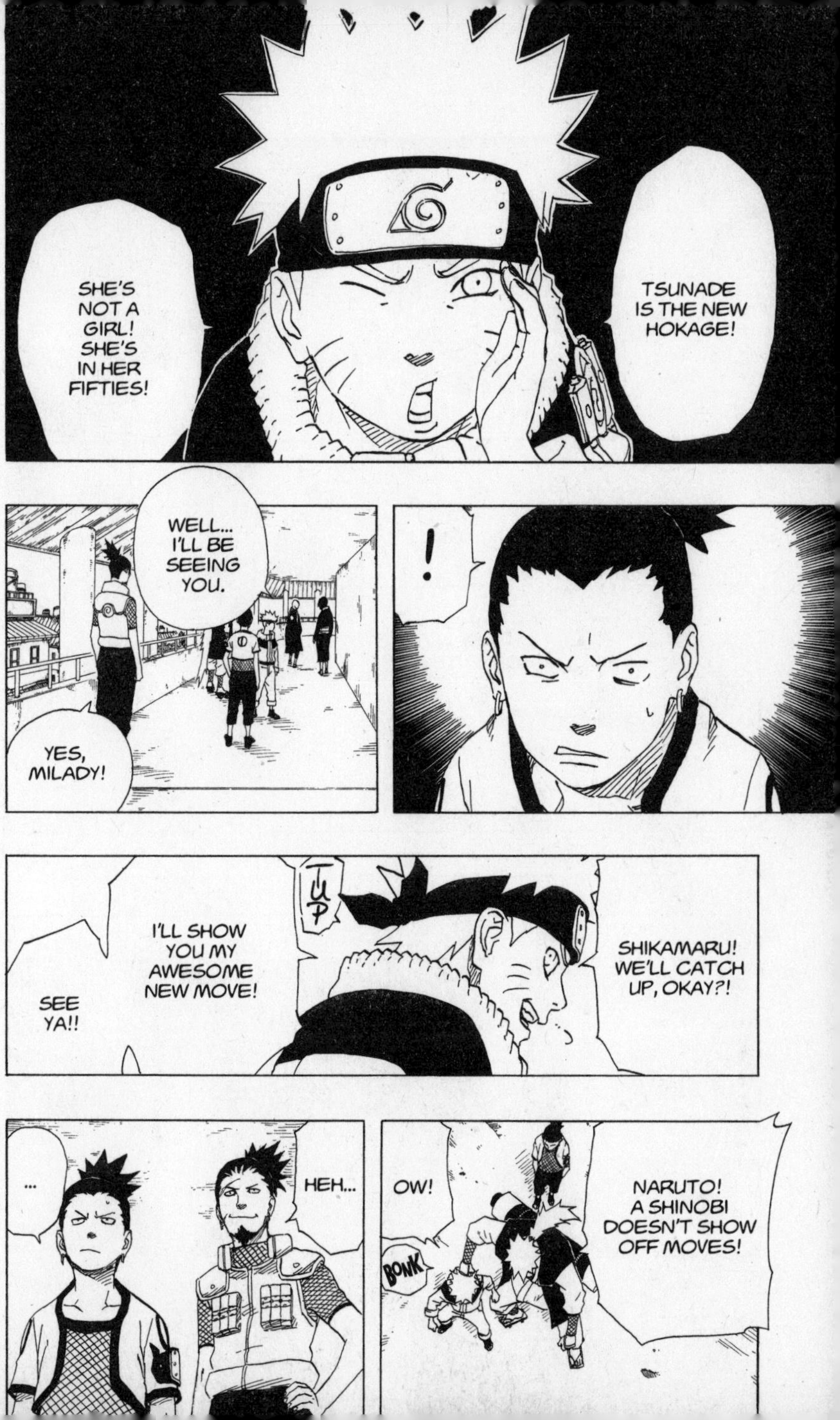
TSUNADE IS THE NEW HOKAGE!
SHE'S NOT A GIRL! SHE'S IN HER FIFTIES!
!
WELL... I'LL BE SEEING YOU.
YES, MILADY!
TUP
SHIKAMARU! WE'LL CATCH UP, OKAY?!
I'LL SHOW YOU MY AWESOME NEW MOVE!
SEE YA!!
NARUTO! A SHINOBI DOESN'T SHOW OFF MOVES!
OW!
BONK
HEH...
...

READ THIS WAY

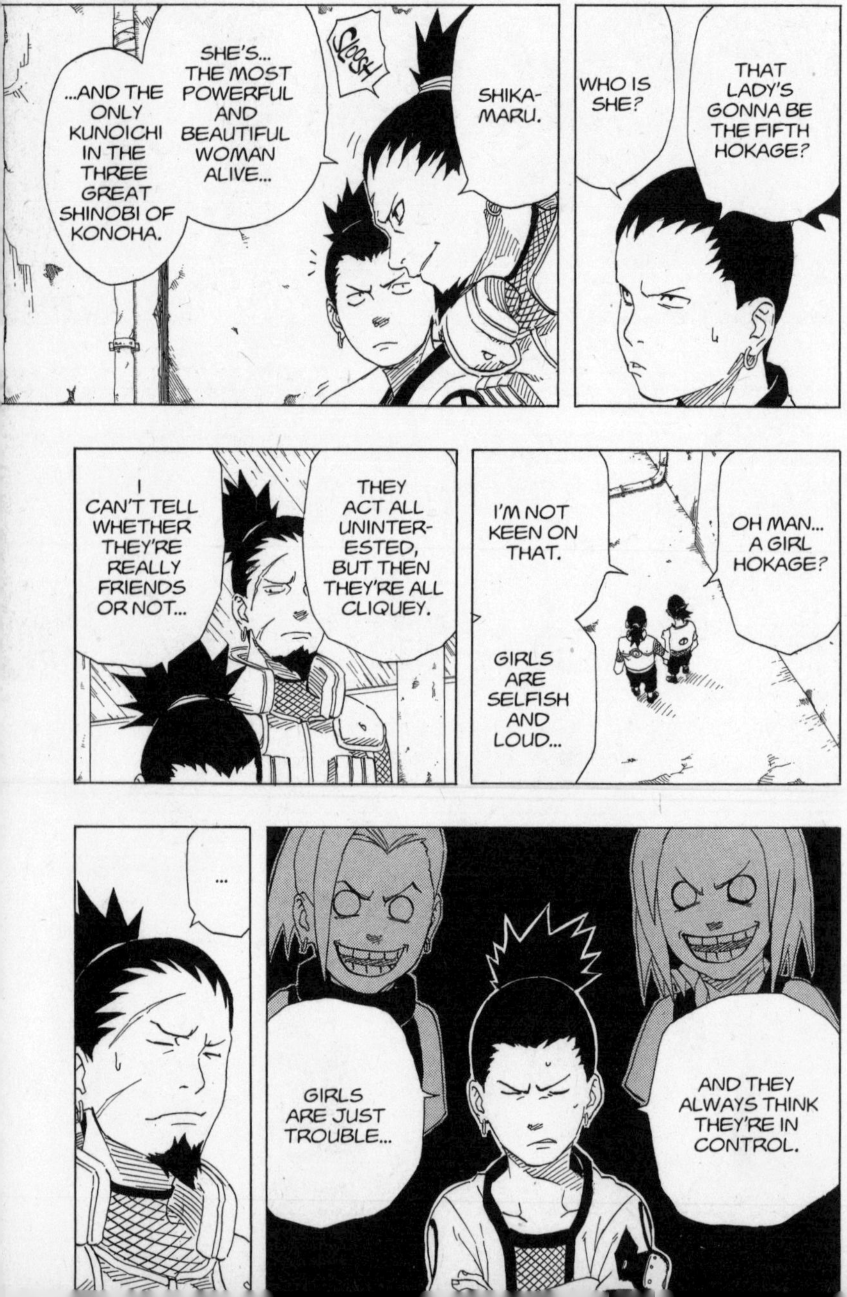
THAT LADY'S GONNA BE THE FIFTH HOKAGE?
WHO IS SHE?
SHIKA-MARU.
SLOSH
SHE'S... THE MOST POWERFUL AND BEAUTIFUL WOMAN ALIVE...
...AND THE ONLY KUNOICHI IN THE THREE GREAT SHINOBI OF KONOHA.
OH MAN... A GIRL HOKAGE?
I'M NOT KEEN ON THAT.
GIRLS ARE SELFISH AND LOUD...
THEY ACT ALL UNINTER-ESTED, BUT THEN THEY'RE ALL CLIQUEY.
I CAN'T TELL WHETHER THEY'RE REALLY FRIENDS OR NOT...
AND THEY ALWAYS THINK THEY'RE IN CONTROL.
GIRLS ARE JUST TROUBLE...
...

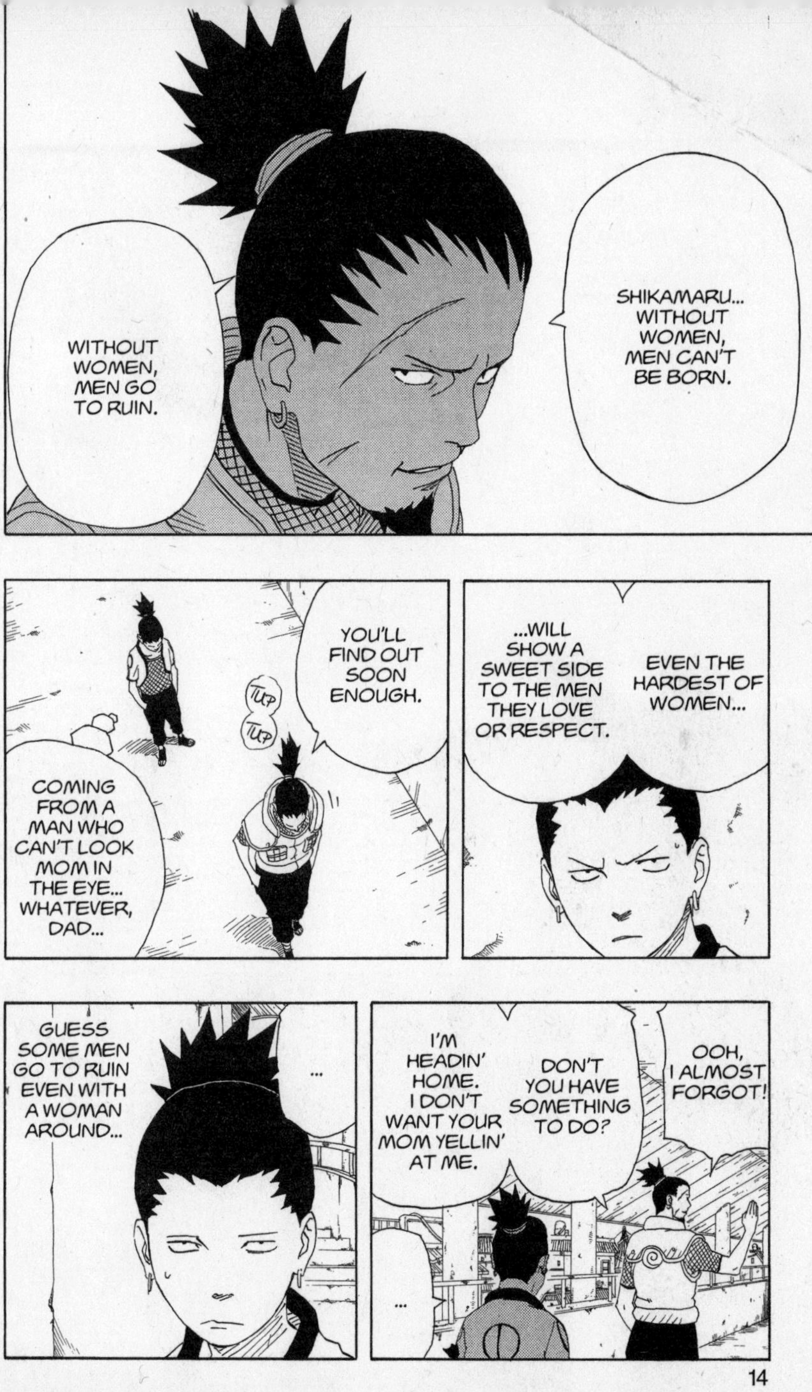
SHIKAMARU... WITHOUT WOMEN, MEN CAN'T BE BORN.
WITHOUT WOMEN, MEN GO TO RUIN.
EVEN THE HARDEST OF WOMEN...
...WILL SHOW A SWEET SIDE TO THE MEN THEY LOVE OR RESPECT.
YOU'LL FIND OUT SOON ENOUGH.
TUP
TUP
COMING FROM A MAN WHO CAN'T LOOK MOM IN THE EYE... WHATEVER, DAD...
OOH, I ALMOST FORGOT!
DON'T YOU HAVE SOMETHING TO DO?
I'M HEADIN' HOME. I DON'T WANT YOUR MOM YELLIN' AT ME.
...
...
GUESS SOME MEN GO TO RUIN EVEN WITH A WOMAN AROUND...

READ THIS WAY

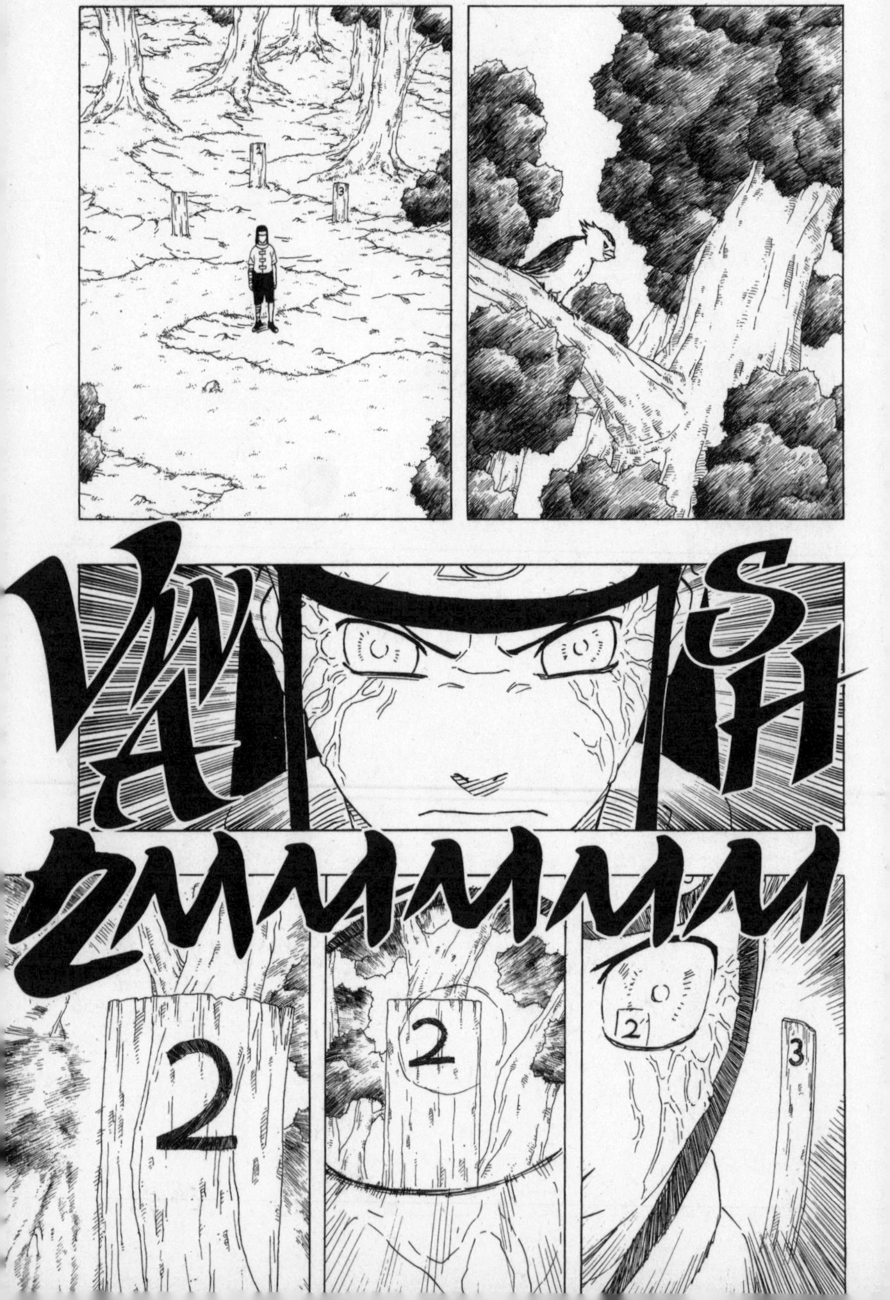
VWASH

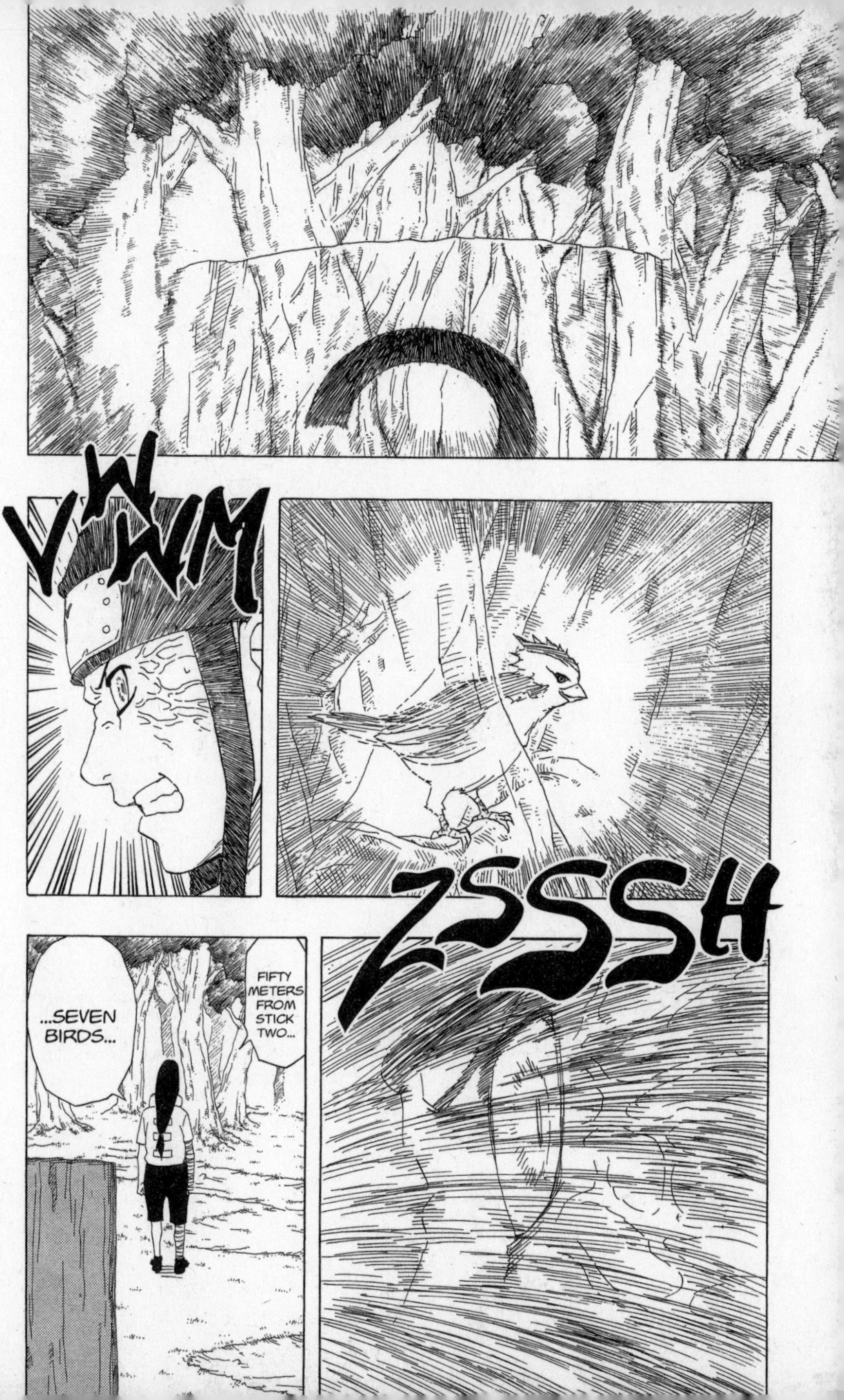
VWM
ZSSH
FIFTY METERS FROM STICK TWO...
...SEVEN BIRDS...

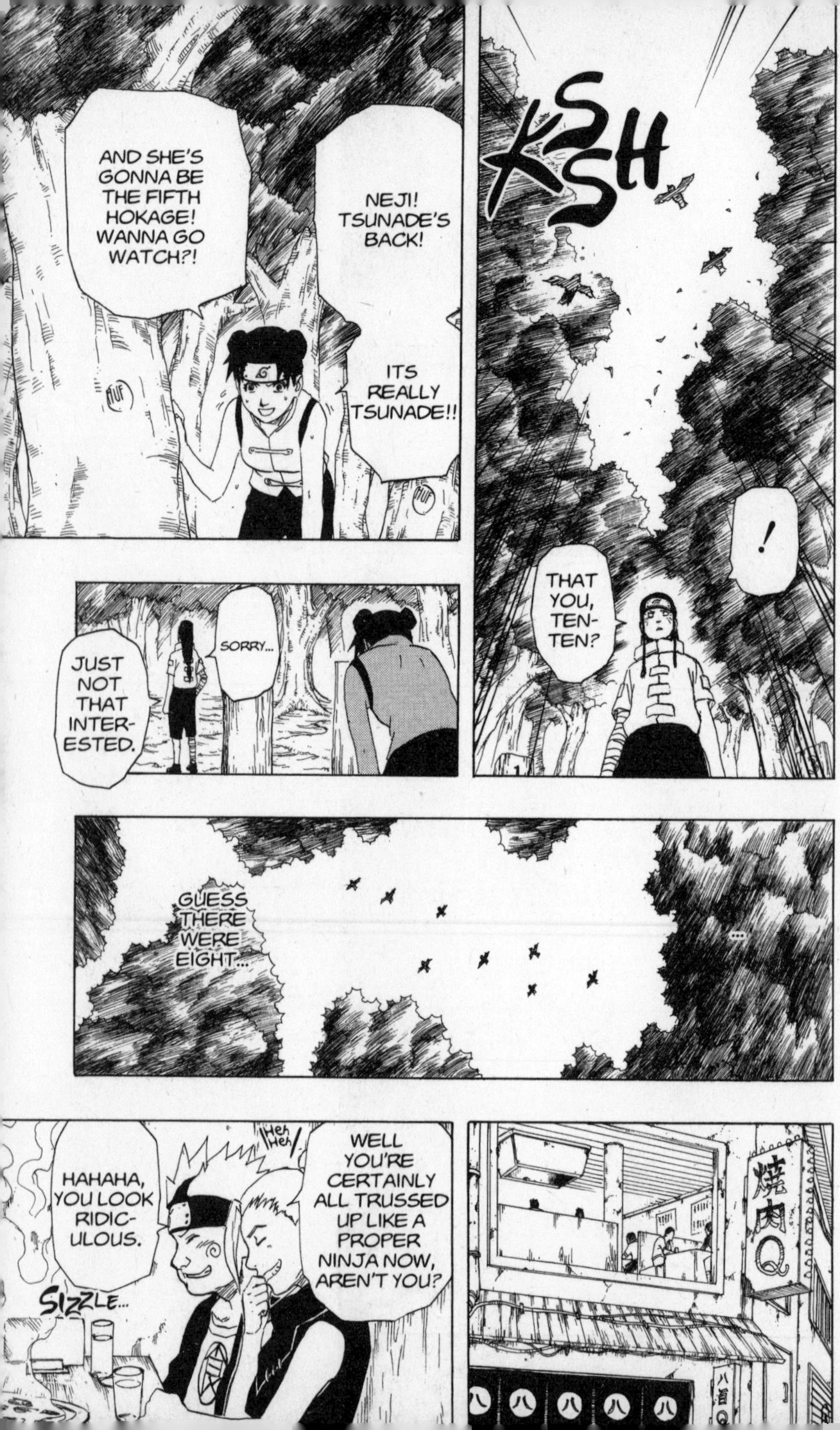
KSH KSH
!
THAT YOU, TEN-TEN?
NEJI! TSUNADE'S BACK!
ITS REALLY TSUNADE!!
AND SHE'S GONNA BE THE FIFTH HOKAGE! WANNA GO WATCH?!
HUF
HUF
SORRY...
JUST NOT THAT INTER-ESTED.
...
GUESS THERE WERE EIGHT...
焼肉Q
Heh Heh
WELL YOU'RE CERTAINLY ALL TRUSSED UP LIKE A PROPER NINJA NOW, AREN'T YOU?
HAHAHA, YOU LOOK RIDIC-ULOUS.
SIZZLE...

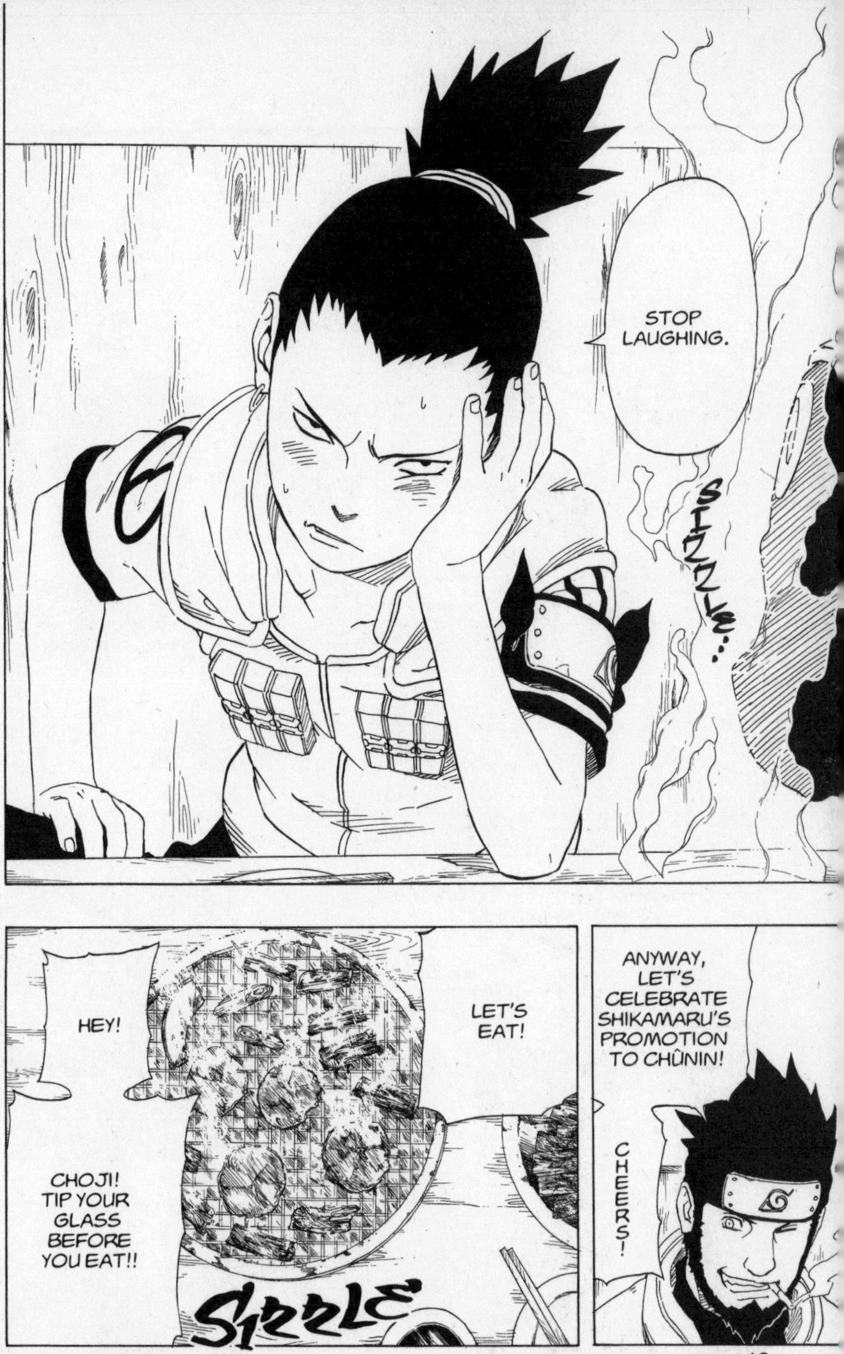
STOP LAUGHING.
SIZZLE...
ANYWAY, LET'S CELEBRATE SHIKAMARU'S PROMOTION TO CHÛNIN!
CHEERS!
LET'S EAT!
HEY!
CHOJI! TIP YOUR GLASS BEFORE YOU EAT!!
SIZZLE

READ THIS WAY

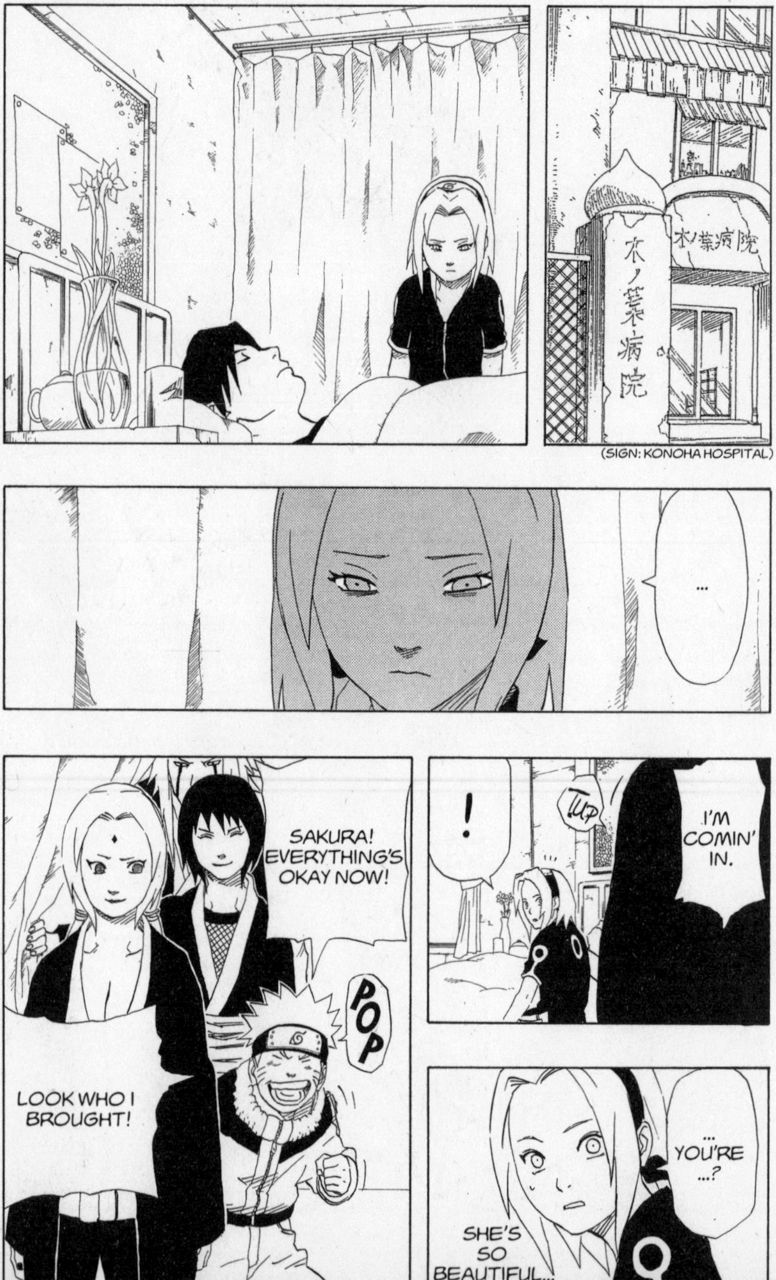

木ノ葉病院
木ノ葉病院
(SIGN: KONOHA HOSPITAL)
...
!
TUP
I'M COMIN' IN.
... YOU'RE ...?
SHE'S SO BEAUTIFUL...
SAKURA! EVERYTHING'S OKAY NOW!
POP
LOOK WHO I BROUGHT!

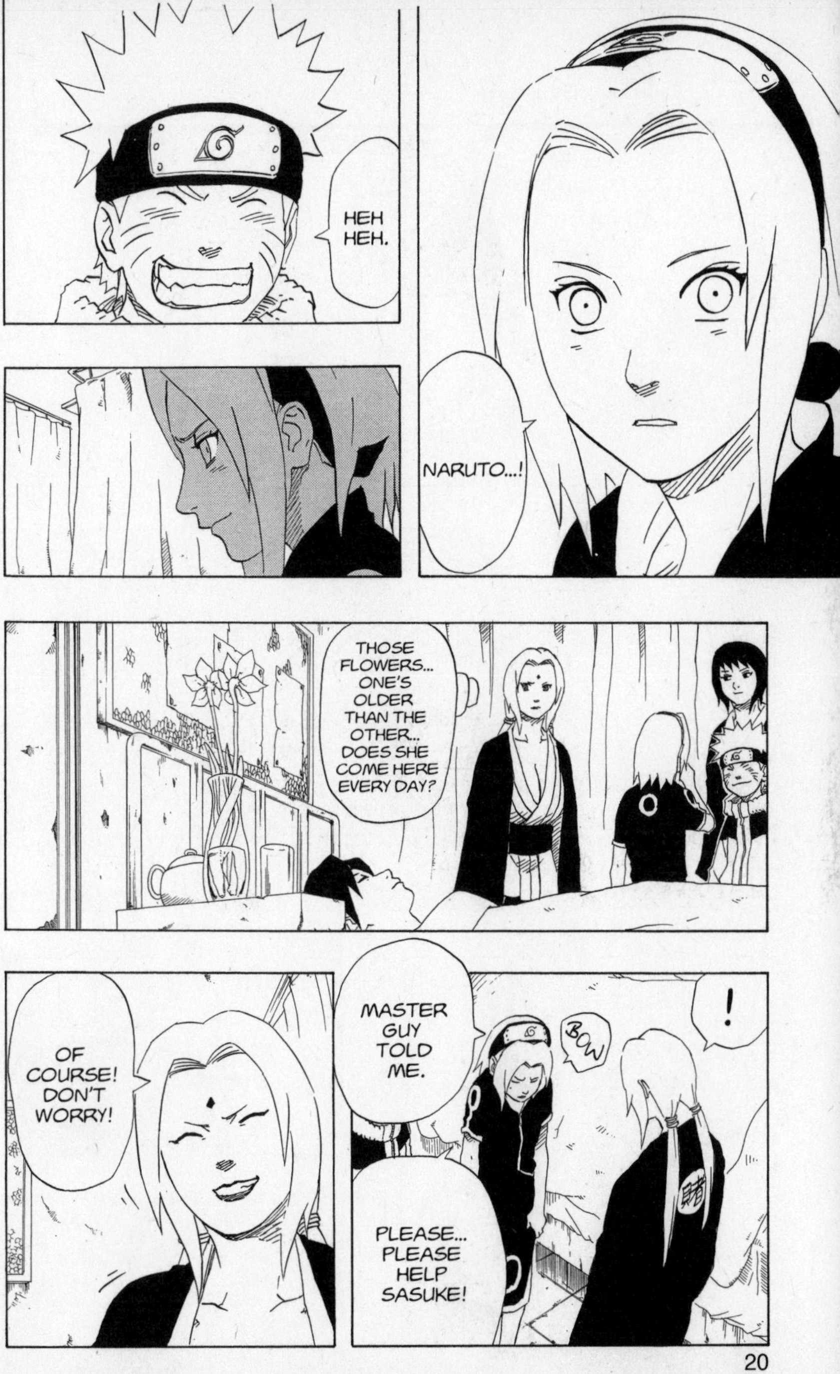

NARUTO...!
HEH HEH.
THOSE FLOWERS... ONE'S OLDER THAN THE OTHER.. DOES SHE COME HERE EVERY DAY?
!
BOW
MASTER GUY TOLD ME.
PLEASE... PLEASE HELP SASUKE!
OF COURSE! DON'T WORRY!

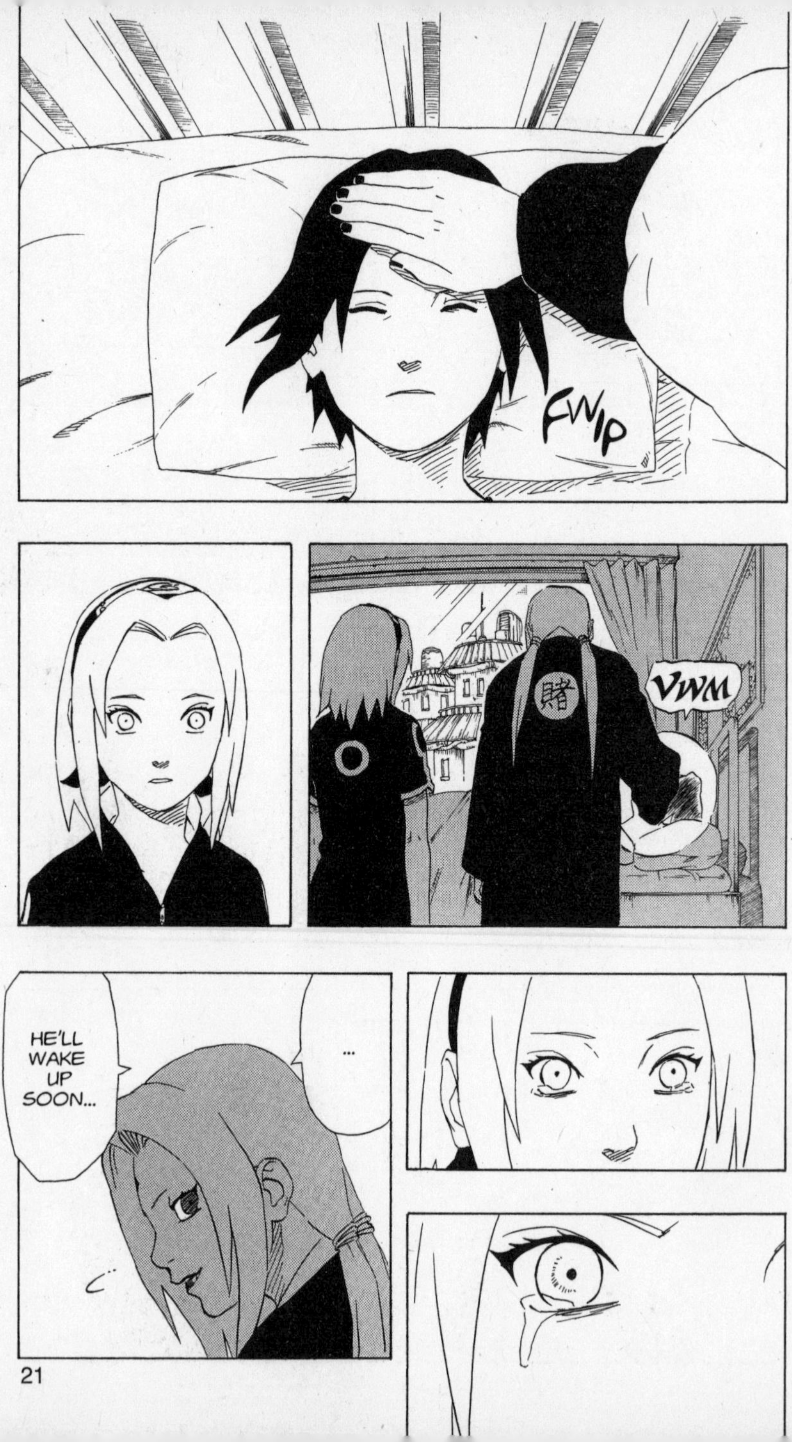
FWIP
VWM
...
HE'LL WAKE UP SOON...

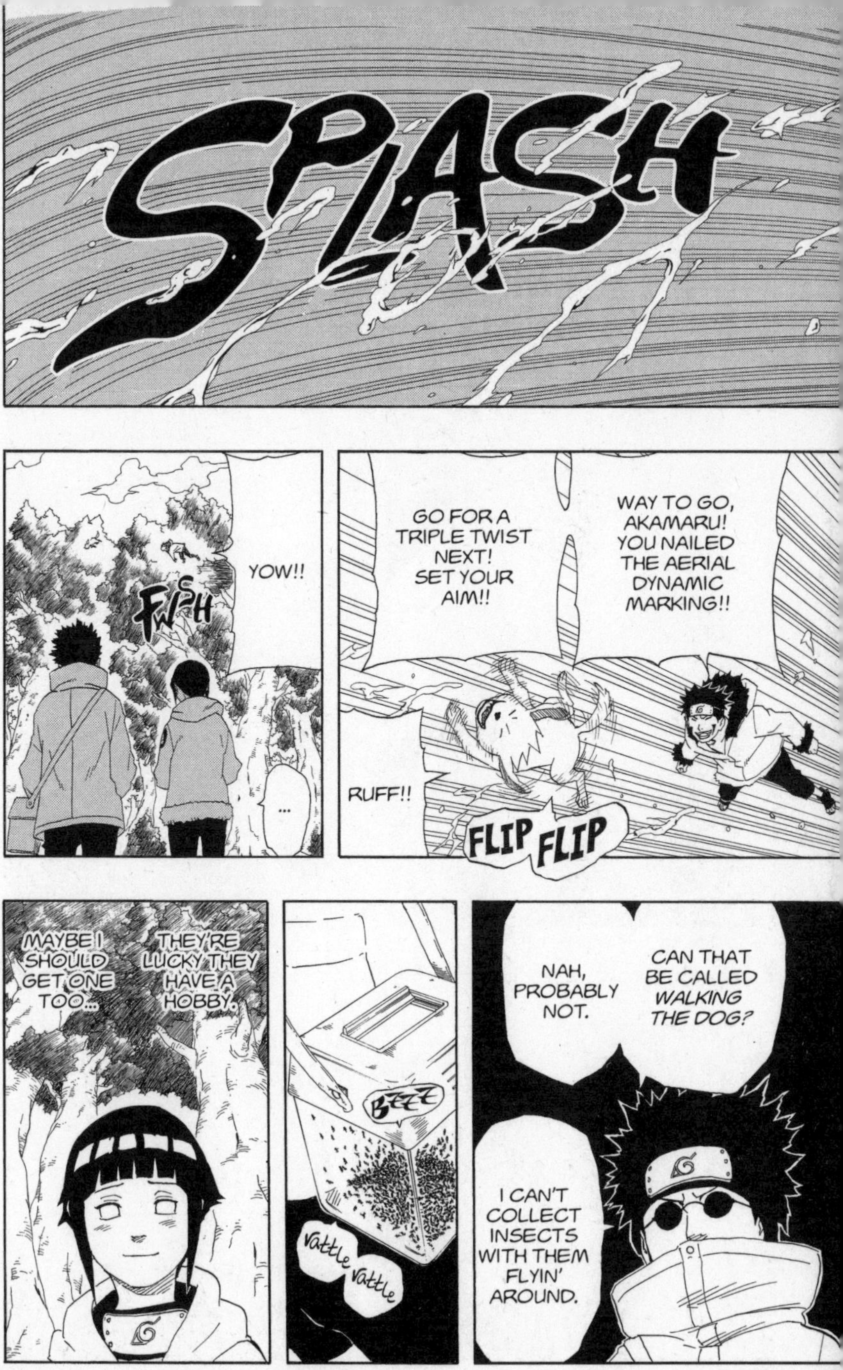

SPLASH
WAY TO GO, AKAMARU! YOU NAILED THE AERIAL DYNAMIC MARKING!!
GO FOR A TRIPLE TWIST NEXT! SET YOUR AIM!!
RUFF!!
FLIP FLIP
YOW!!
FWSH
...
CAN THAT BE CALLED *WALKING THE DOG?*
NAH, PROBABLY NOT.
I CAN'T COLLECT INSECTS WITH THEM FLYIN' AROUND.
BZZZ
rattle rattle
THEY'RE LUCKY THEY HAVE A HOBBY.
MAYBE I SHOULD GET ONE TOO...

READ THIS WAY

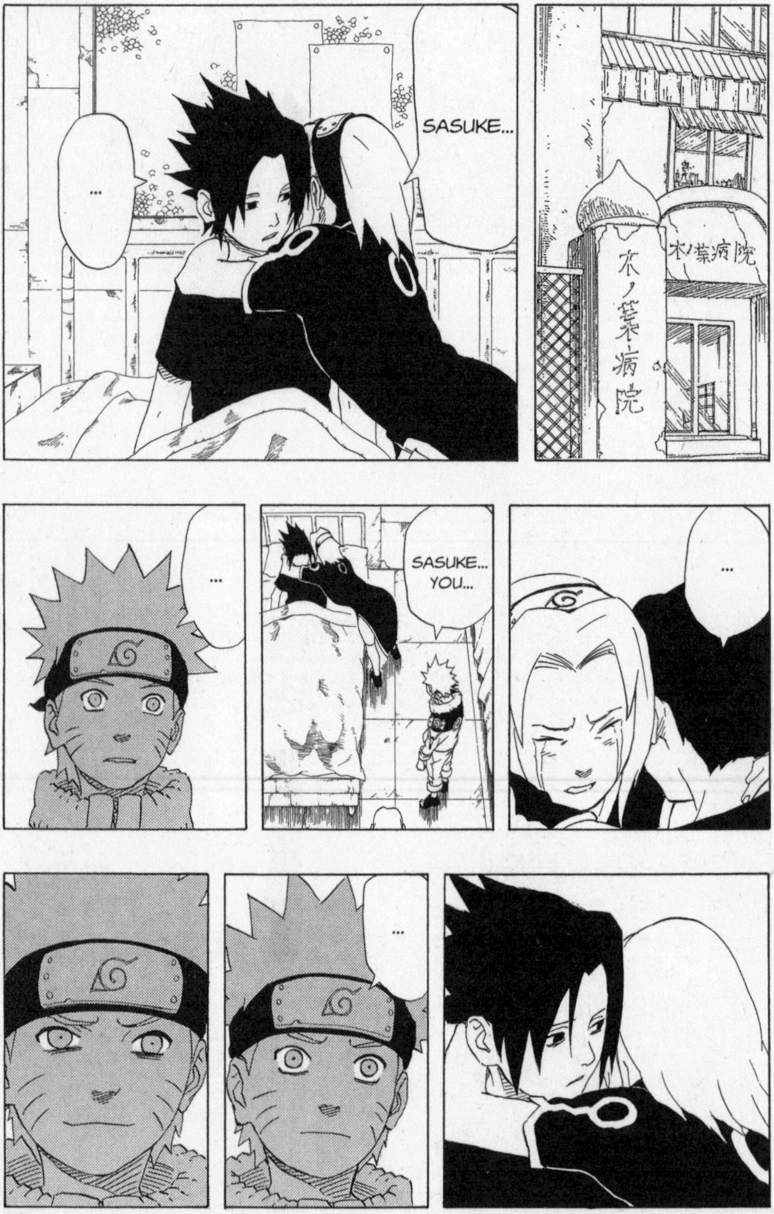
木ノ葉病院
木ノ葉病院
SASUKE...
...
...
SASUKE... YOU...
...
...

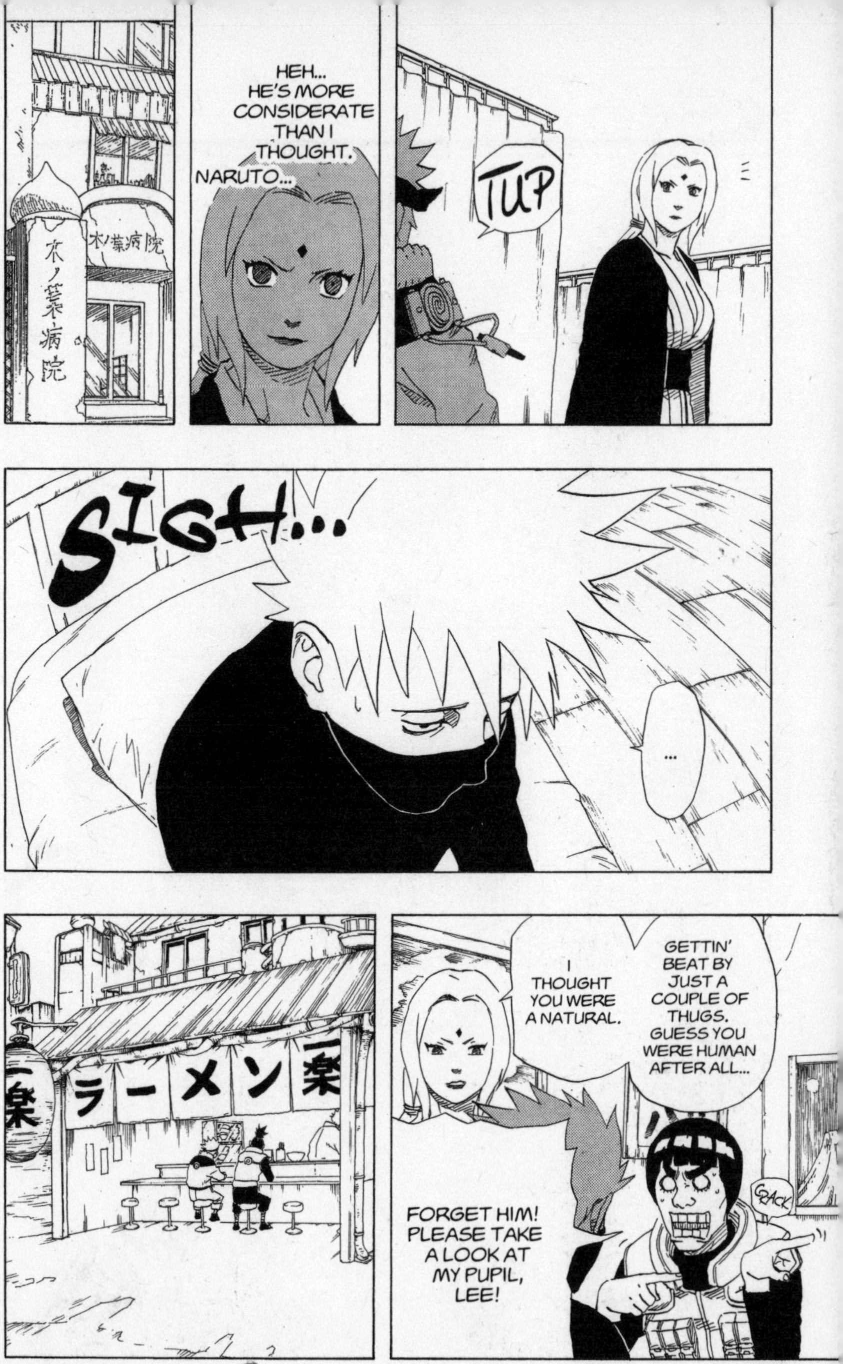
TUP
HEH... HE'S MORE CONSIDERATE THAN I THOUGHT.
NARUTO...
木ノ葉病院
木ノ葉病院
SIGH...
...
GETTIN' BEAT BY JUST A COUPLE OF THUGS. GUESS YOU WERE HUMAN AFTER ALL...
I THOUGHT YOU WERE A NATURAL.
FORGET HIM! PLEASE TAKE A LOOK AT MY PUPIL, LEE!
CRACK
一楽
ラーメン
一楽

READ THIS WAY

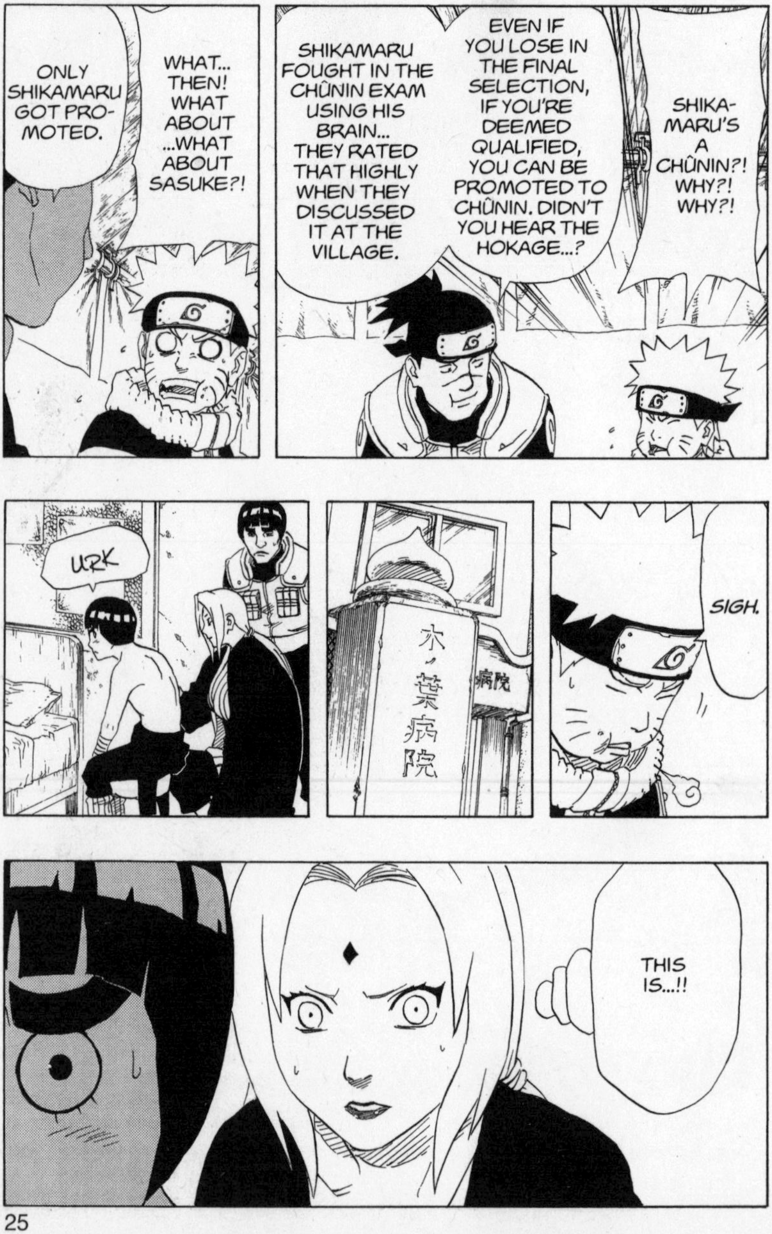
SHIKA-MARU'S A CHÛNIN?! WHY?! WHY?!
EVEN IF YOU LOSE IN THE FINAL SELECTION, IF YOU'RE DEEMED QUALIFIED, YOU CAN BE PROMOTED TO CHÛNIN. DIDN'T YOU HEAR THE HOKAGE...?
SHIKAMARU FOUGHT IN THE CHÛNIN EXAM USING HIS BRAIN... THEY RATED THAT HIGHLY WHEN THEY DISCUSSED IT AT THE VILLAGE.
WHAT... THEN! WHAT ABOUT ...WHAT ABOUT SASUKE?!
ONLY SHIKAMARU GOT PRO-MOTED.
SIGH.
木ノ葉病院
病院
URK
THIS IS...!!

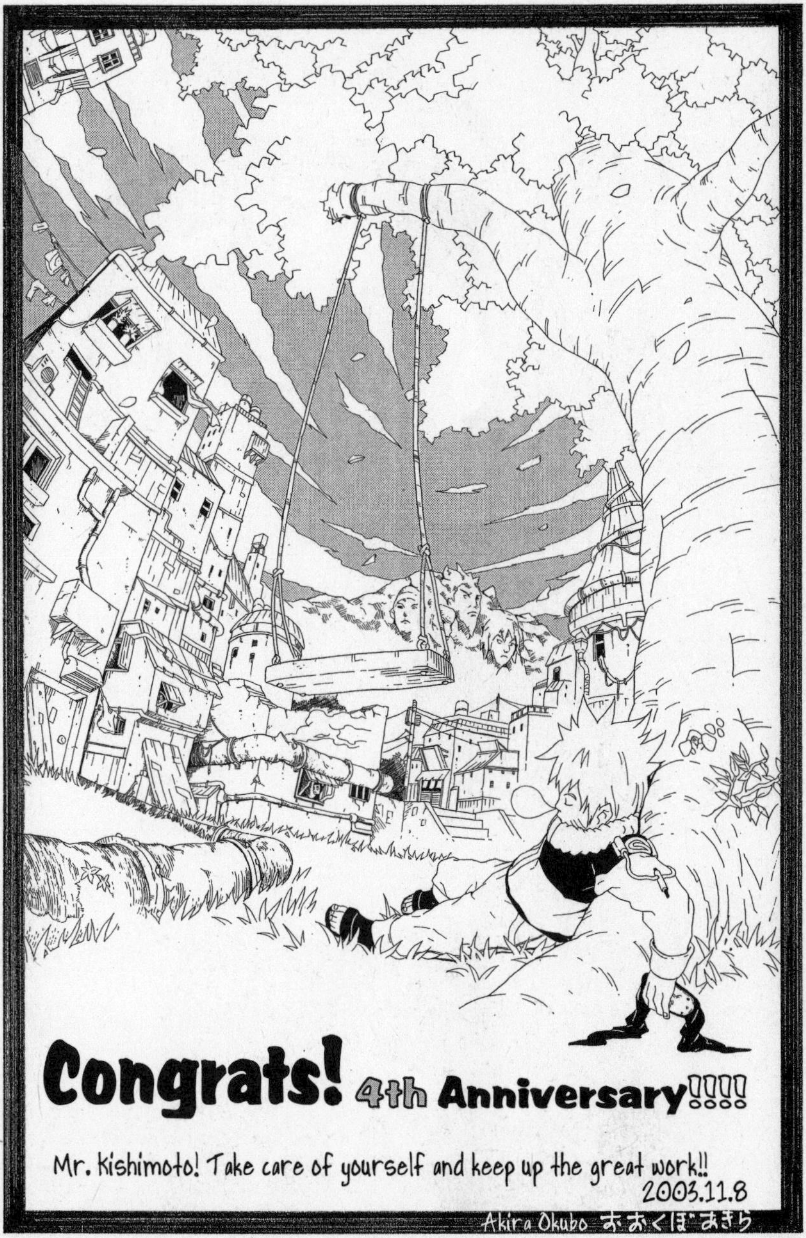
Congrats! 4th Anniversary!!!!!
Mr. Kishimoto! Take care of yourself and keep up the great work!!
2003.11.8
Akira Okubo おおくぼあきら

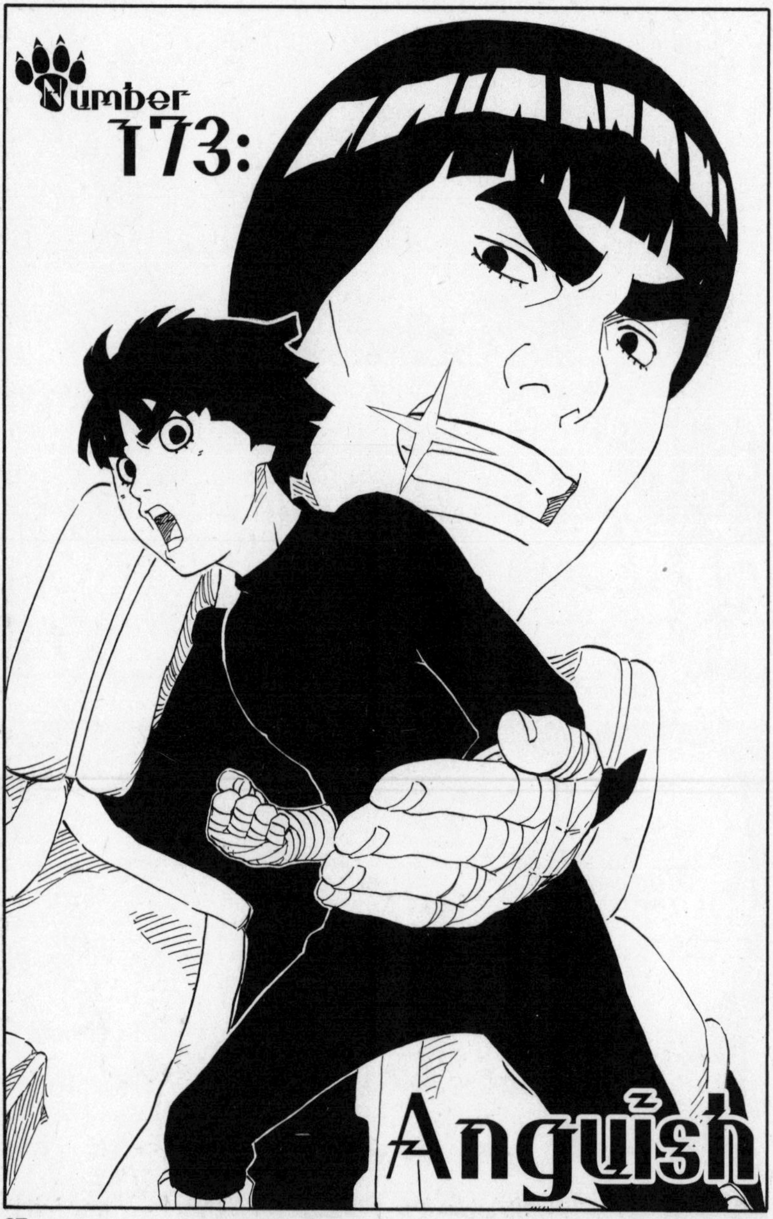
Number 173:
Anguish

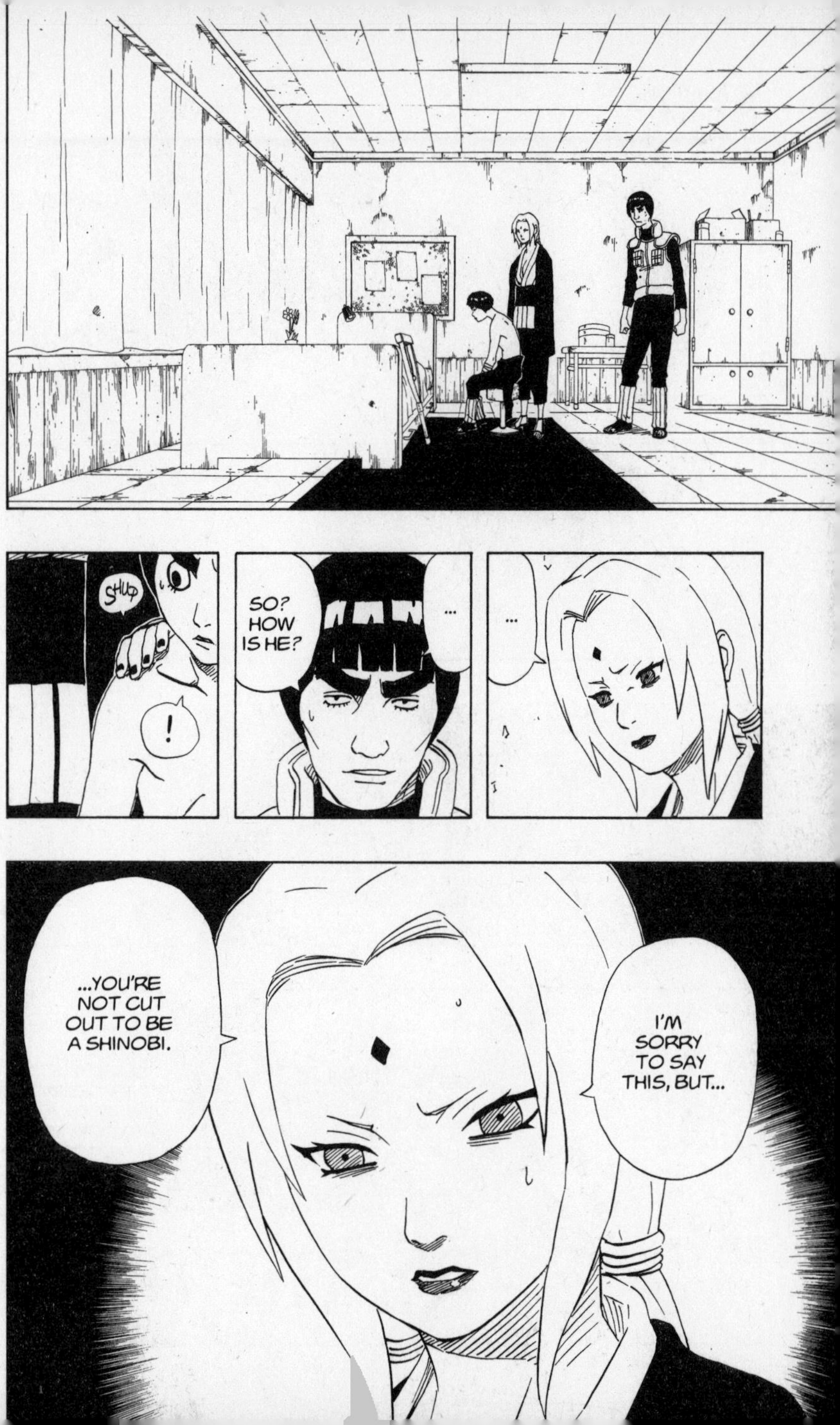
...
...
SO? HOW IS HE?
SHUP
!
I'M SORRY TO SAY THIS, BUT...
...YOU'RE NOT CUT OUT TO BE A SHINOBI.

READ THIS WAY

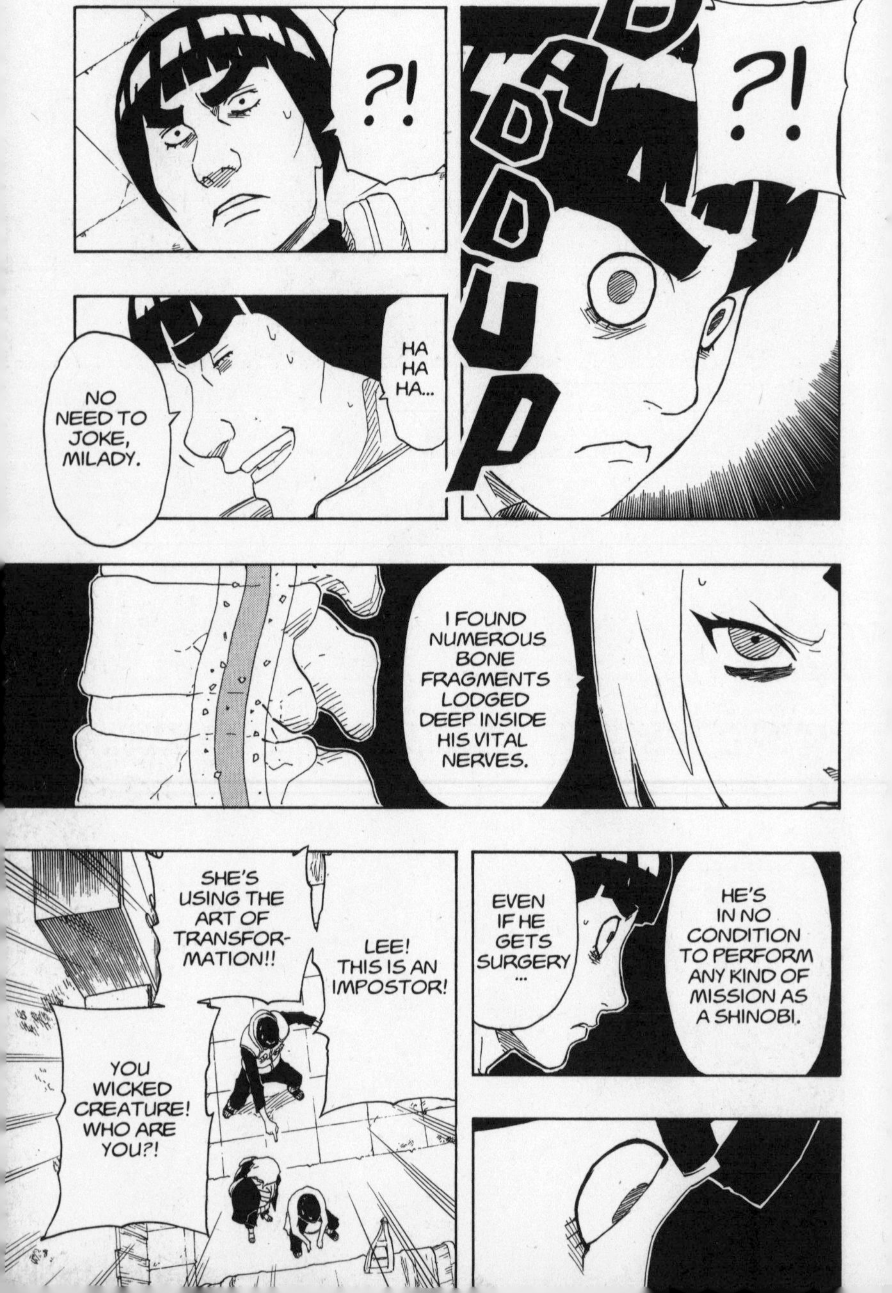
DADDUP
?!
?!
HA HA HA...
NO NEED TO JOKE, MILADY.
I FOUND NUMEROUS BONE FRAGMENTS LODGED DEEP INSIDE HIS VITAL NERVES.
HE'S IN NO CONDITION TO PERFORM ANY KIND OF MISSION AS A SHINOBI.
EVEN IF HE GETS SURGERY...
LEE! THIS IS AN IMPOSTOR!
SHE'S USING THE ART OF TRANSFORMATION!!
YOU WICKED CREATURE! WHO ARE YOU?!

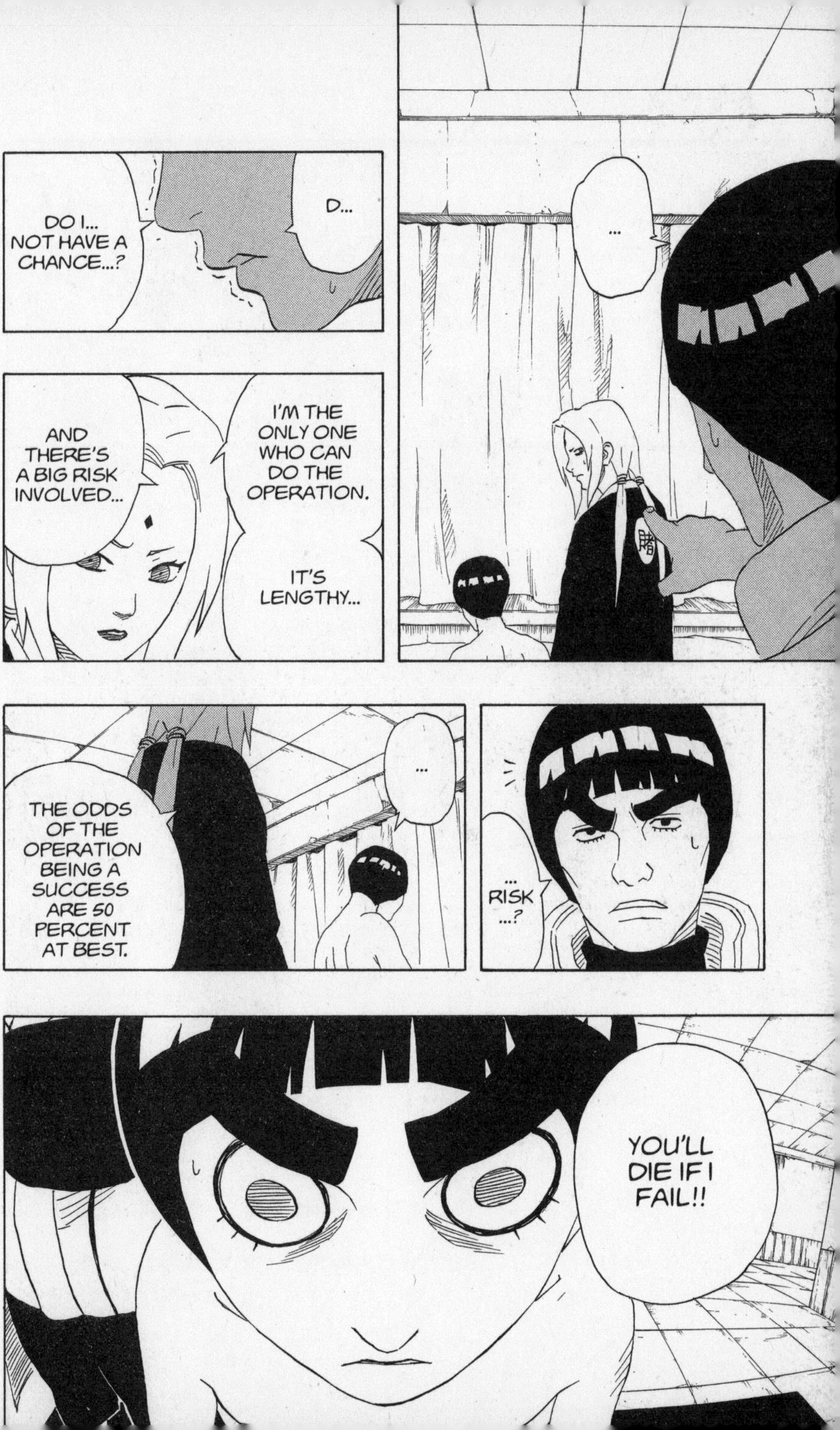
...
D...
DO I... NOT HAVE A CHANCE...?
I'M THE ONLY ONE WHO CAN DO THE OPERATION.
IT'S LENGTHY...
AND THERE'S A BIG RISK INVOLVED...
... RISK ...?
...
THE ODDS OF THE OPERATION BEING A SUCCESS ARE 50 PERCENT AT BEST.
YOU'LL DIE IF I FAIL!!

READ THIS WAY

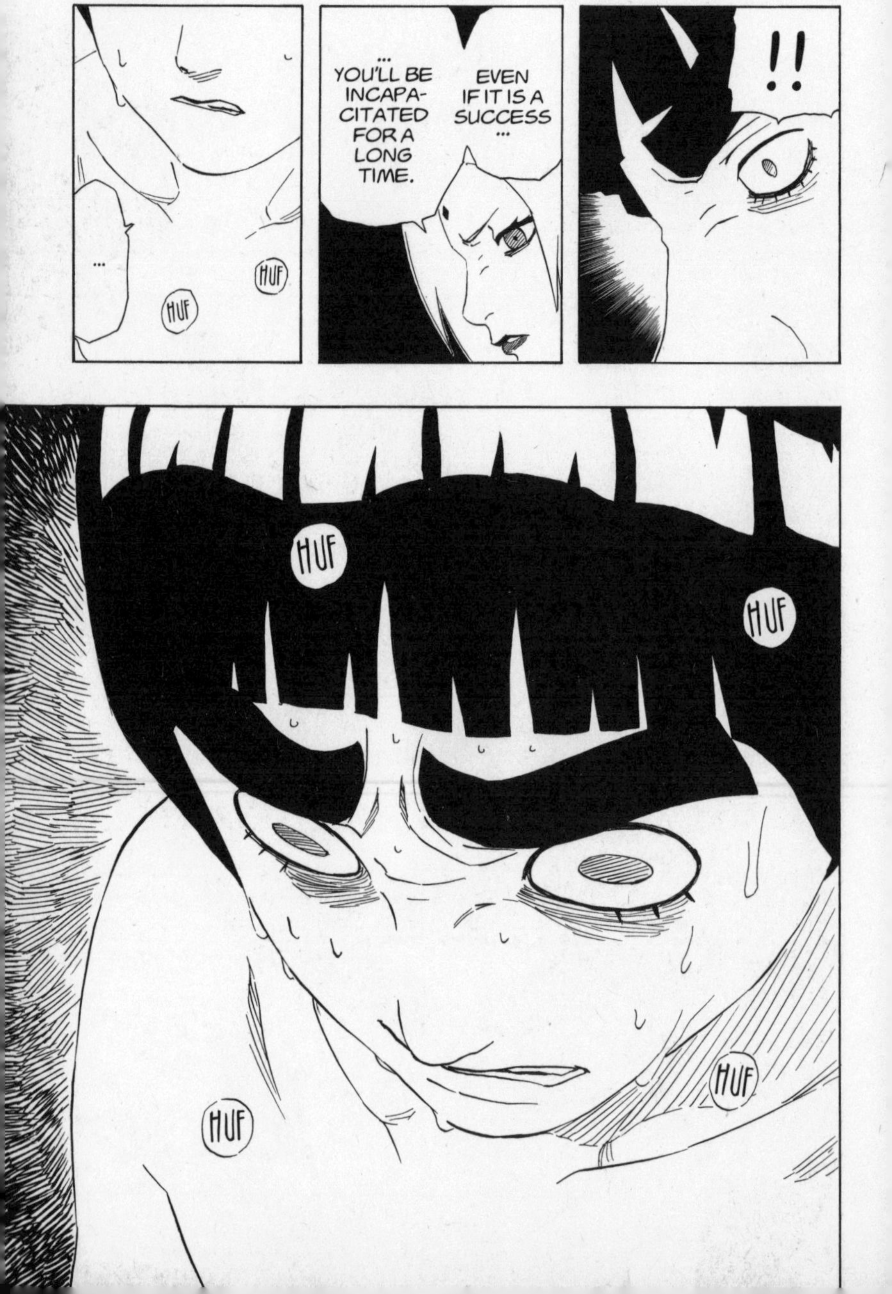
!!
EVEN IF IT IS A SUCCESS ...
... YOU'LL BE INCAPACITATED FOR A LONG TIME.
HUF
...
HUF
HUF
HUF
HUF
HUF

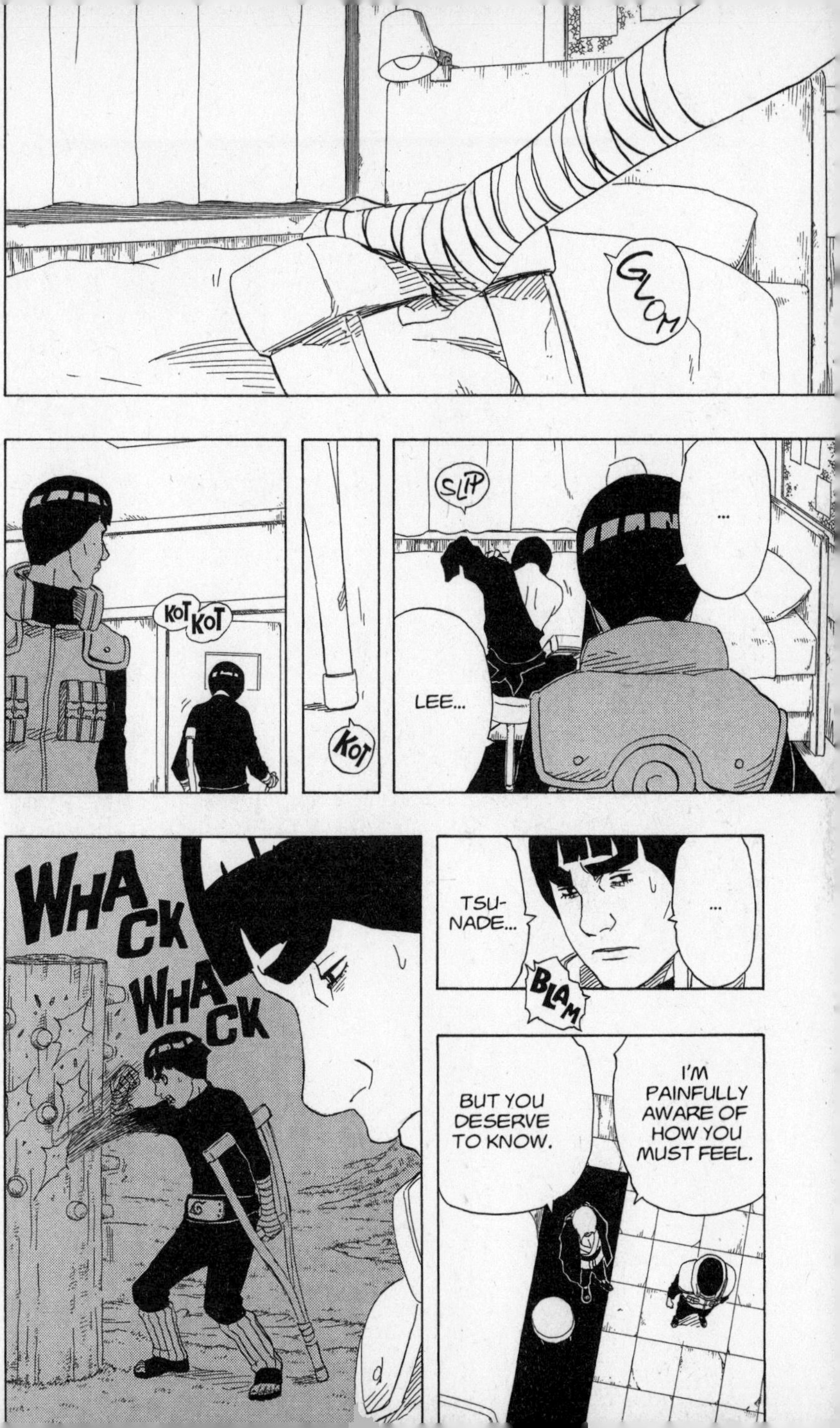
GLOM
...
SLIP
LEE...
KOT
KOT KOT
...
TSU-NADE...
BLAM
I'M PAINFULLY AWARE OF HOW YOU MUST FEEL.
BUT YOU DESERVE TO KNOW.
WHACK
WHACK

READ THIS WAY

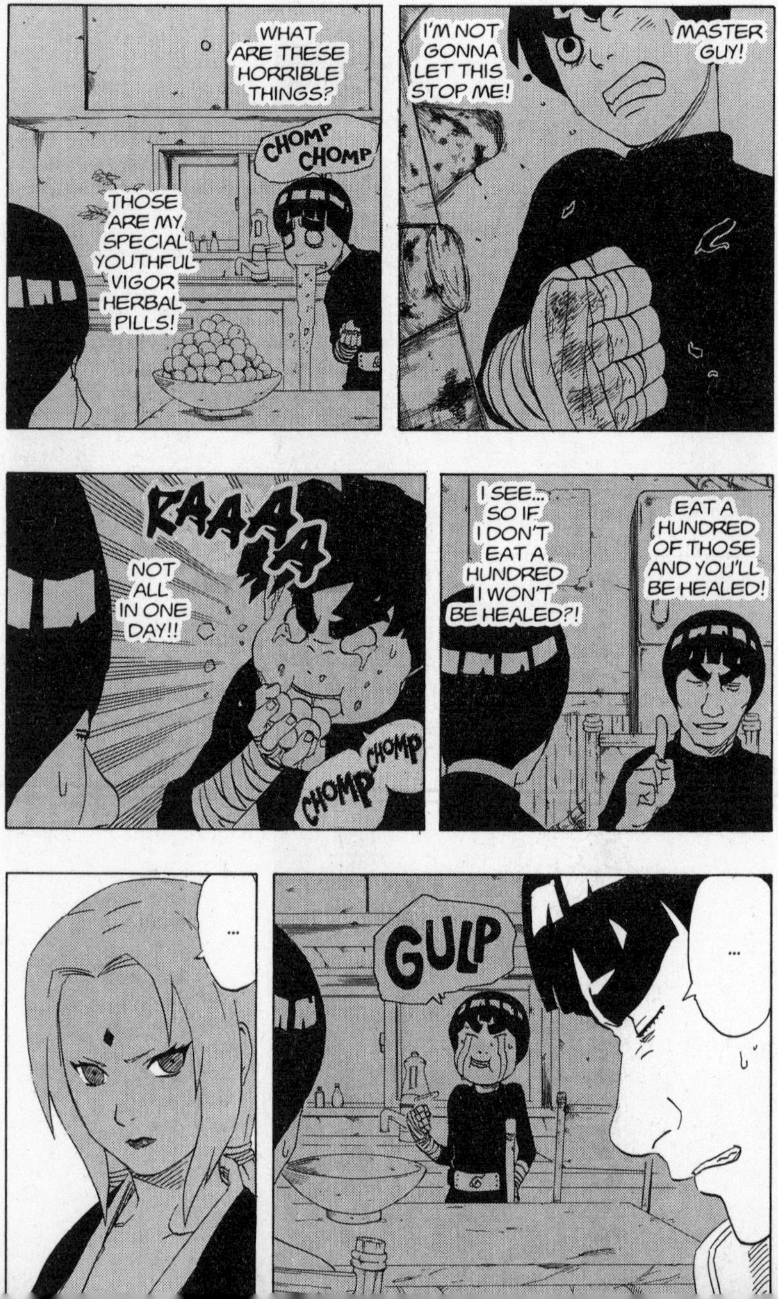
MASTER GUY!
I'M NOT GONNA LET THIS STOP ME!
WHAT ARE THESE HORRIBLE THINGS?
CHOMP CHOMP
THOSE ARE MY SPECIAL YOUTHFUL VIGOR HERBAL PILLS!
EAT A HUNDRED OF THOSE AND YOU'LL BE HEALED!
I SEE... SO IF I DON'T EAT A HUNDRED I WON'T BE HEALED?!
RAAAAA
NOT ALL IN ONE DAY!!
CHOMP CHOMP
...
GULP
...

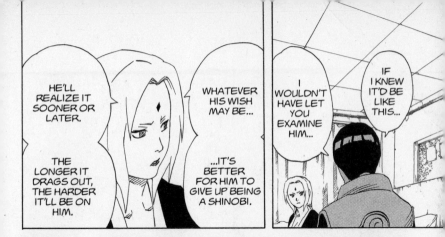

IF I KNEW IT'D BE LIKE THIS...
I WOULDN'T HAVE LET YOU EXAMINE HIM...
WHATEVER HIS WISH MAY BE...
...IT'S BETTER FOR HIM TO GIVE UP BEING A SHINOBI.
HE'LL REALIZE IT SOONER OR LATER.
THE LONGER IT DRAGS OUT, THE HARDER IT'LL BE ON HIM.
...
焼肉
Q

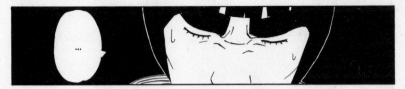

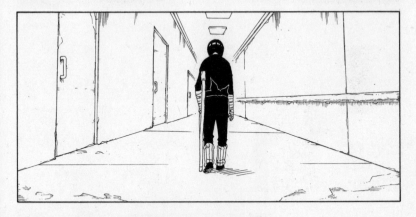

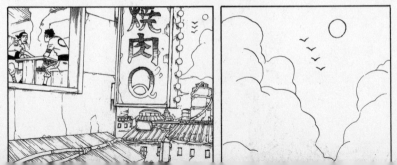

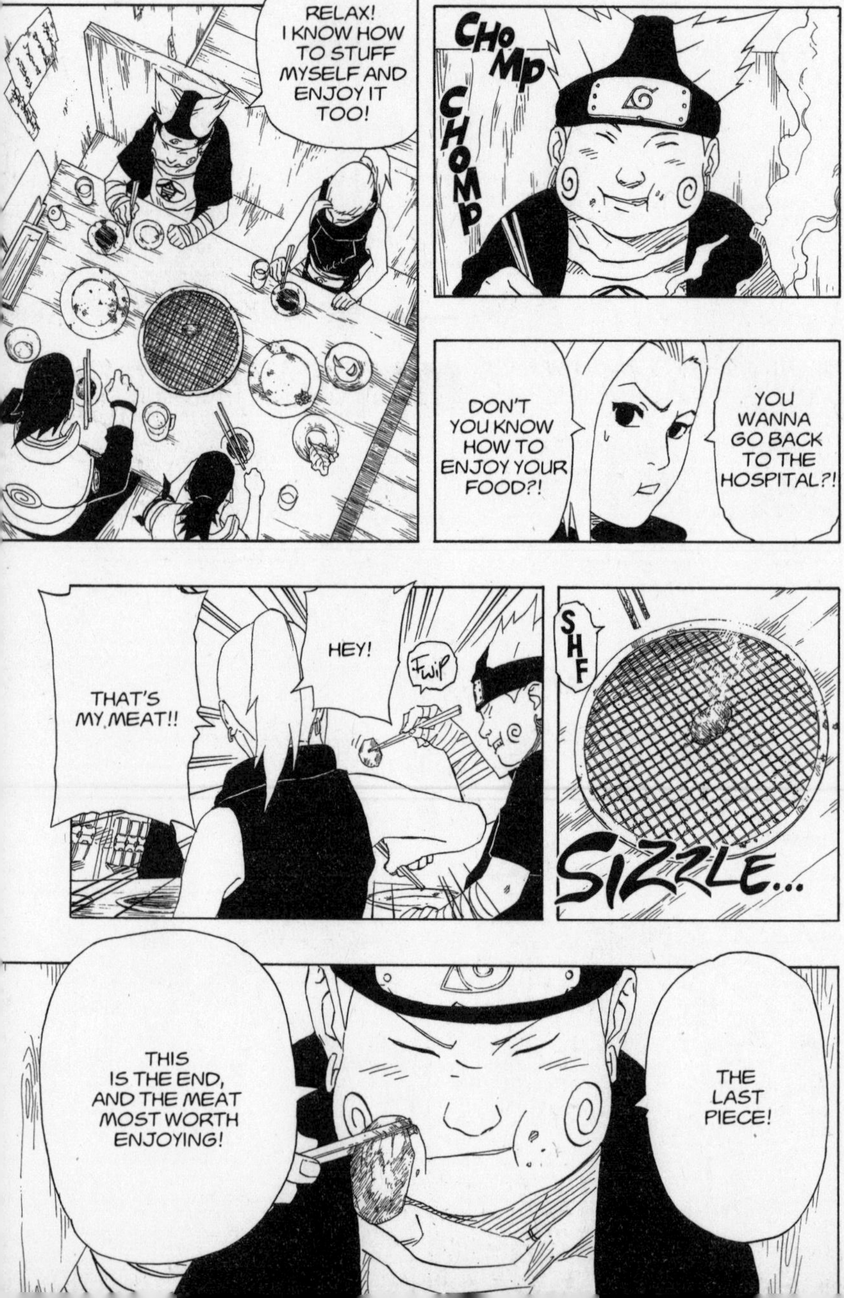
CHOMP
CHOMP
YOU WANNA GO BACK TO THE HOSPITAL?!
DON'T YOU KNOW HOW TO ENJOY YOUR FOOD?!
RELAX! I KNOW HOW TO STUFF MYSELF AND ENJOY IT TOO!
SHF
SIZZLE...
FWIP
HEY!
THAT'S MY MEAT!!
THE LAST PIECE!
THIS IS THE END, AND THE MEAT MOST WORTH ENJOYING!

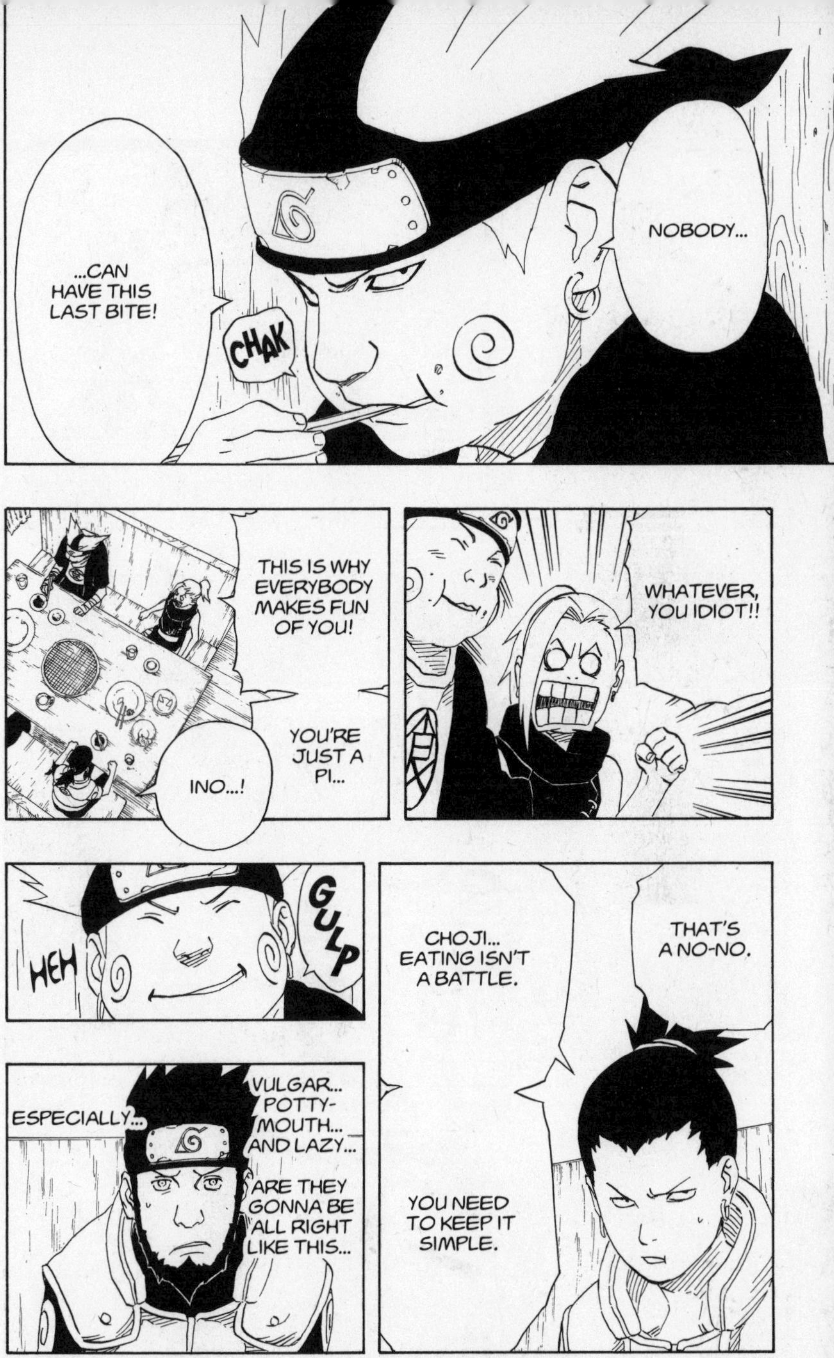
NOBODY...
...CAN HAVE THIS LAST BITE!
CHAK
WHATEVER, YOU IDIOT!!
THIS IS WHY EVERYBODY MAKES FUN OF YOU!
YOU'RE JUST A PI...
INO...!
THAT'S A NO-NO.
CHOJI... EATING ISN'T A BATTLE.
YOU NEED TO KEEP IT SIMPLE.
GULP
HEH
VULGAR... POTTY-MOUTH... AND LAZY...
ESPECIALLY...
ARE THEY GONNA BE ALL RIGHT LIKE THIS...

READ THIS WAY

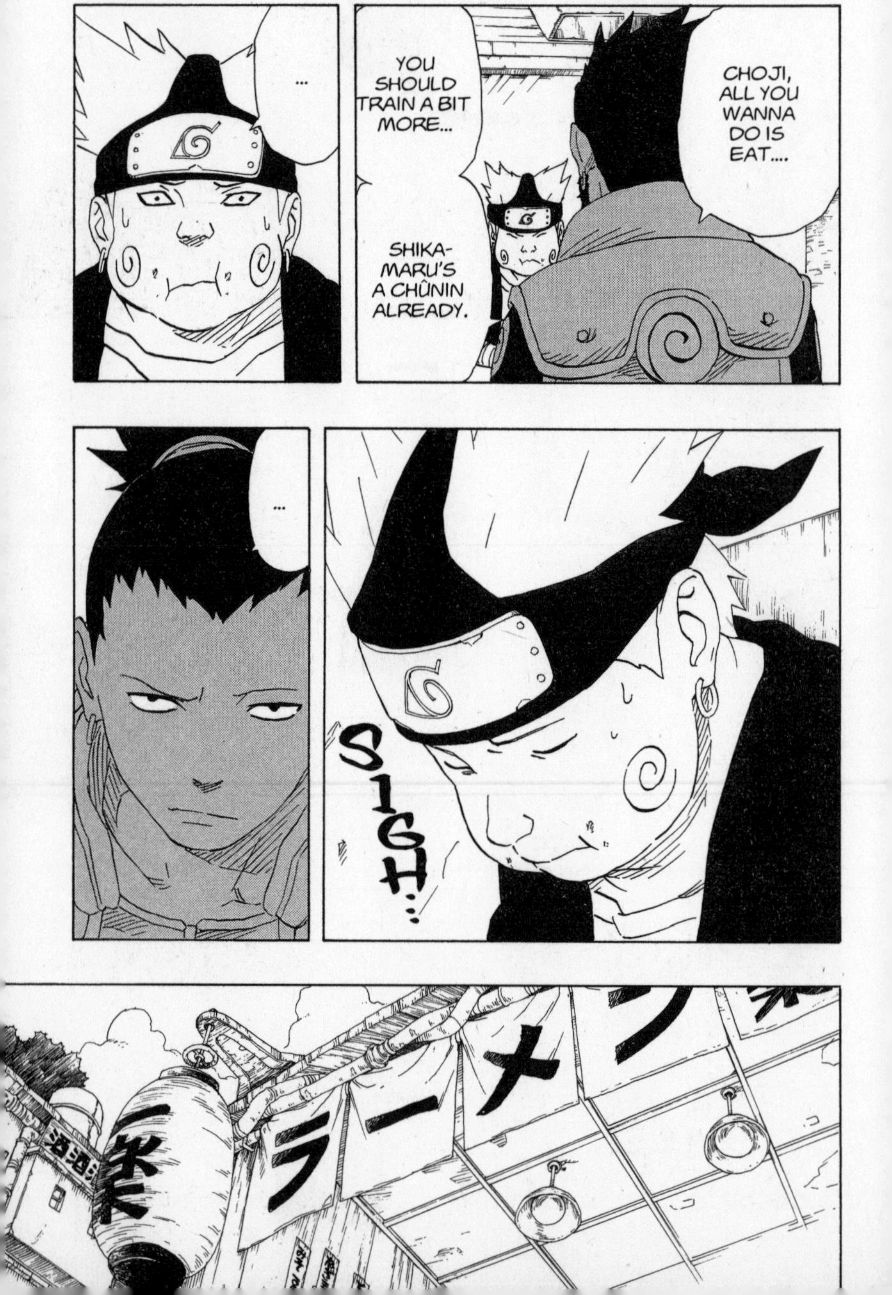
CHOJI, ALL YOU WANNA DO IS EAT....
YOU SHOULD TRAIN A BIT MORE...
SHIKA-MARU'S A CHÛNIN ALREADY.
...
SIGH...
...
ラーメン

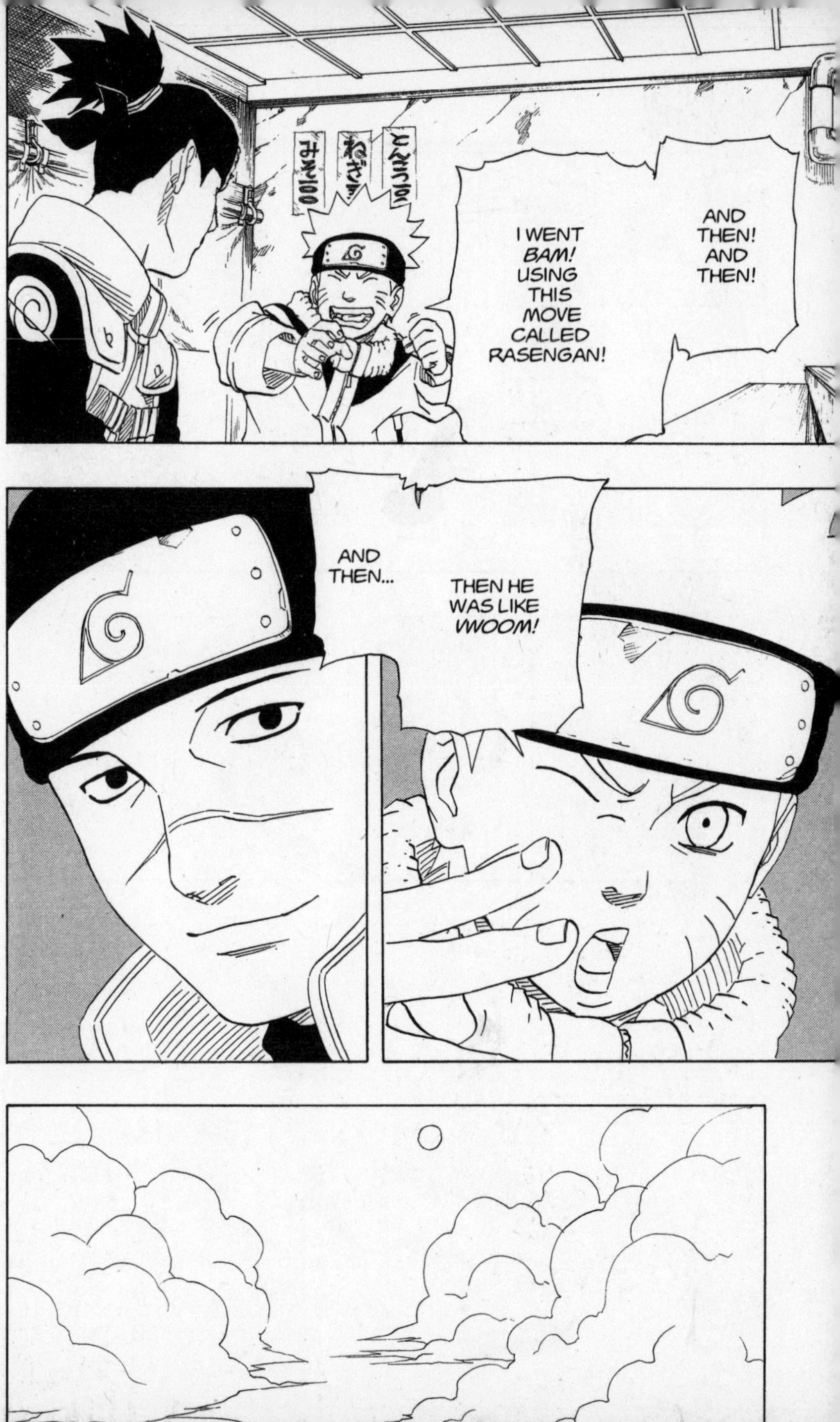
AND THEN! AND THEN!
I WENT *BAM!* USING THIS MOVE CALLED RASENGAN!
AND THEN...
THEN HE WAS LIKE *VWOOM!*

READ THIS WAY

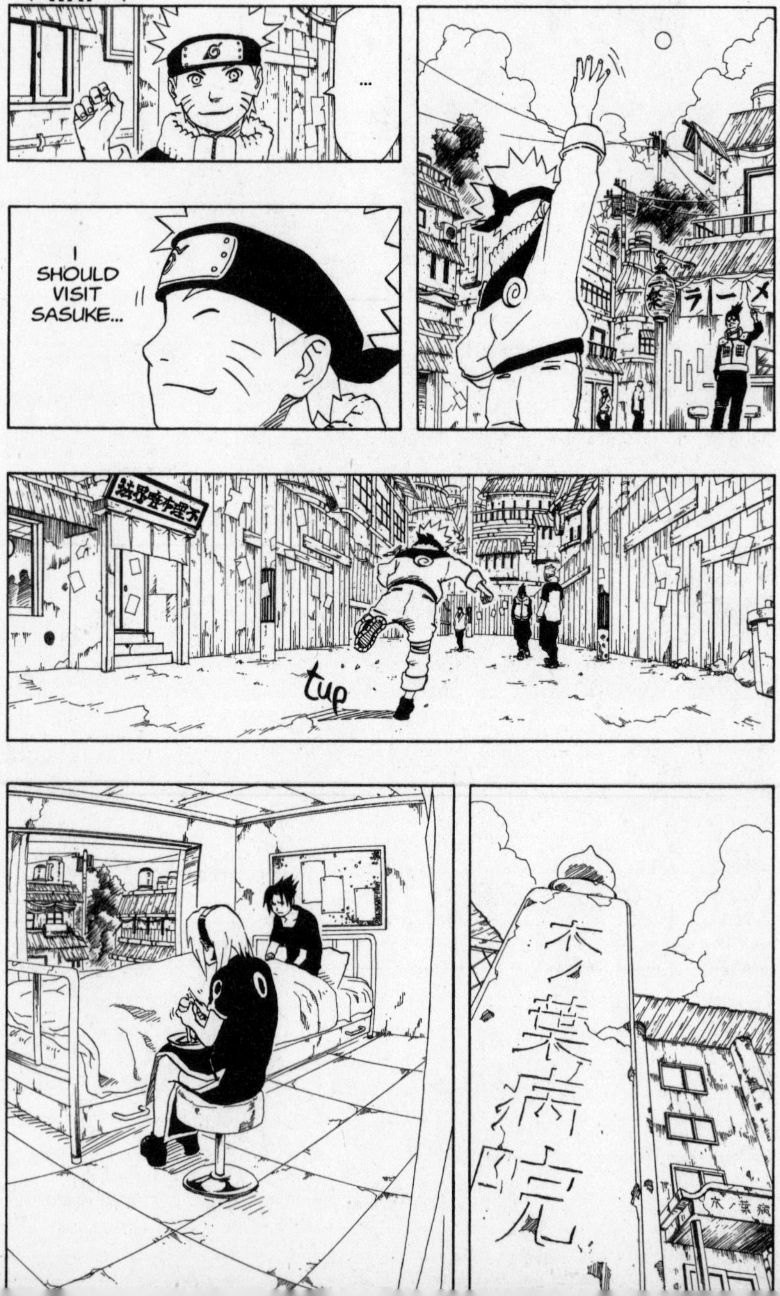
一楽
ラーメ
...
I SHOULD VISIT SASUKE...
tup
木ノ葉病院
木ノ葉病

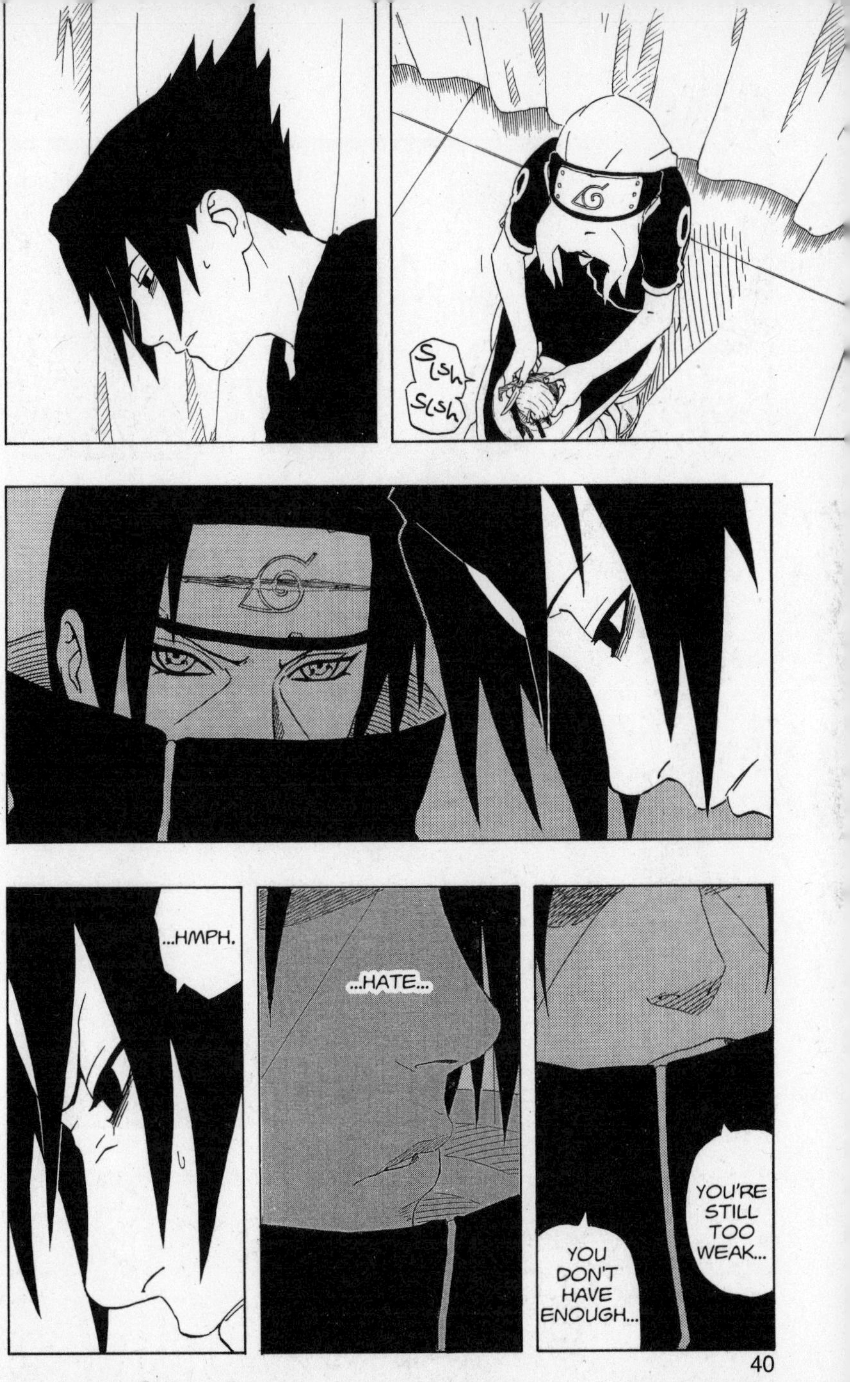
Slsh
Slsh
YOU'RE STILL TOO WEAK...
YOU DON'T HAVE ENOUGH...
...HATE...
...HMPH.

READ THIS WAY

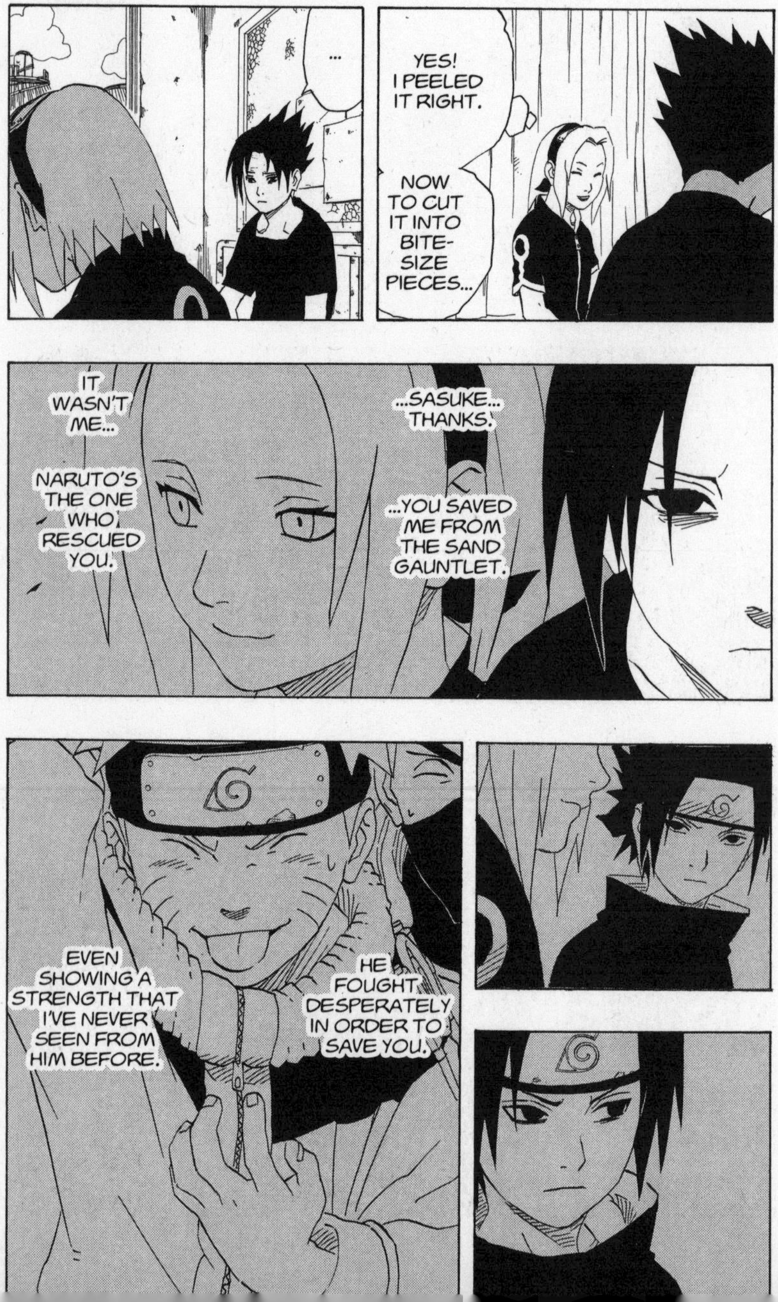
YES! I PEELED IT RIGHT.
NOW TO CUT IT INTO BITE-SIZE PIECES...
...
...SASUKE... THANKS.
...YOU SAVED ME FROM THE SAND GAUNTLET.
IT WASN'T ME...
NARUTO'S THE ONE WHO RESCUED YOU.
HE FOUGHT DESPERATELY IN ORDER TO SAVE YOU.
EVEN SHOWING A STRENGTH THAT I'VE NEVER SEEN FROM HIM BEFORE.

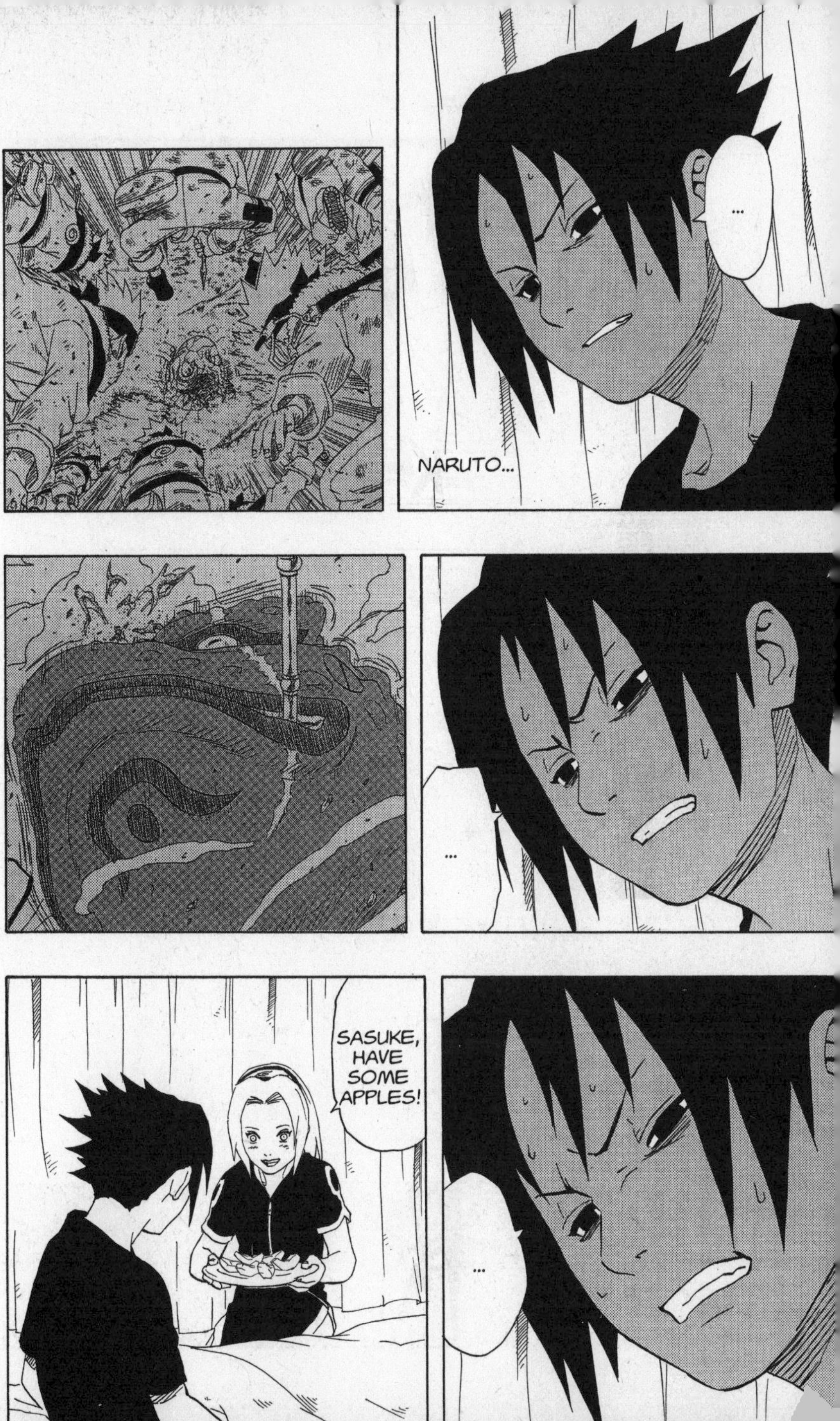
...
NARUTO...
...
...
SASUKE, HAVE SOME APPLES!

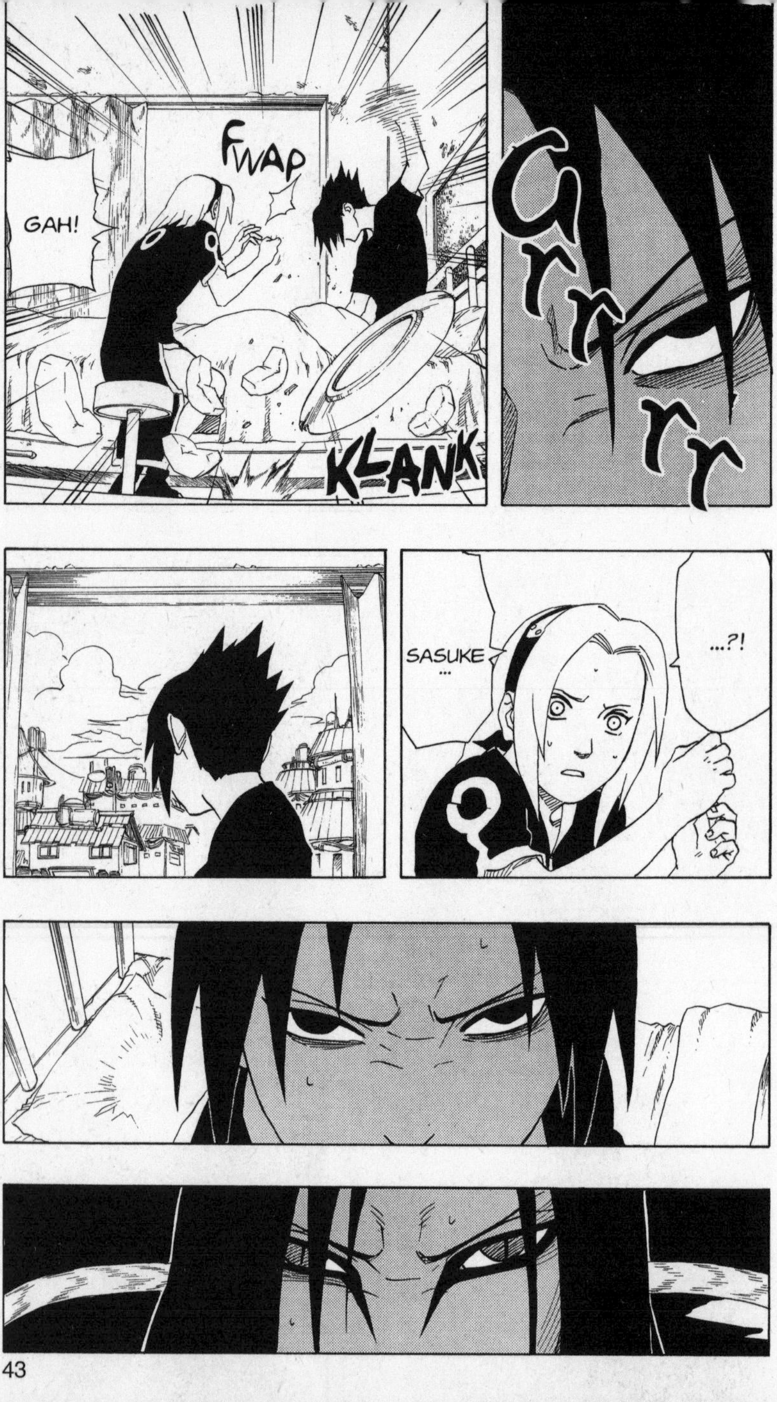
Grrrrr
FWAP
GAH!
KLANK
...?!
SASUKE ...

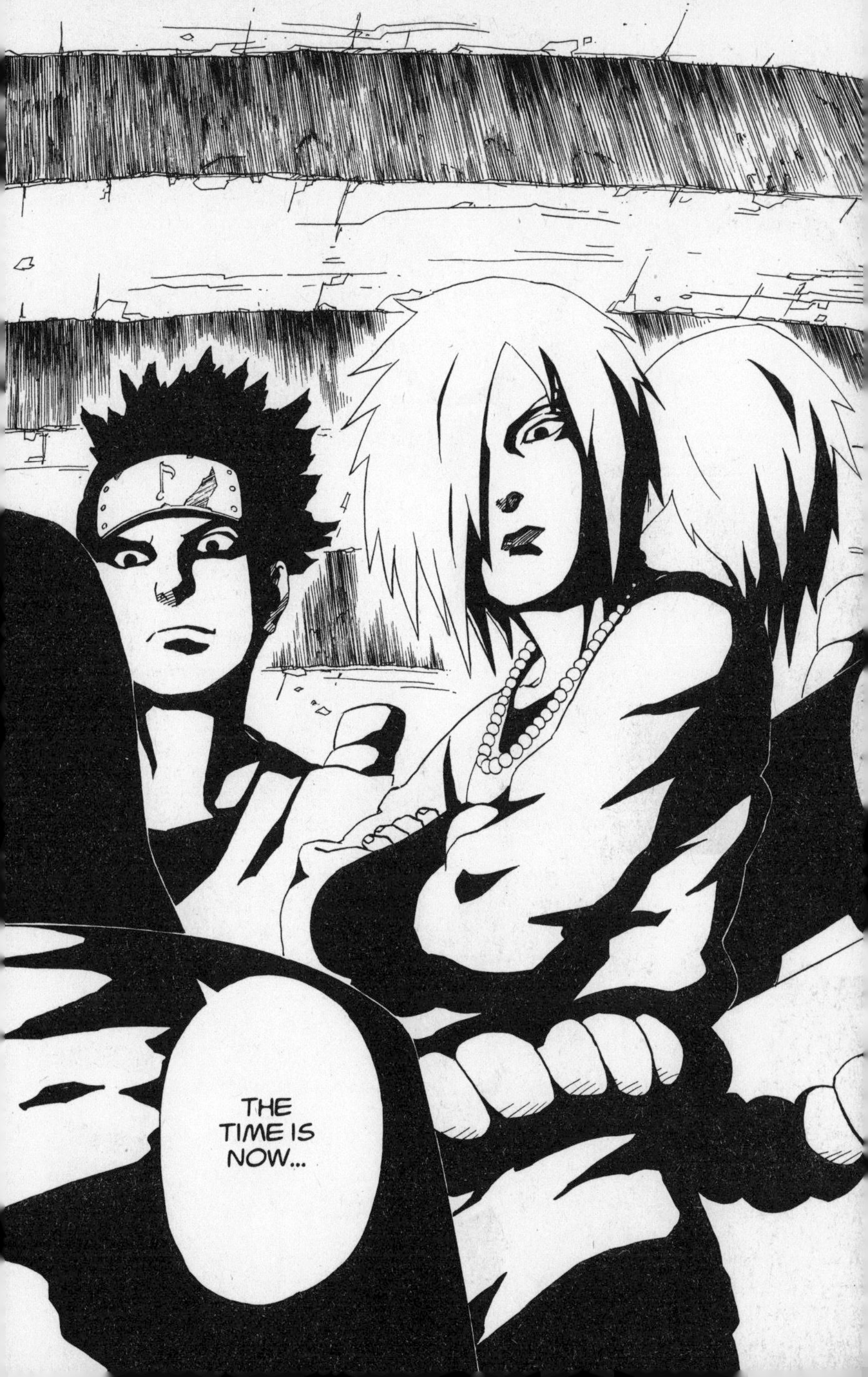
THE TIME IS NOW...

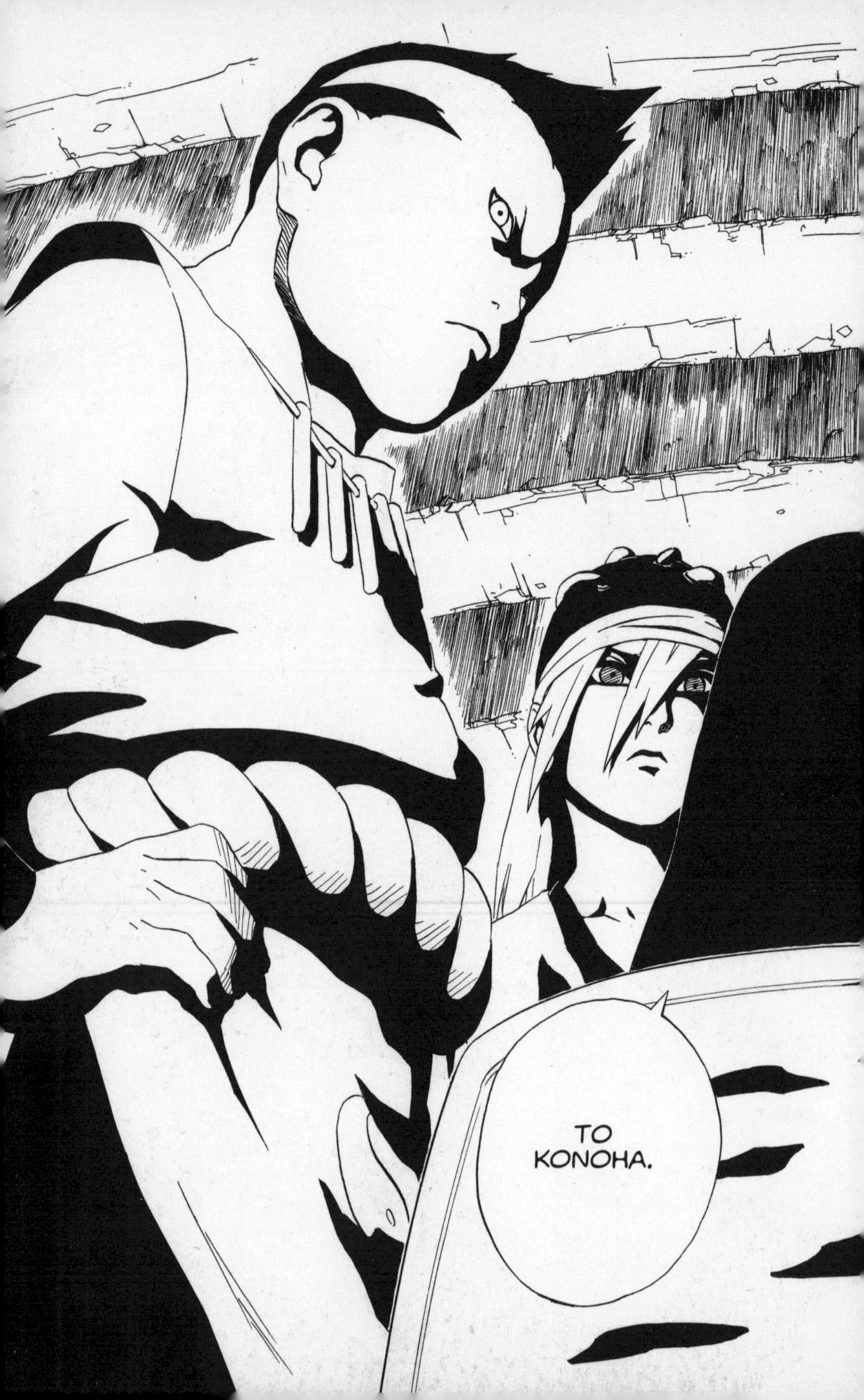
TO KONOHA.

Number 174: Feelings...!

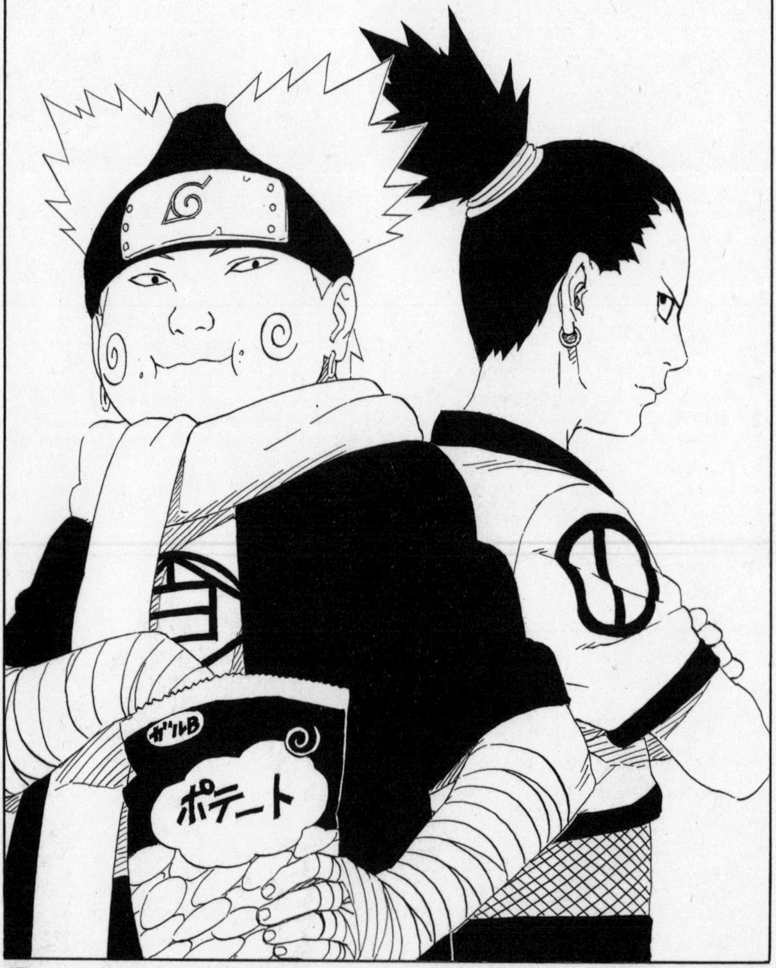
ガルB
ポテート

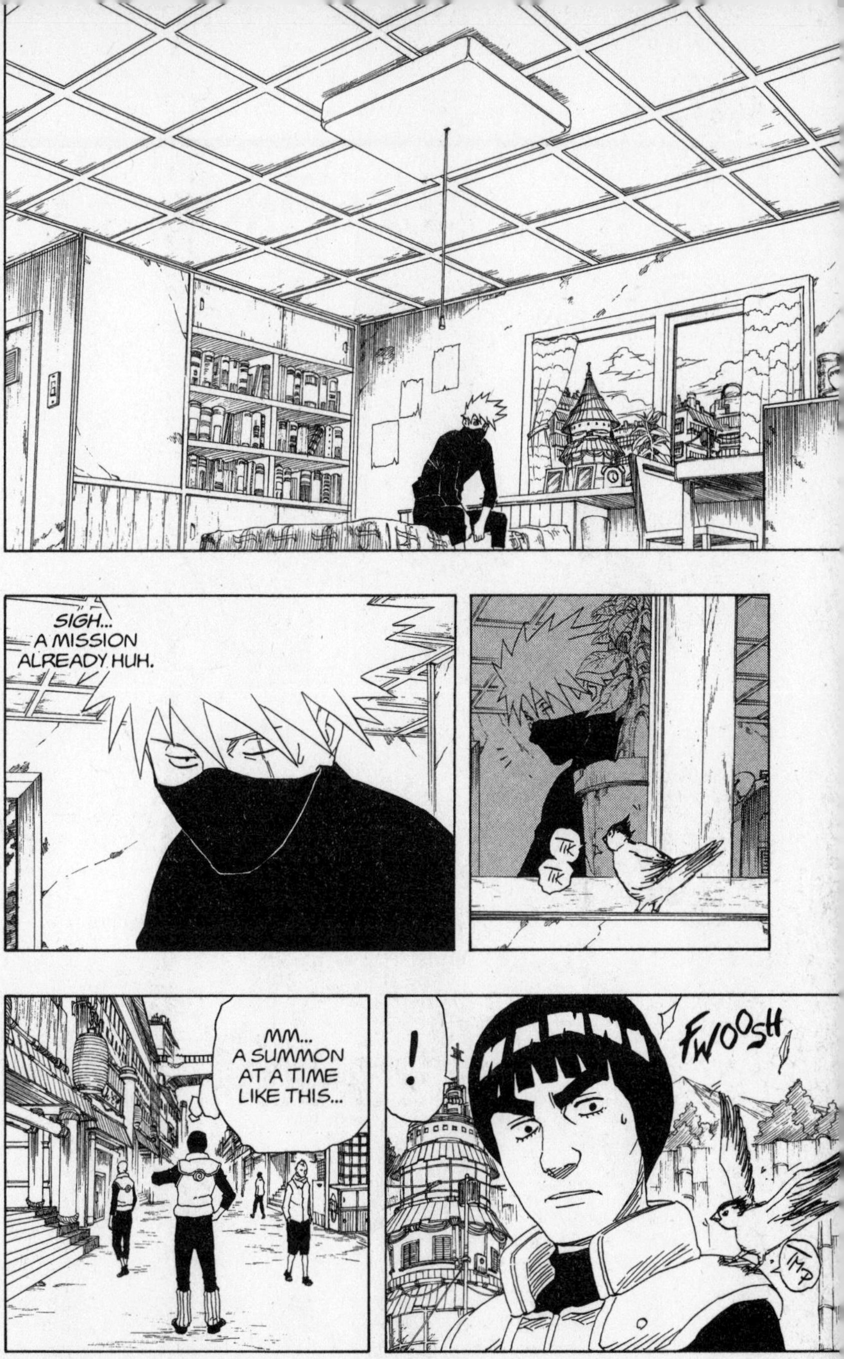

TIK
TIK
SIGH... A MISSION ALREADY HUH.
!
FWOOSH
TMP
MM... A SUMMON AT A TIME LIKE THIS...

READ THIS WAY

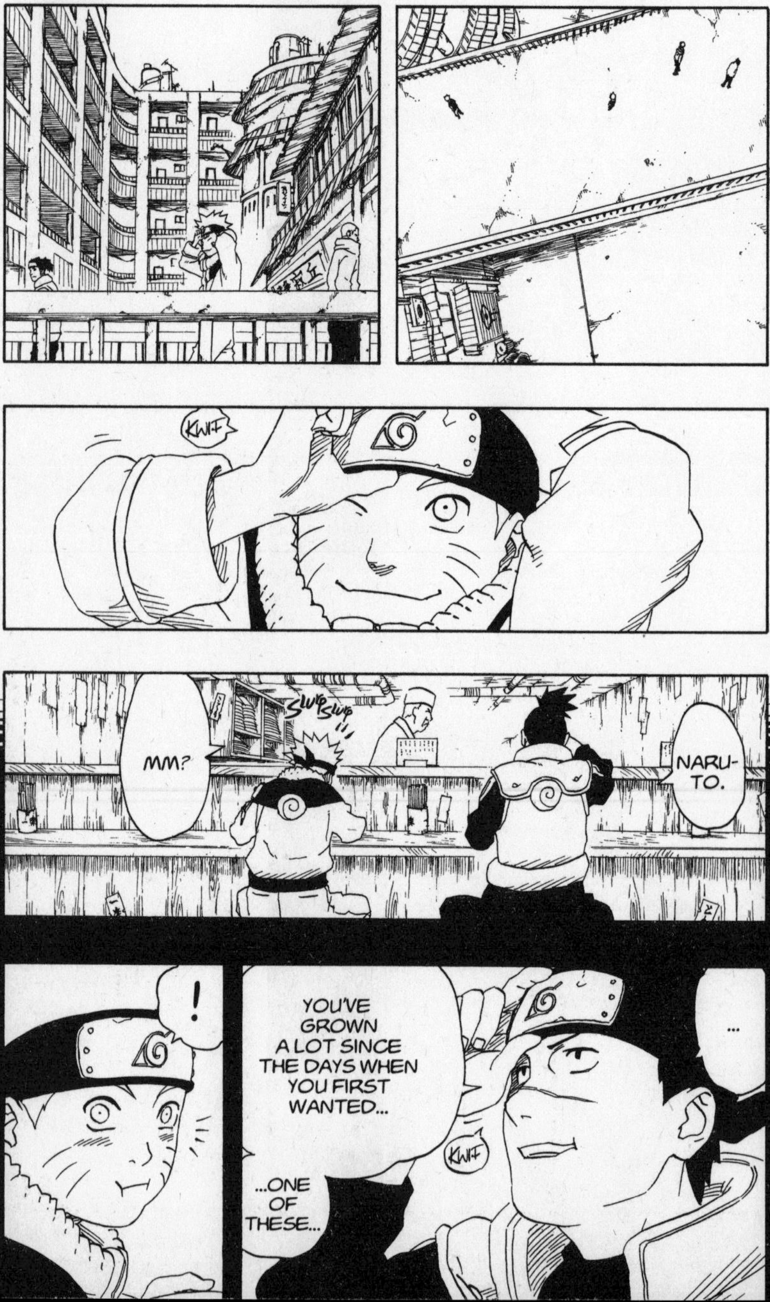
KWIF
NARU-TO.
SLURP SLURP
MM?
...
YOU'VE GROWN A LOT SINCE THE DAYS WHEN YOU FIRST WANTED...
KWIF
...ONE OF THESE...
!

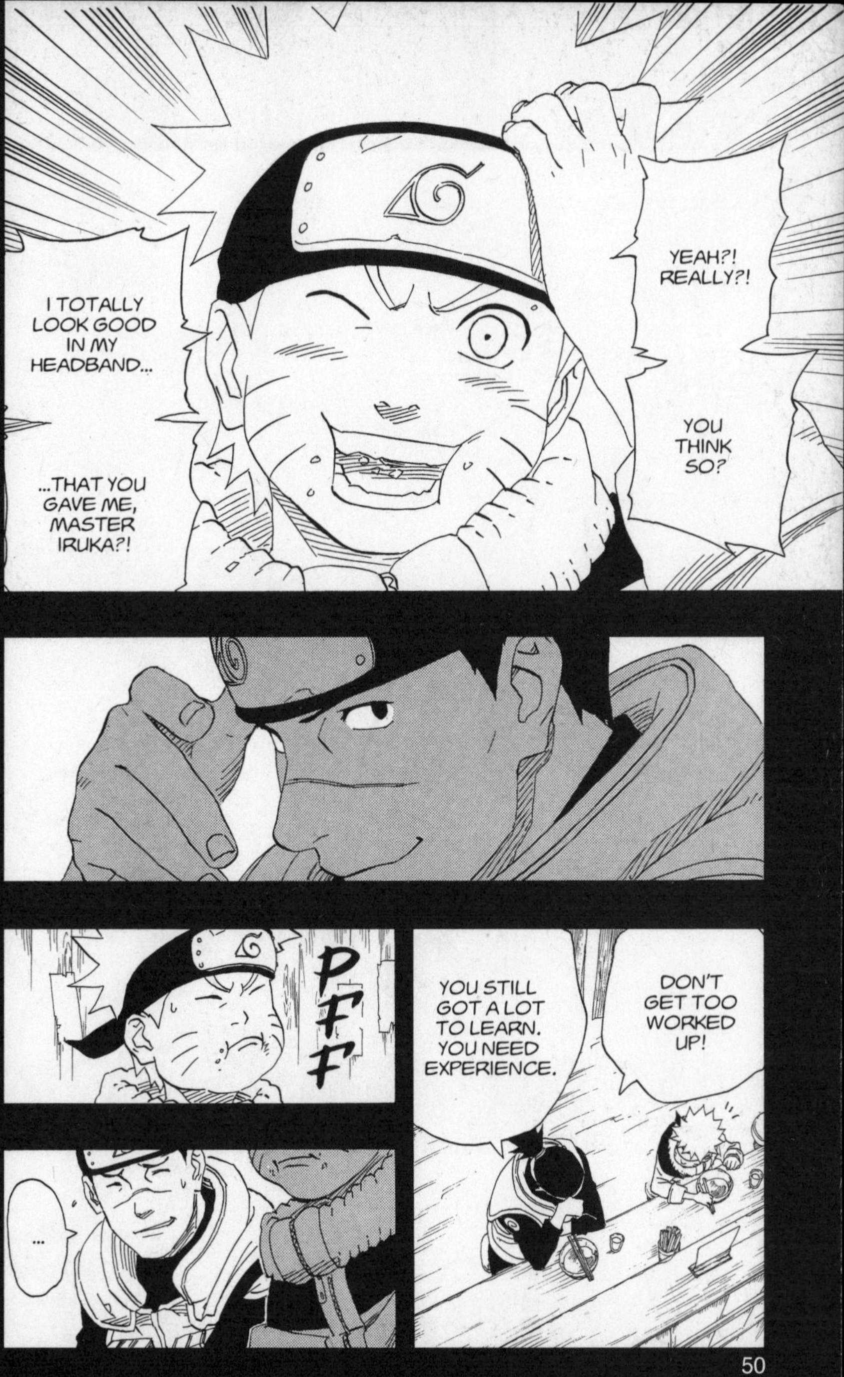
YEAH?! REALLY?!
YOU THINK SO?
I TOTALLY LOOK GOOD IN MY HEADBAND...
...THAT YOU GAVE ME, MASTER IRUKA?!
DON'T GET TOO WORKED UP!
YOU STILL GOT A LOT TO LEARN. YOU NEED EXPERIENCE.
PFF
...

READ THIS WAY

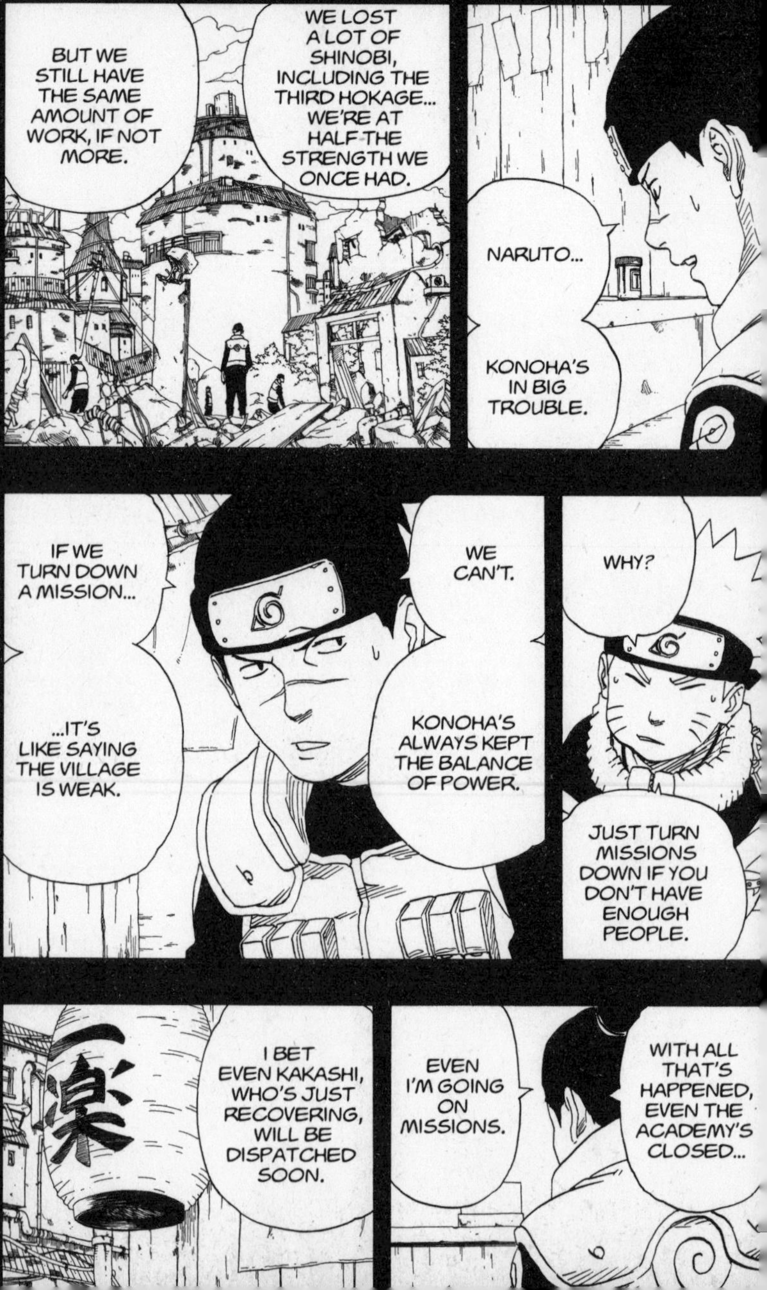
NARUTO...
KONOHA'S IN BIG TROUBLE.
WE LOST A LOT OF SHINOBI, INCLUDING THE THIRD HOKAGE... WE'RE AT HALF THE STRENGTH WE ONCE HAD.
BUT WE STILL HAVE THE SAME AMOUNT OF WORK, IF NOT MORE.
WHY?
JUST TURN MISSIONS DOWN IF YOU DON'T HAVE ENOUGH PEOPLE.
WE CAN'T.
KONOHA'S ALWAYS KEPT THE BALANCE OF POWER.
IF WE TURN DOWN A MISSION...
...IT'S LIKE SAYING THE VILLAGE IS WEAK.
WITH ALL THAT'S HAPPENED, EVEN THE ACADEMY'S CLOSED...
EVEN I'M GOING ON MISSIONS.
I BET EVEN KAKASHI, WHO'S JUST RECOVERING, WILL BE DISPATCHED SOON.

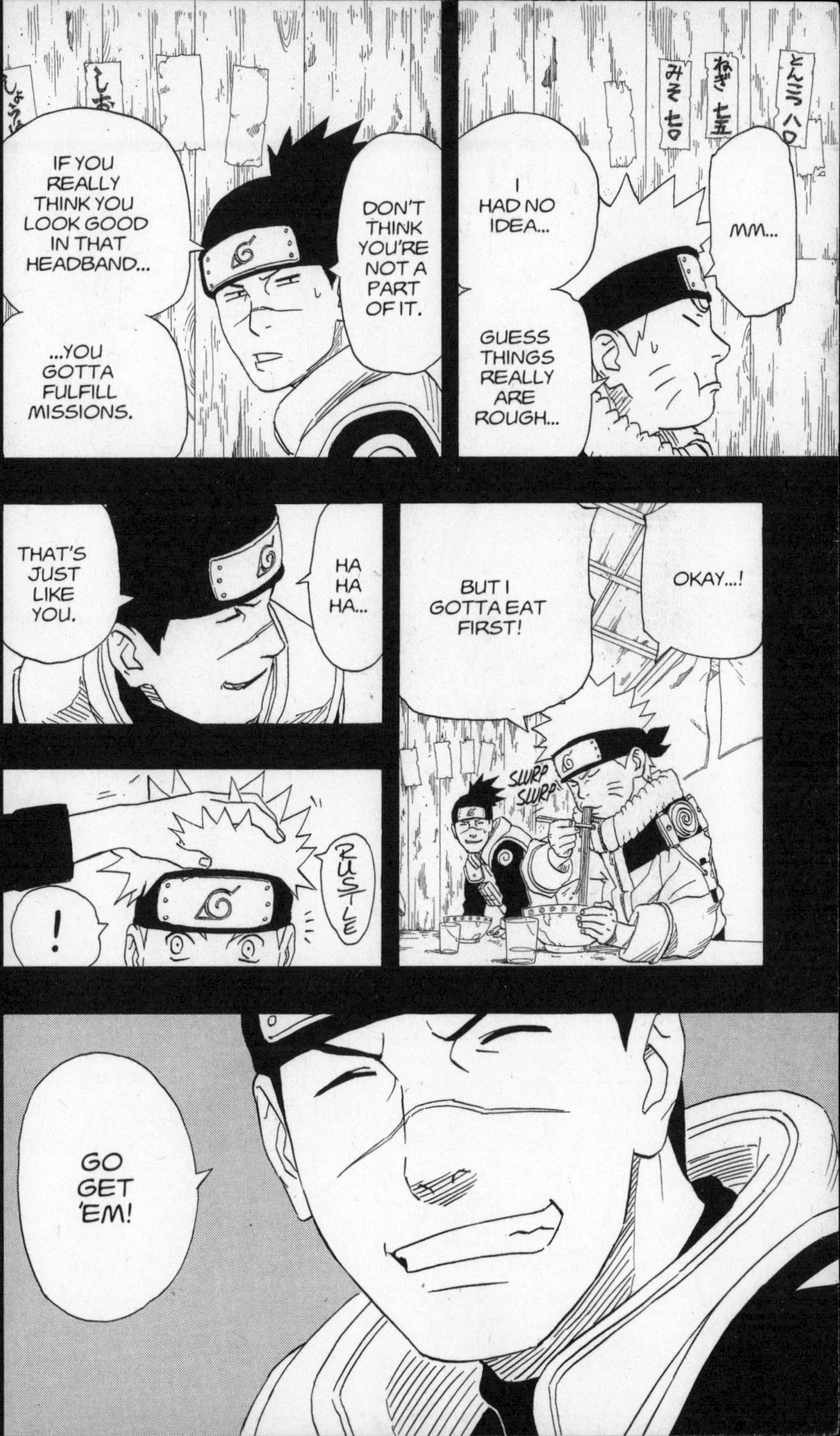

とんこつ 八〇
ねぎ 七五
みそ 七〇
MM...
I HAD NO IDEA...
GUESS THINGS REALLY ARE ROUGH...
しお
DON'T THINK YOU'RE NOT A PART OF IT.
IF YOU REALLY THINK YOU LOOK GOOD IN THAT HEADBAND...
...YOU GOTTA FULFILL MISSIONS.
OKAY...!
BUT I GOTTA EAT FIRST!
SLURP SLURP
HA HA HA...
THAT'S JUST LIKE YOU.
RUSTLE
!
GO GET 'EM!

READ THIS WAY

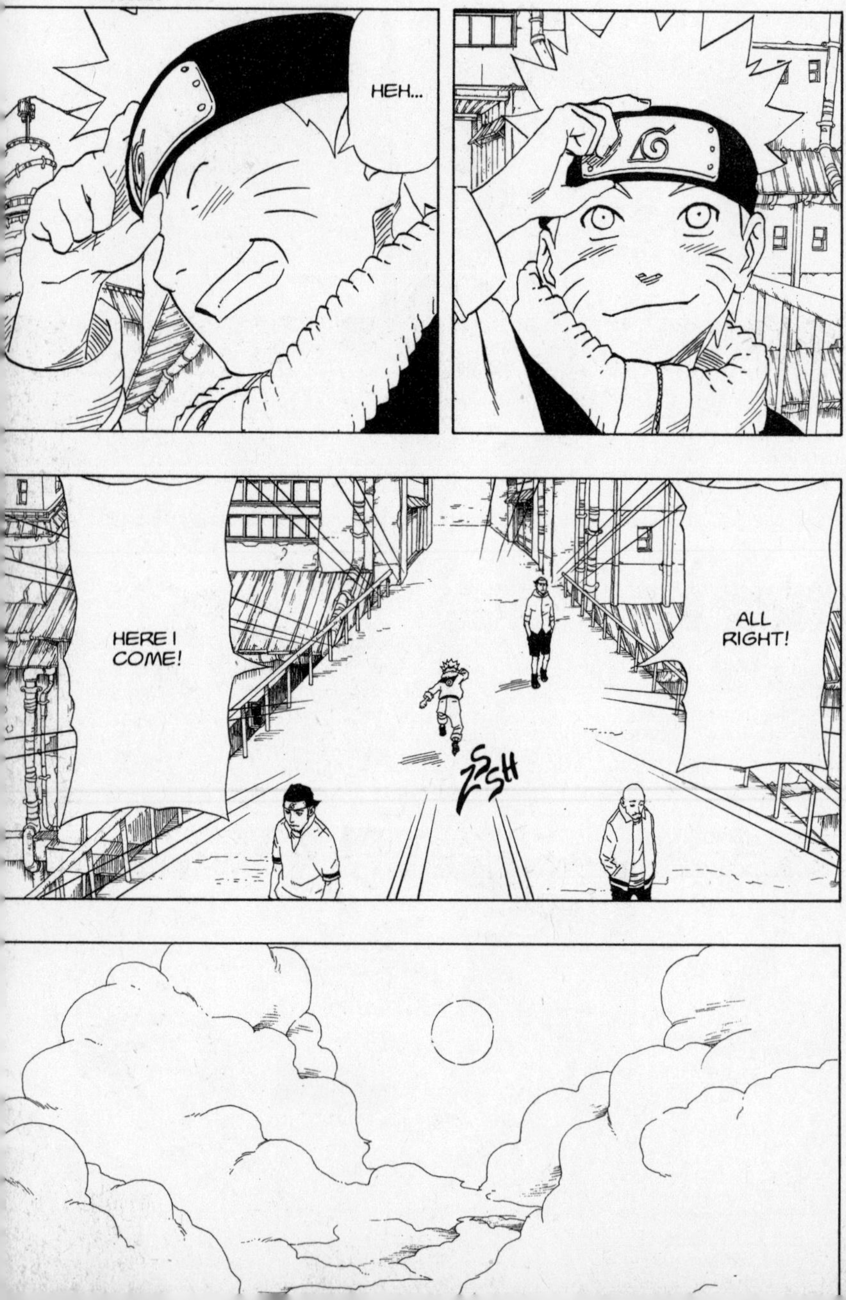
HEH...
ALL RIGHT!
HERE I COME!
ZSSH

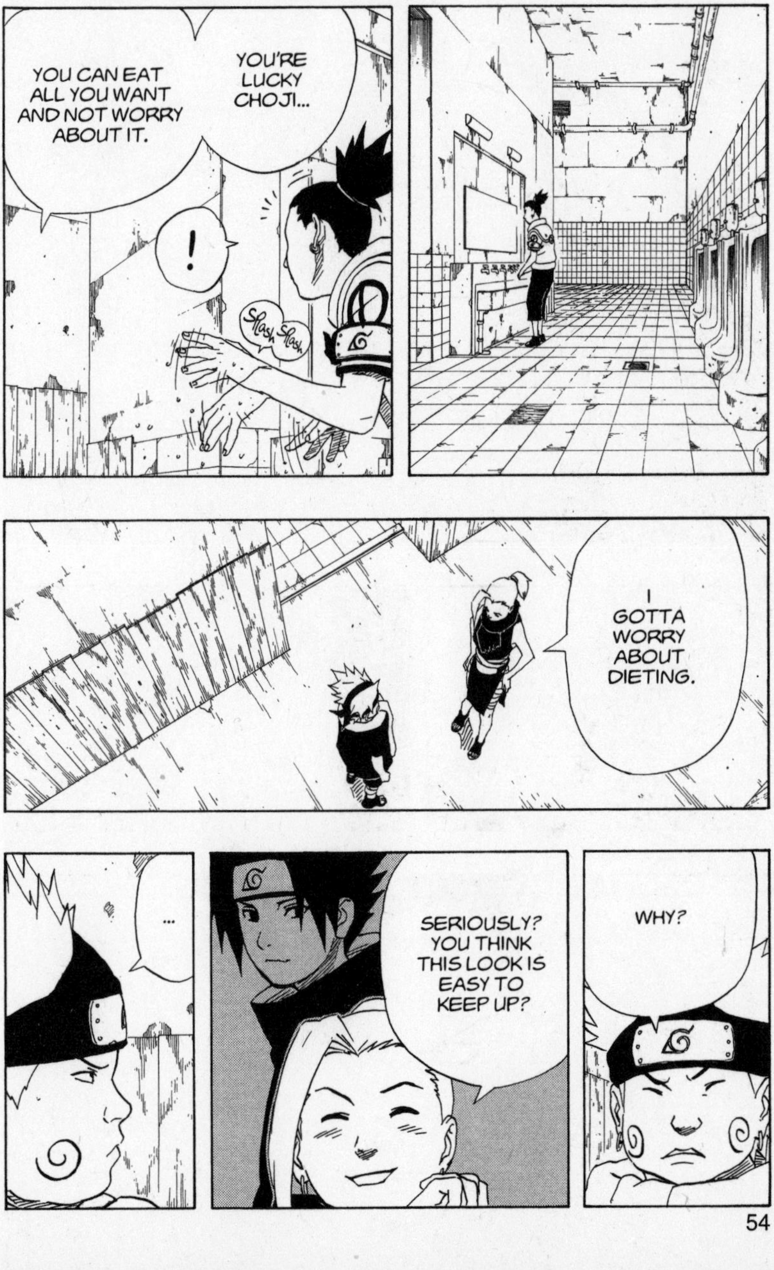
YOU'RE LUCKY CHOJI...
YOU CAN EAT ALL YOU WANT AND NOT WORRY ABOUT IT.
!
Slash Slash
I GOTTA WORRY ABOUT DIETING.
WHY?
SERIOUSLY? YOU THINK THIS LOOK IS EASY TO KEEP UP?
...

READ THIS WAY

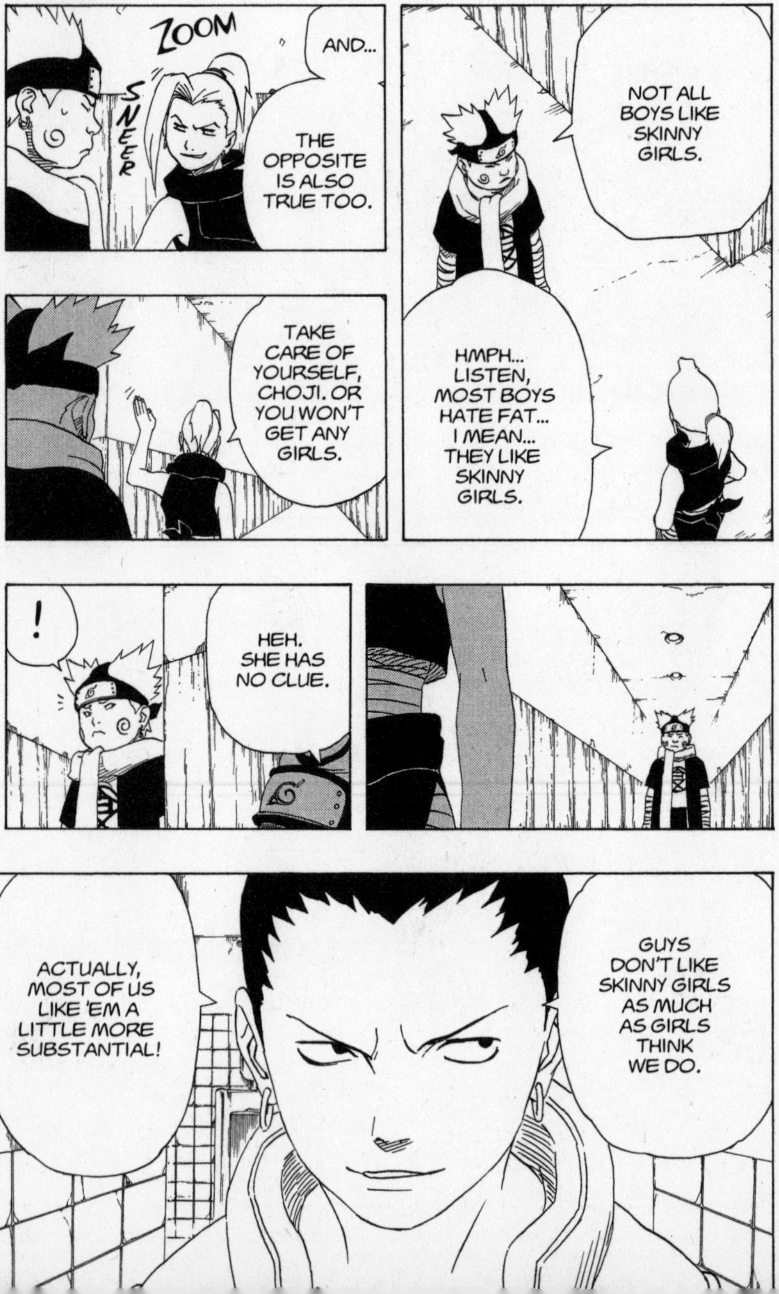
NOT ALL BOYS LIKE SKINNY GIRLS.
HMPH... LISTEN, MOST BOYS HATE FAT... I MEAN... THEY LIKE SKINNY GIRLS.
AND...
THE OPPOSITE IS ALSO TRUE TOO.
ZOOM
SNEER
TAKE CARE OF YOURSELF, CHOJI. OR YOU WON'T GET ANY GIRLS.
HEH. SHE HAS NO CLUE.
!
GUYS DON'T LIKE SKINNY GIRLS AS MUCH AS GIRLS THINK WE DO.
ACTUALLY, MOST OF US LIKE 'EM A LITTLE MORE SUBSTANTIAL!

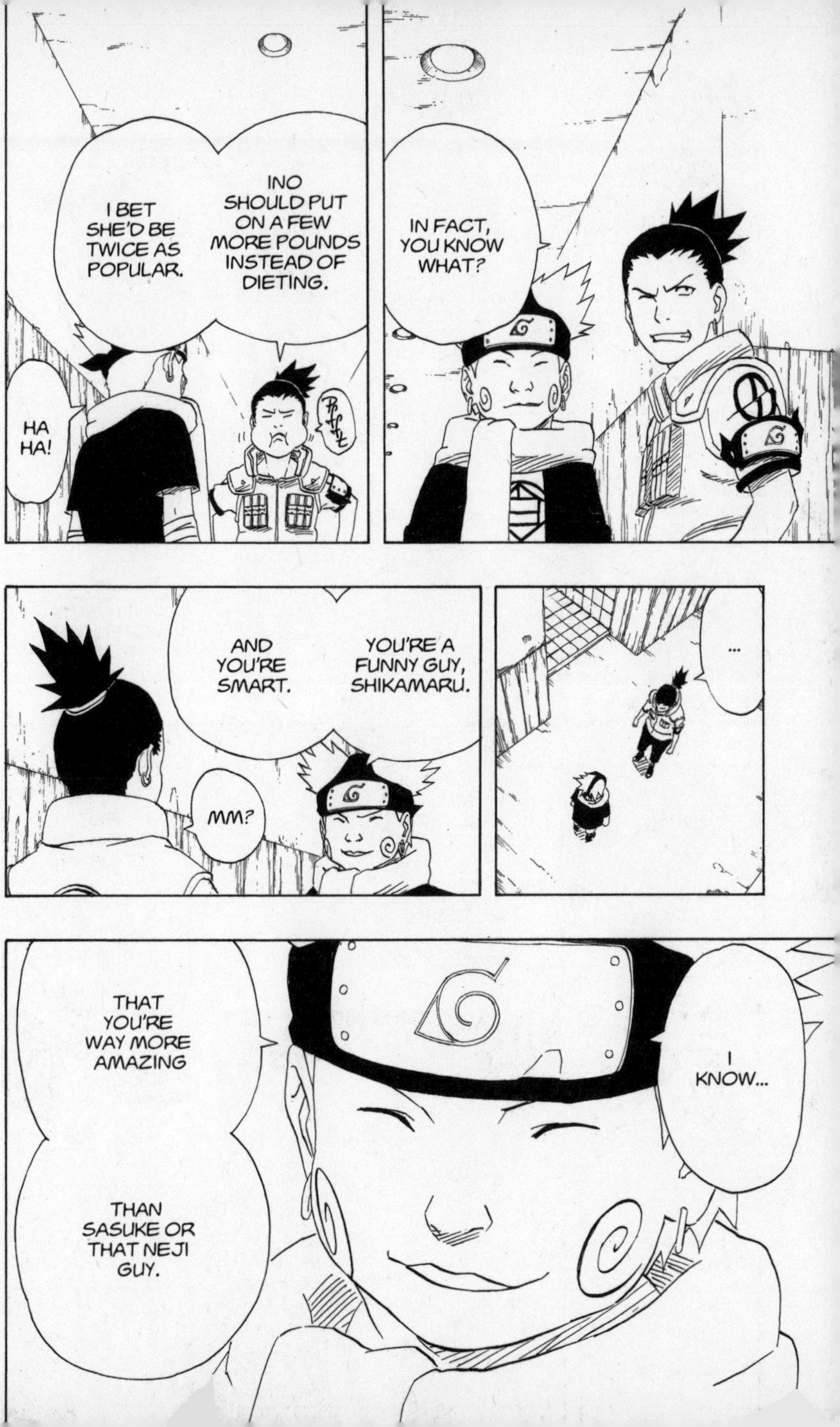
IN FACT, YOU KNOW WHAT?
INO SHOULD PUT ON A FEW MORE POUNDS INSTEAD OF DIETING.
I BET SHE'D BE TWICE AS POPULAR.
Pfft
HA HA!
...
YOU'RE A FUNNY GUY, SHIKAMARU.
AND YOU'RE SMART.
MM?
I KNOW...
THAT YOU'RE WAY MORE AMAZING
THAN SASUKE OR THAT NEJI GUY.

READ THIS WAY

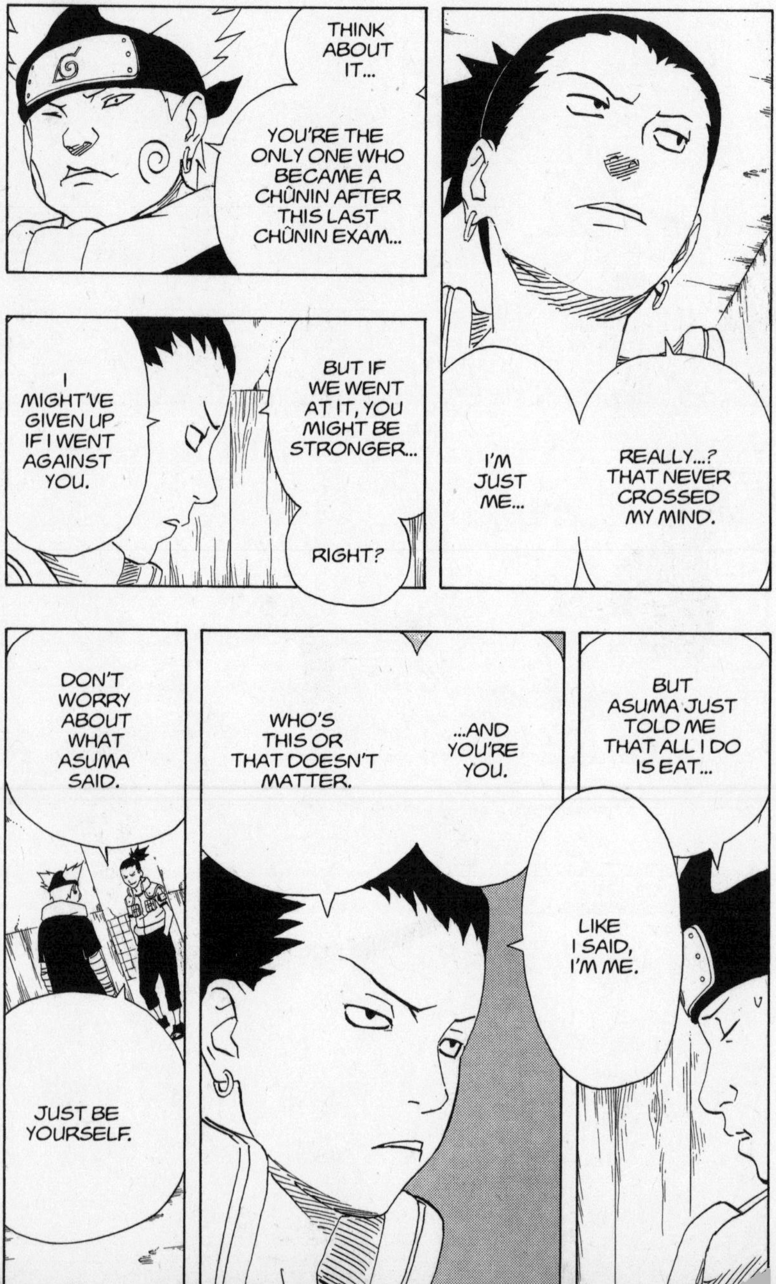
REALLY...? THAT NEVER CROSSED MY MIND.
I'M JUST ME...
THINK ABOUT IT...
YOU'RE THE ONLY ONE WHO BECAME A CHÛNIN AFTER THIS LAST CHÛNIN EXAM...
BUT IF WE WENT AT IT, YOU MIGHT BE STRONGER...
RIGHT?
I MIGHT'VE GIVEN UP IF I WENT AGAINST YOU.
BUT ASUMA JUST TOLD ME THAT ALL I DO IS EAT...
LIKE I SAID, I'M ME.
...AND YOU'RE YOU.
WHO'S THIS OR THAT DOESN'T MATTER.
DON'T WORRY ABOUT WHAT ASUMA SAID.
JUST BE YOURSELF.

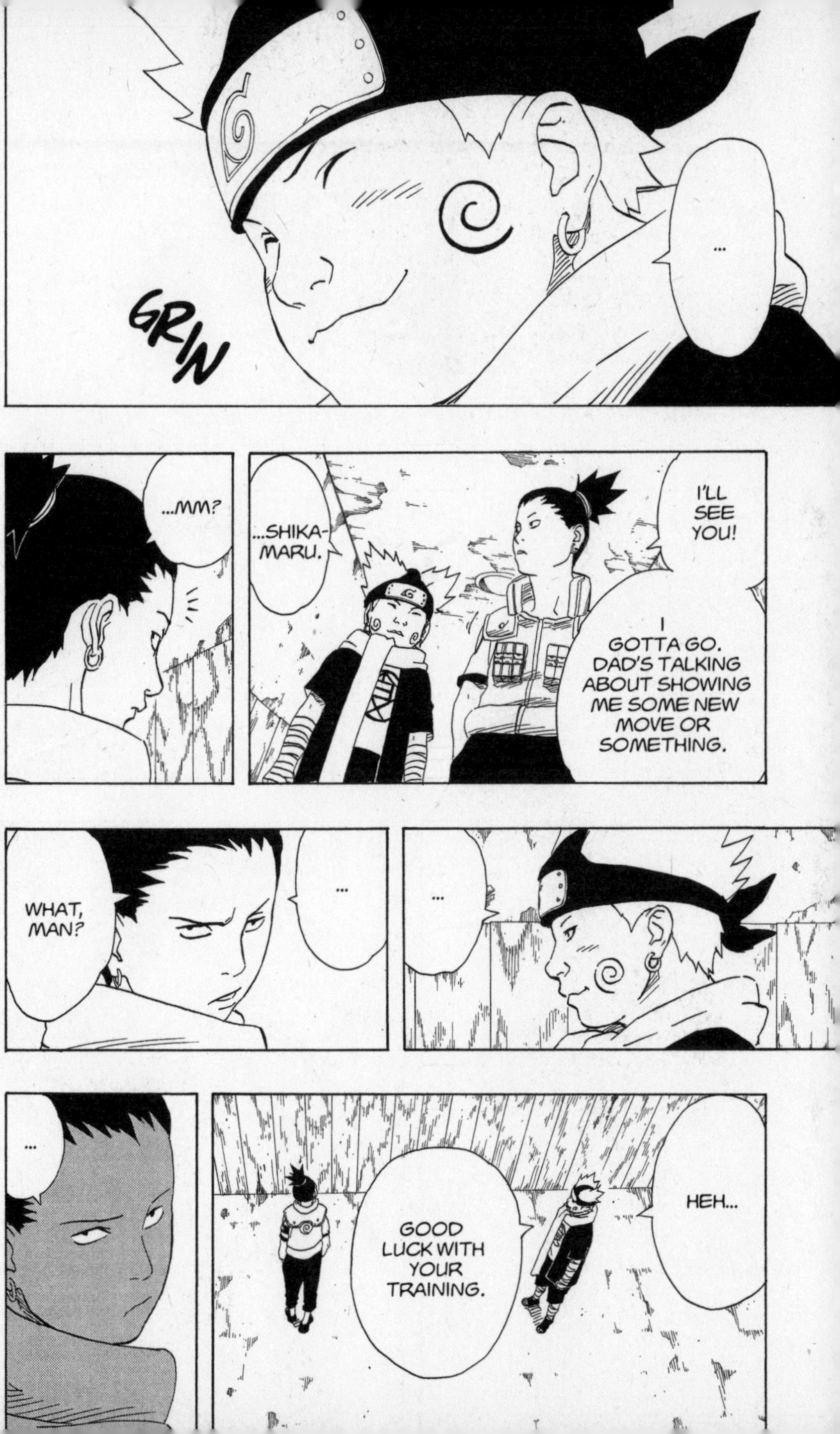
...
GRIN
I'LL SEE YOU!
I GOTTA GO. DAD'S TALKING ABOUT SHOWING ME SOME NEW MOVE OR SOMETHING.
...SHIKA-MARU.
...MM?
...
...
WHAT, MAN?
HEH...
GOOD LUCK WITH YOUR TRAINING.
...

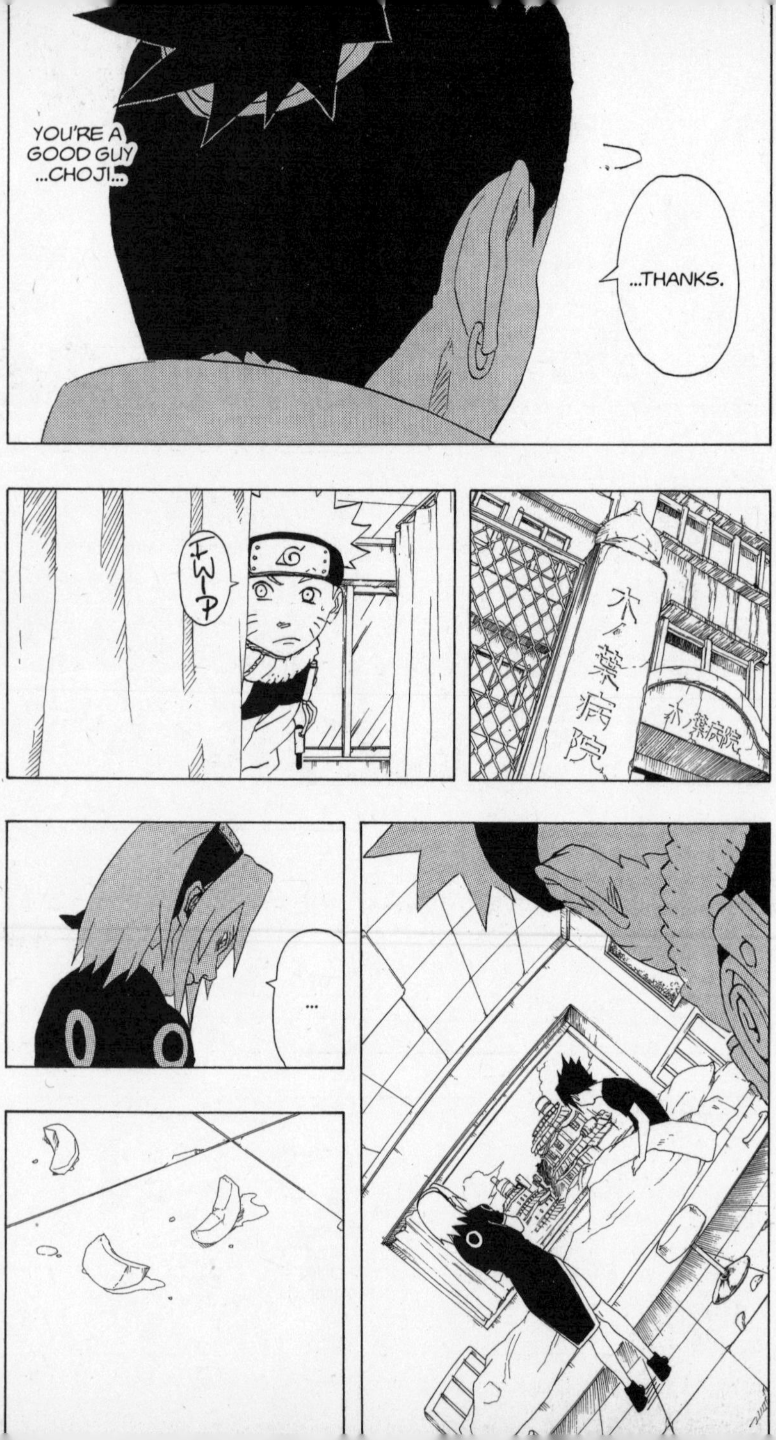
...THANKS.
YOU'RE A GOOD GUY ...CHOJI...
木ノ葉病院
木ノ葉病院
FWIP
...

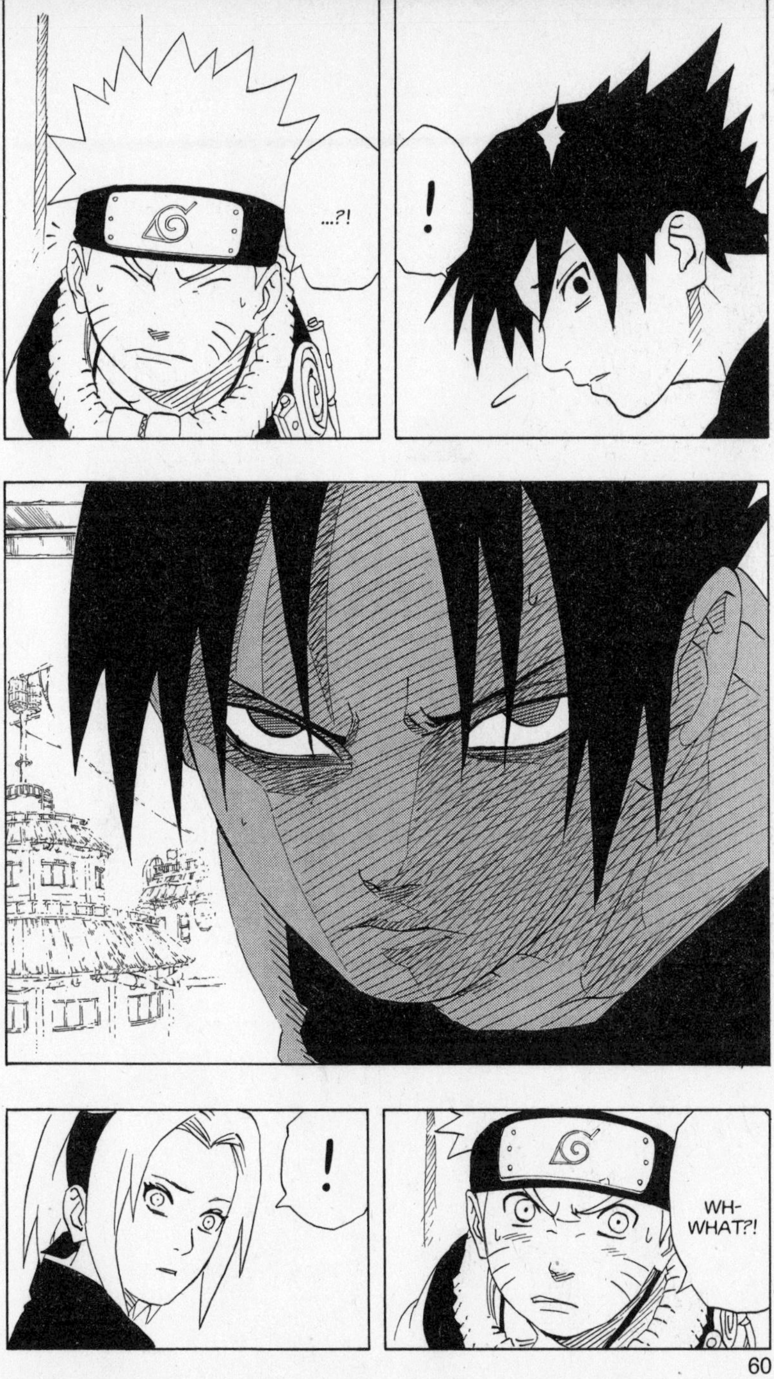
!
...?!
WH- WHAT?!
!

READ THIS WAY

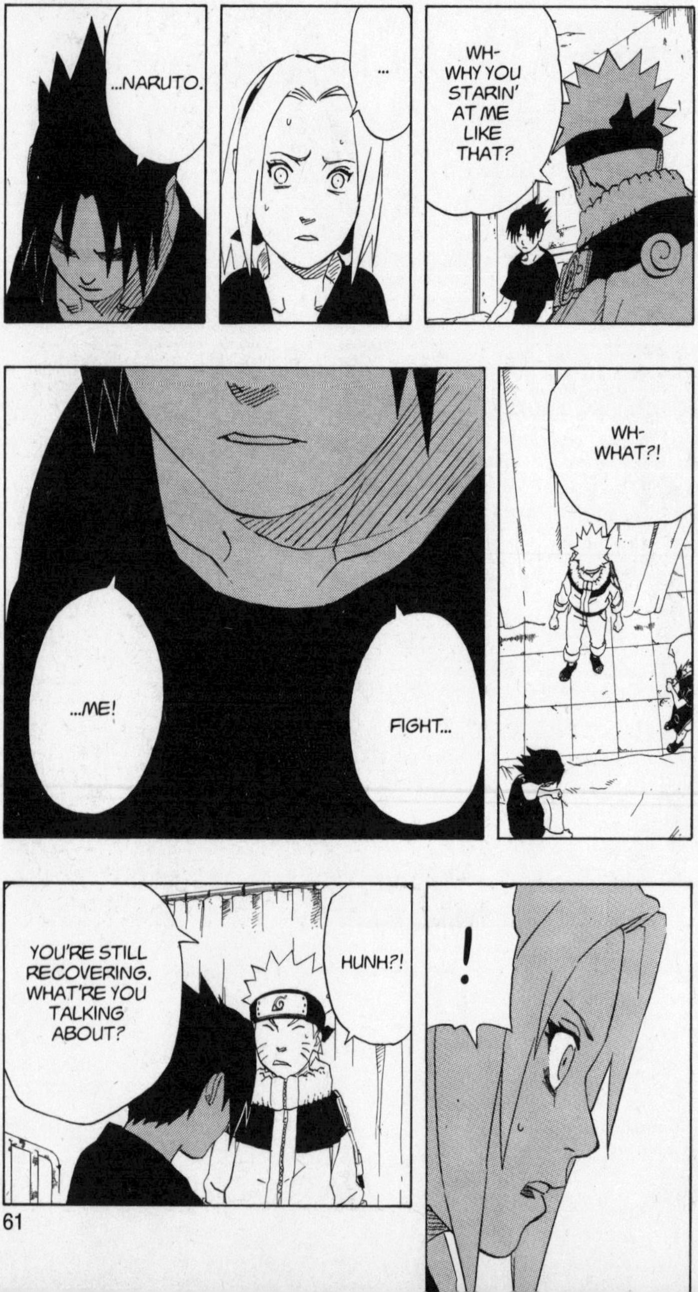

WH- WHY YOU STARIN' AT ME LIKE THAT?
...
...NARUTO.
WH- WHAT?!
FIGHT...
...ME!
!
HUNH?!
YOU'RE STILL RECOVERING. WHAT'RE YOU TALKING ABOUT?

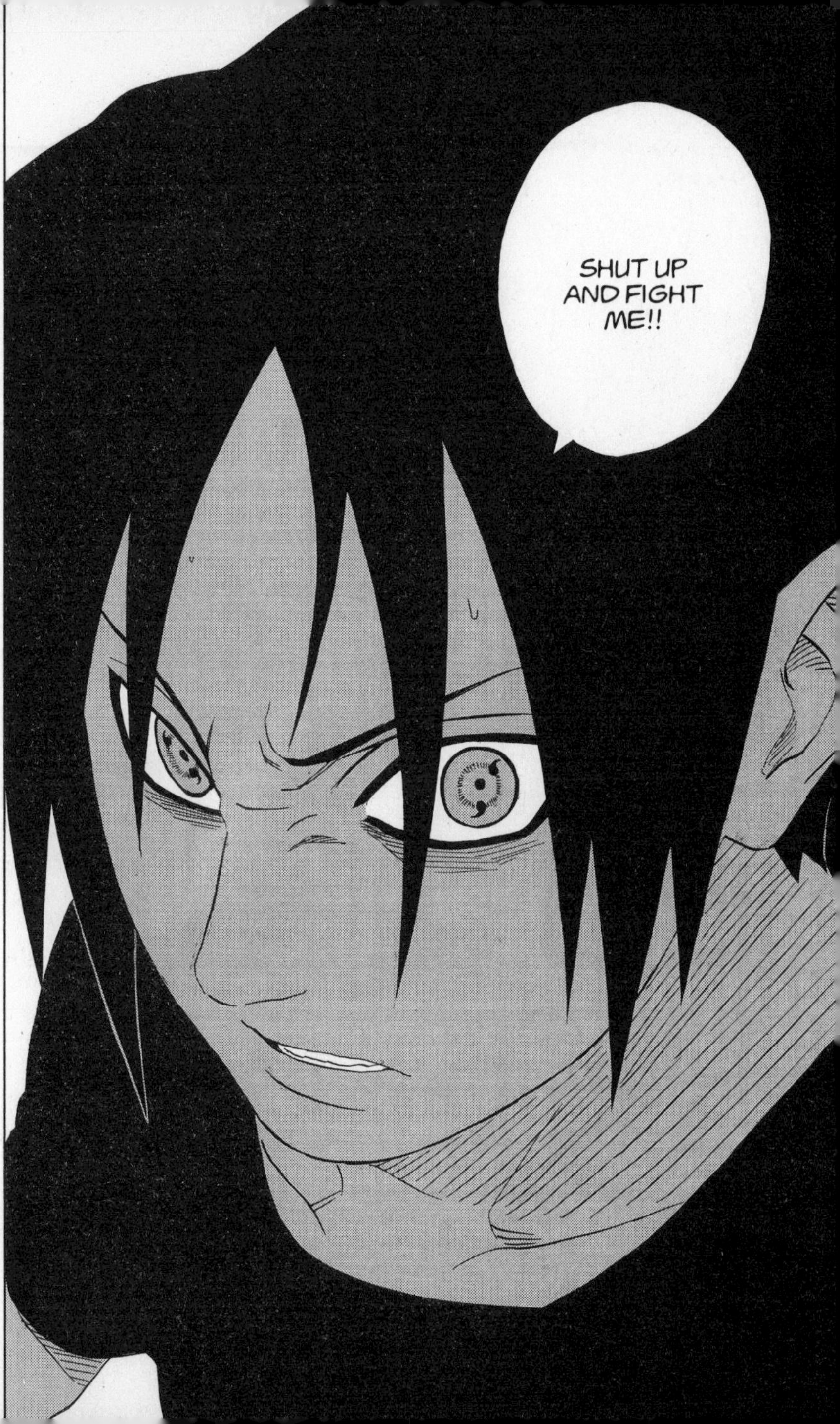
SHUT UP AND FIGHT ME!!

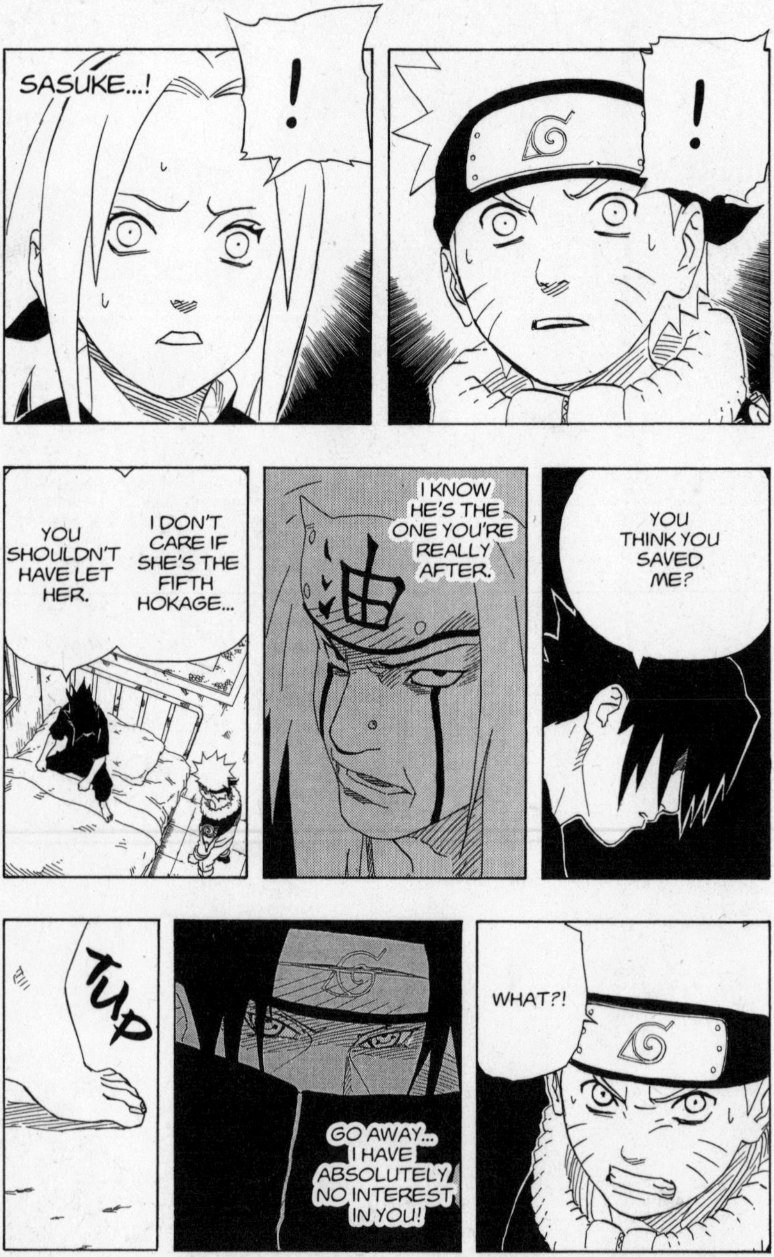
!
!
SASUKE...!
YOU THINK YOU SAVED ME?
I KNOW HE'S THE ONE YOU'RE REALLY AFTER.
I DON'T CARE IF SHE'S THE FIFTH HOKAGE...
YOU SHOULDN'T HAVE LET HER.
WHAT?!
GO AWAY... I HAVE ABSOLUTELY NO INTEREST IN YOU!
TUP

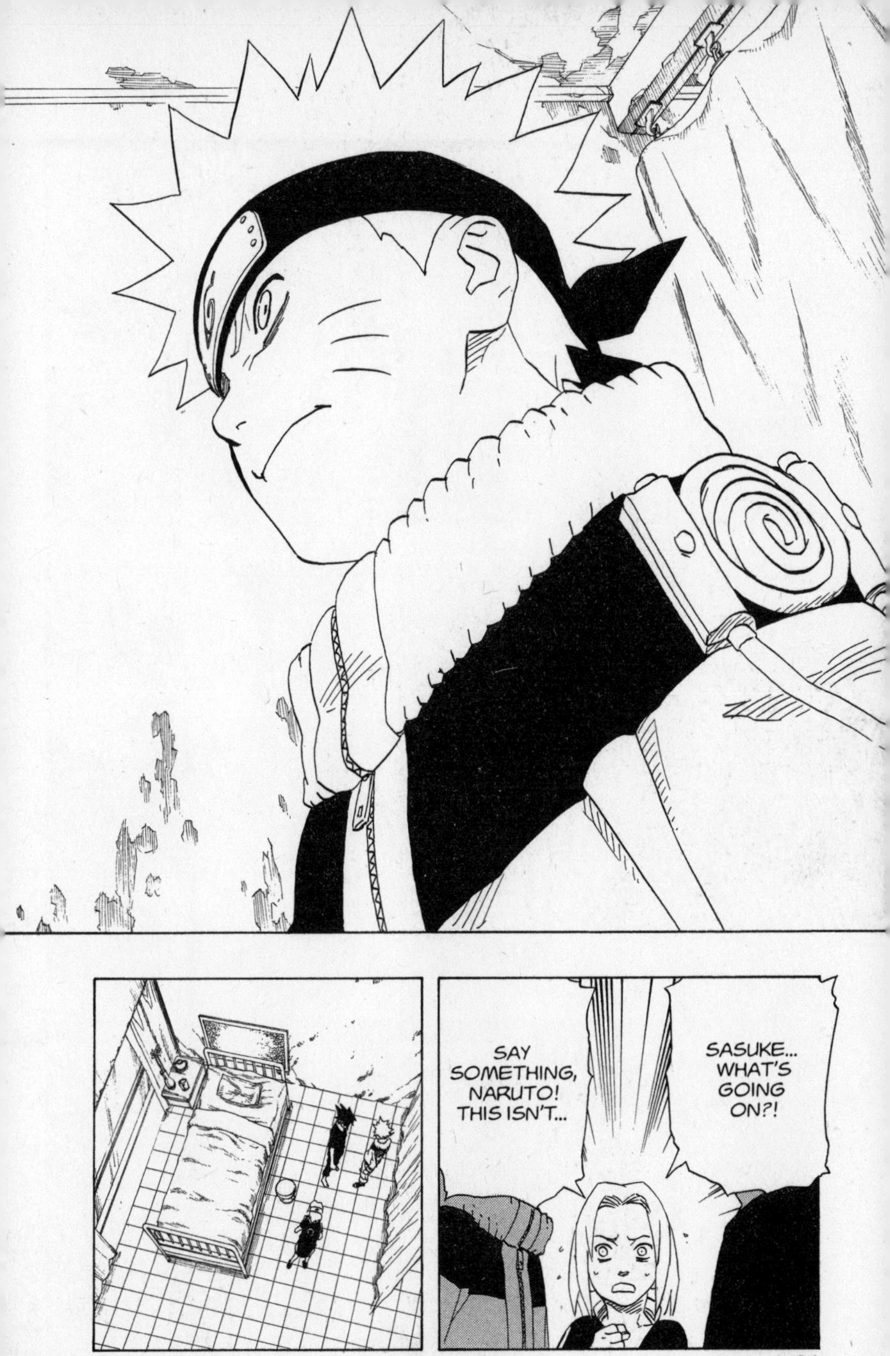
SASUKE... WHAT'S GOING ON?!
SAY SOMETHING, NARUTO! THIS ISN'T...

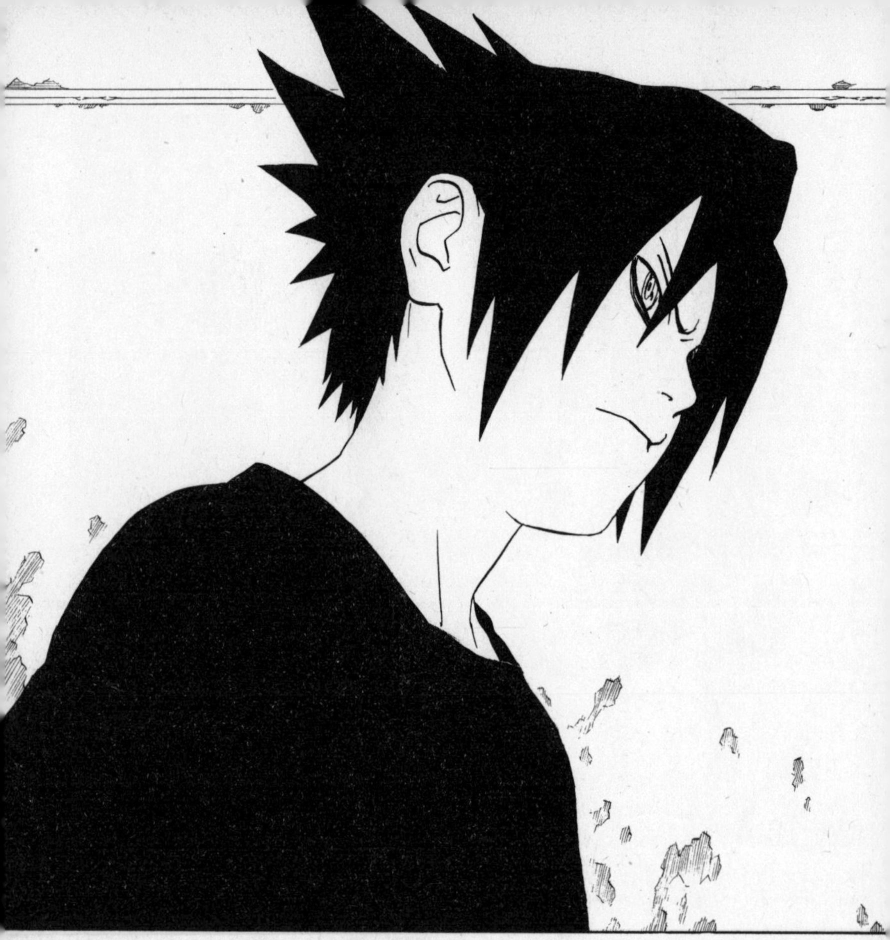
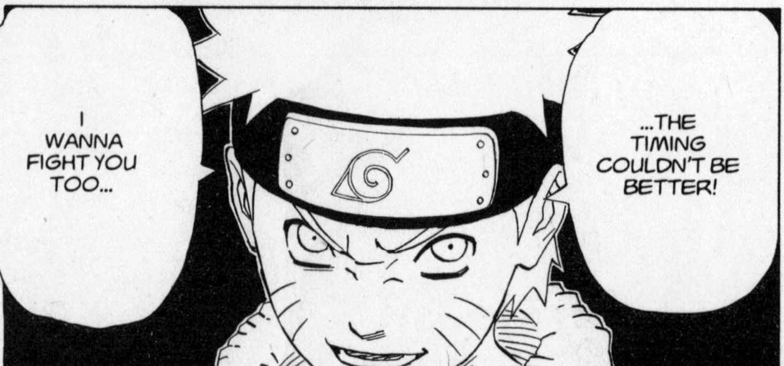
...THE TIMING COULDN'T BE BETTER!
I WANNA FIGHT YOU TOO...

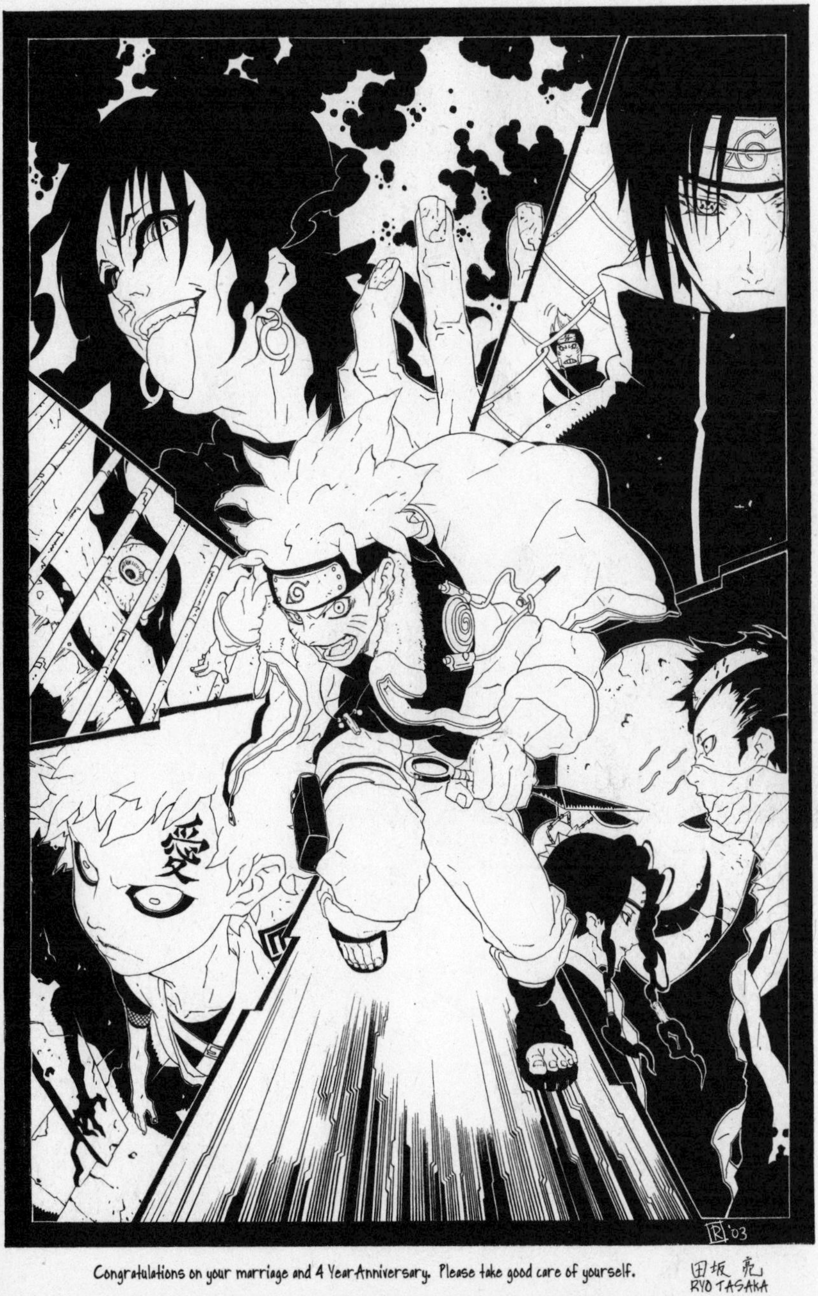
愛
R '03

Congratulations on your marriage and 4 Year Anniversary. Please take good care of yourself.

田坂亮
RYO TASAKA

Number 175: Naruto vs. Sasuke!!

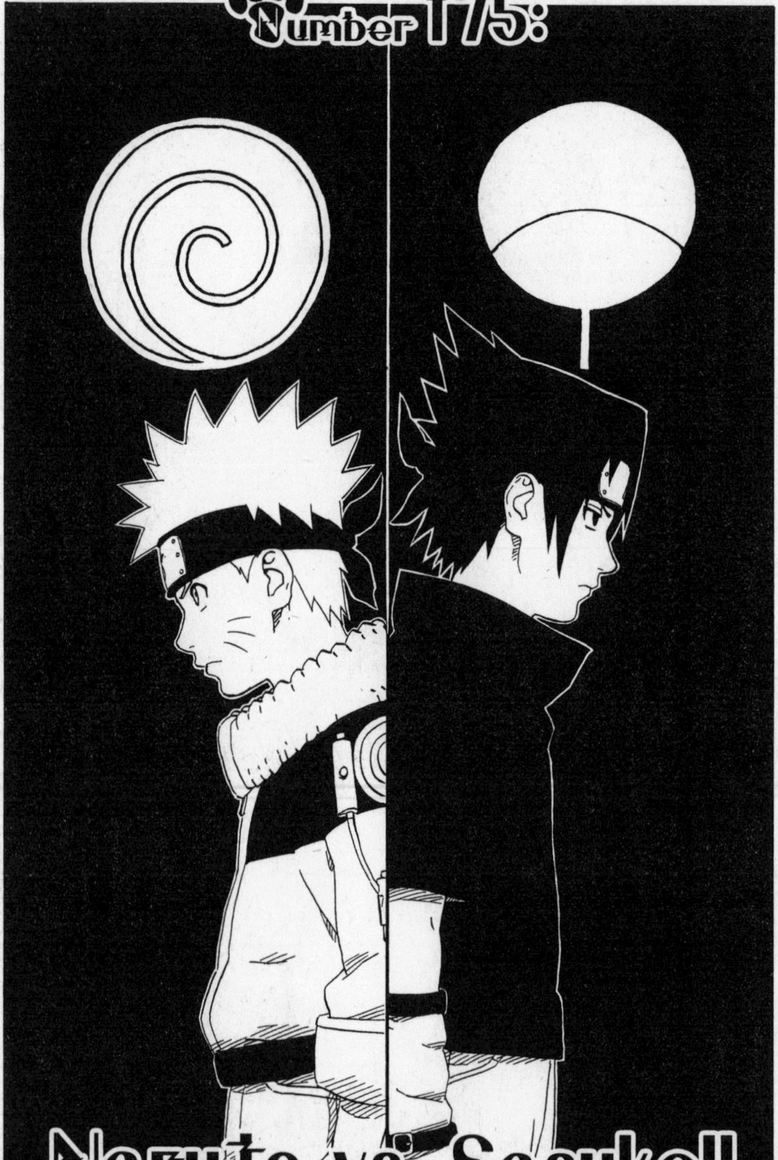

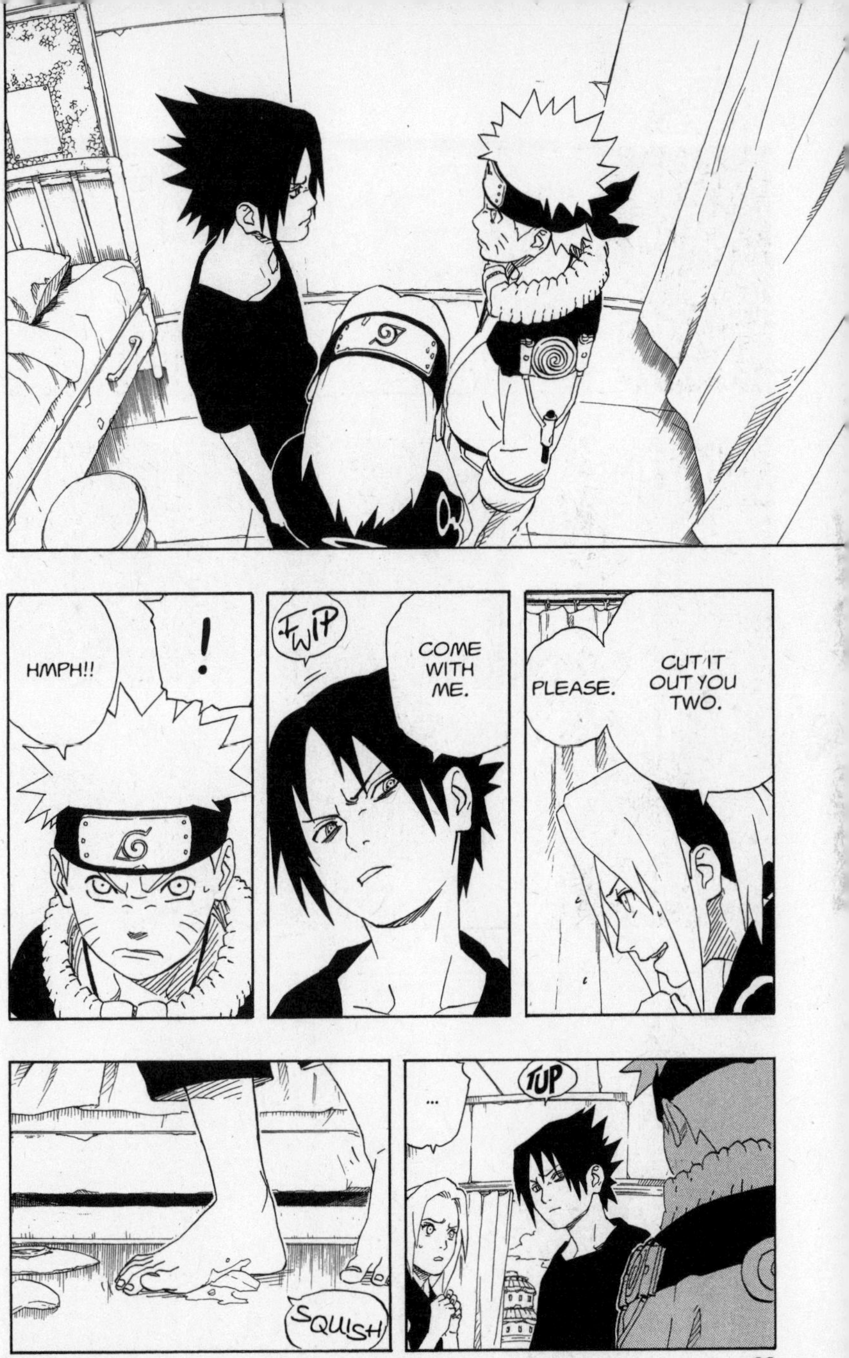
CUT IT OUT YOU TWO.
PLEASE.
FWIP
COME WITH ME.
!
HMPH!!
TUP
...
SQUISH

READ THIS WAY

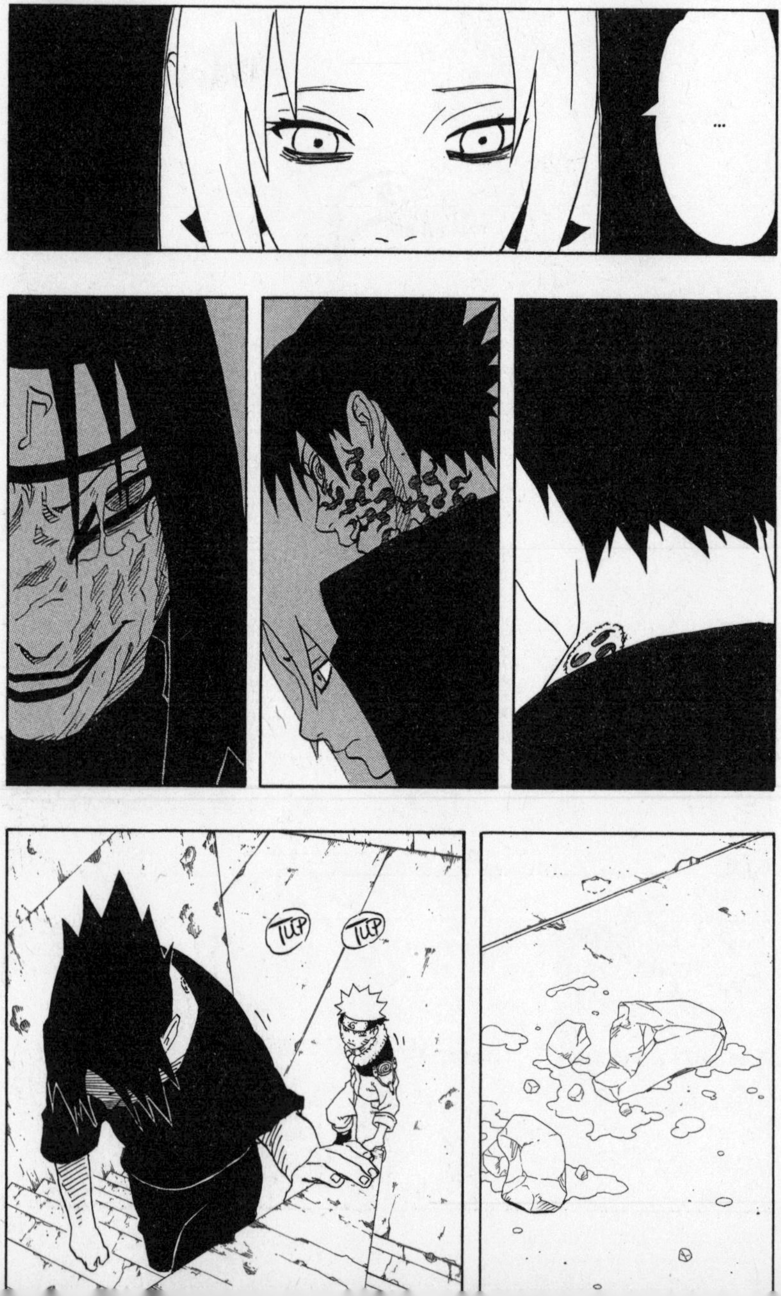
...
TUP
TUP

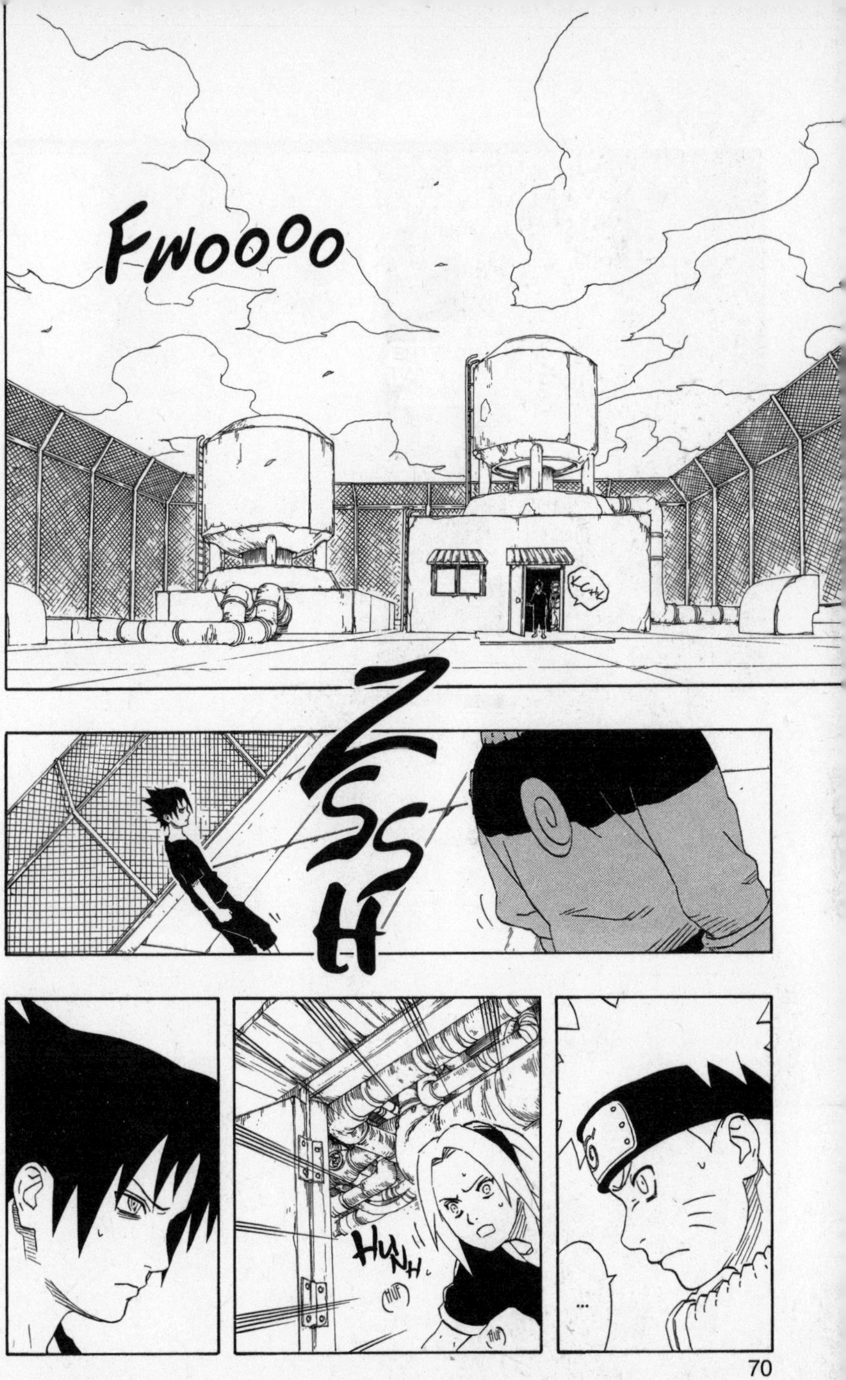
FWOOOO
KCHK
ZSSH
...
HUNH
HUF
HUF

READ THIS WAY

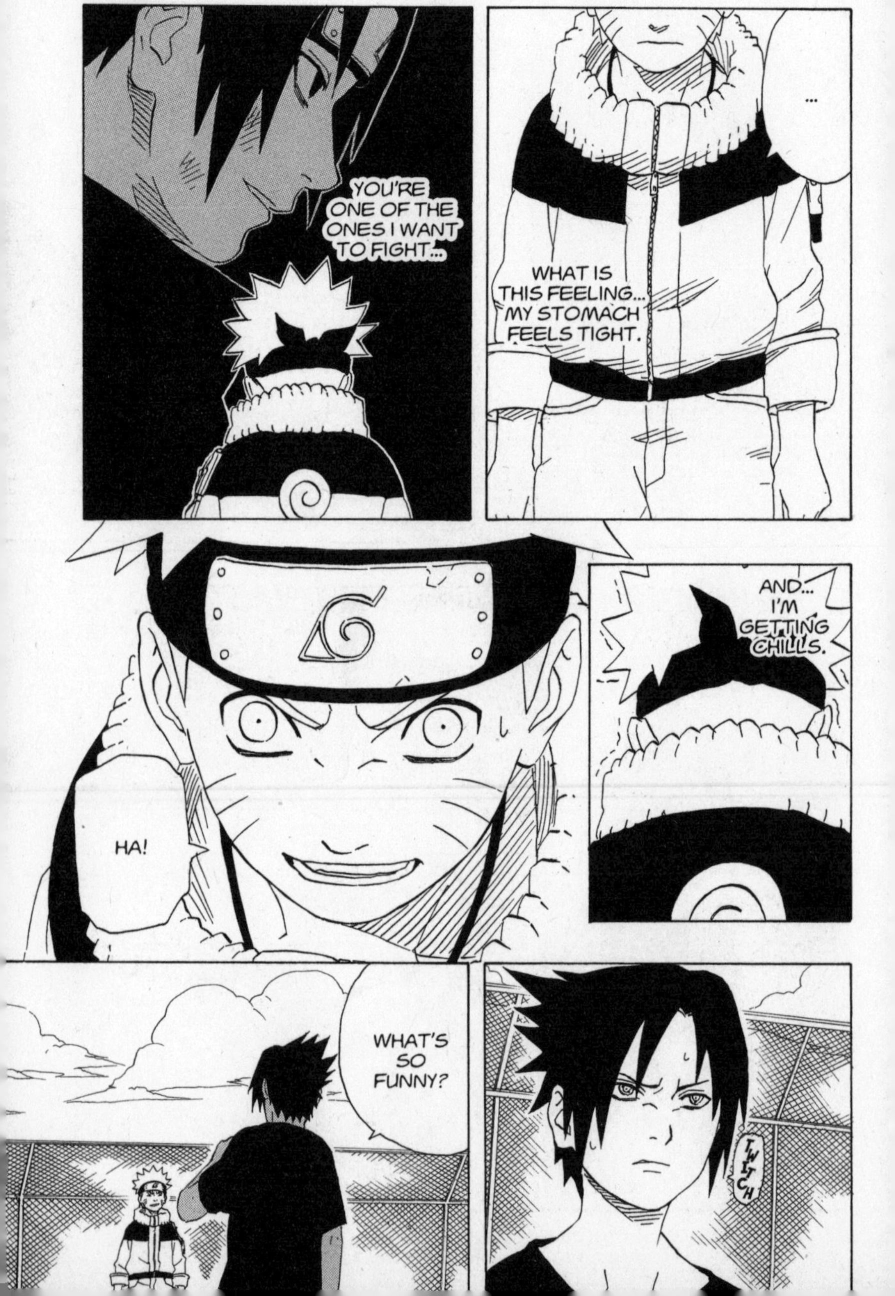
...
WHAT IS THIS FEELING... MY STOMACH FEELS TIGHT.
YOU'RE ONE OF THE ONES I WANT TO FIGHT...
AND... I'M GETTING CHILLS.
HA!
TWITCH
WHAT'S SO FUNNY?

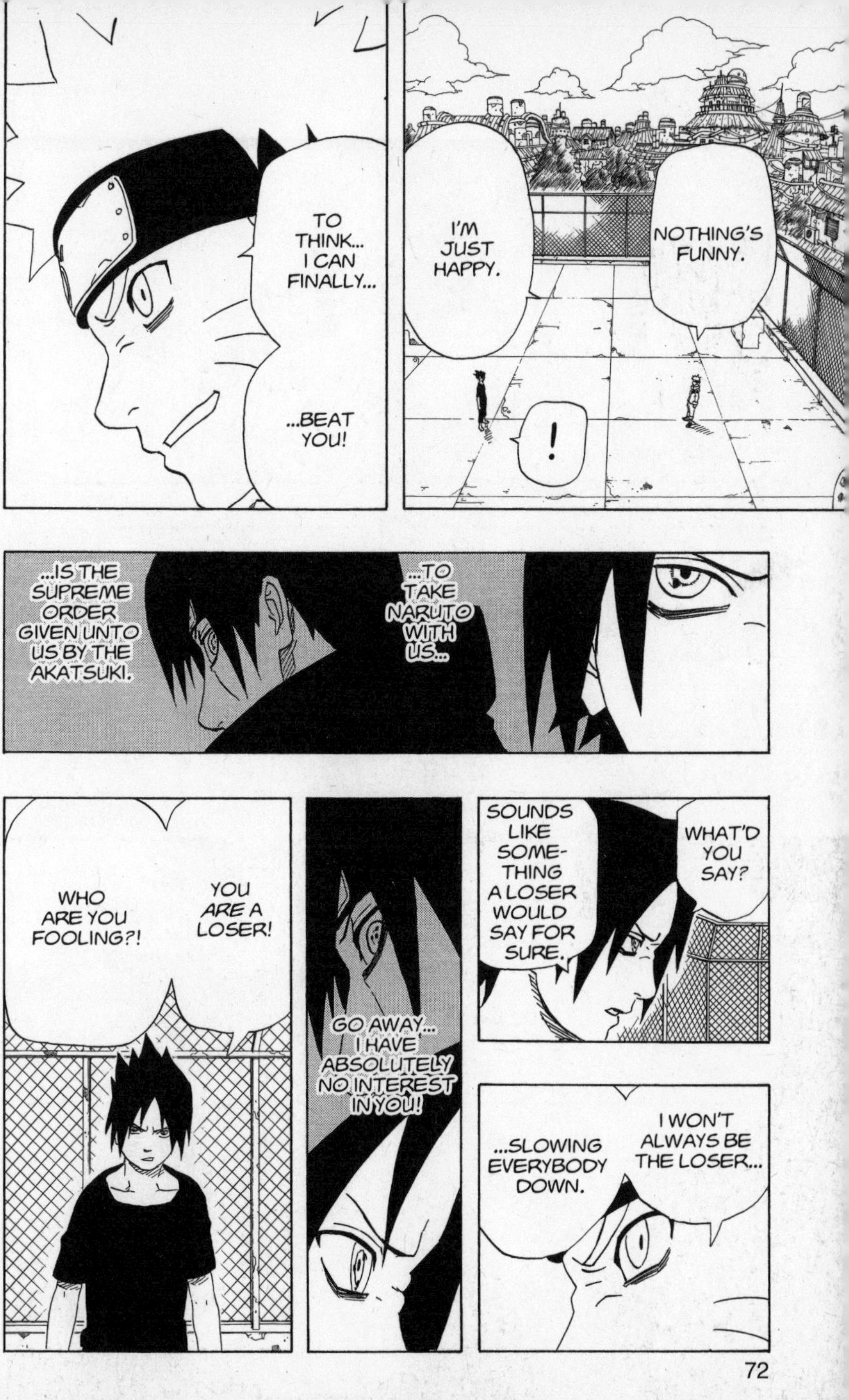
NOTHING'S FUNNY.
I'M JUST HAPPY.
!
TO THINK... I CAN FINALLY...
...BEAT YOU!
...TO TAKE NARUTO WITH US...
...IS THE SUPREME ORDER GIVEN UNTO US BY THE AKATSUKI.
WHAT'D YOU SAY?
SOUNDS LIKE SOME-THING A LOSER WOULD SAY FOR SURE.
I WON'T ALWAYS BE THE LOSER...
...SLOWING EVERYBODY DOWN.
GO AWAY... I HAVE ABSOLUTELY NO INTEREST IN YOU!
YOU ARE A LOSER!
WHO ARE YOU FOOLING?!

READ THIS WAY

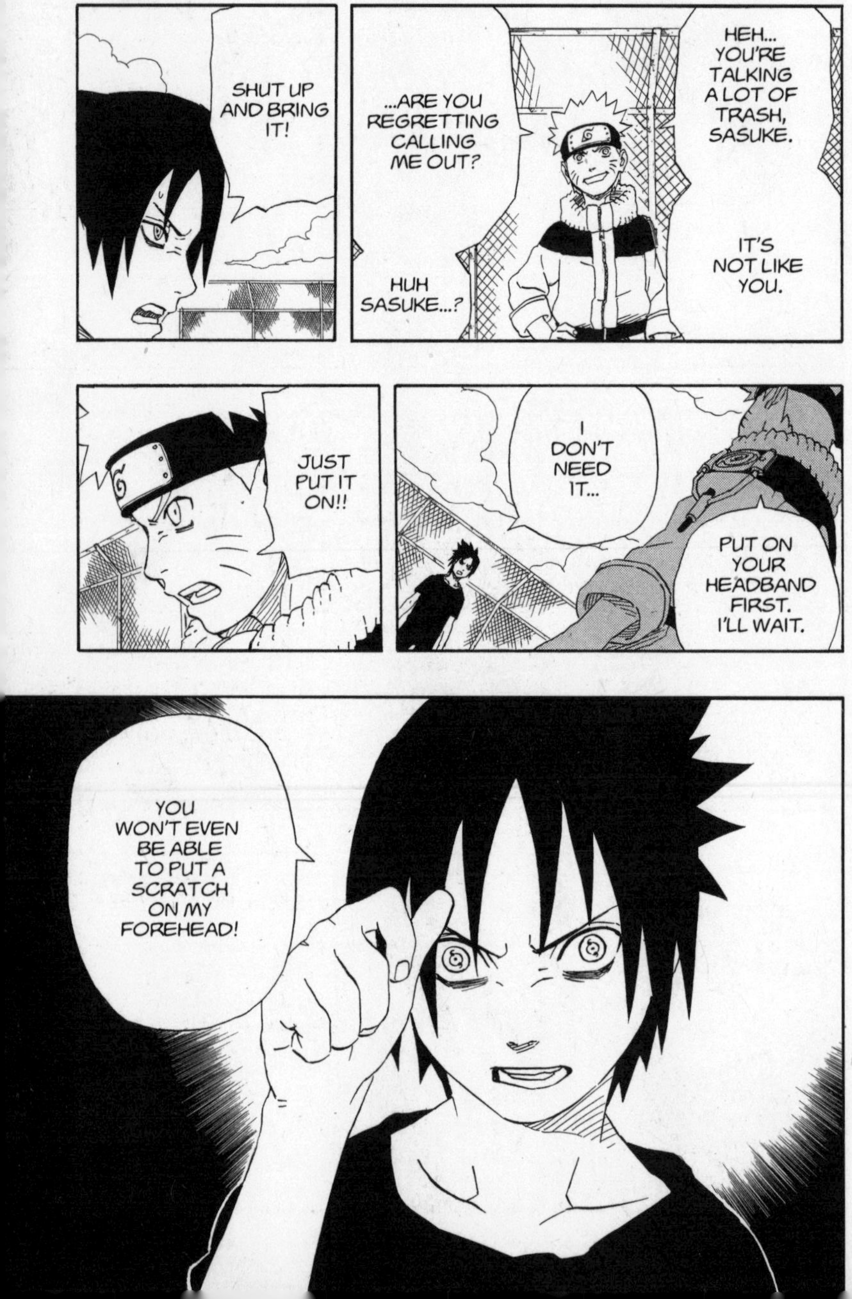
HEH... YOU'RE TALKING A LOT OF TRASH, SASUKE.
IT'S NOT LIKE YOU.
...ARE YOU REGRETTING CALLING ME OUT?
HUH SASUKE...?
SHUT UP AND BRING IT!
PUT ON YOUR HEADBAND FIRST. I'LL WAIT.
I DON'T NEED IT...
JUST PUT IT ON!!
YOU WON'T EVEN BE ABLE TO PUT A SCRATCH ON MY FOREHEAD!

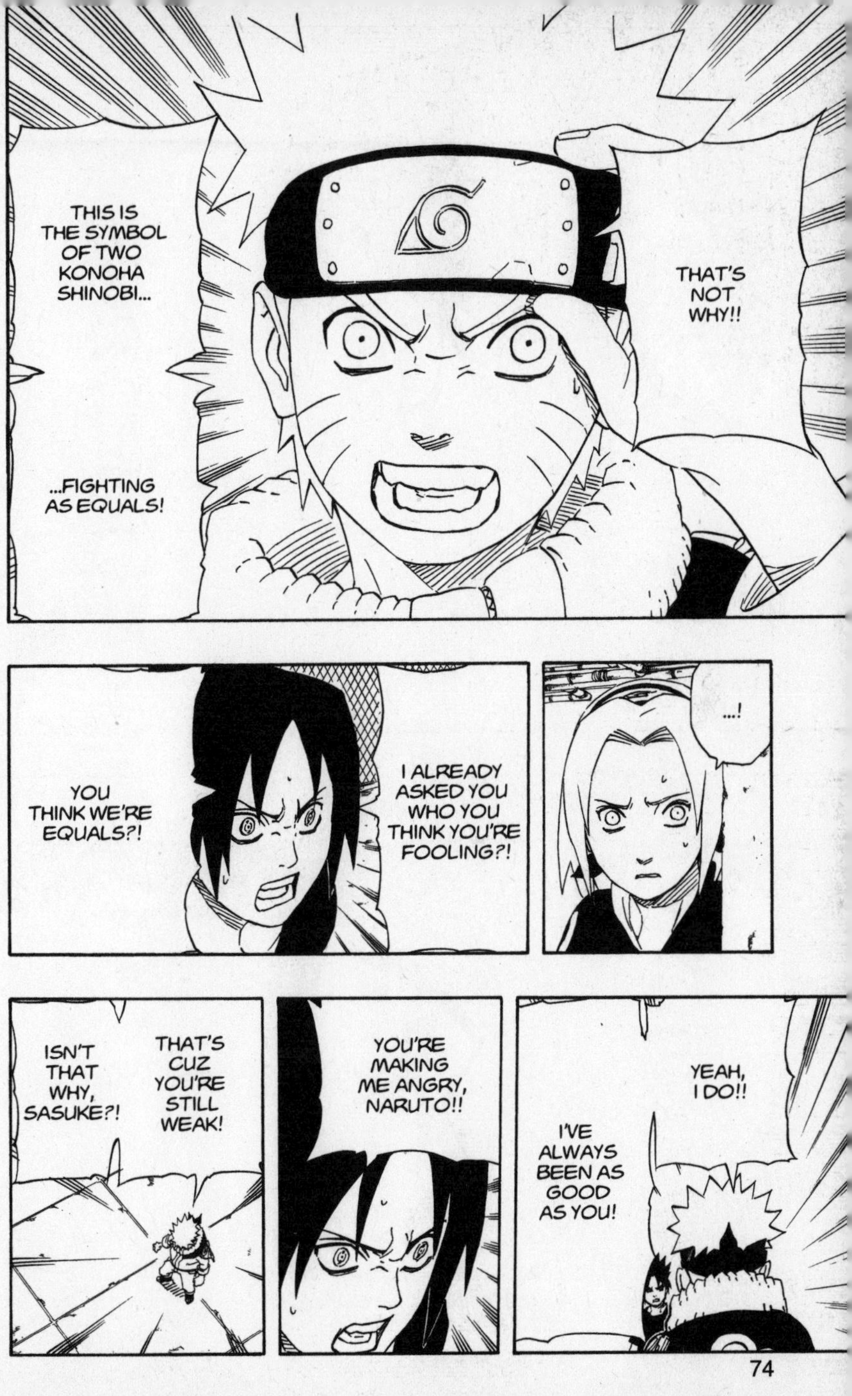
THAT'S NOT WHY!!
THIS IS THE SYMBOL OF TWO KONOHA SHINOBI...
...FIGHTING AS EQUALS!
...!
I ALREADY ASKED YOU WHO YOU THINK YOU'RE FOOLING?!
YOU THINK WE'RE EQUALS?!
YEAH, I DO!!
I'VE ALWAYS BEEN AS GOOD AS YOU!
YOU'RE MAKING ME ANGRY, NARUTO!!
THAT'S CUZ YOU'RE STILL WEAK!
ISN'T THAT WHY, SASUKE?!

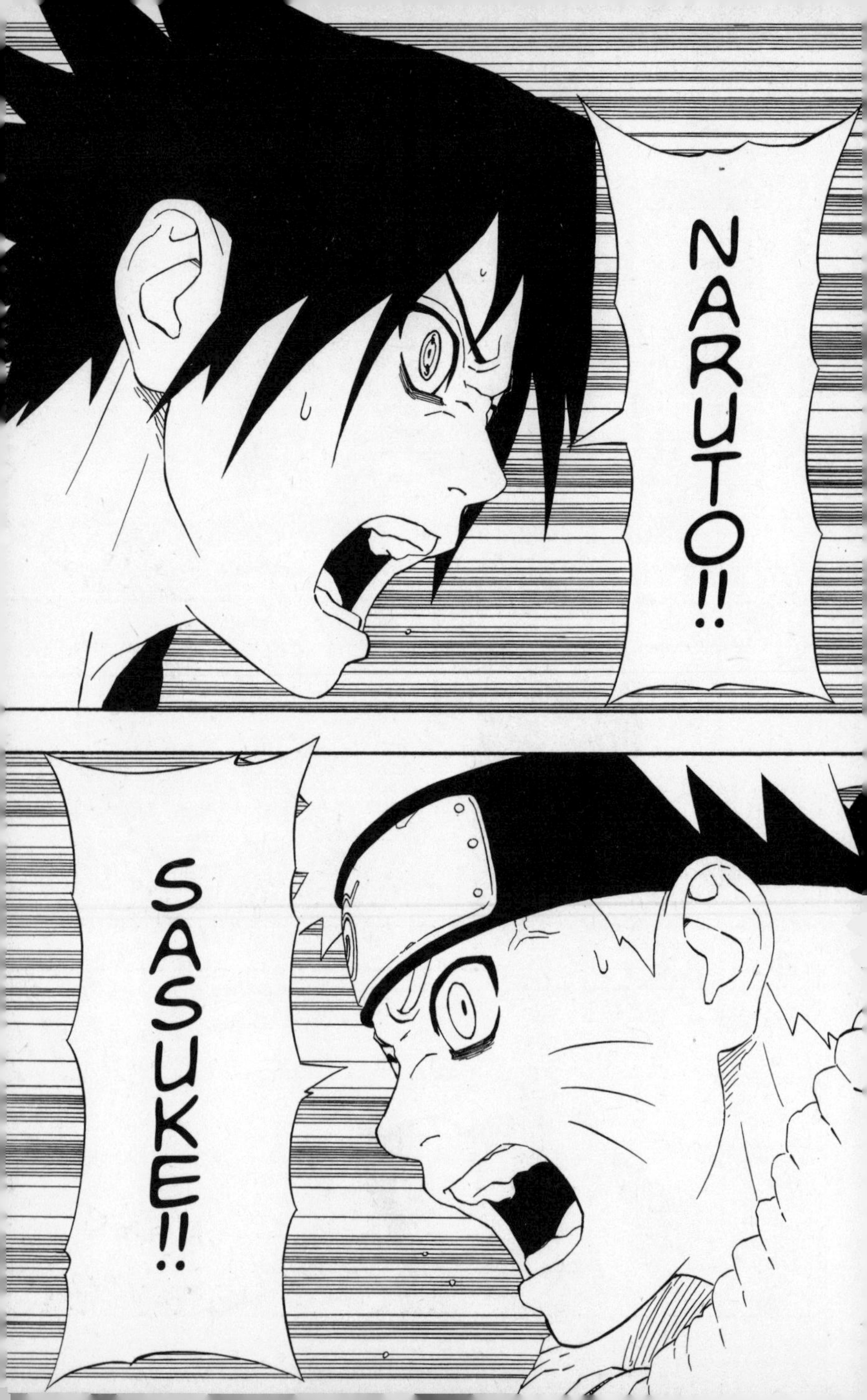
NARUTO!!
SASUKE!!

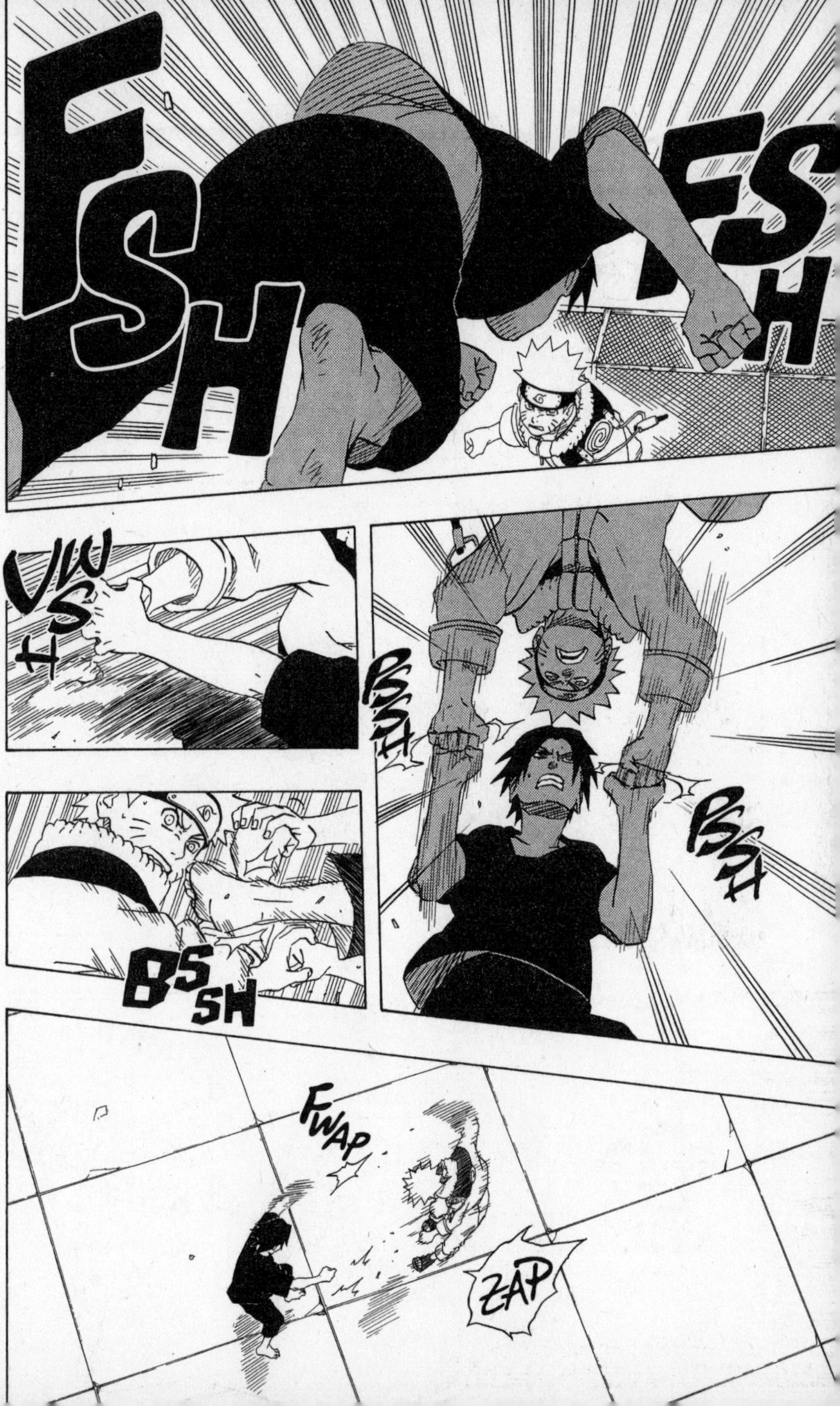

FSH
FSH
PSSH
PSSH
VWSH
BSSH
ZAP
FWAP

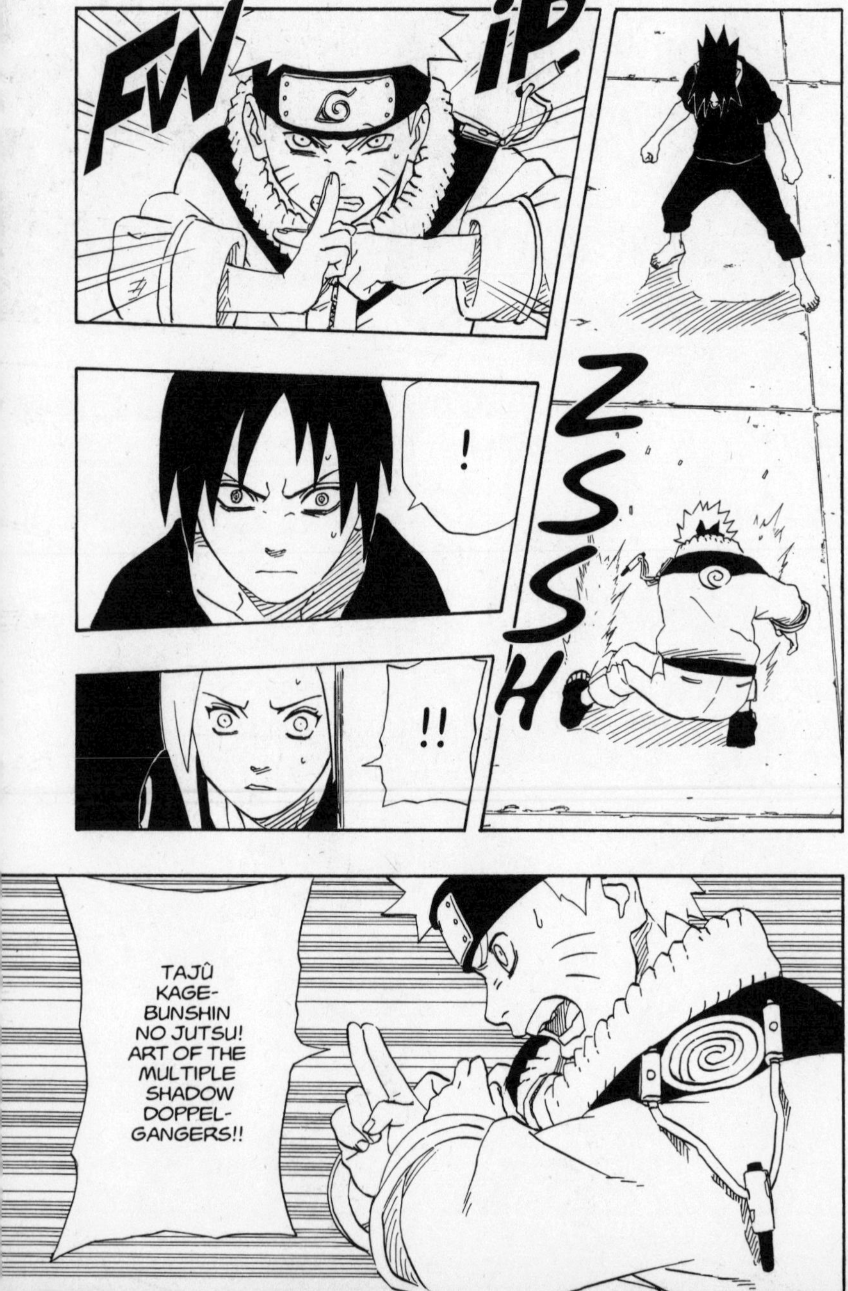
ZSSSH
FWIP
!
!!
TAJÛ KAGE-BUNSHIN NO JUTSU! ART OF THE MULTIPLE SHADOW DOPPEL-GANGERS!!

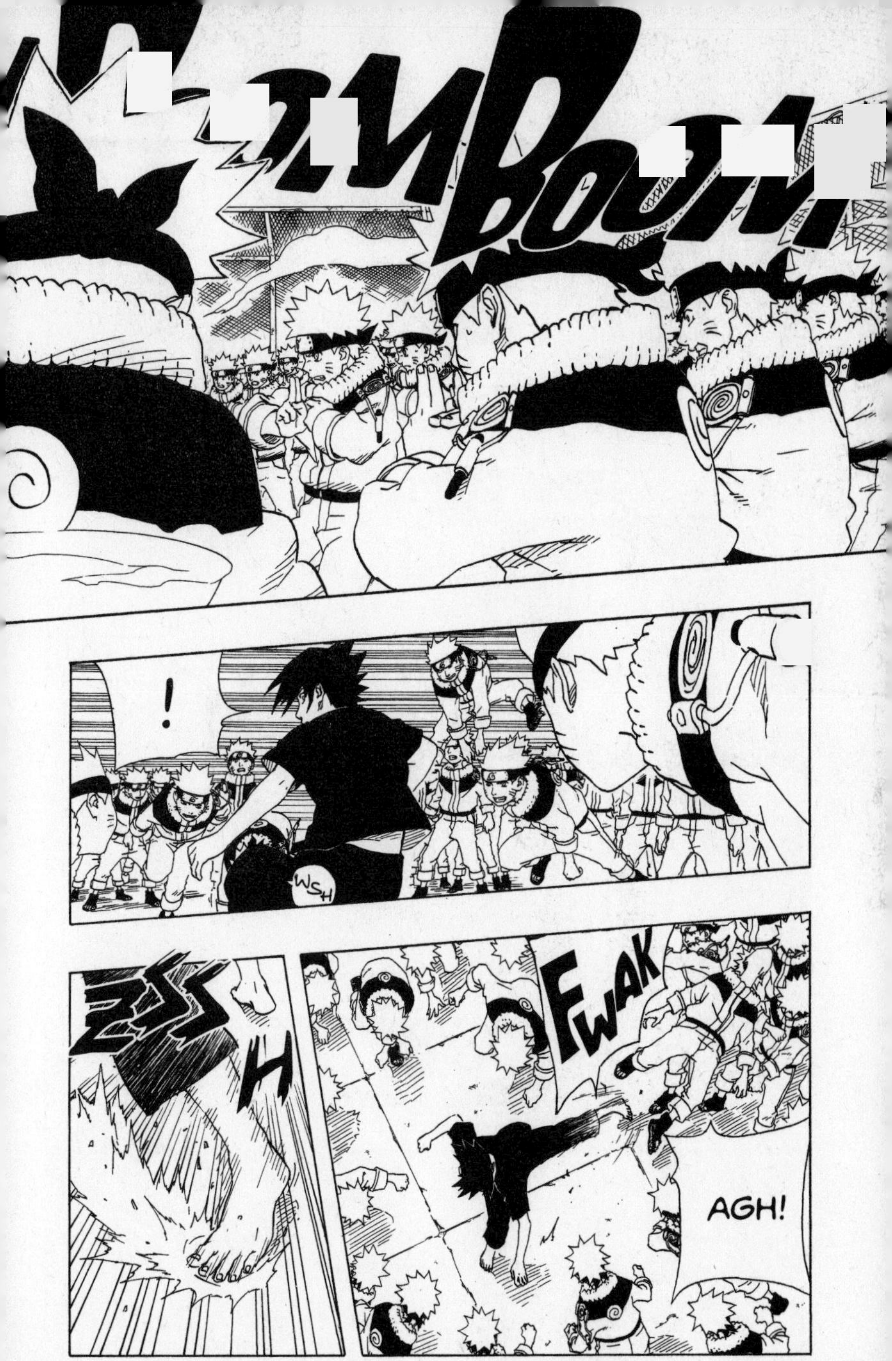
!
WSH
FWAK
AGH!

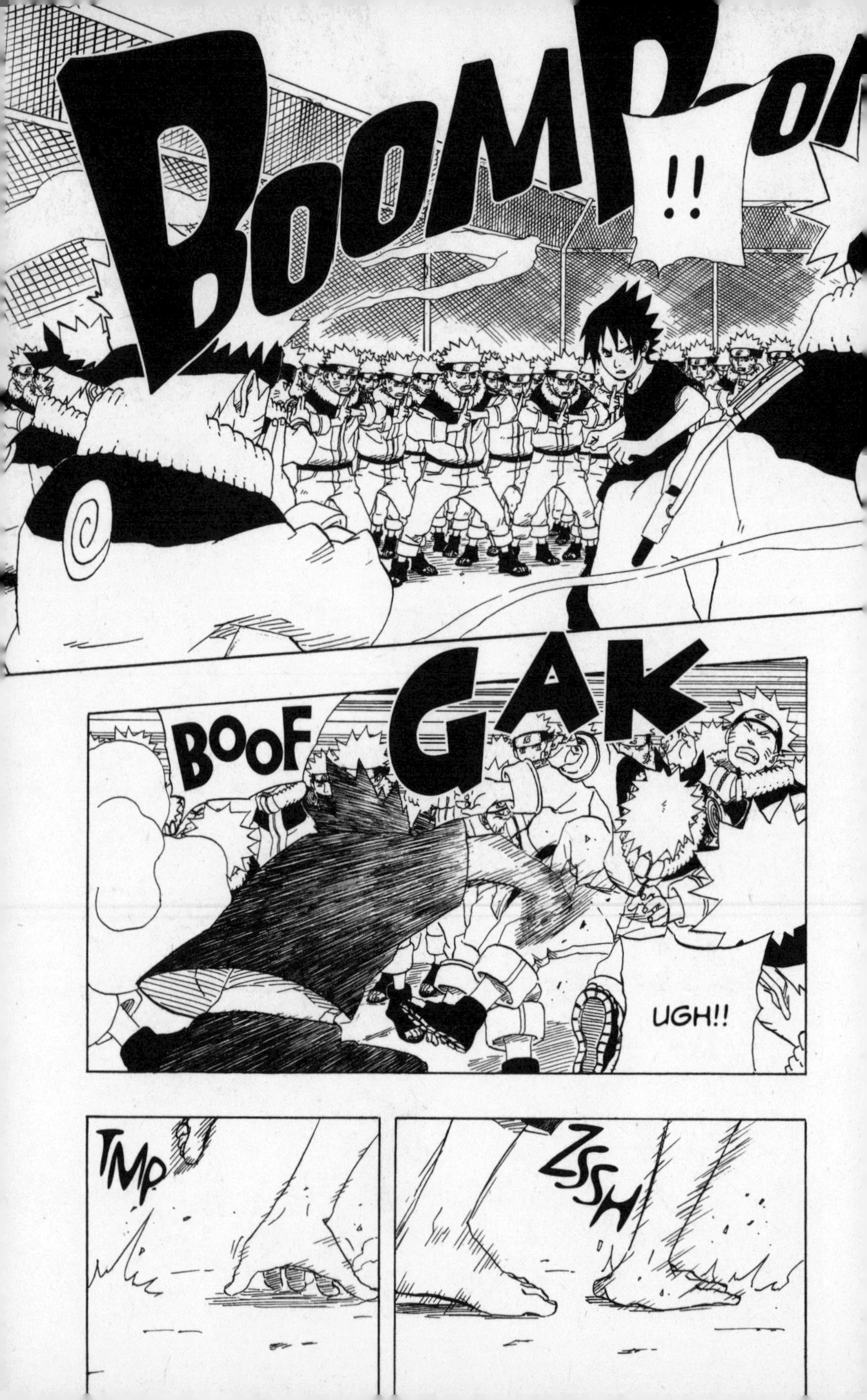
BOOMP-OF
!!
GAK
BOOF
UGH!!
ZSSH
TMP

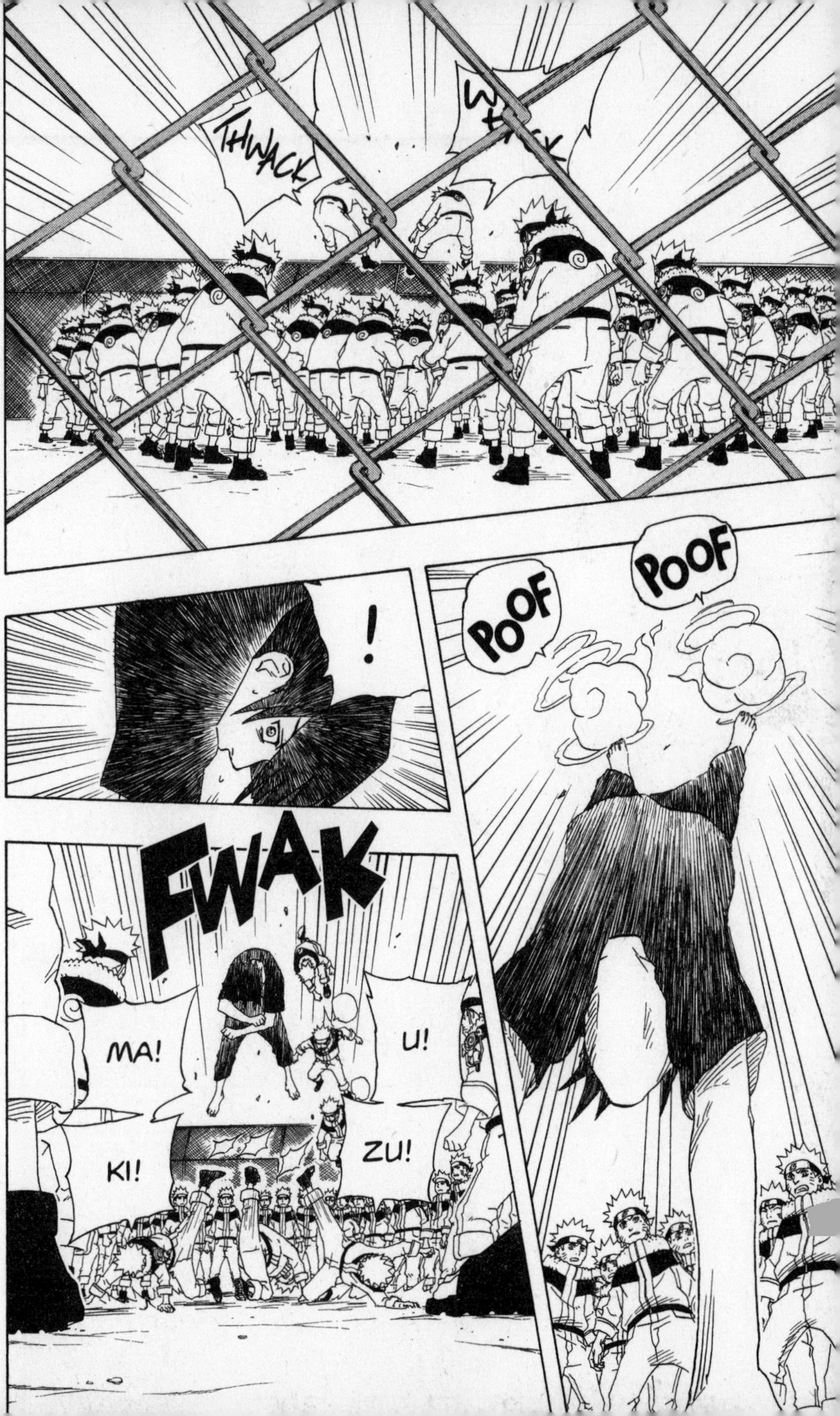
WHACK
THWACK
POOF
POOF
!
FWAK
U!
ZU!
MA!
KI!

READ THIS WAY

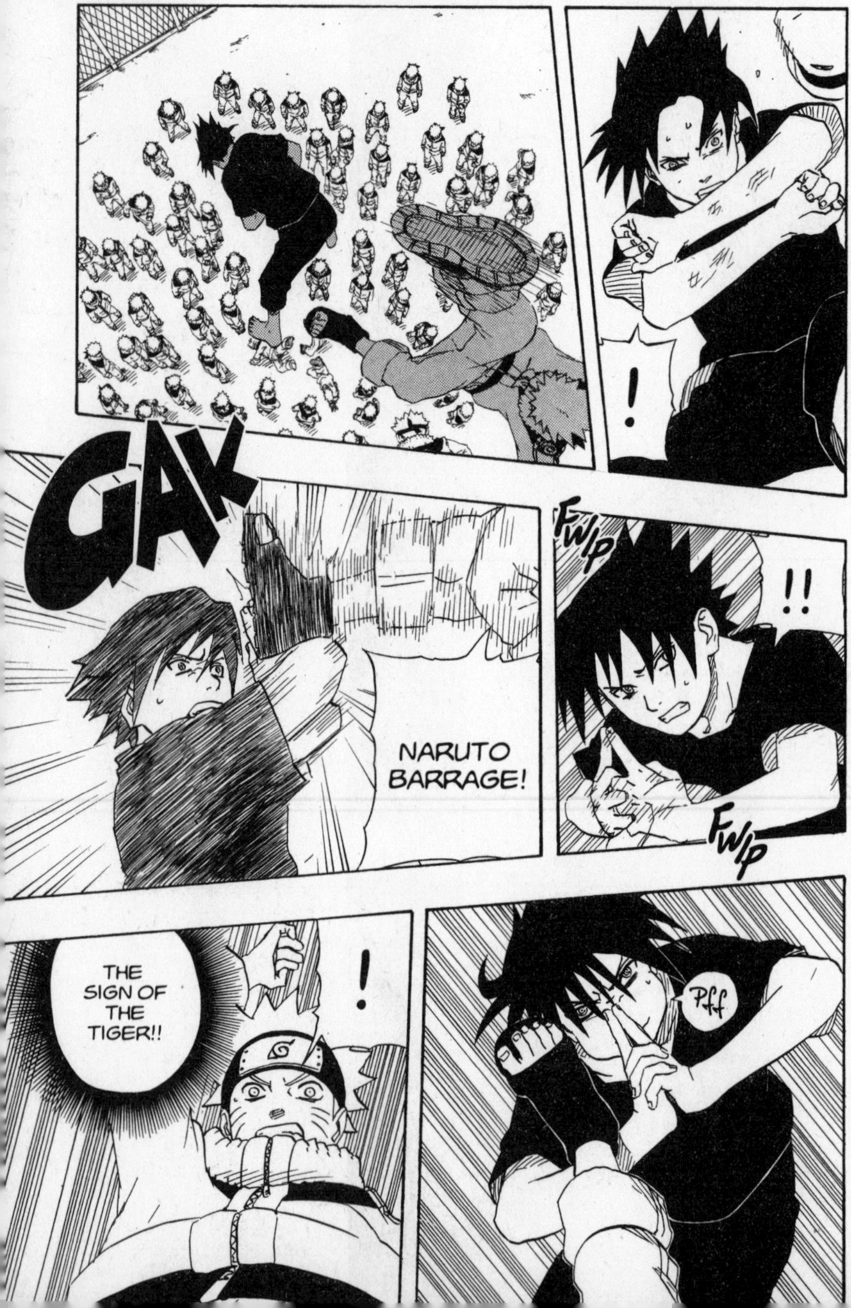
!
FWIP
!!
FWIP
GAK
NARUTO BARRAGE!
Pff
!
THE SIGN OF THE TIGER!!

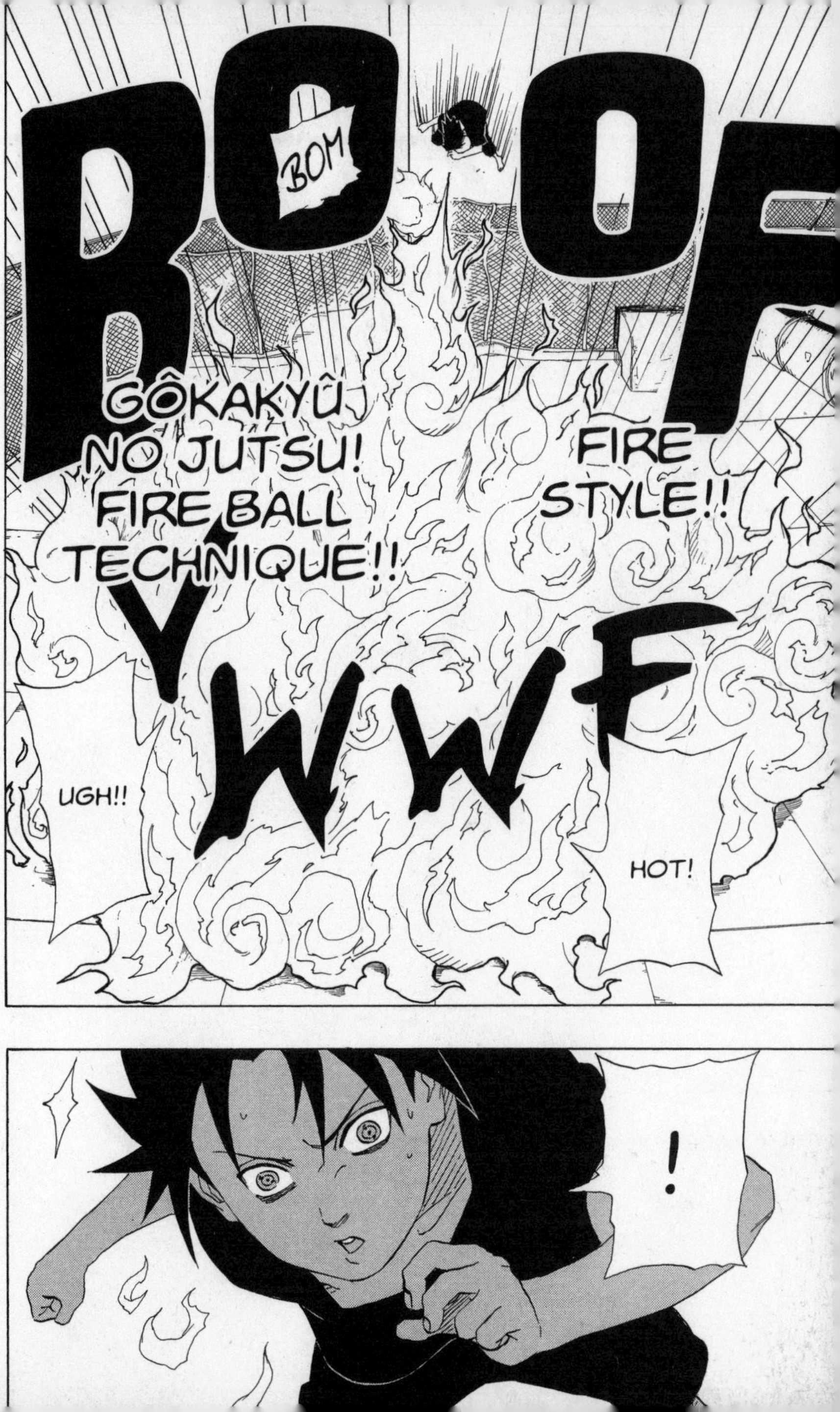
BOOF
BOM
FIRE STYLE!!
GÔKAKYÛ NO JUTSU! FIRE BALL TECHNIQUE!!
YWF
HOT!
UGH!!
!

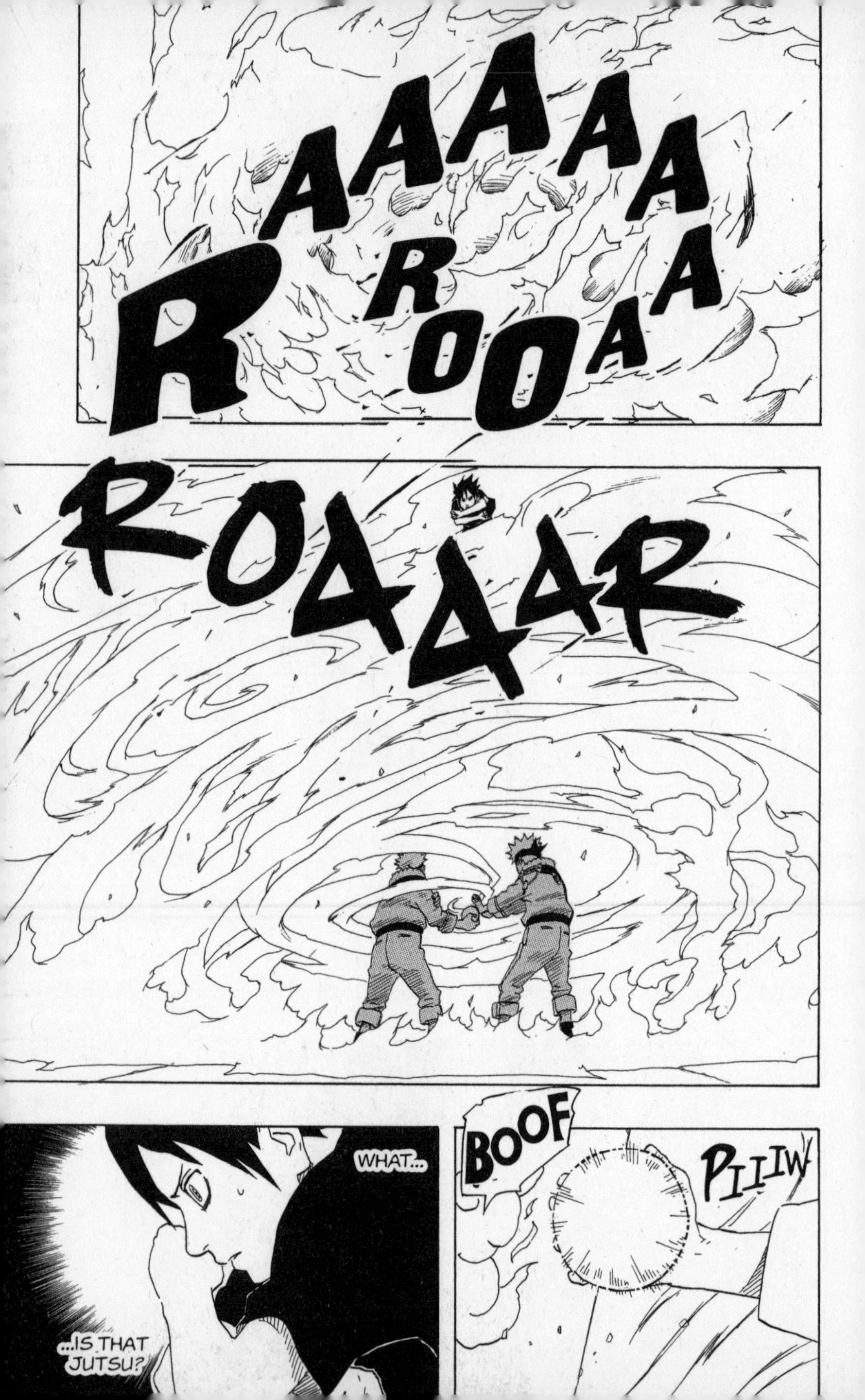
RAAAAAA
ROOAA
ROAAAR
BOOF
PIIW
WHAT...
...IS THAT JUTSU?

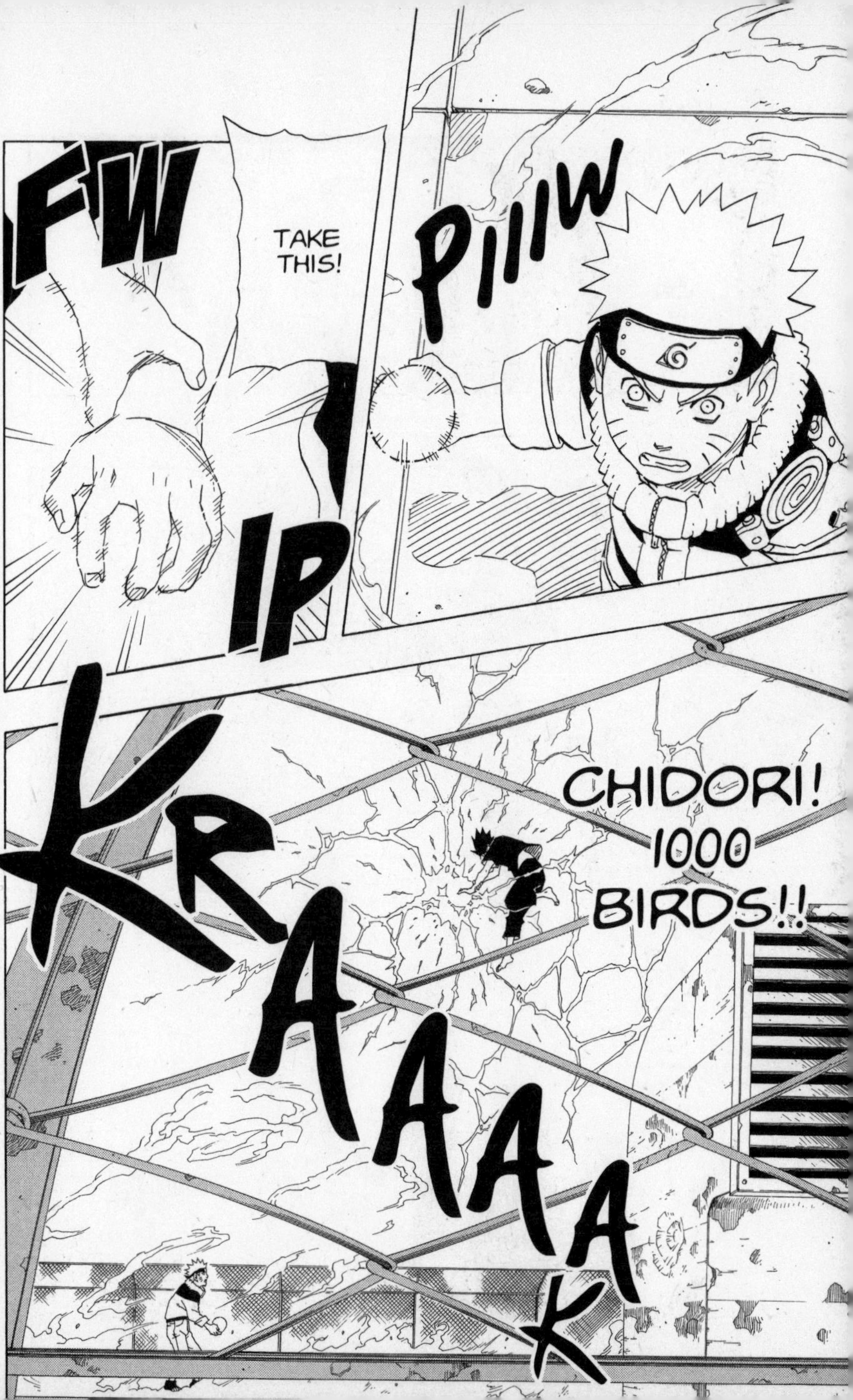
PIIIW
FWIP
TAKE THIS!
CHIDORI! 1000 BIRDS!!
KRAAAAAK

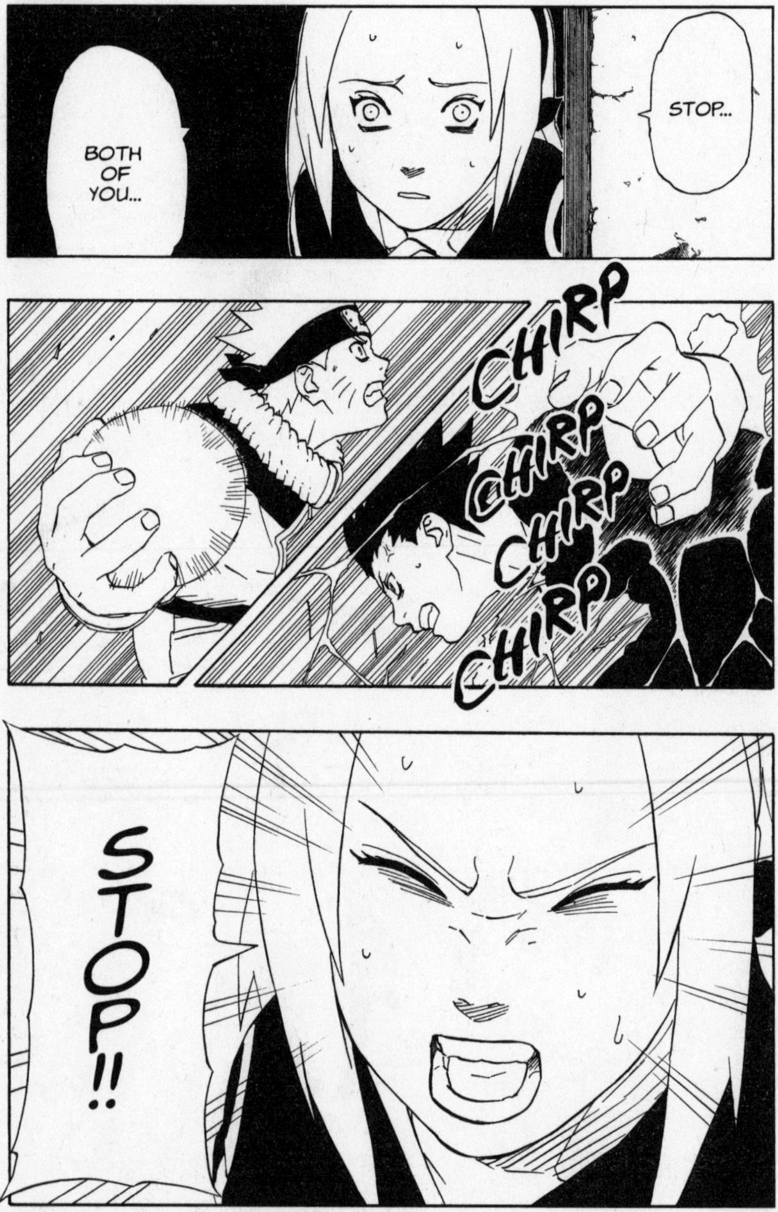
STOP...
BOTH OF YOU...
CHIRP
CHIRP
CHIRP
CHIRP
CHIRP
STOP!!

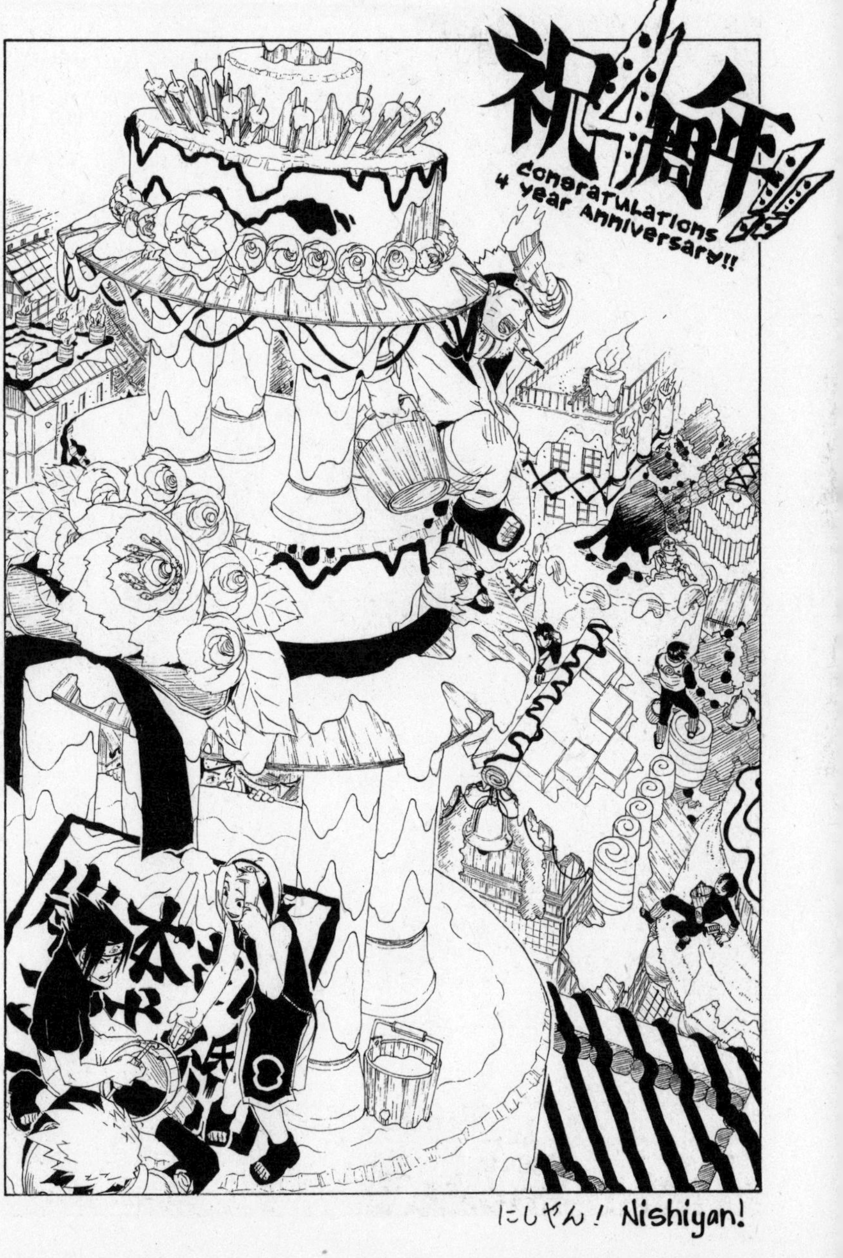
祝4周年!!
Congratulations 4 year Anniversary!!

にしやん! Nishiyan!

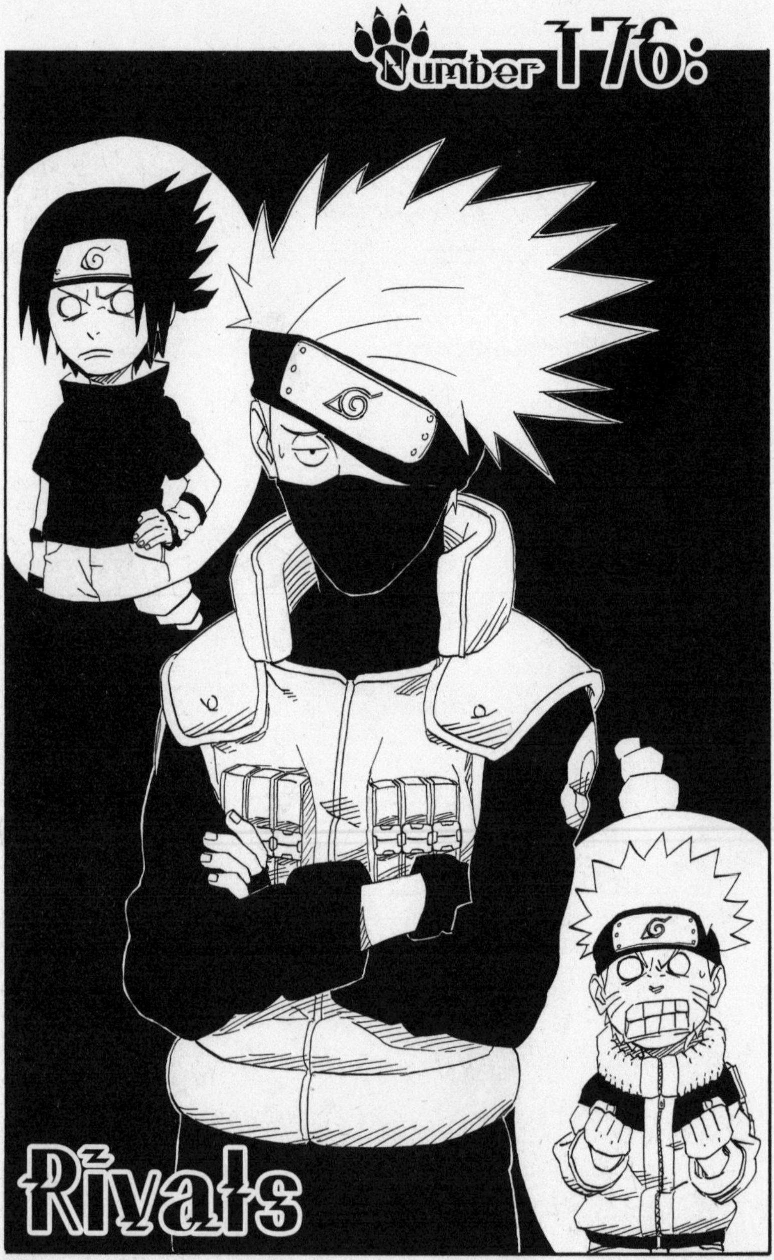
Number 176:
Rivals

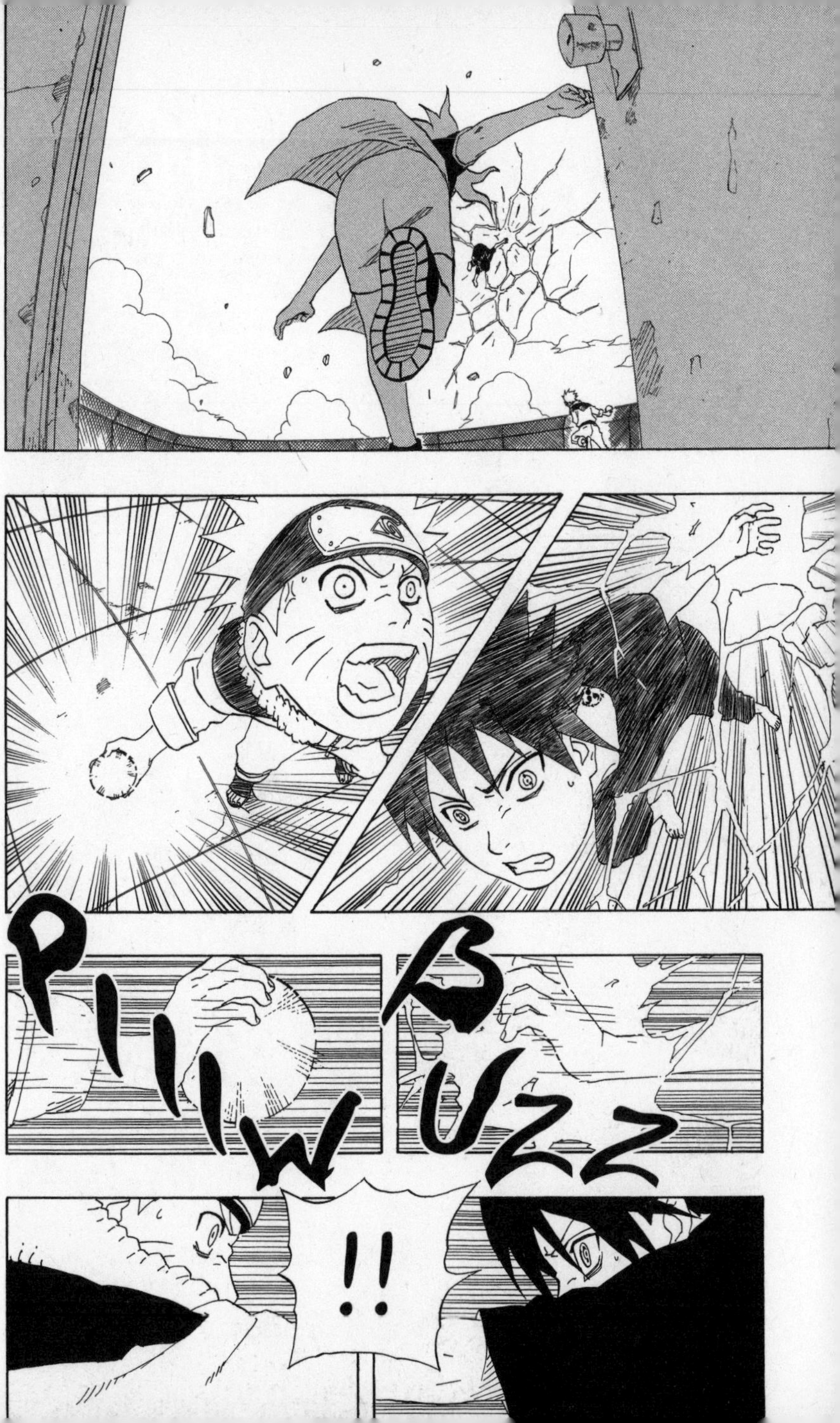
BUZZ
PIIIW
!!

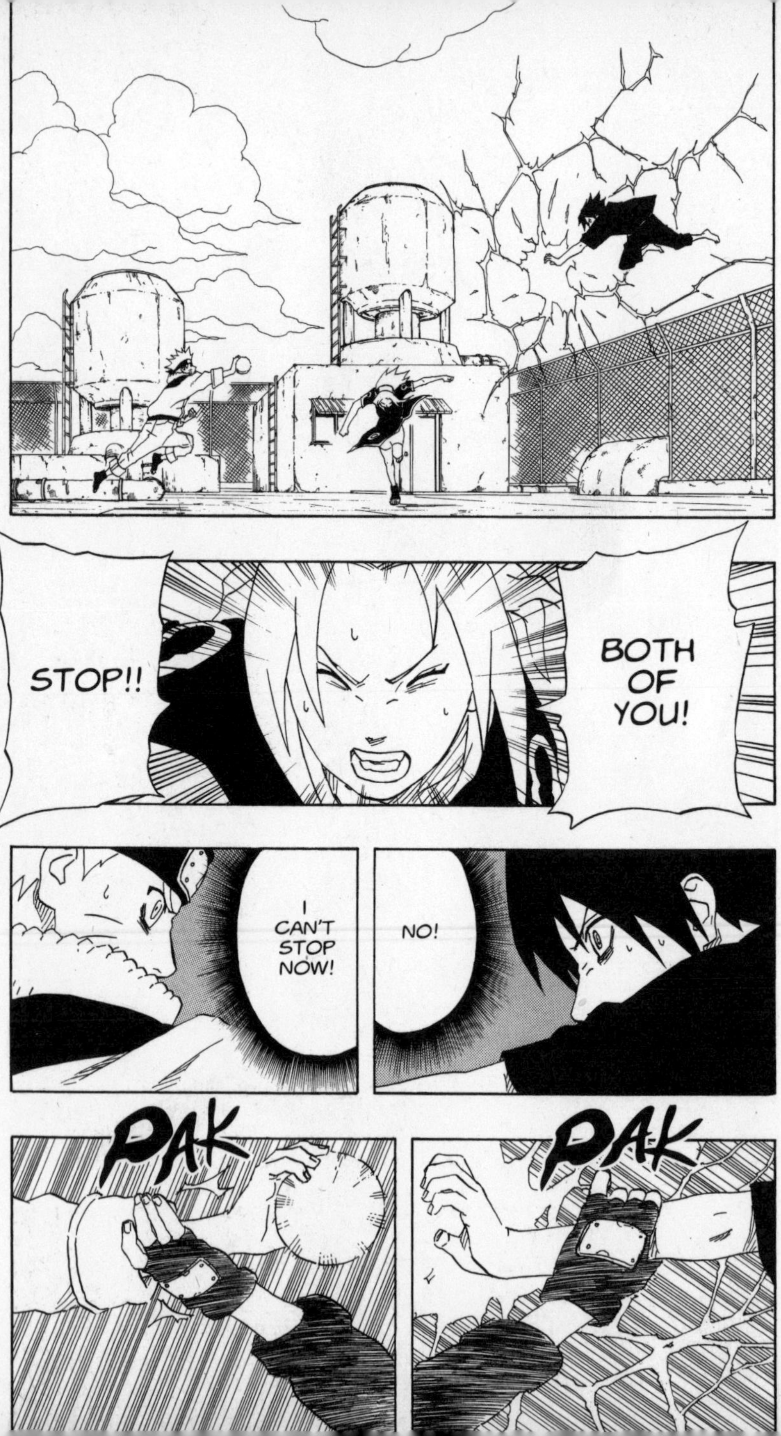
STOP!!
BOTH OF YOU!
NO!
I CAN'T STOP NOW!
PAK
PAK

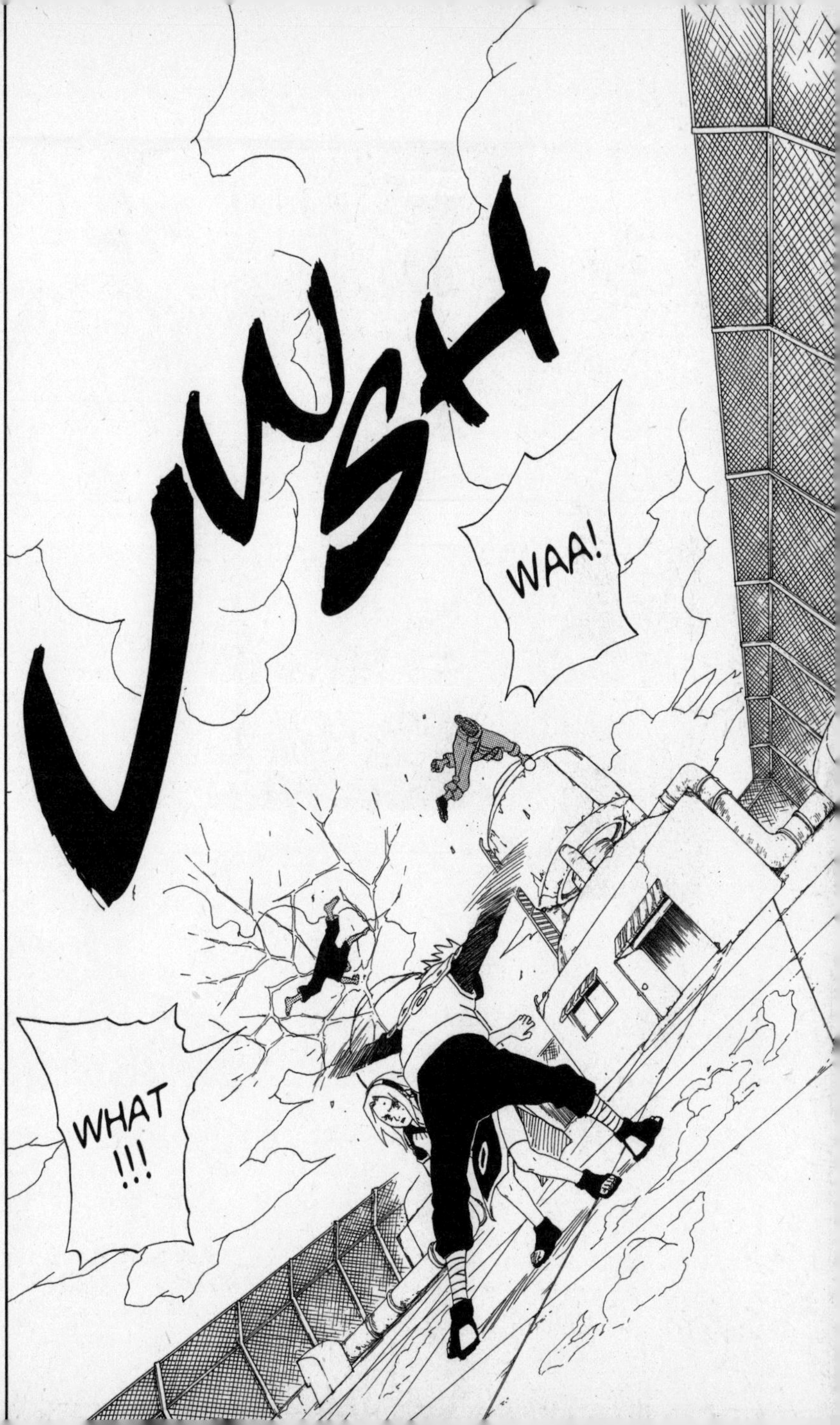
WAA!
WHAT !!!

READ THIS WAY

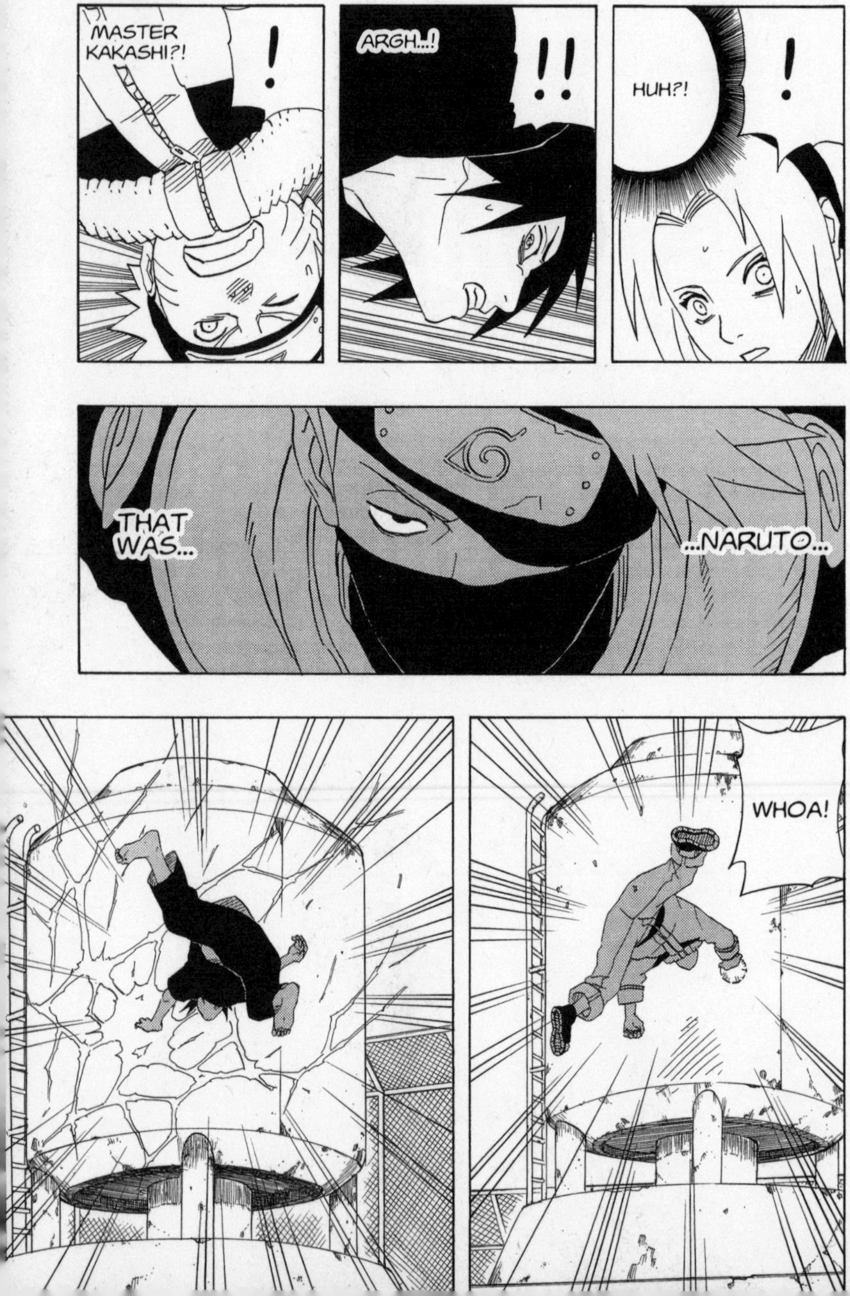
!
HUH?!
!!
ARGH...!
!
MASTER KAKASHI?!
...NARUTO...
THAT WAS...
WHOA!

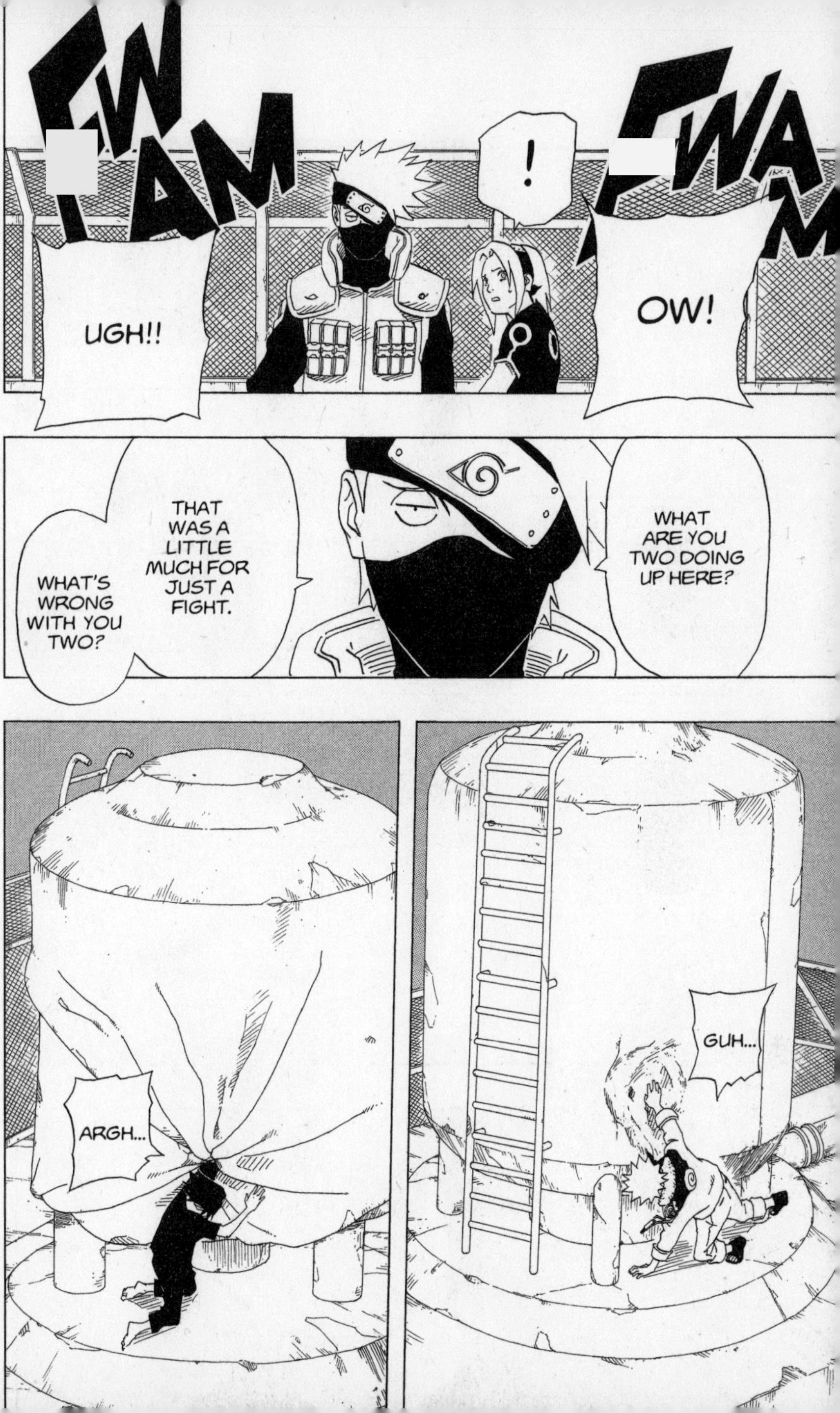
FWAM
OW!
!
FWAM
UGH!!
WHAT ARE YOU TWO DOING UP HERE?
THAT WAS A LITTLE MUCH FOR JUST A FIGHT.
WHAT'S WRONG WITH YOU TWO?
GUH...
ARGH...

READ THIS WAY

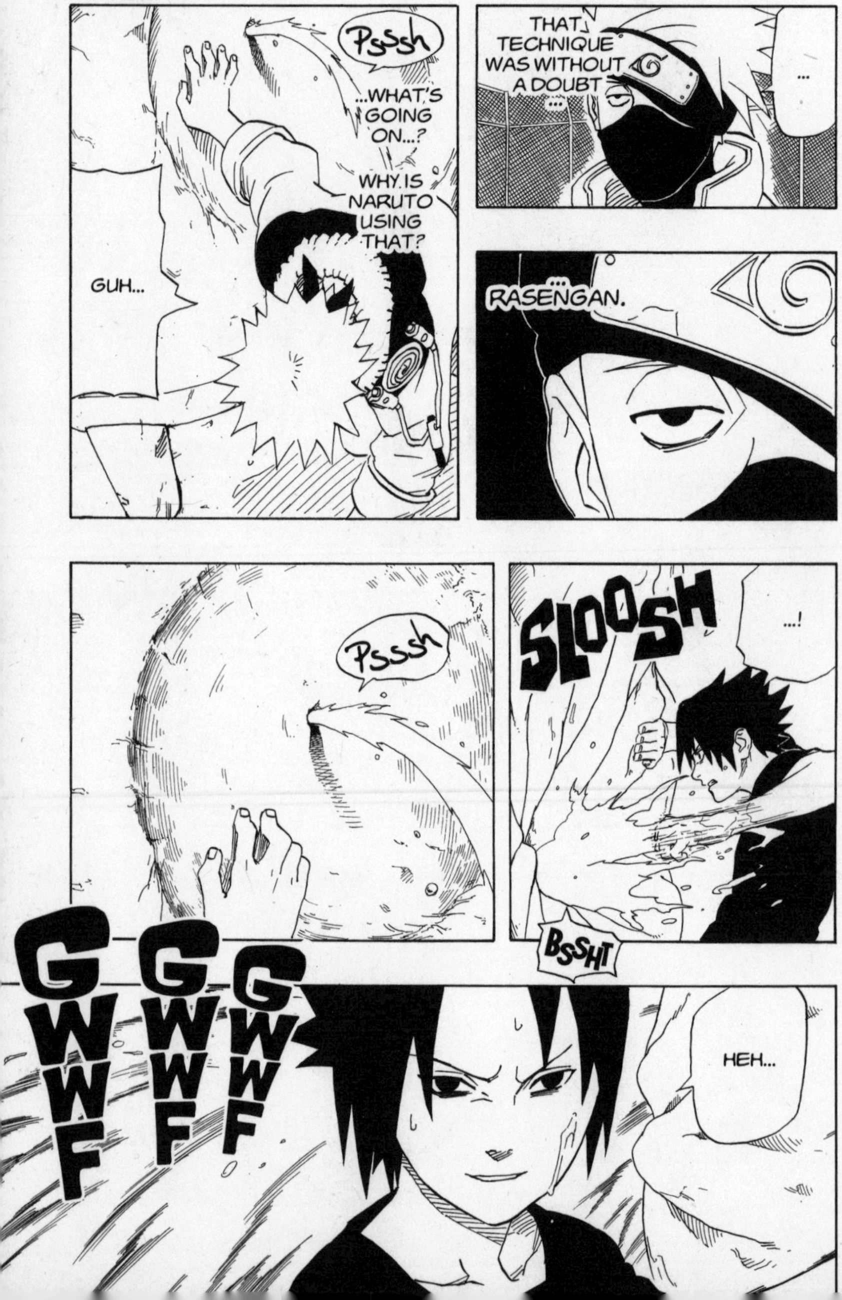
THAT TECHNIQUE WAS WITHOUT A DOUBT ...
...
... RASENGAN.
Pssh
...WHAT'S GOING ON...?
WHY IS NARUTO USING THAT?
GUH...
SLOOSH
...!
BSSHT
Psssh
GWWF
GWWF
GWWF
HEH...

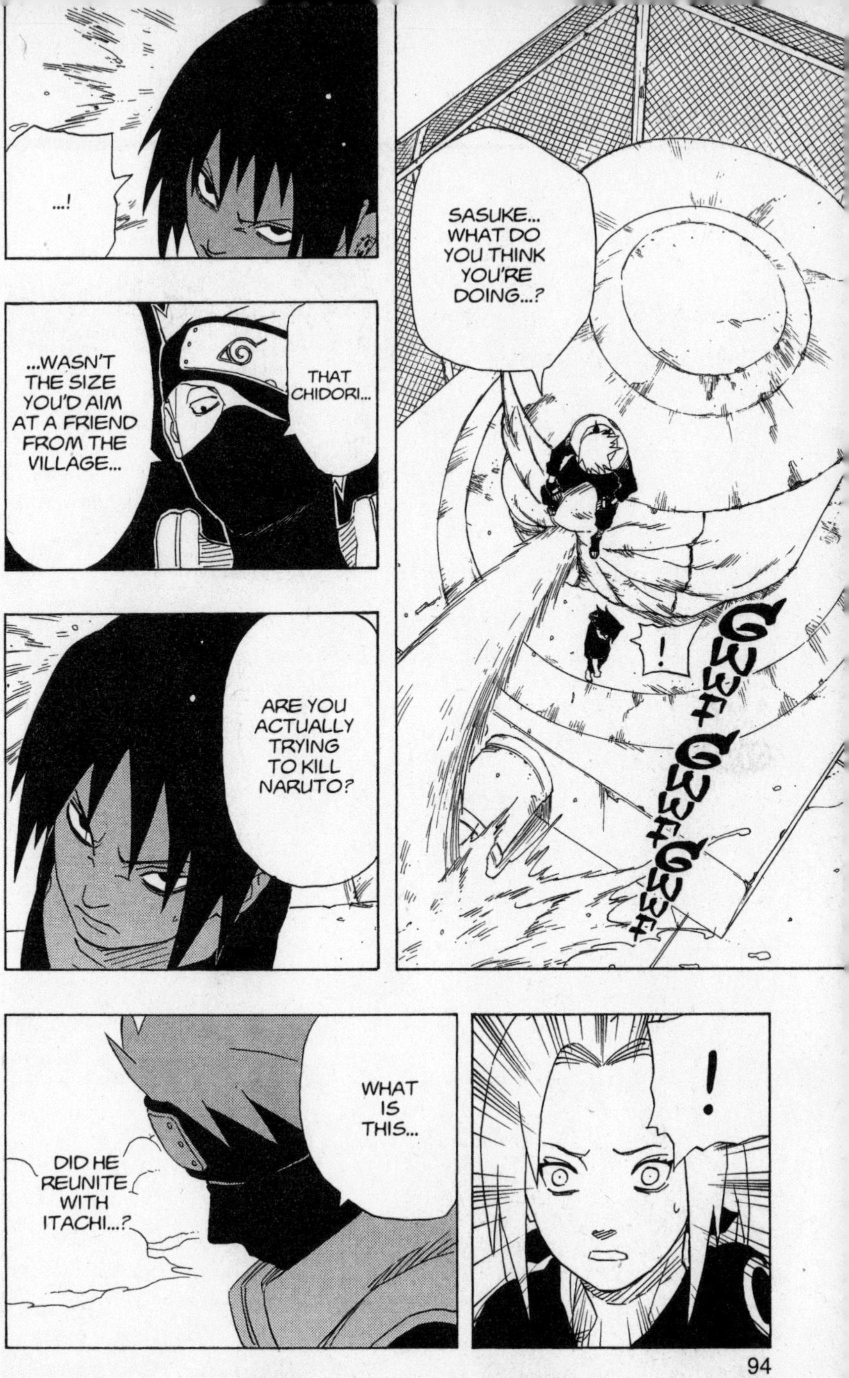
SASUKE... WHAT DO YOU THINK YOU'RE DOING...?
!
GWWF GWWF GWWF
...!
THAT CHIDORI...
...WASN'T THE SIZE YOU'D AIM AT A FRIEND FROM THE VILLAGE...
ARE YOU ACTUALLY TRYING TO KILL NARUTO?
!
WHAT IS THIS...
DID HE REUNITE WITH ITACHI...?

READ THIS WAY

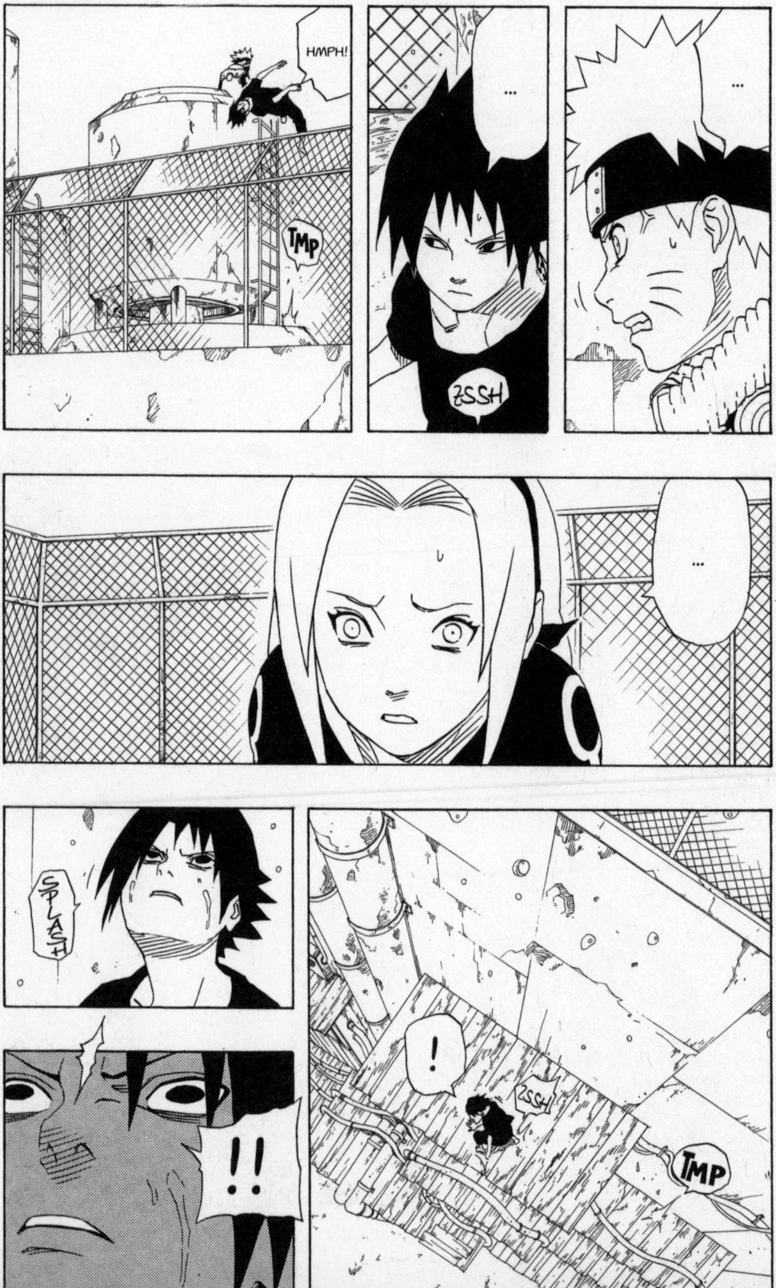
...
...
ZSSH
HMPH!
TMP
...
!
ZSSH
TMP
SPLASH
!!

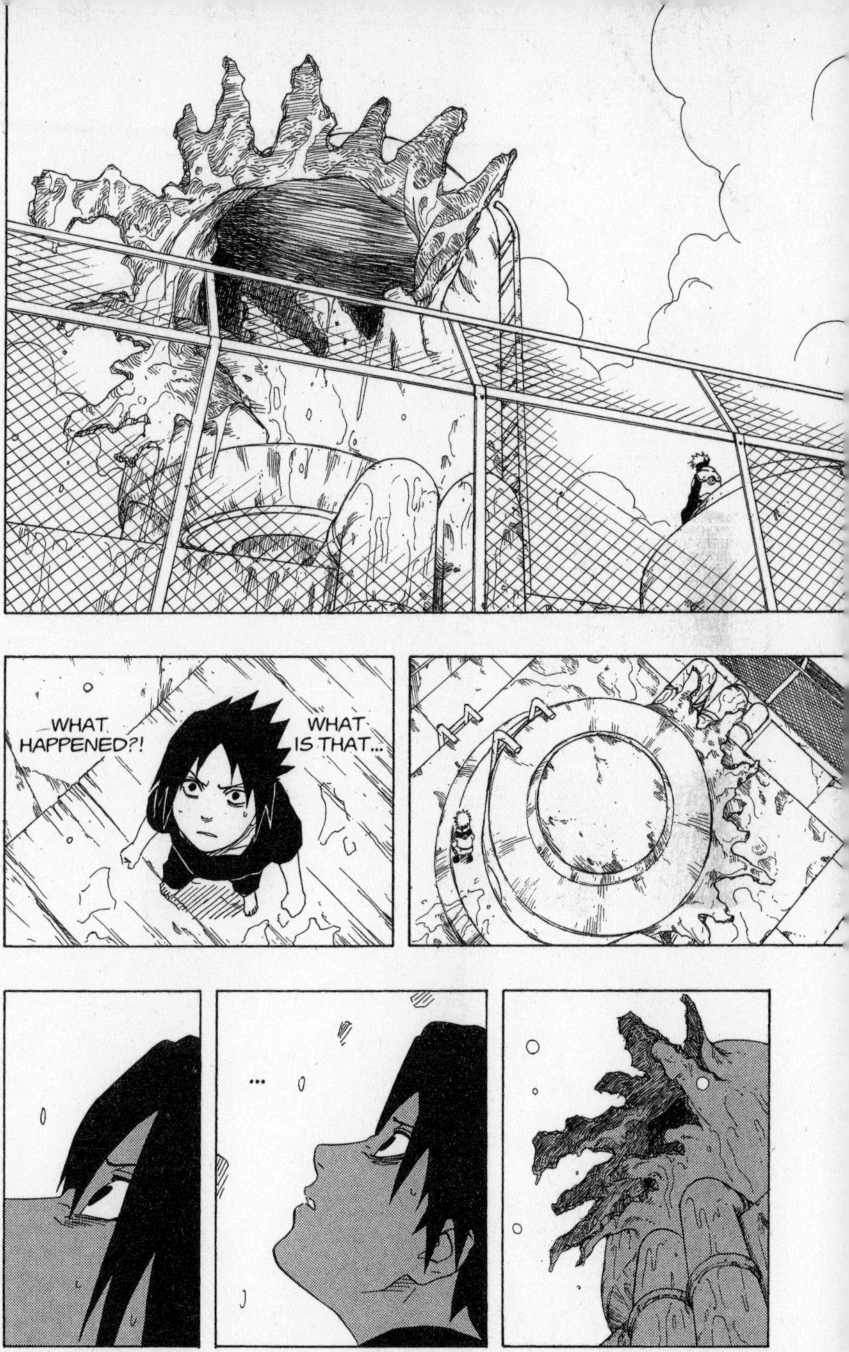
WHAT IS THAT...
WHAT HAPPENED?!
...

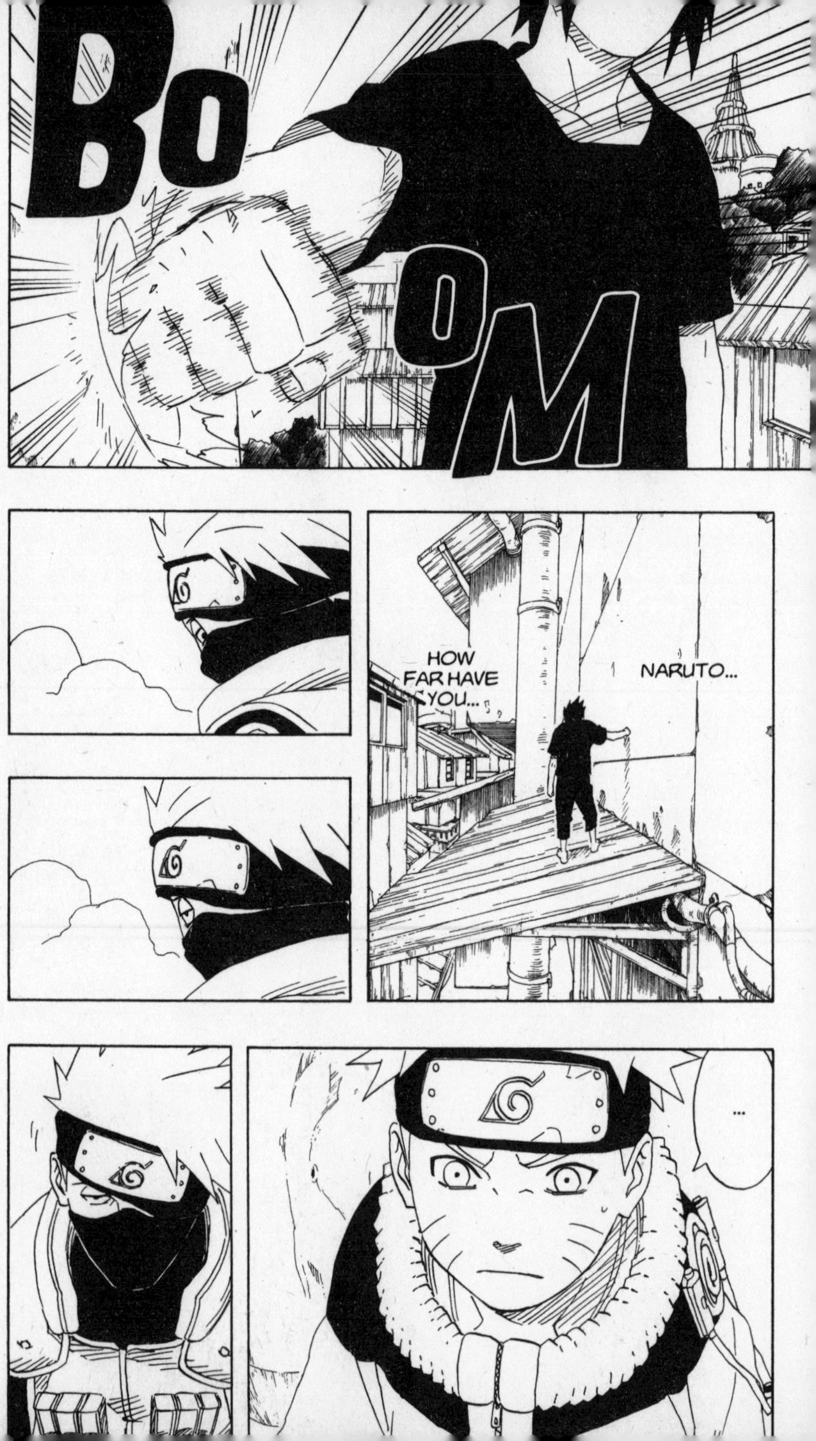
BOOM
NARUTO...
HOW FAR HAVE YOU...
...

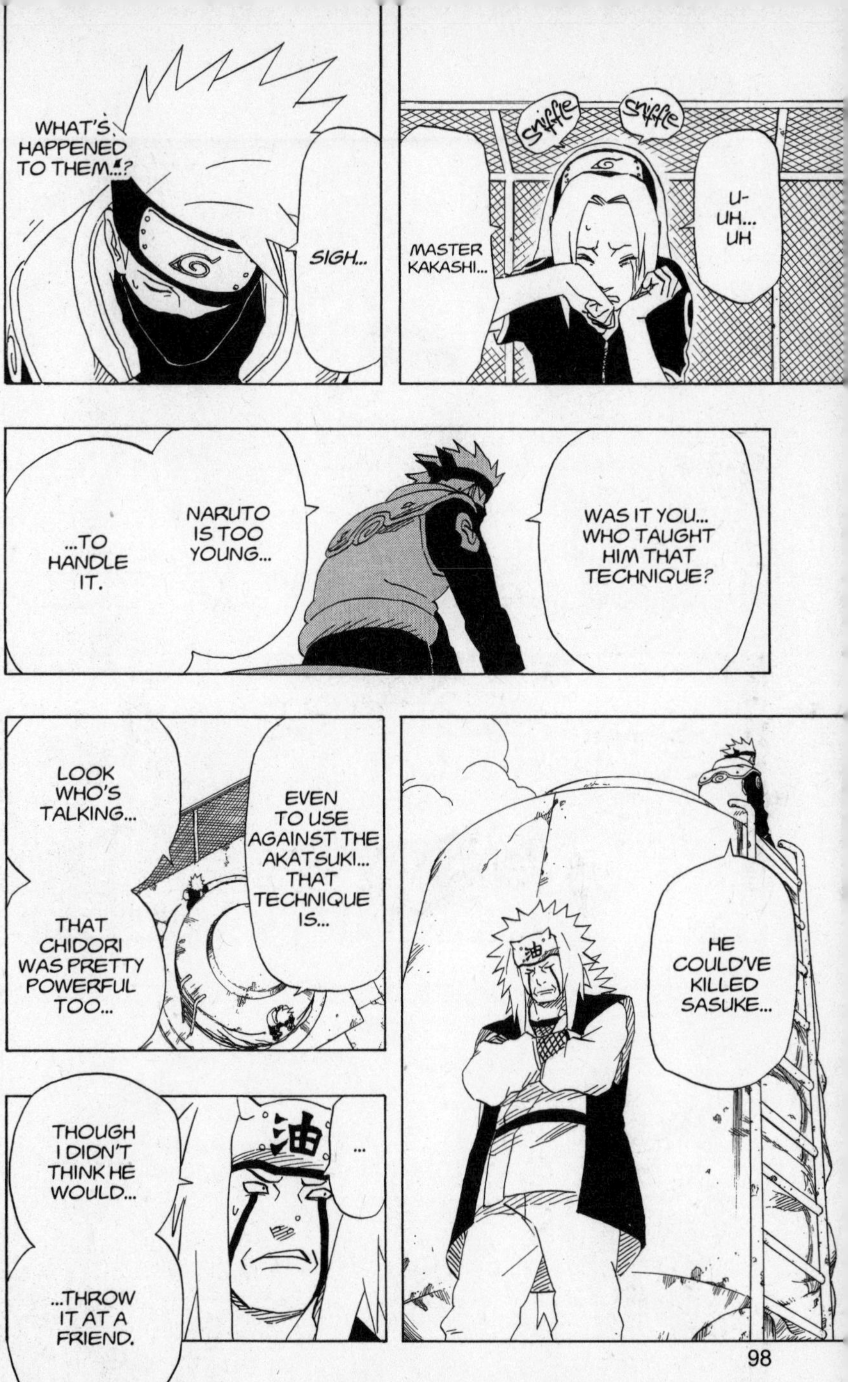
SNIFFLE
SNIFFLE
U- UH... UH
MASTER KAKASHI...
SIGH...
WHAT'S HAPPENED TO THEM...?
WAS IT YOU... WHO TAUGHT HIM THAT TECHNIQUE?
NARUTO IS TOO YOUNG...
...TO HANDLE IT.
HE COULD'VE KILLED SASUKE...
EVEN TO USE AGAINST THE AKATSUKI... THAT TECHNIQUE IS...
LOOK WHO'S TALKING...
THAT CHIDORI WAS PRETTY POWERFUL TOO...
...
THOUGH I DIDN'T THINK HE WOULD...
...THROW IT AT A FRIEND.

READ THIS WAY

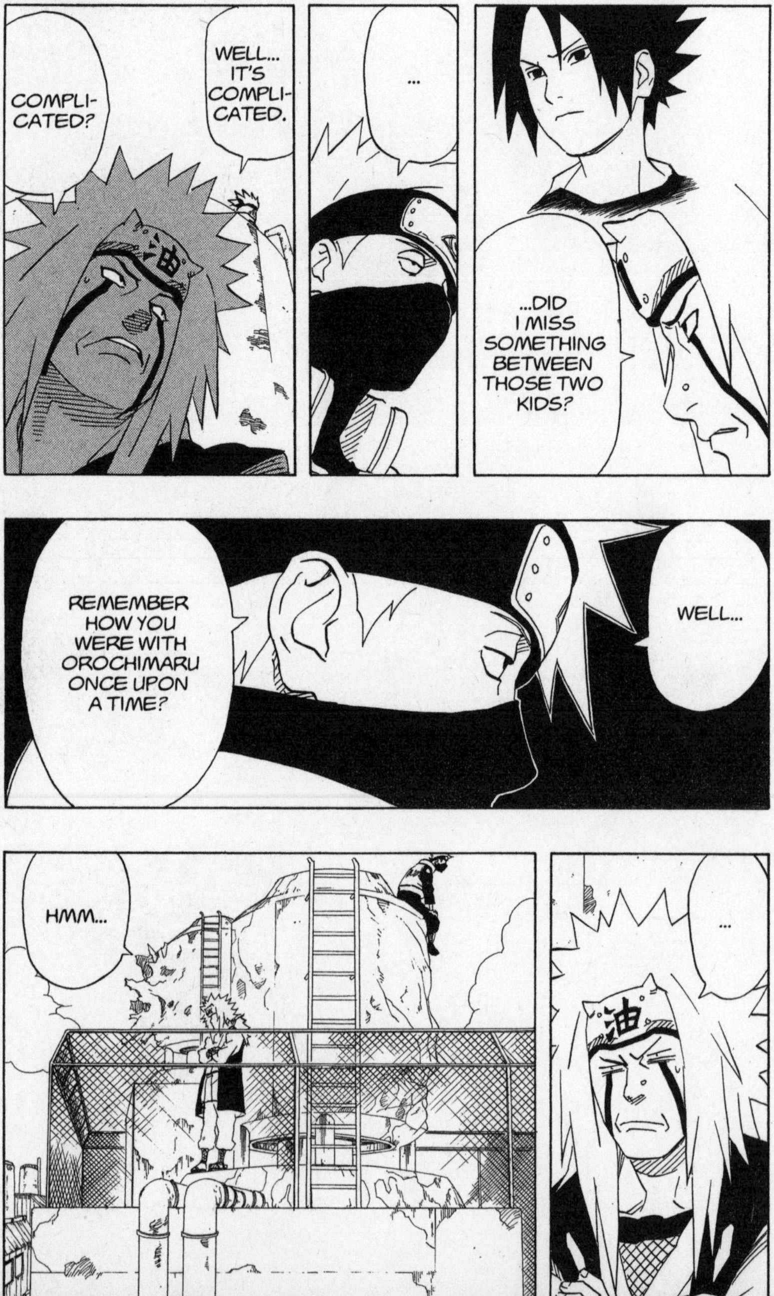
...DID I MISS SOMETHING BETWEEN THOSE TWO KIDS?
...
WELL... IT'S COMPLICATED.
COMPLICATED?
WELL...
REMEMBER HOW YOU WERE WITH OROCHIMARU ONCE UPON A TIME?
...
HMM...

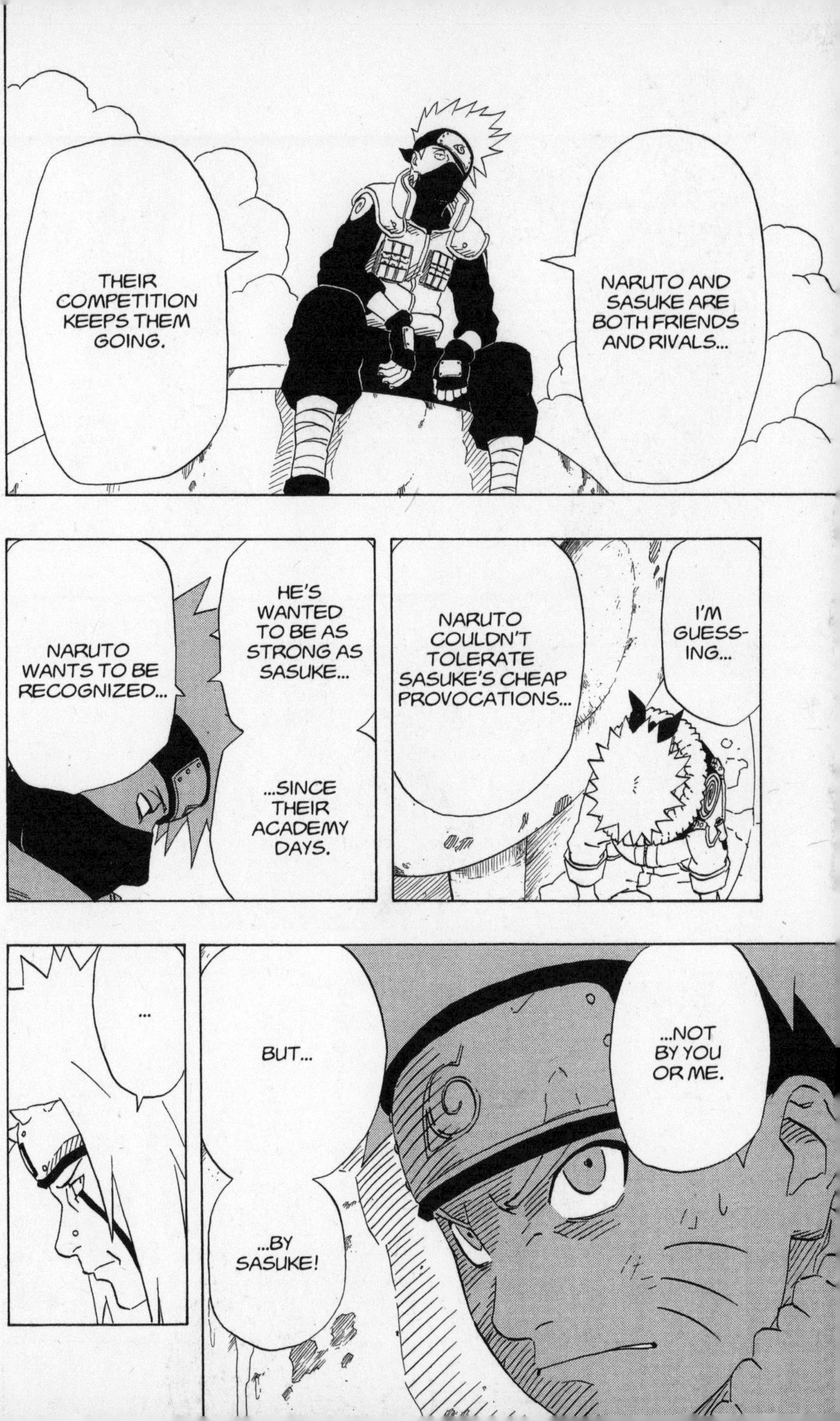
NARUTO AND SASUKE ARE BOTH FRIENDS AND RIVALS...
THEIR COMPETITION KEEPS THEM GOING.
I'M GUESSING...
NARUTO COULDN'T TOLERATE SASUKE'S CHEAP PROVOCATIONS...
HE'S WANTED TO BE AS STRONG AS SASUKE...
...SINCE THEIR ACADEMY DAYS.
NARUTO WANTS TO BE RECOGNIZED...
...NOT BY YOU OR ME.
BUT...
...BY SASUKE!
...

READ THIS WAY

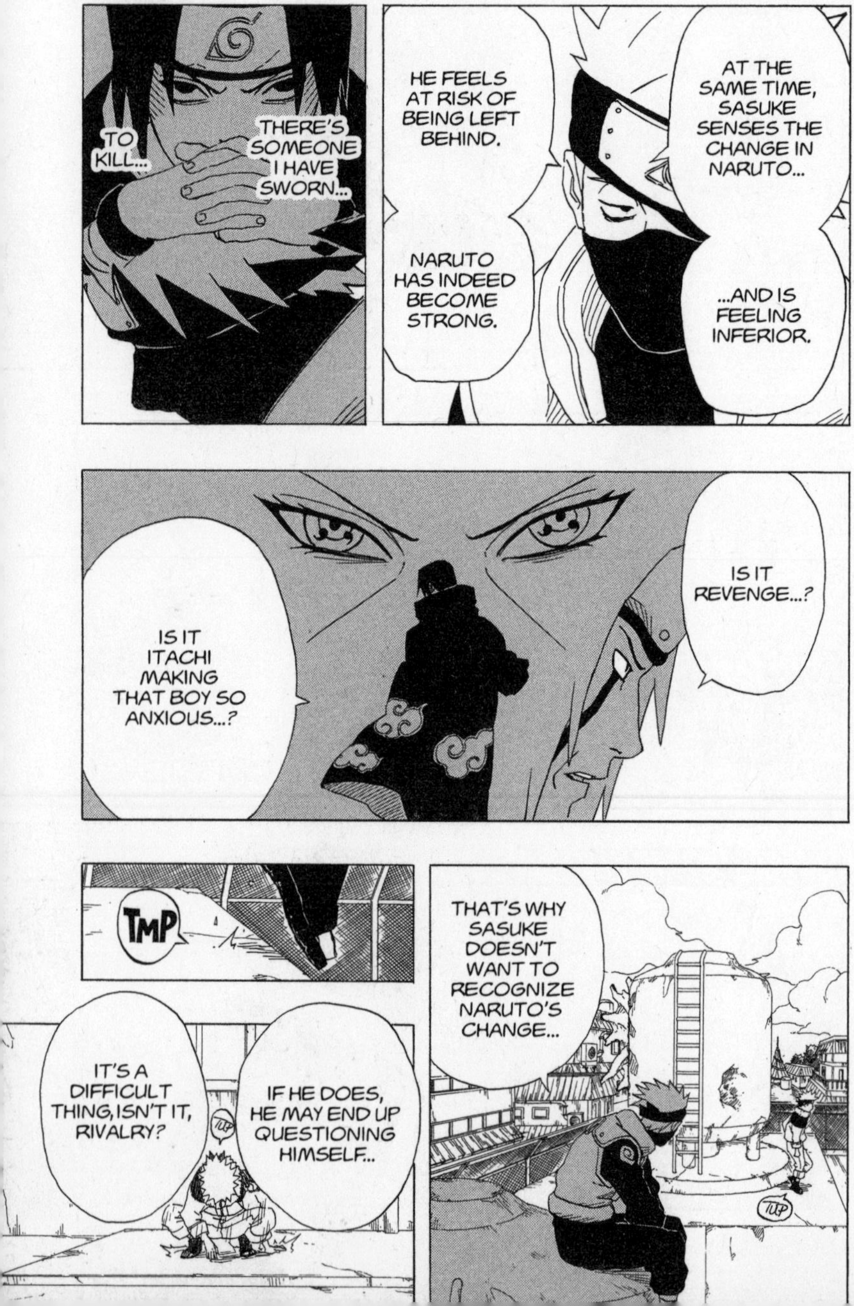
AT THE SAME TIME, SASUKE SENSES THE CHANGE IN NARUTO...
...AND IS FEELING INFERIOR.
HE FEELS AT RISK OF BEING LEFT BEHIND.
NARUTO HAS INDEED BECOME STRONG.
THERE'S SOMEONE I HAVE SWORN...
TO KILL...
IS IT REVENGE...?
IS IT ITACHI MAKING THAT BOY SO ANXIOUS...?
THAT'S WHY SASUKE DOESN'T WANT TO RECOGNIZE NARUTO'S CHANGE...
TUP
TMP
IF HE DOES, HE MAY END UP QUESTIONING HIMSELF...
IT'S A DIFFICULT THING, ISN'T IT, RIVALRY?
TUP

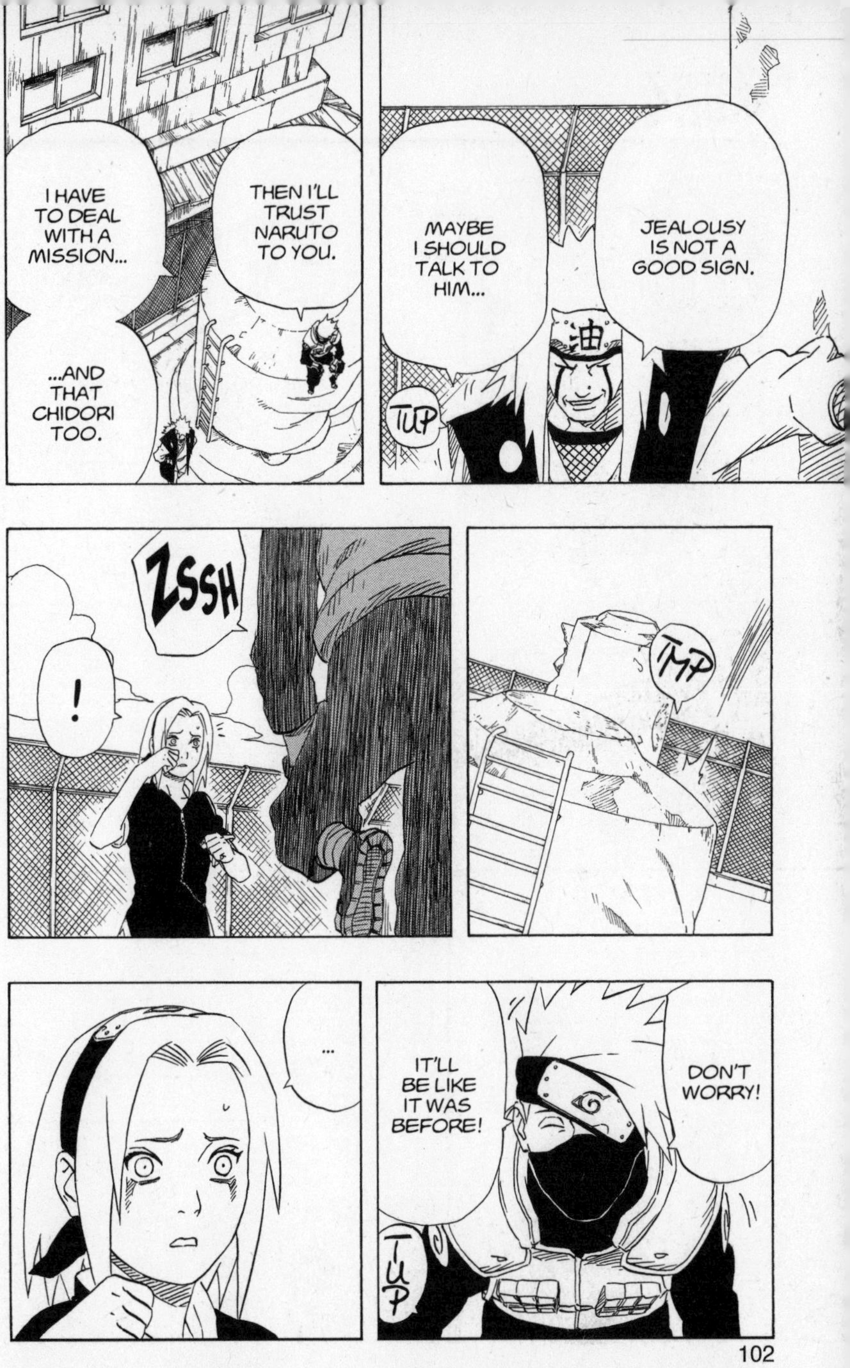
JEALOUSY IS NOT A GOOD SIGN.
MAYBE I SHOULD TALK TO HIM...
TUP
THEN I'LL TRUST NARUTO TO YOU.
I HAVE TO DEAL WITH A MISSION...
...AND THAT CHIDORI TOO.
TMP
ZSSH
!
DON'T WORRY!
IT'LL BE LIKE IT WAS BEFORE!
TUP
...

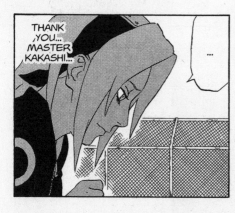

THANK YOU... MASTER KAKASHI...

...

ZSSH

!

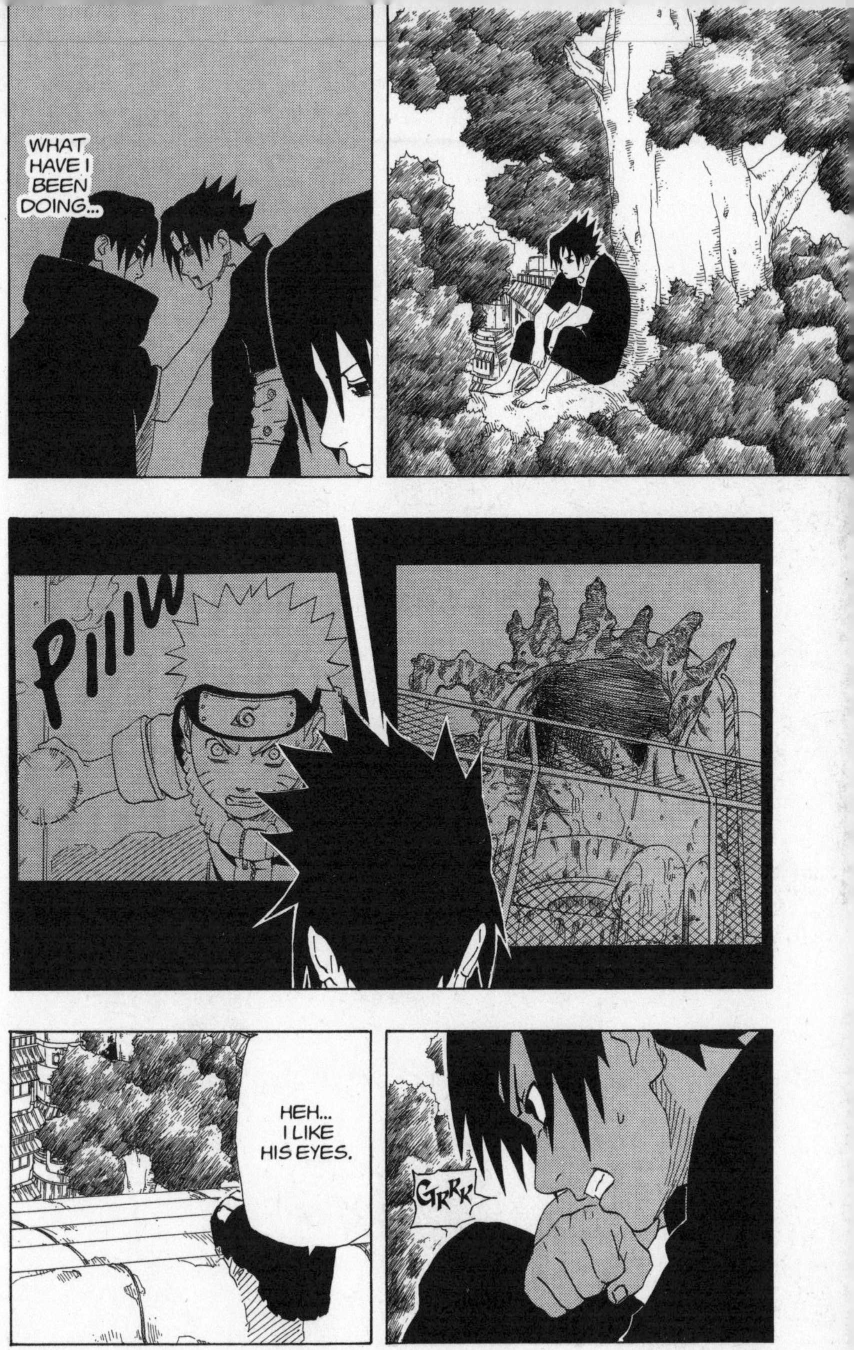
WHAT HAVE I BEEN DOING...
PIIIW
HEH... I LIKE HIS EYES.
GRRK

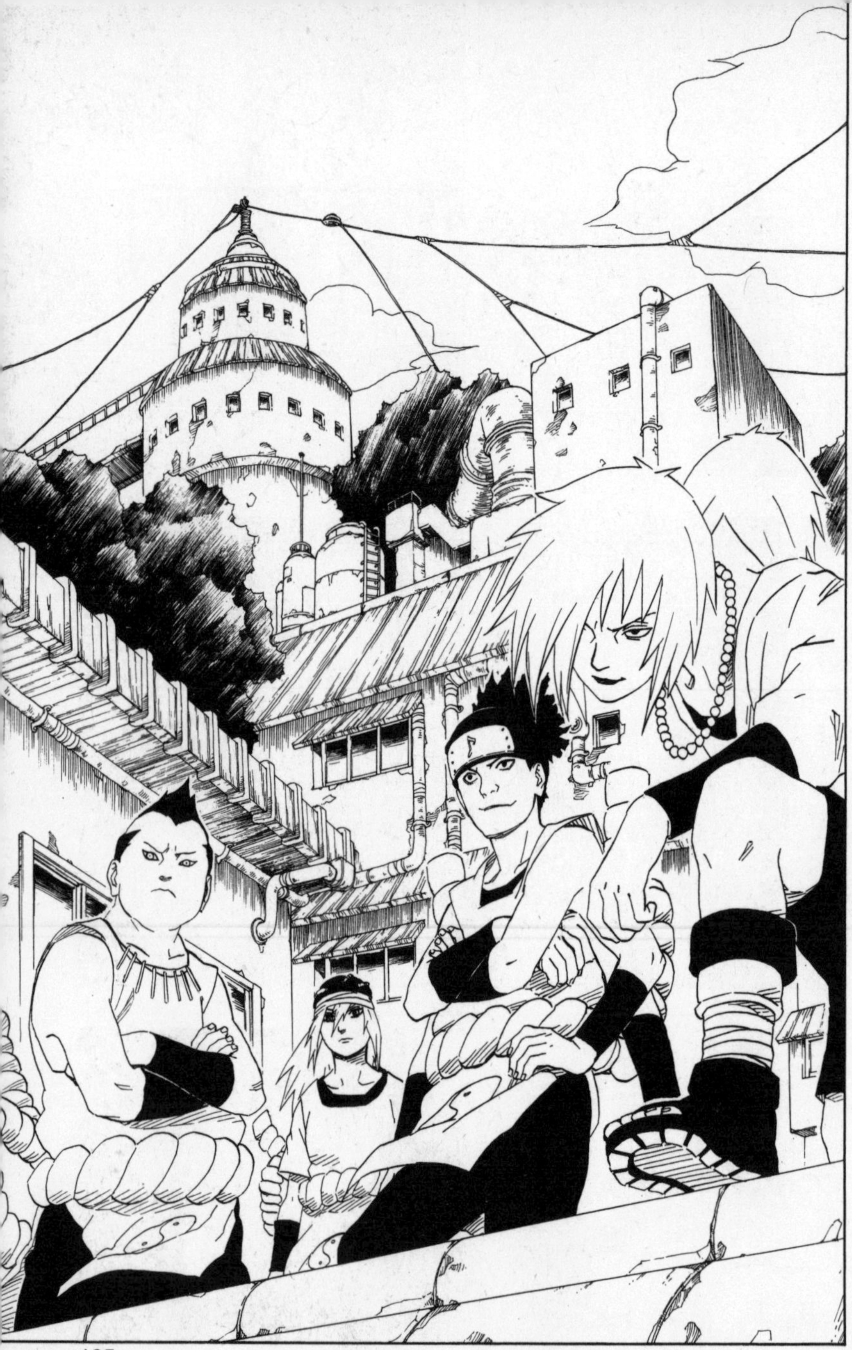

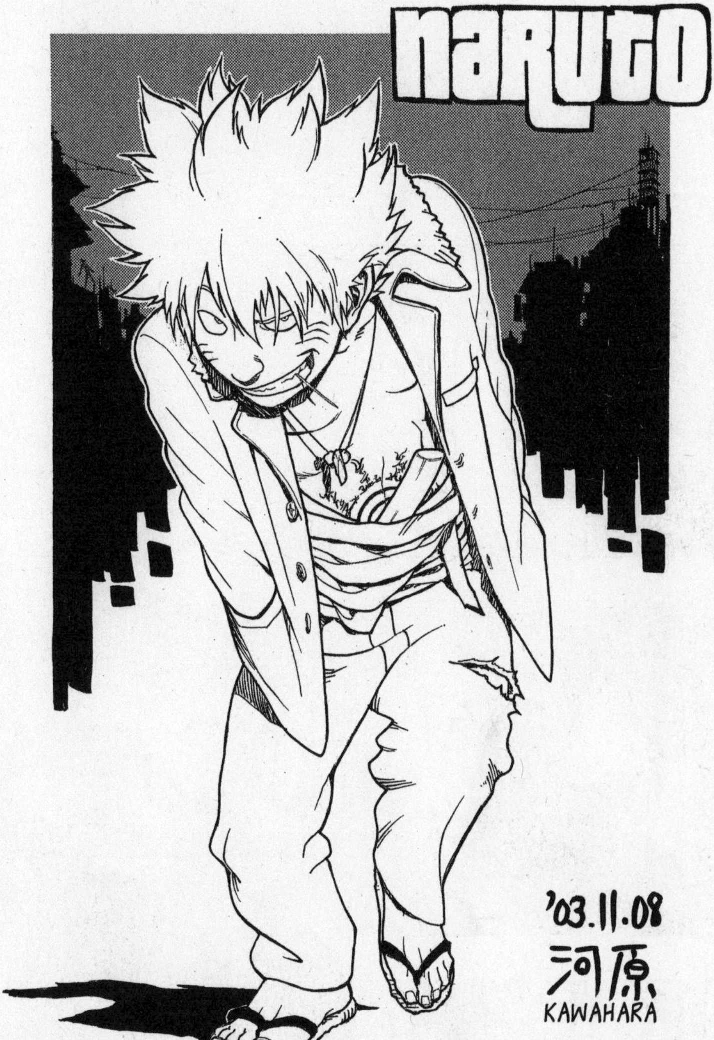
NARUTO
'03.11.08
河原
KAWAHARA

Congratulations, on your marriage and 4 year anniversary (and birthday)--!!!

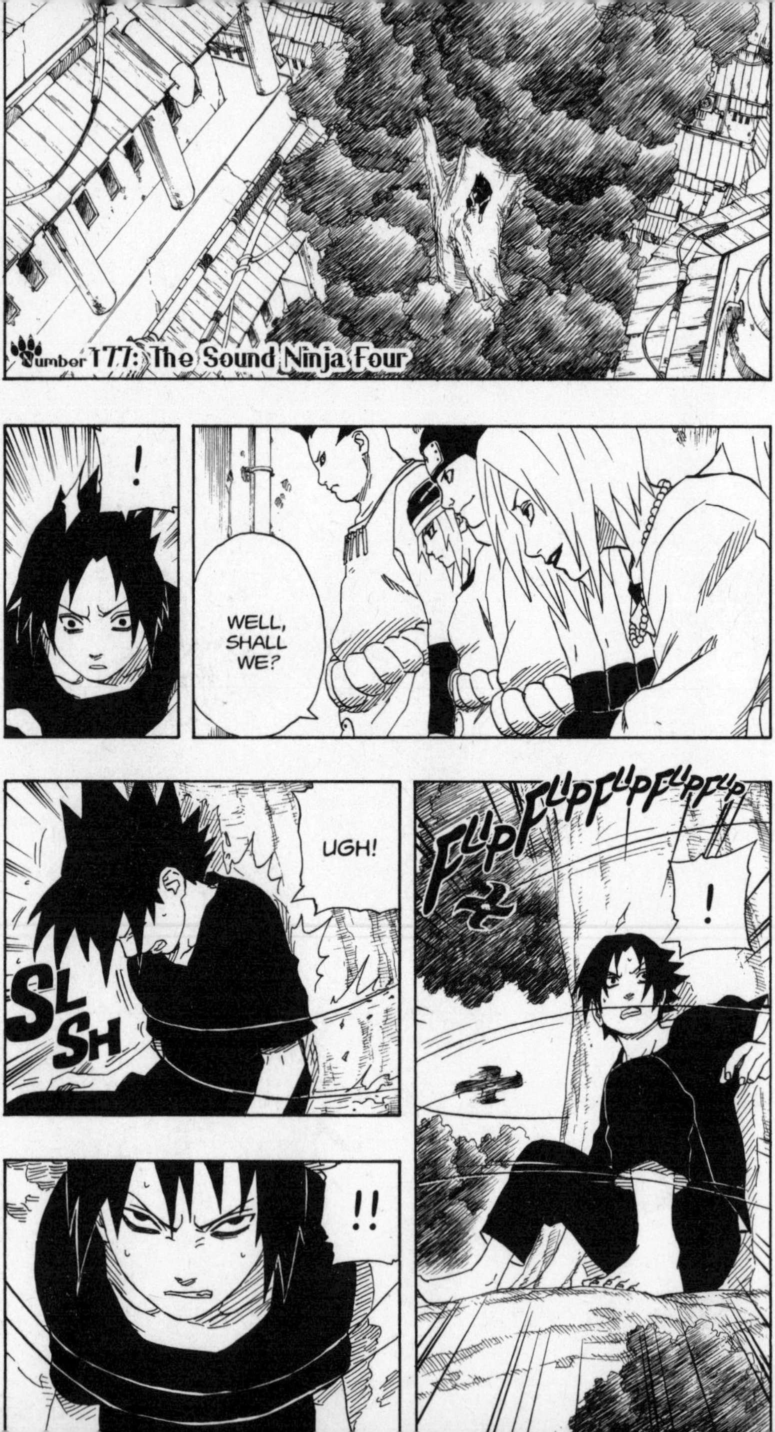
Number 177: The Sound Ninja Four
WELL, SHALL WE?
!
FLIPFLIPFLIPFLIPFLIP
!
UGH!
SLSH
!!

Number 177: The Sound Ninja Four

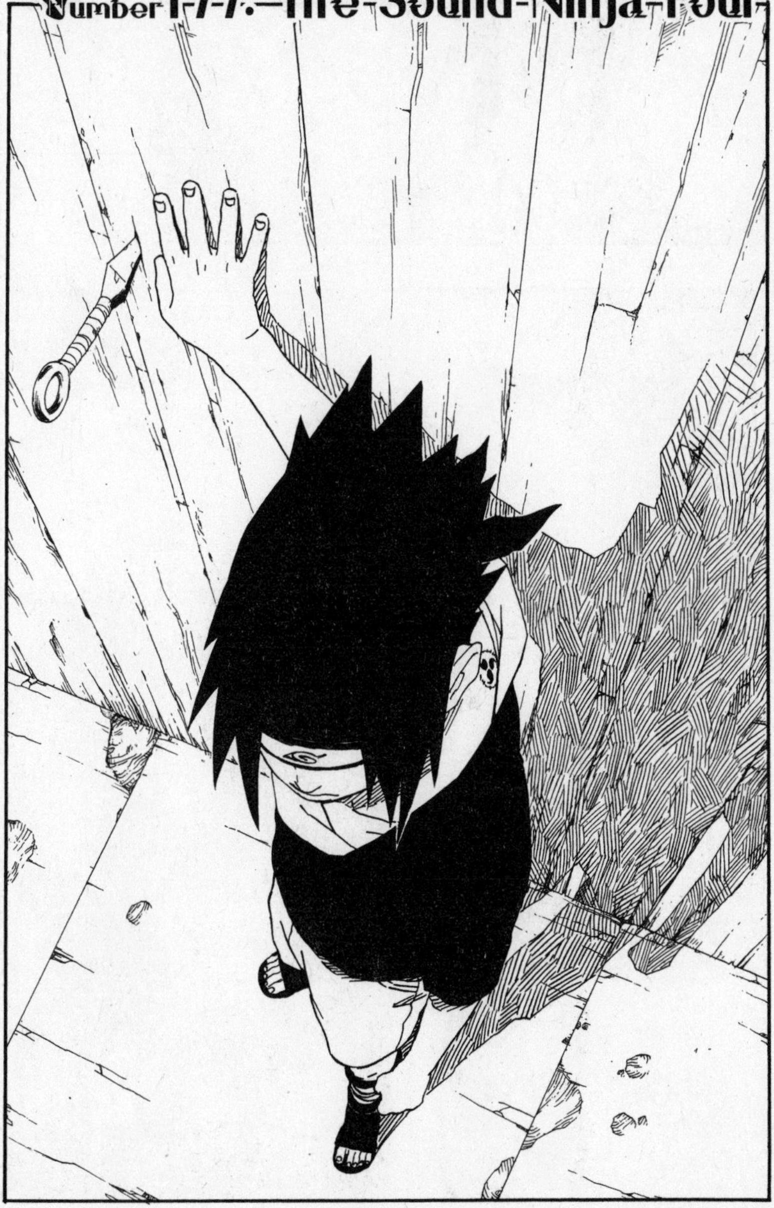

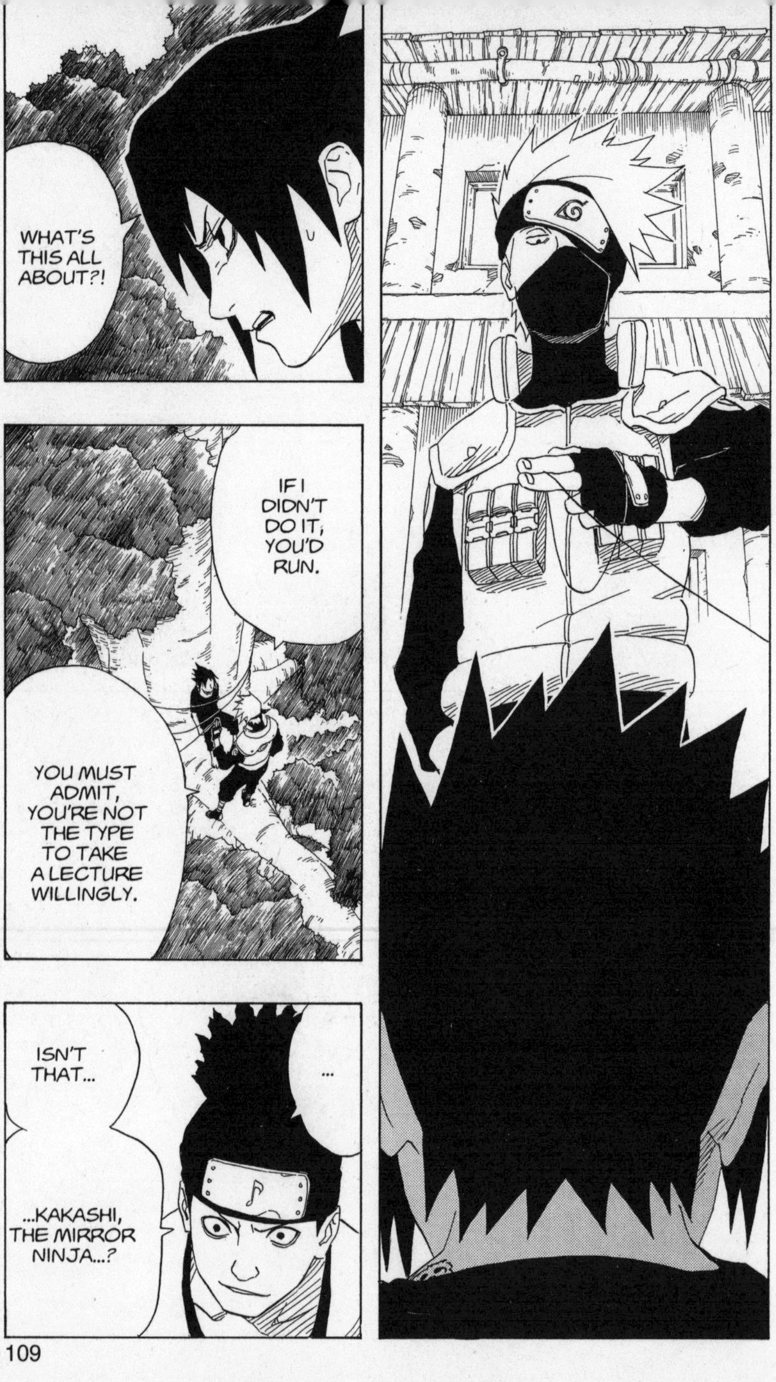
WHAT'S THIS ALL ABOUT?!
IF I DIDN'T DO IT, YOU'D RUN.
YOU MUST ADMIT, YOU'RE NOT THE TYPE TO TAKE A LECTURE WILLINGLY.
...
ISN'T THAT...
...KAKASHI, THE MIRROR NINJA...?

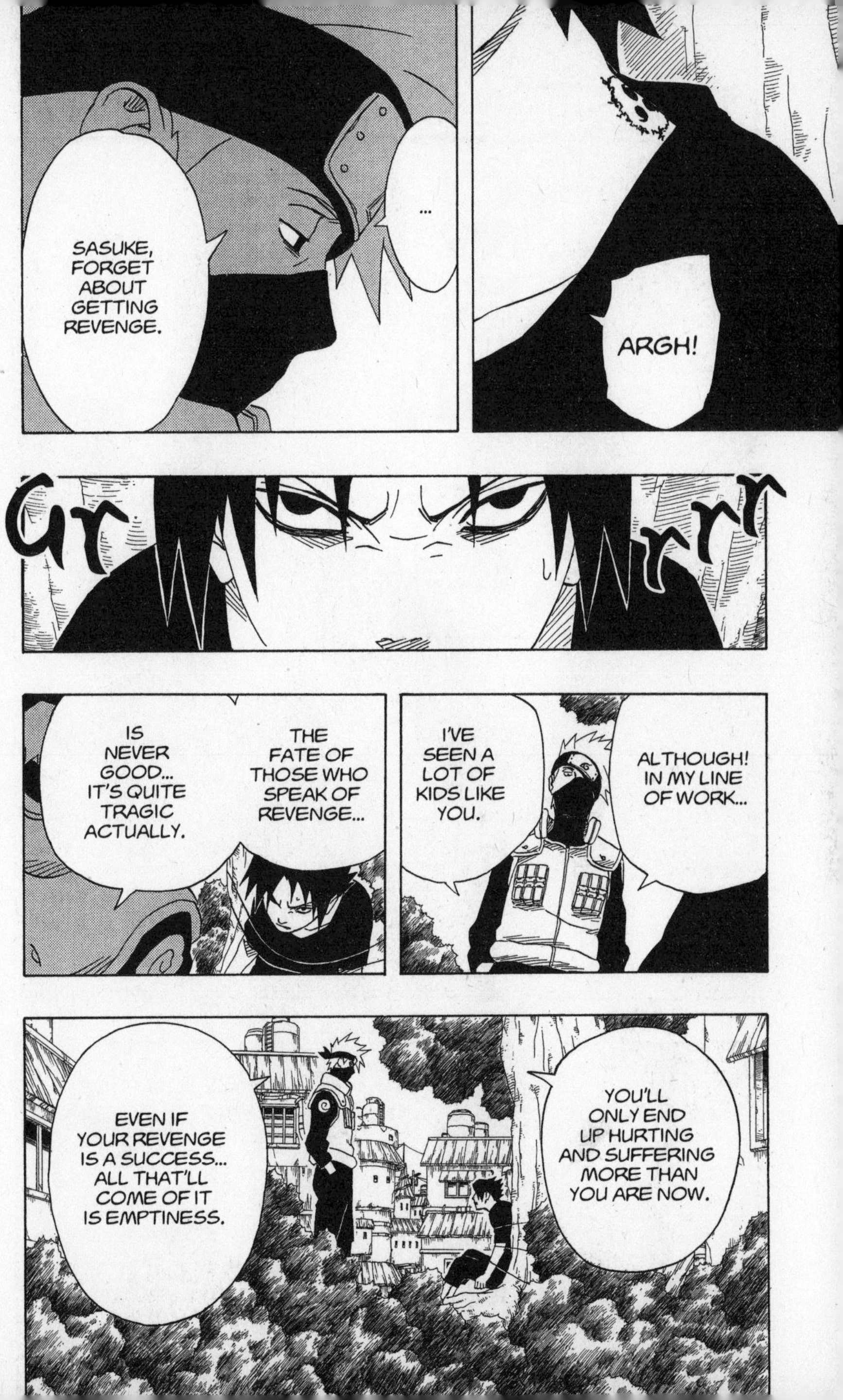
ARGH!
...
SASUKE, FORGET ABOUT GETTING REVENGE.
Grrrr
ALTHOUGH! IN MY LINE OF WORK...
I'VE SEEN A LOT OF KIDS LIKE YOU.
THE FATE OF THOSE WHO SPEAK OF REVENGE...
IS NEVER GOOD... IT'S QUITE TRAGIC ACTUALLY.
YOU'LL ONLY END UP HURTING AND SUFFERING MORE THAN YOU ARE NOW.
EVEN IF YOUR REVENGE IS A SUCCESS... ALL THAT'LL COME OF IT IS EMPTINESS.

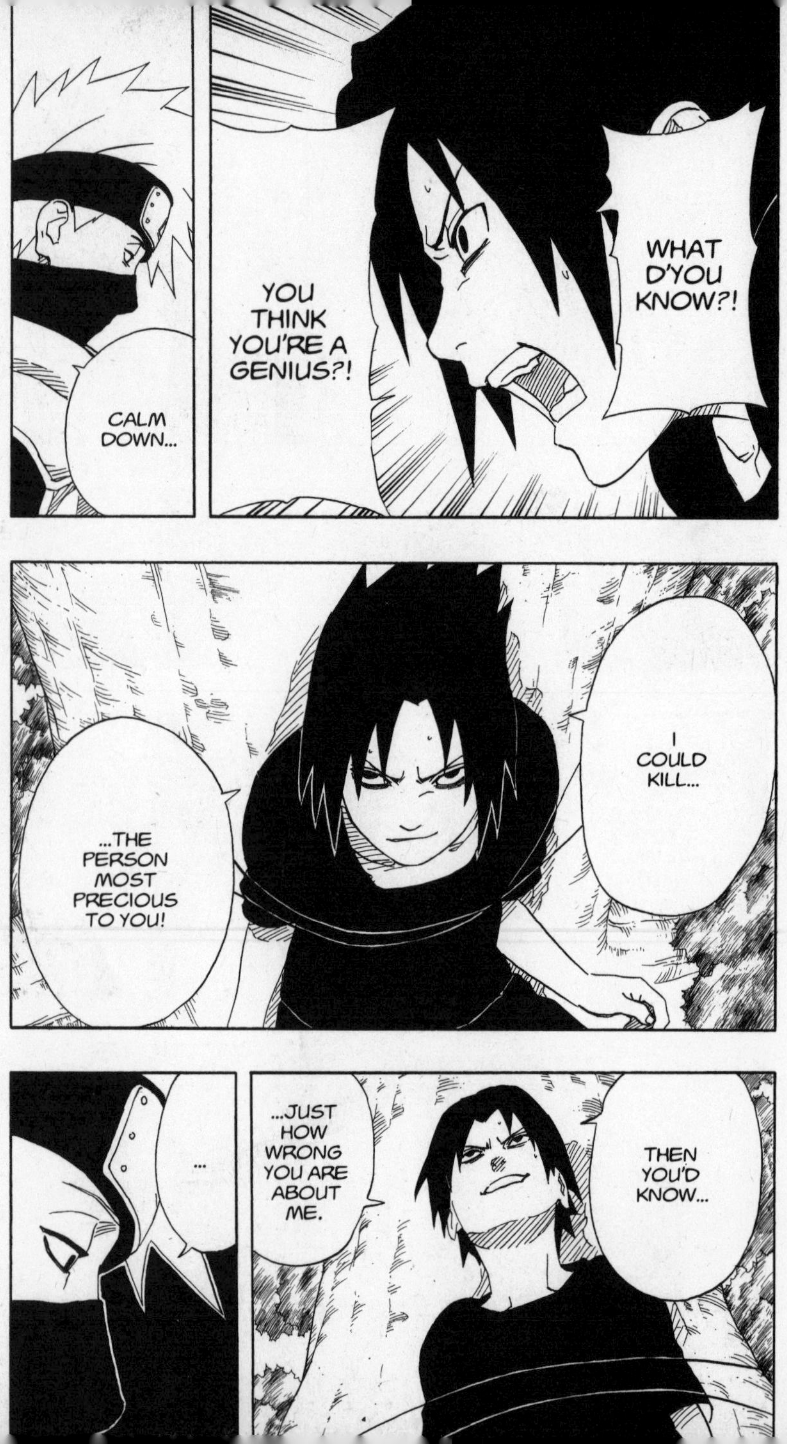
WHAT D'YOU KNOW?!
YOU THINK YOU'RE A GENIUS?!
CALM DOWN...
I COULD KILL...
...THE PERSON MOST PRECIOUS TO YOU!
THEN YOU'D KNOW...
...JUST HOW WRONG YOU ARE ABOUT ME.
...

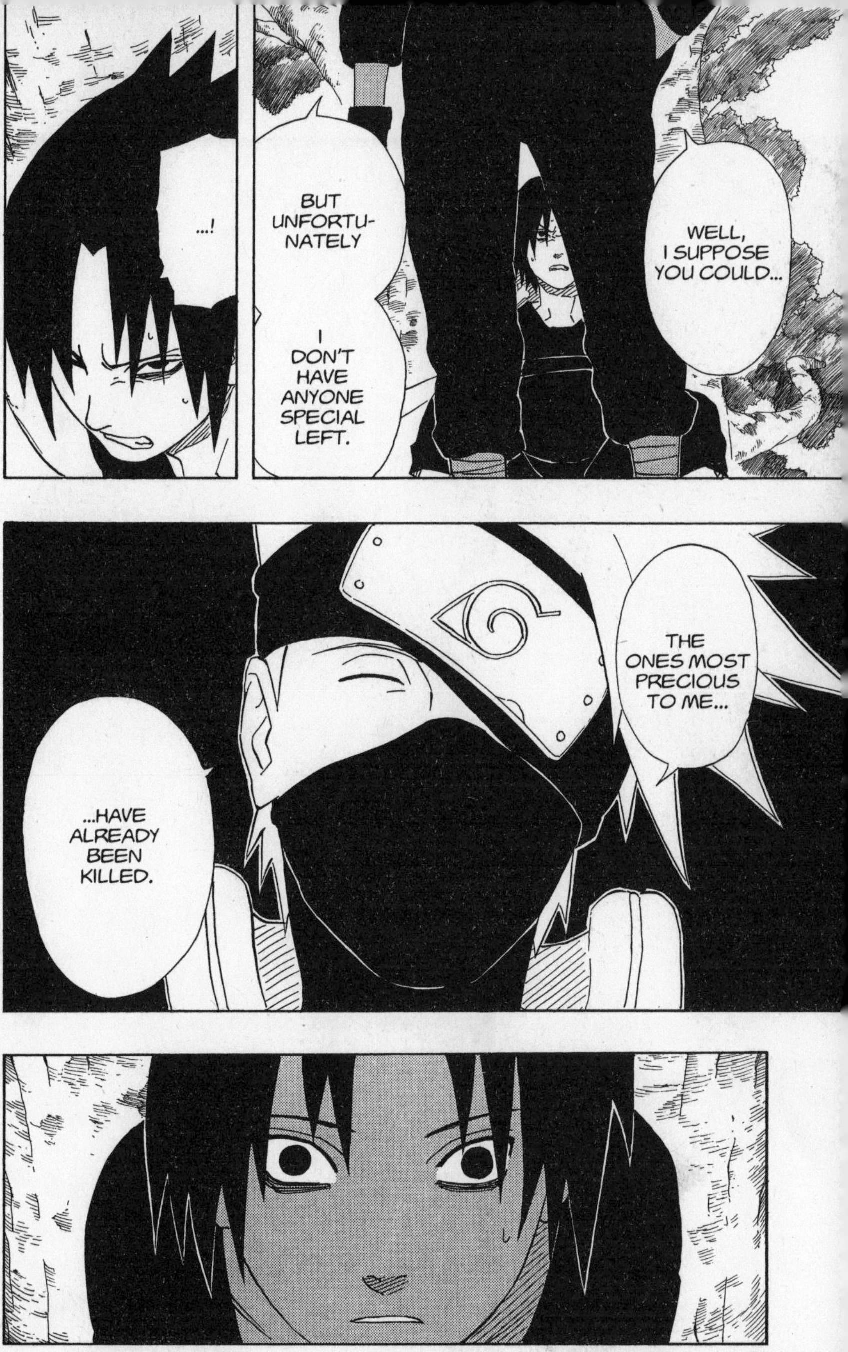
WELL, I SUPPOSE YOU COULD...
BUT UNFORTU-NATELY
I DON'T HAVE ANYONE SPECIAL LEFT.
...!
THE ONES MOST PRECIOUS TO ME...
...HAVE ALREADY BEEN KILLED.

READ THIS WAY

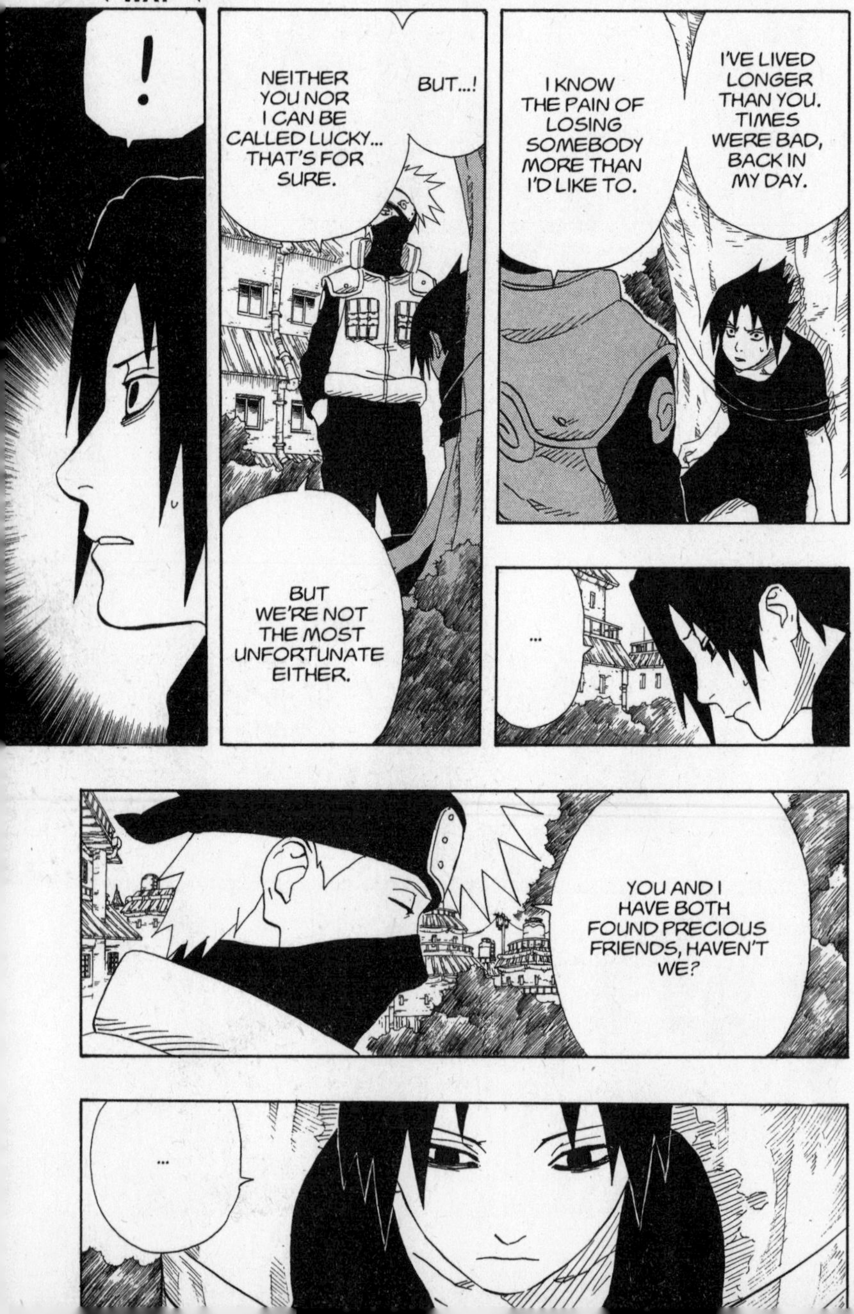
I'VE LIVED LONGER THAN YOU. TIMES WERE BAD, BACK IN MY DAY.
I KNOW THE PAIN OF LOSING SOMEBODY MORE THAN I'D LIKE TO.
...
BUT...!
NEITHER YOU NOR I CAN BE CALLED LUCKY... THAT'S FOR SURE.
BUT WE'RE NOT THE MOST UNFORTUNATE EITHER.
!
YOU AND I HAVE BOTH FOUND PRECIOUS FRIENDS, HAVEN'T WE?
...

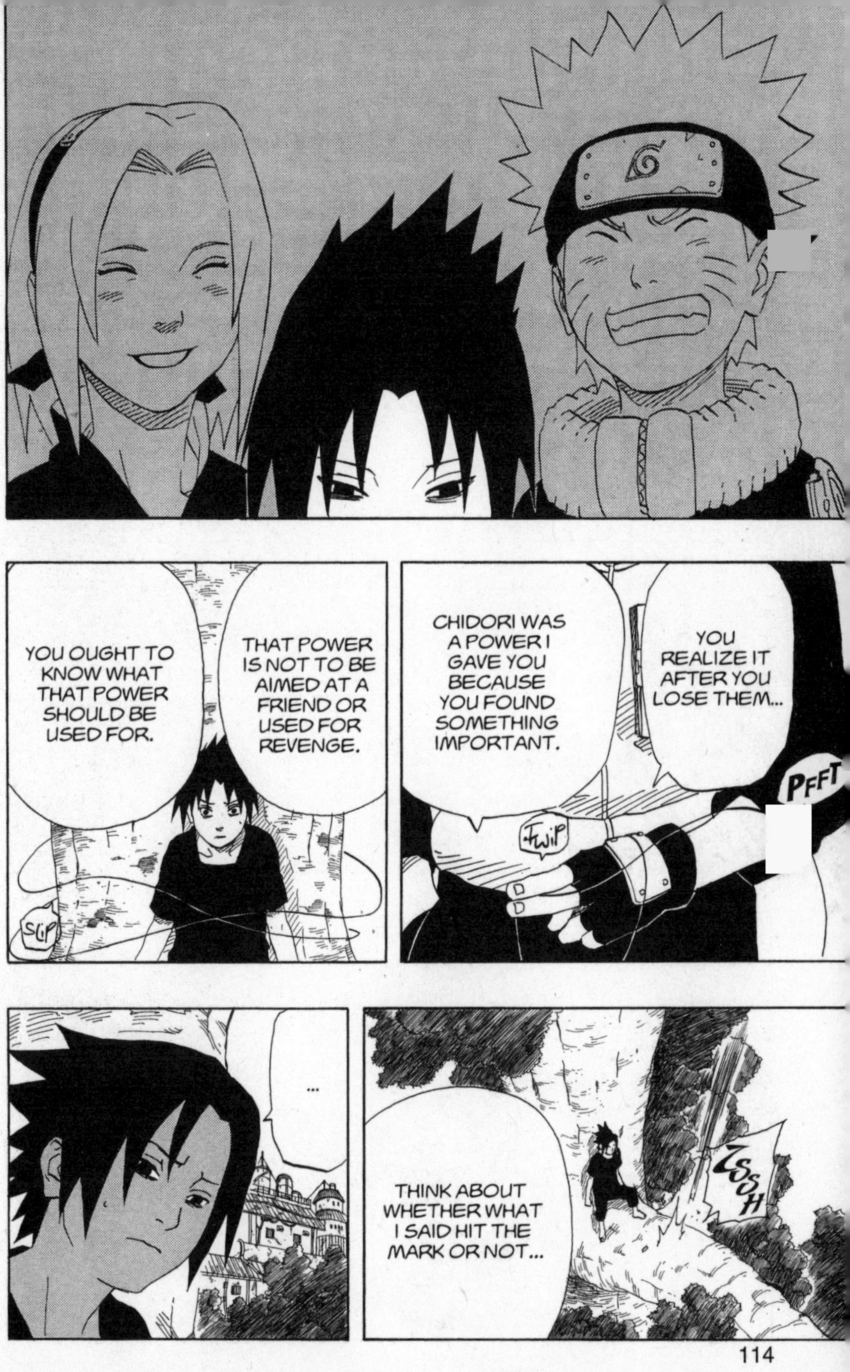
YOU REALIZE IT AFTER YOU LOSE THEM...
CHIDORI WAS A POWER I GAVE YOU BECAUSE YOU FOUND SOMETHING IMPORTANT.
PFFT
TWIP
THAT POWER IS NOT TO BE AIMED AT A FRIEND OR USED FOR REVENGE.
YOU OUGHT TO KNOW WHAT THAT POWER SHOULD BE USED FOR.
SLIP
THINK ABOUT WHETHER WHAT I SAID HIT THE MARK OR NOT...
ZSSH
...

READ THIS WAY

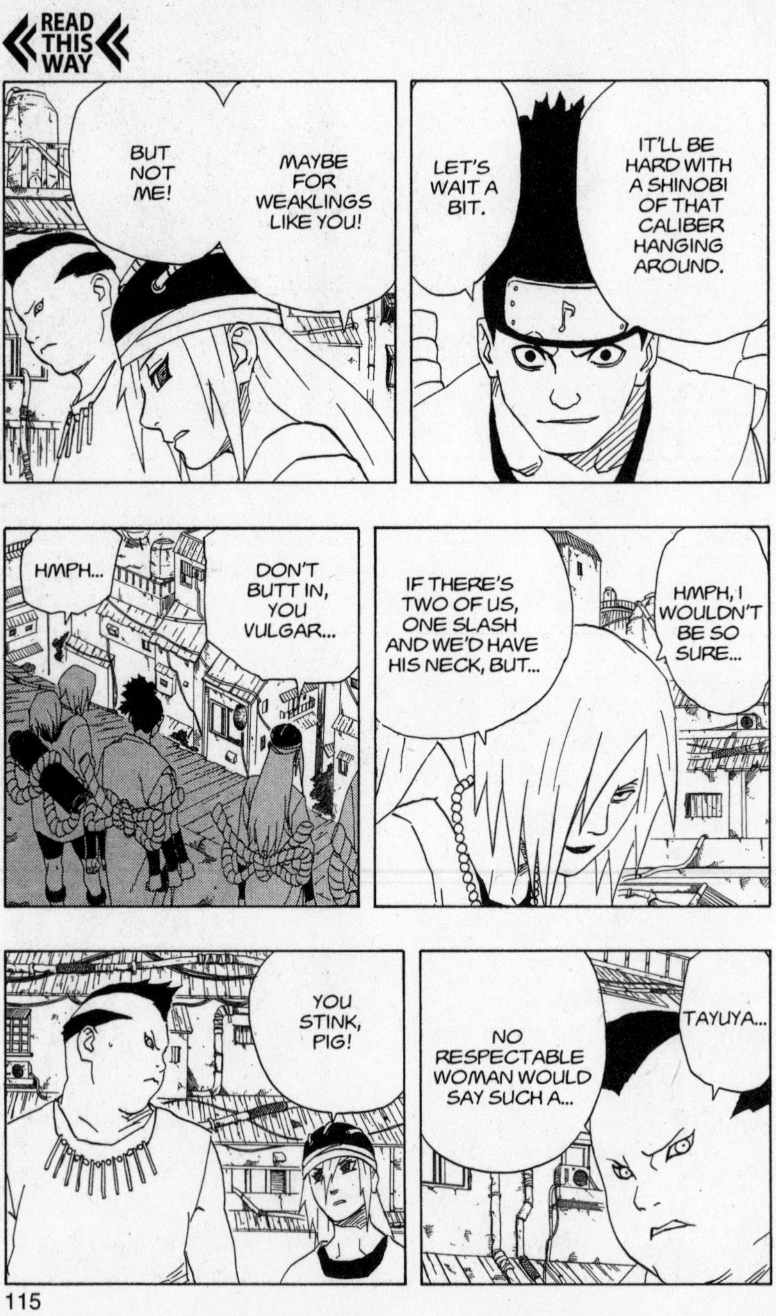
IT'LL BE HARD WITH A SHINOBI OF THAT CALIBER HANGING AROUND.
LET'S WAIT A BIT.
MAYBE FOR WEAKLINGS LIKE YOU!
BUT NOT ME!
HMPH, I WOULDN'T BE SO SURE...
IF THERE'S TWO OF US, ONE SLASH AND WE'D HAVE HIS NECK, BUT...
DON'T BUTT IN, YOU VULGAR...
HMPH...
TAYUYA...
NO RESPECTABLE WOMAN WOULD SAY SUCH A...
YOU STINK, PIG!

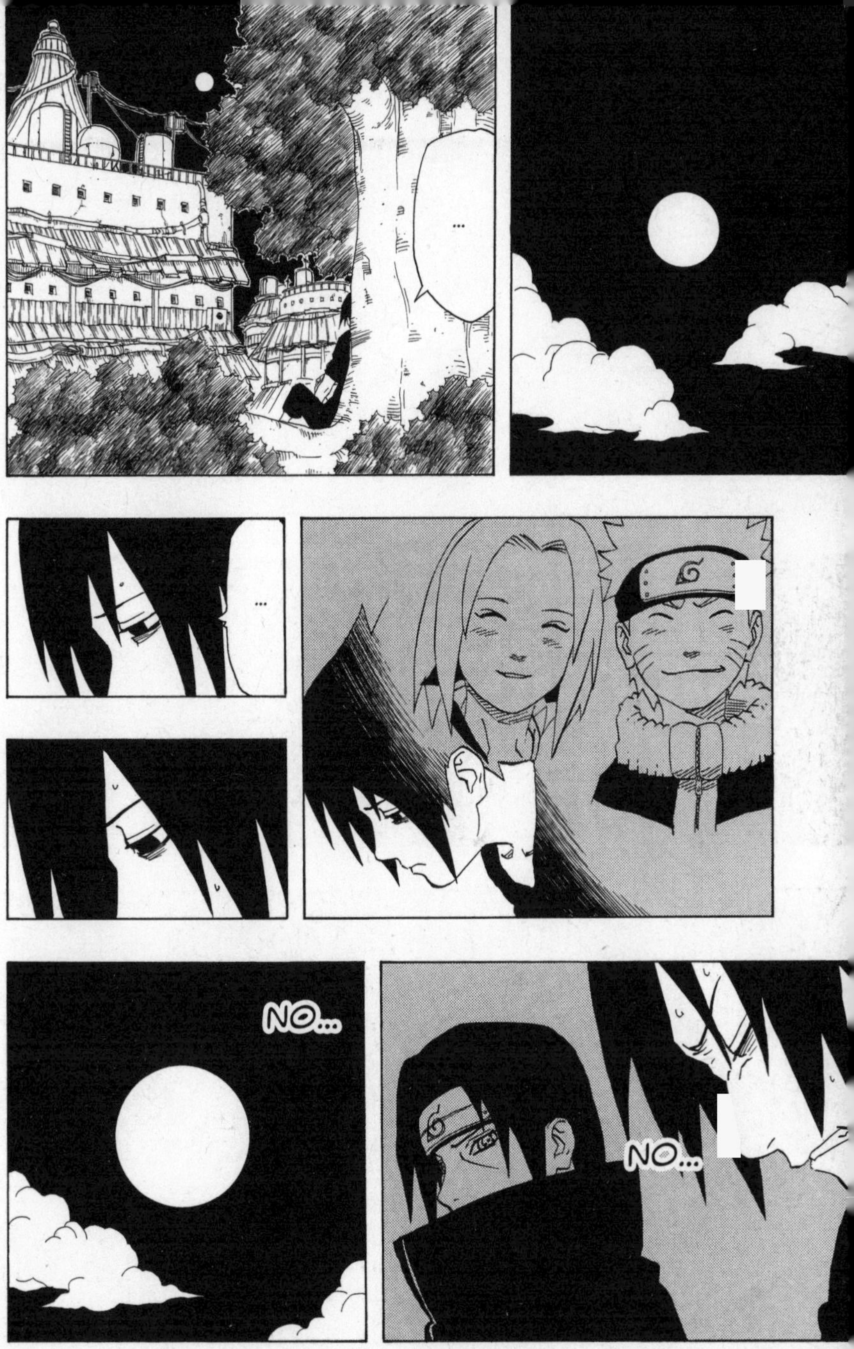
...
...
NO...
NO...

READ THIS WAY

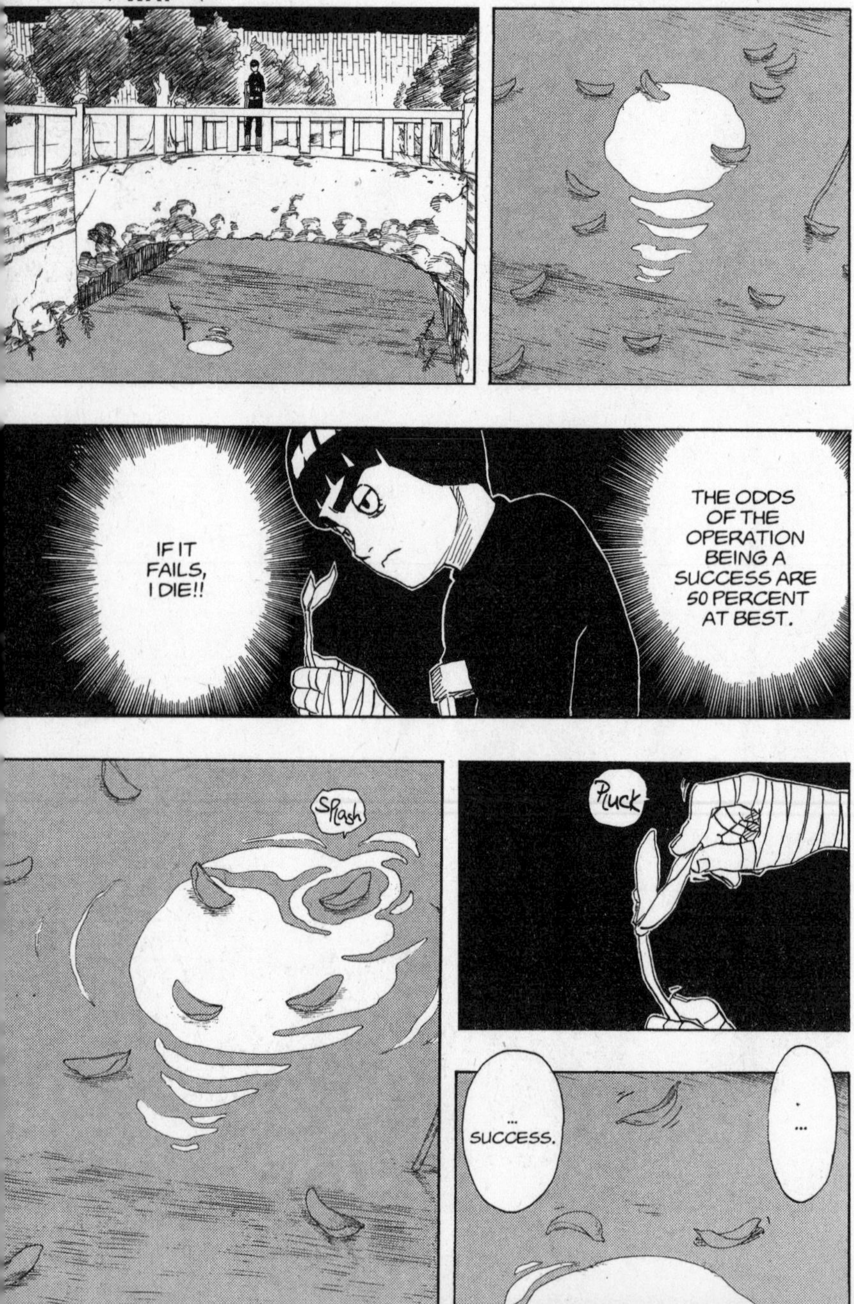
THE ODDS OF THE OPERATION BEING A SUCCESS ARE 50 PERCENT AT BEST.
IF IT FAILS, I DIE!!
Pluck
. ...
... SUCCESS.
Splash

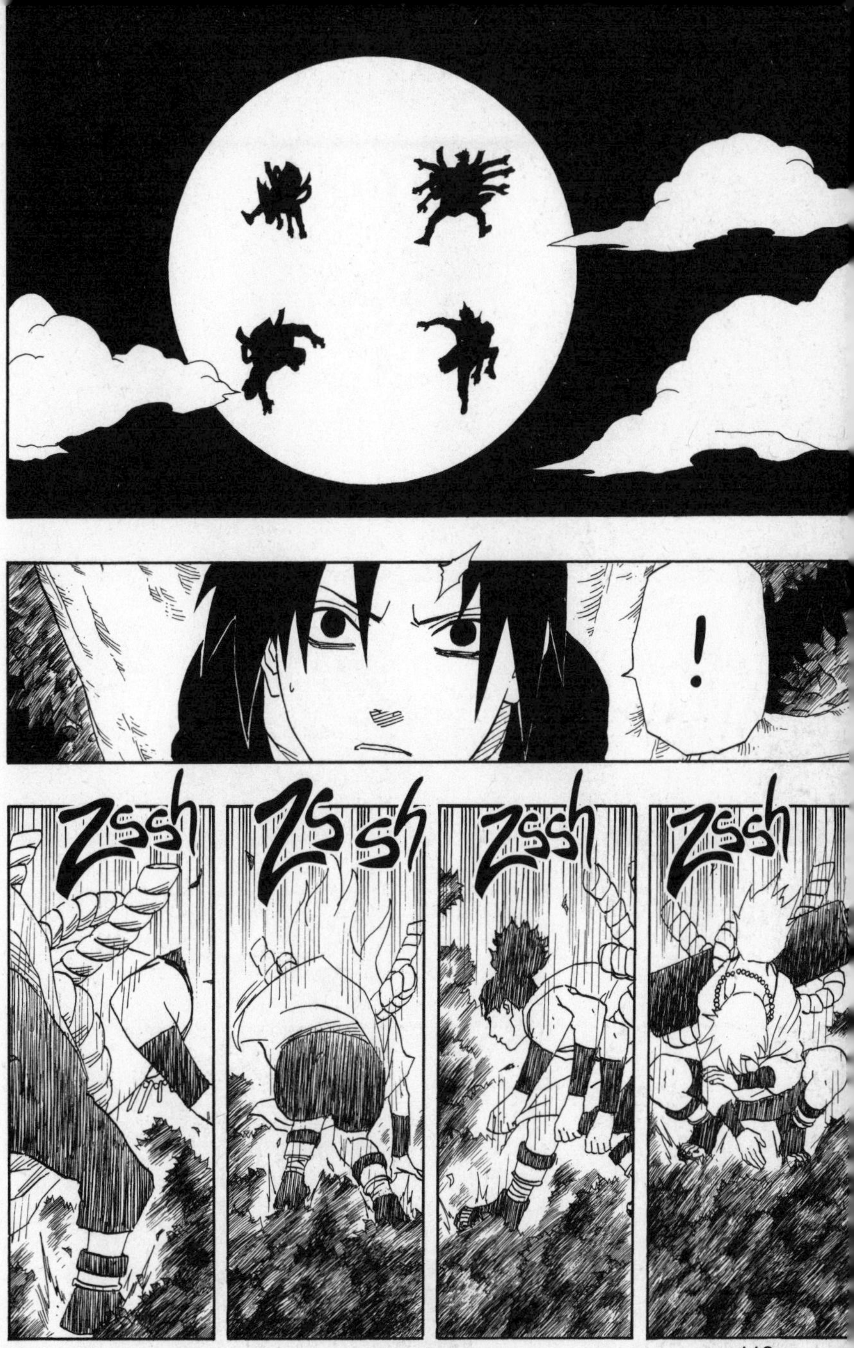
!
Zssh
Zssh
Zssh
Zssh

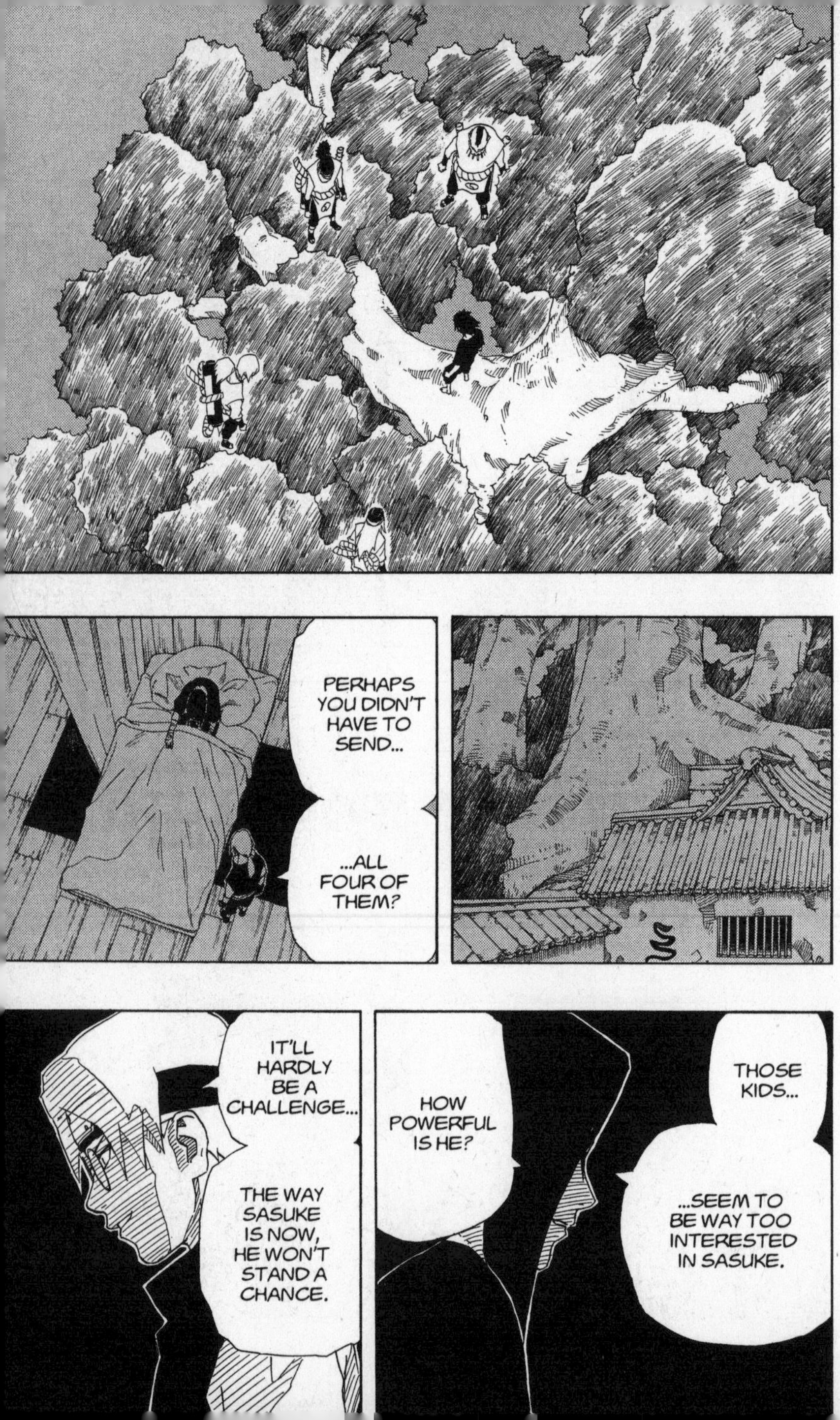
PERHAPS YOU DIDN'T HAVE TO SEND...
...ALL FOUR OF THEM?
THOSE KIDS...
...SEEM TO BE WAY TOO INTERESTED IN SASUKE.
HOW POWERFUL IS HE?
IT'LL HARDLY BE A CHALLENGE...
THE WAY SASUKE IS NOW, HE WON'T STAND A CHANCE.

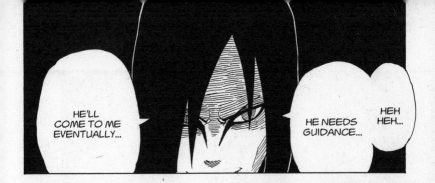

HEH HEH...
HE NEEDS GUIDANCE...
HE'LL COME TO ME EVENTUALLY...
WHO ARE YOU...?
THE SOUND FOUR.
KIDOMARU OF THE EAST GATE.
LIKE-WISE.
JIROBO OF THE SOUTH GATE.
LIKE-WISE.
SAKON OF THE WEST GATE.
LIKE-WISE.
TAYUYA OF THE NORTH GATE.

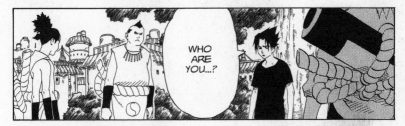

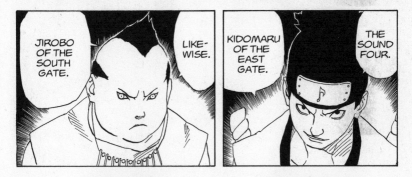

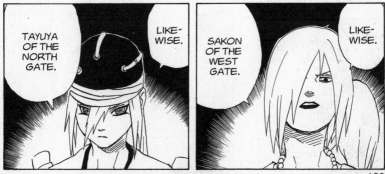

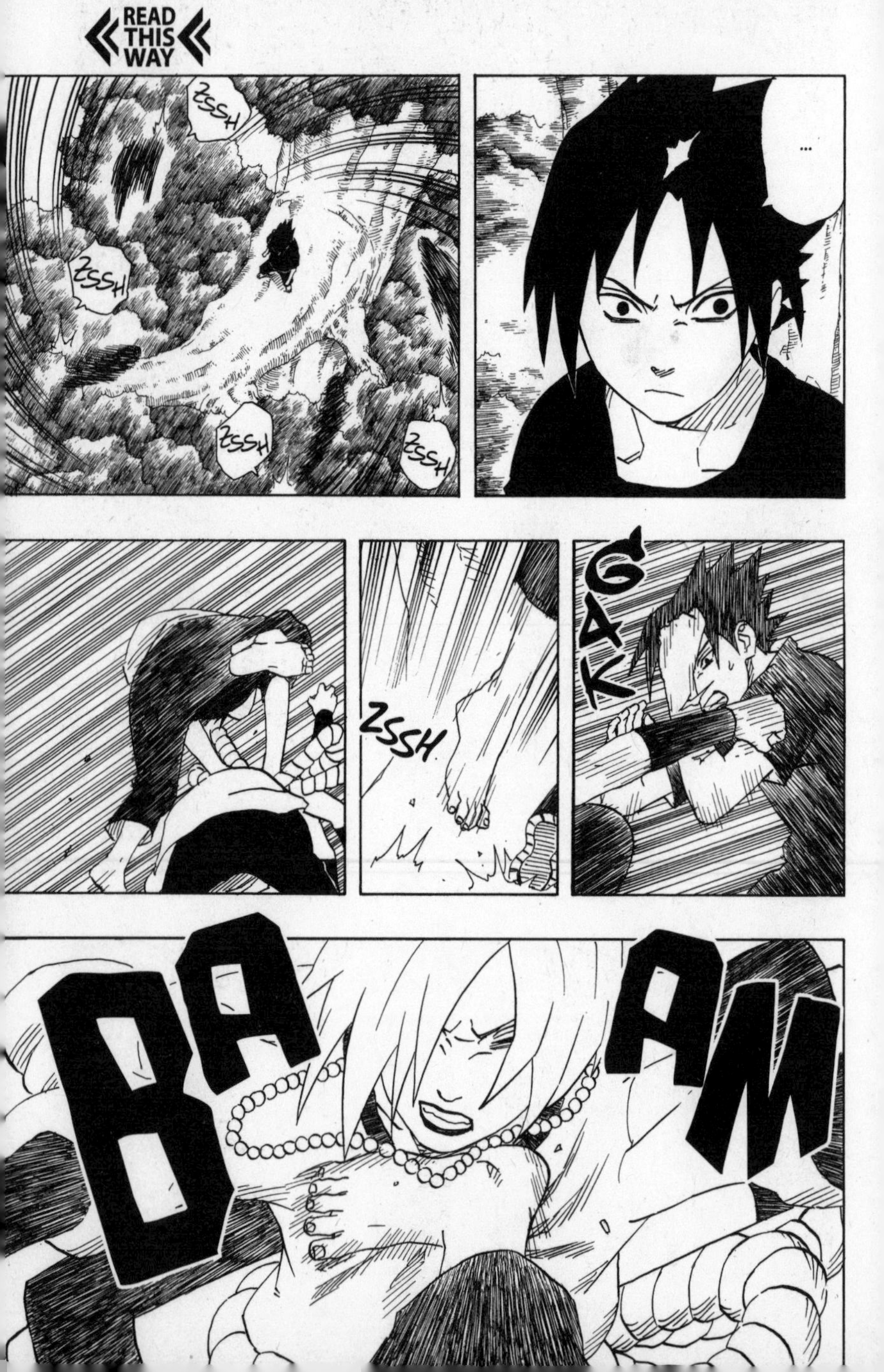
READ THIS WAY
...
ZSSH
ZSSH
ZSSH
ZSSH
GAK
ZSSH
BA
AM

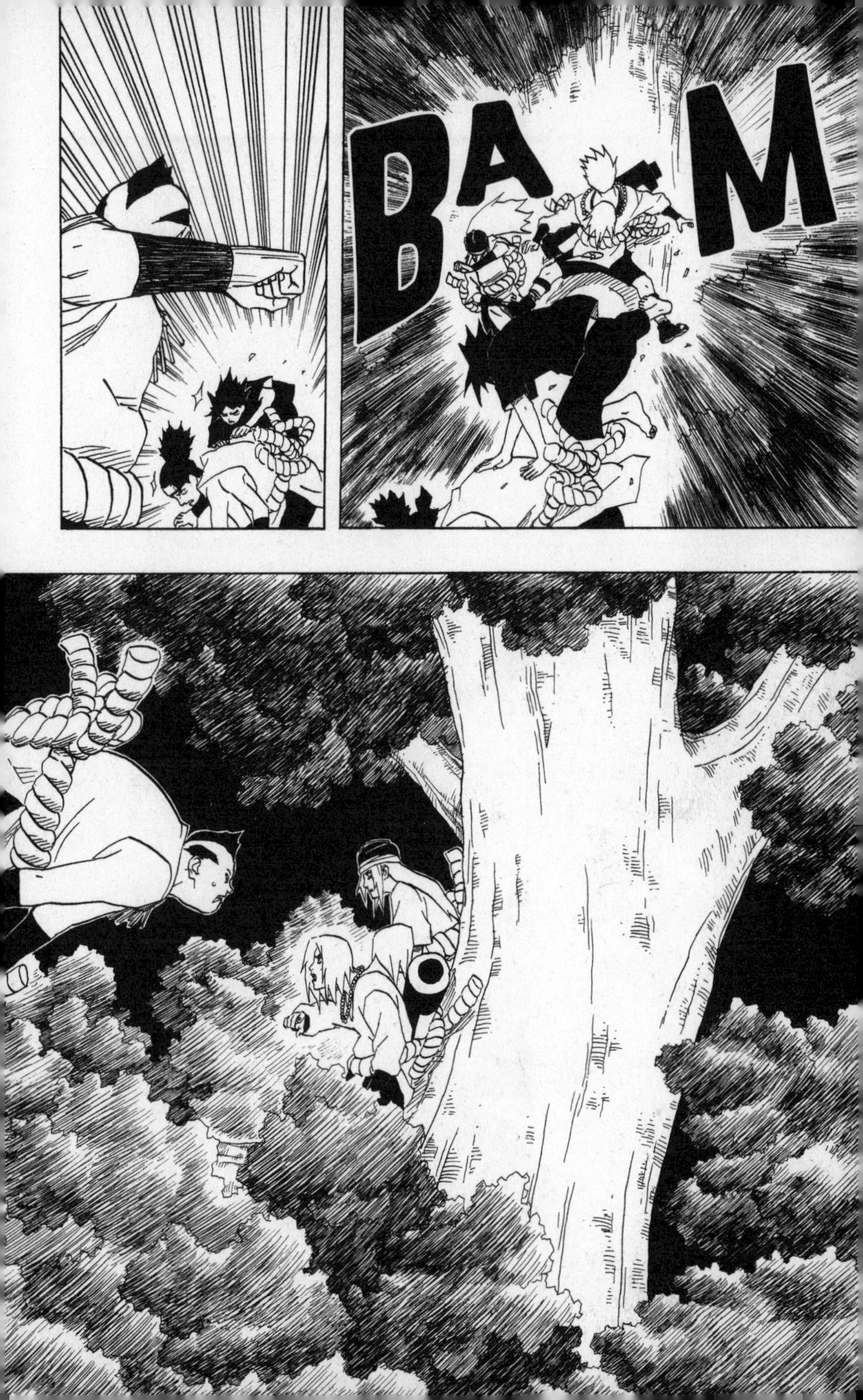
BAM

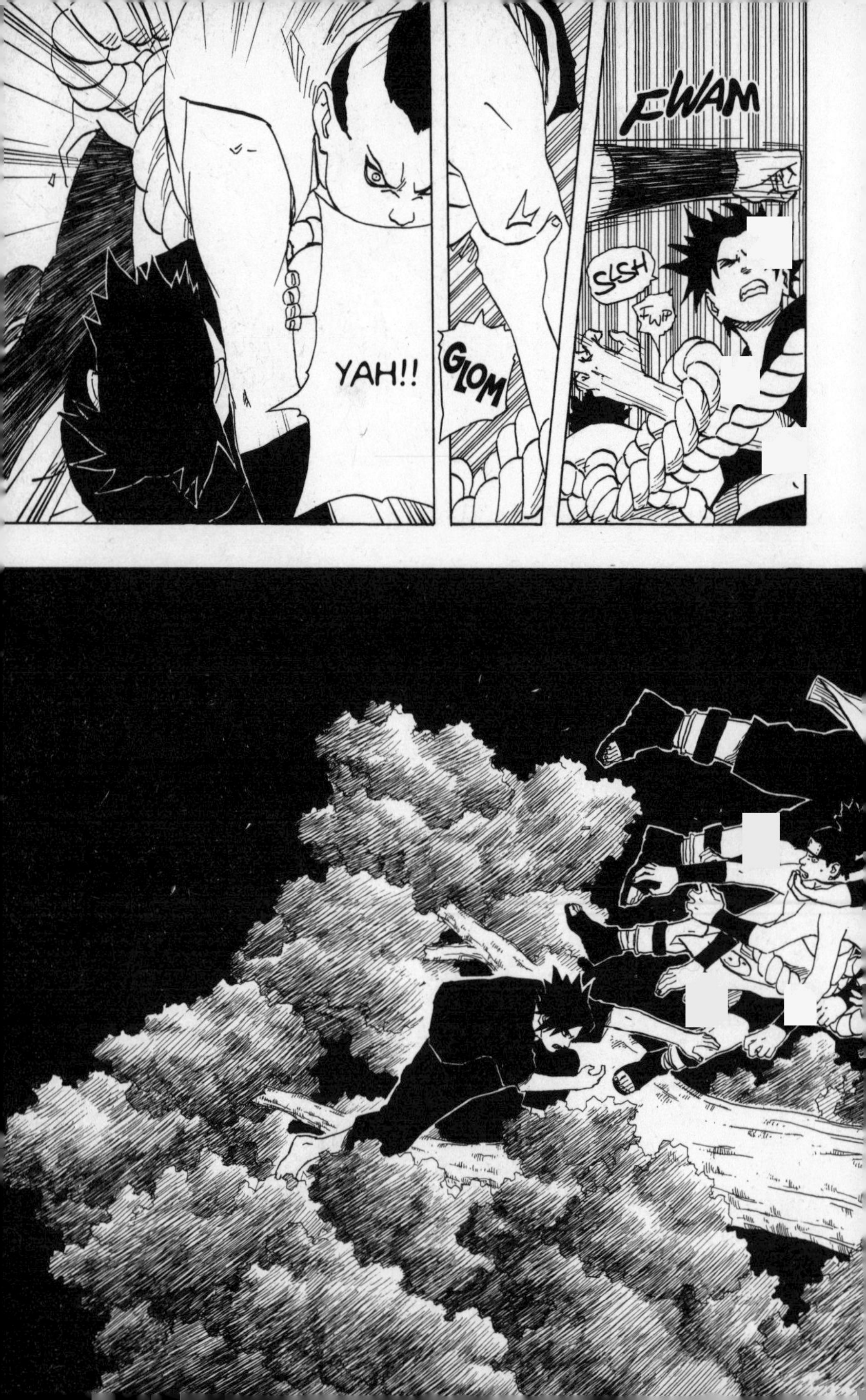
FWAM
SLSH
FWIP
GLOM
YAH!!

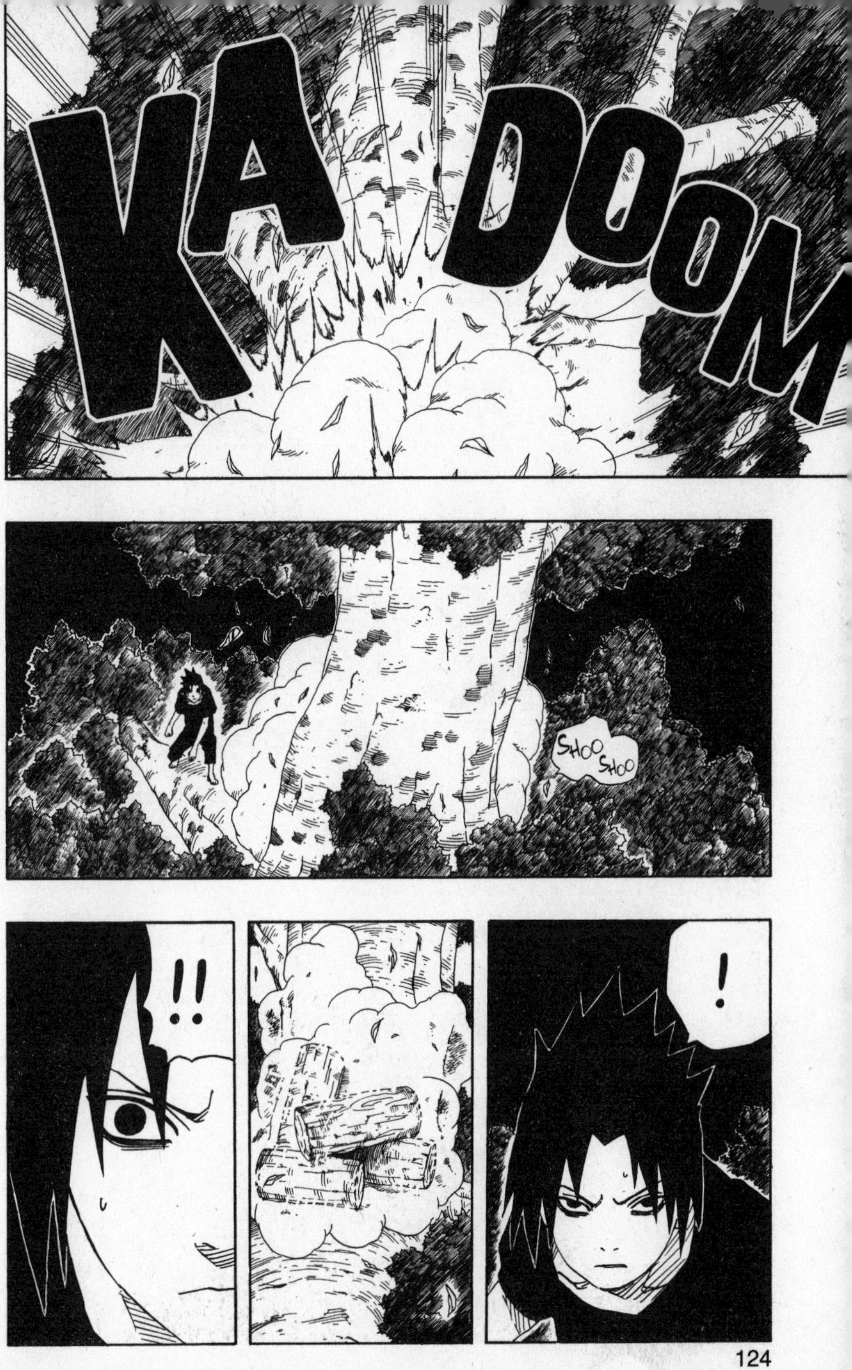
KA DOOM
SHOO SHOO
!
!!

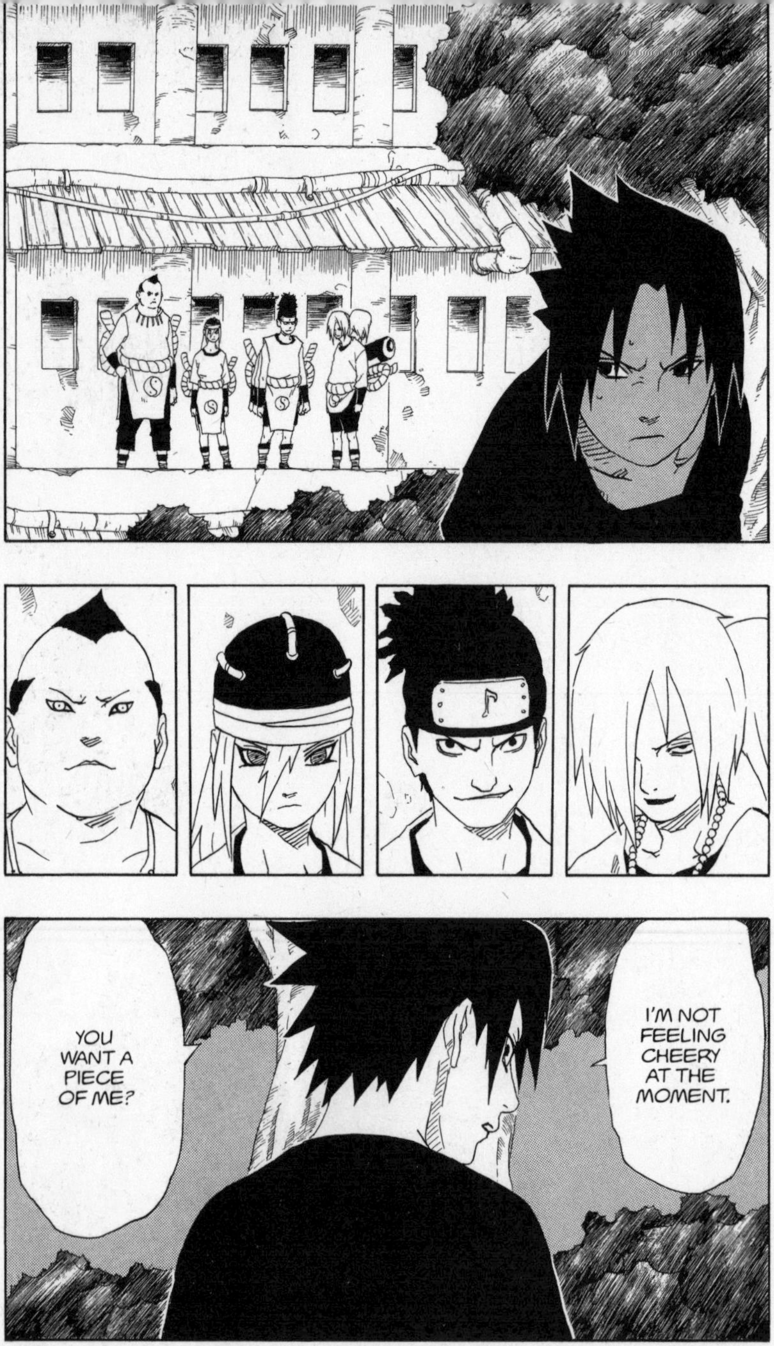
I'M NOT FEELING CHEERY AT THE MOMENT.
YOU WANT A PIECE OF ME?

Number 178:

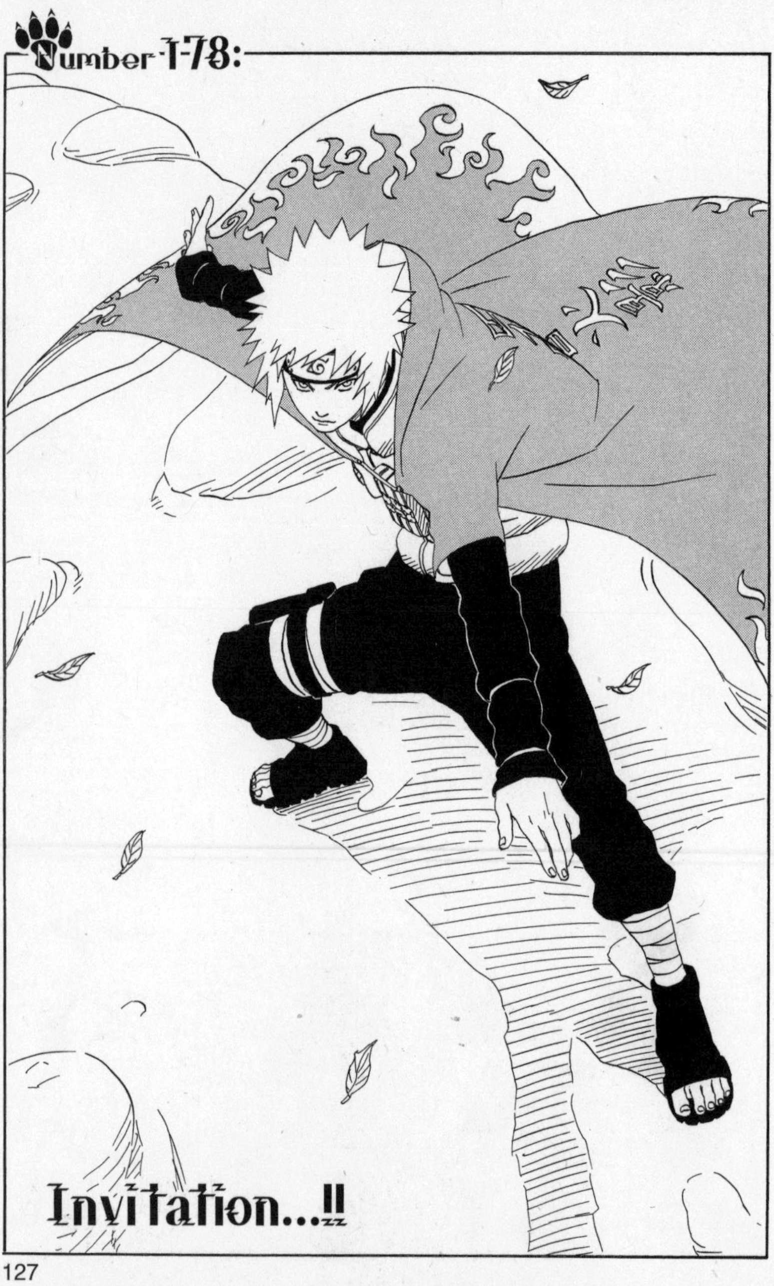
Invitation...!!

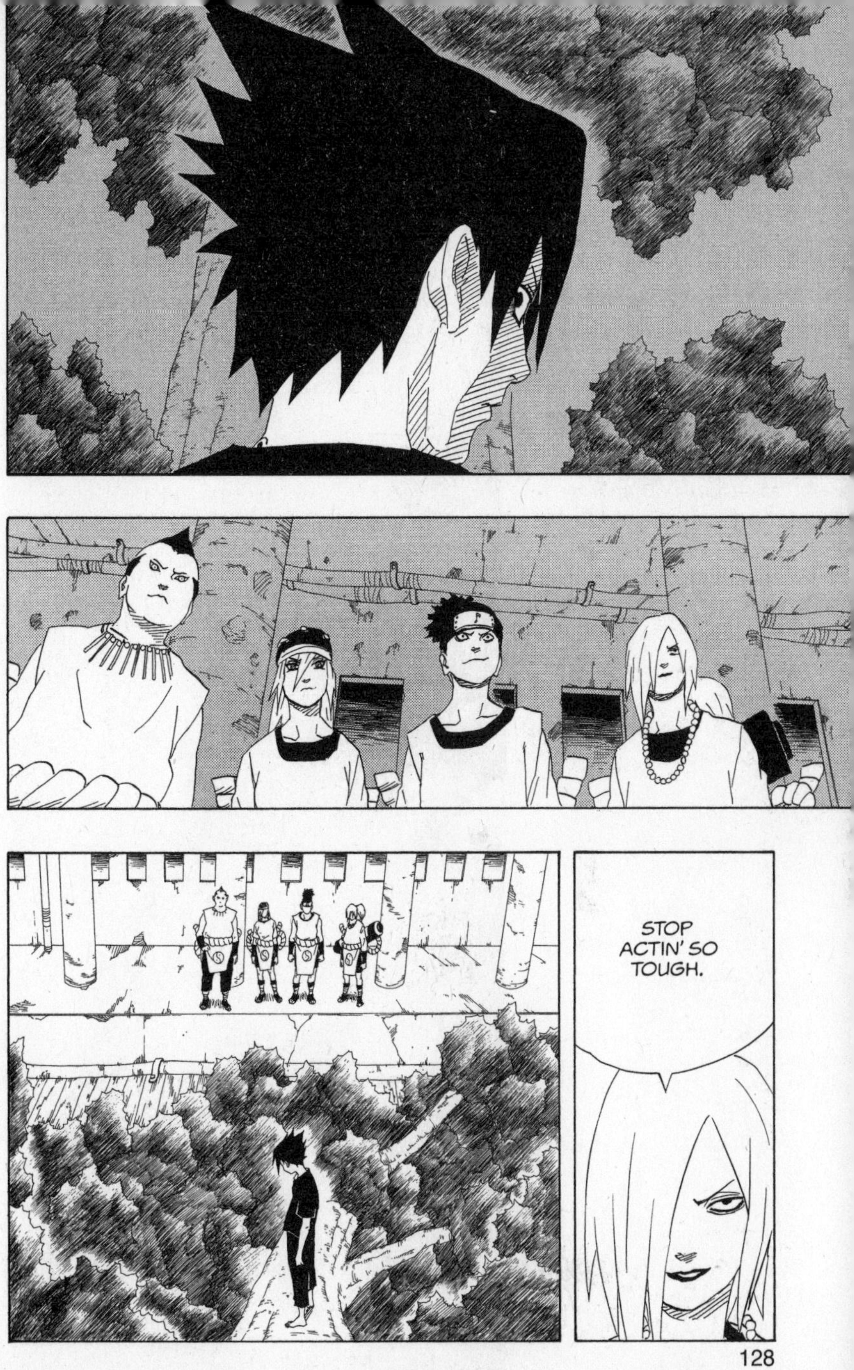
STOP ACTIN' SO TOUGH.

READ THIS WAY

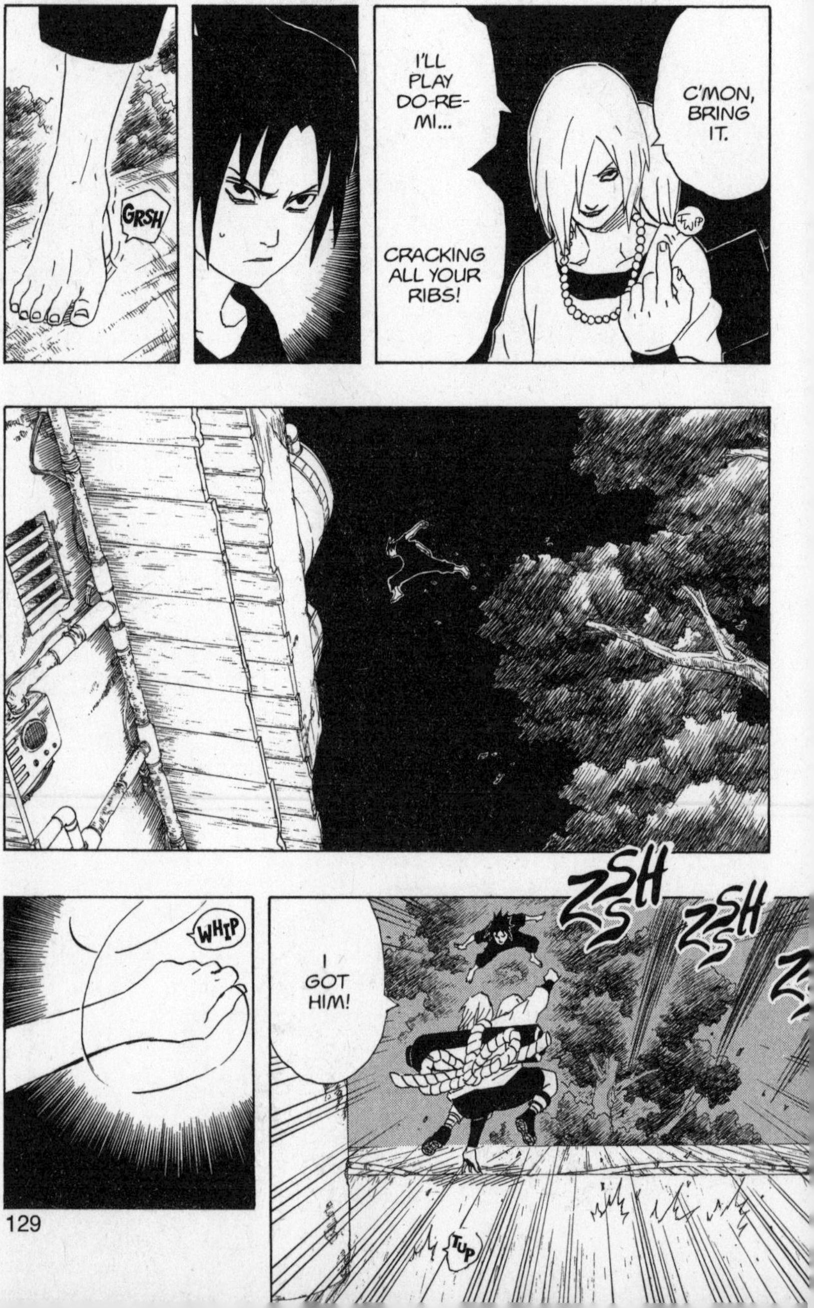
C'MON, BRING IT.
FWIP
I'LL PLAY DO-RE-MI...
CRACKING ALL YOUR RIBS!
GRSH
ZSSH
ZSSH
I GOT HIM!
TUP
WHIP

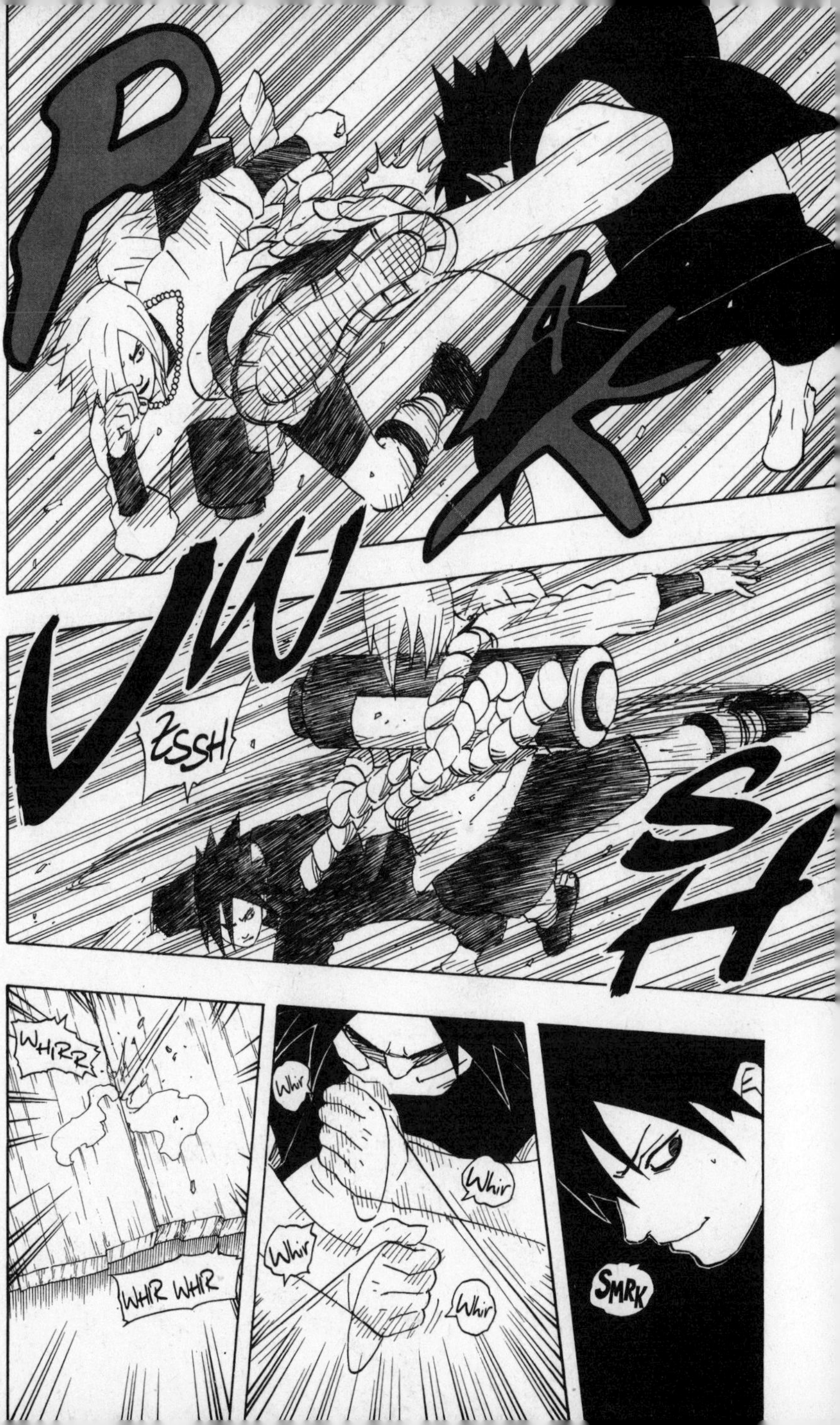
PAK
VWSSH
ZSSH
SMRK
Whir
Whir
Whir
Whir
WHIRR
WHIR WHIR

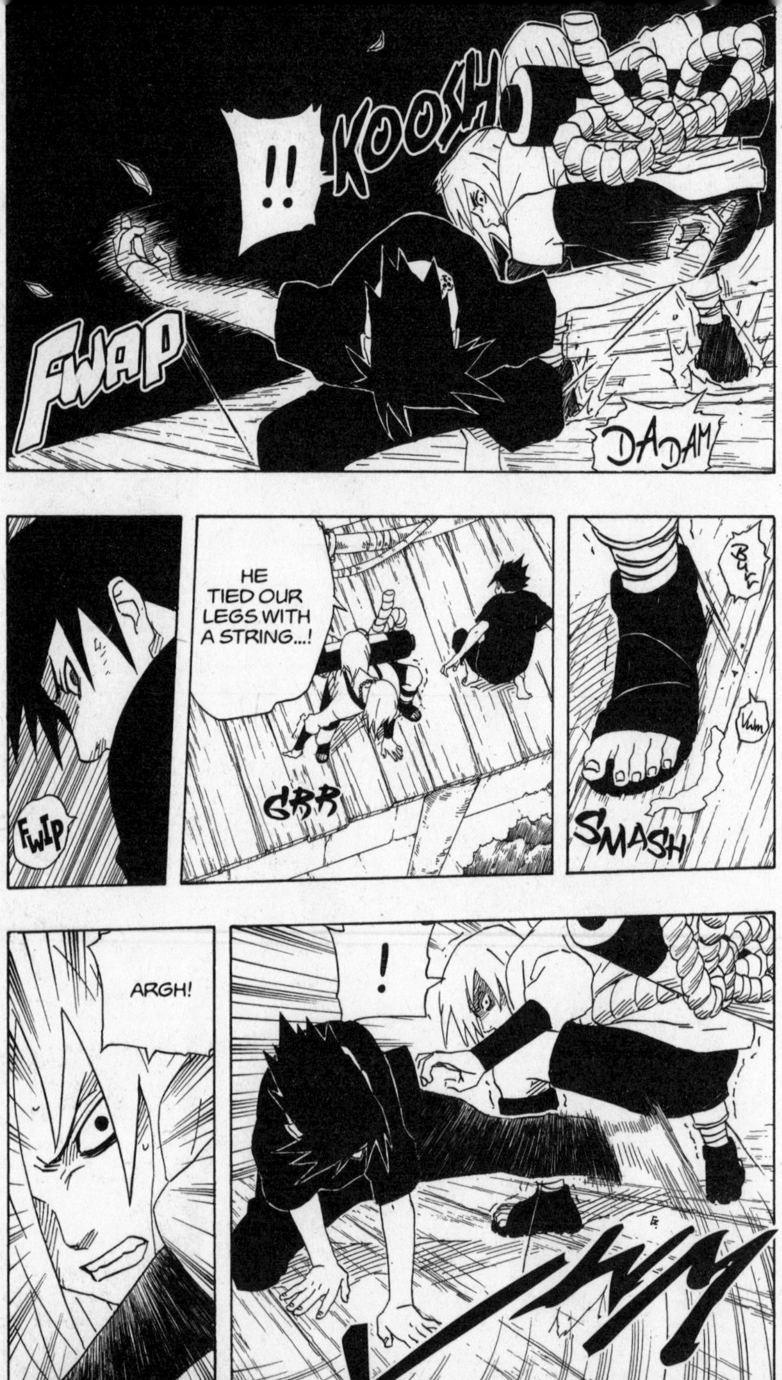
KOOSH
!!
DADAM
FWAP
Burr
Vwm
SMASH
HE TIED OUR LEGS WITH A STRING...!
GRR
FWIP
!
VWM
ARGH!

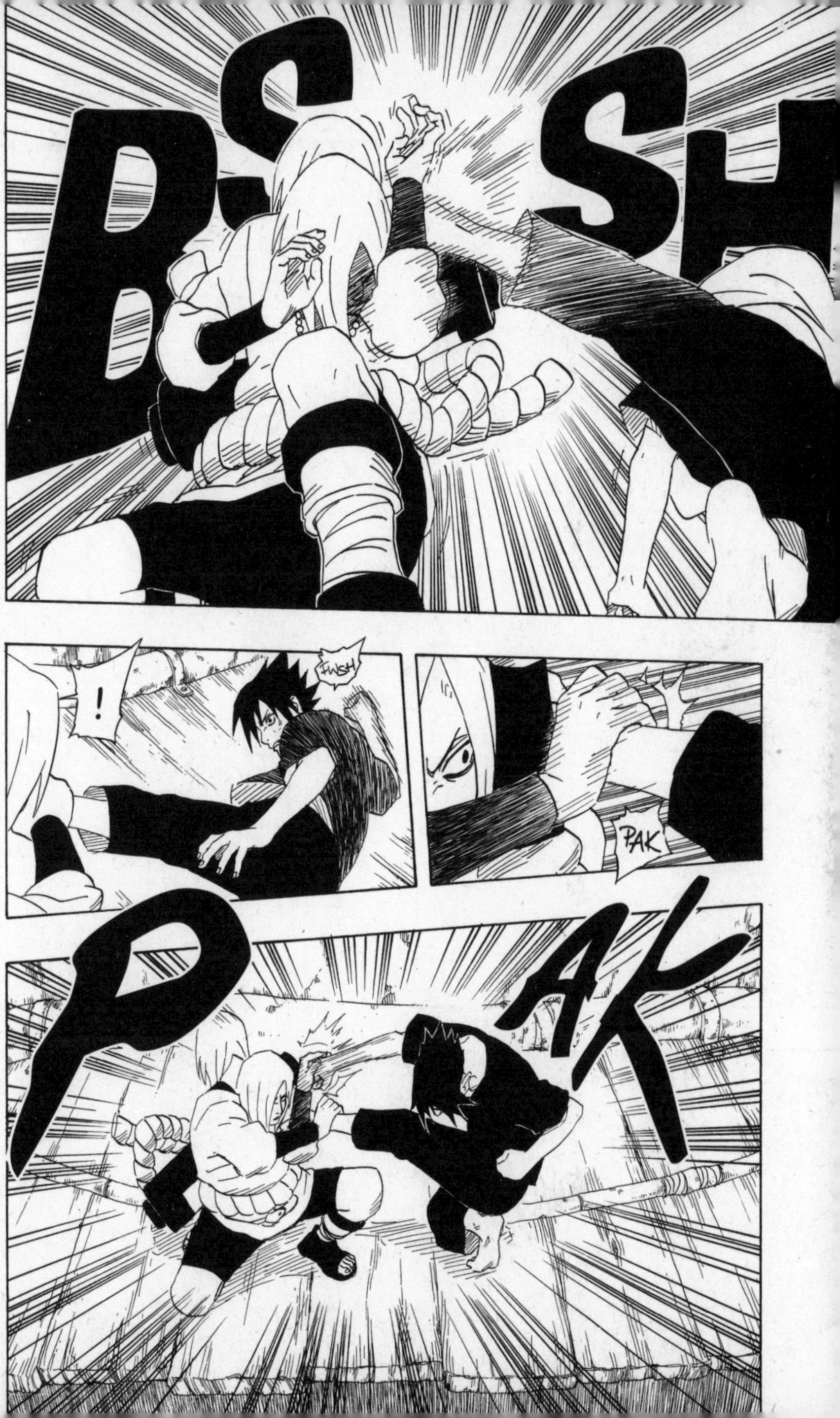
BSSH
PAK
FWSH
!
PAK

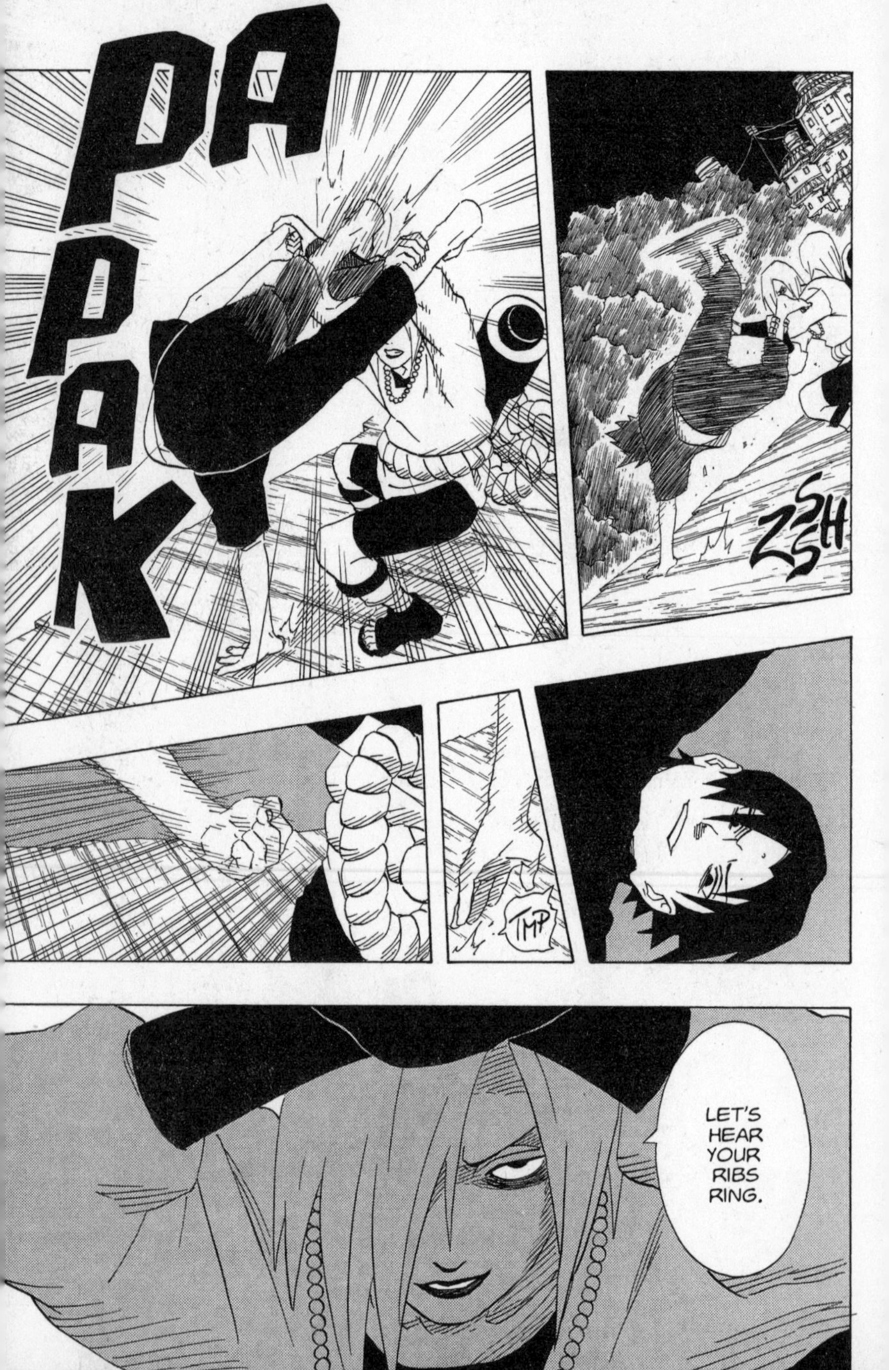
ZSSH
DA PA PAK
TMP
LET'S HEAR YOUR RIBS RING.

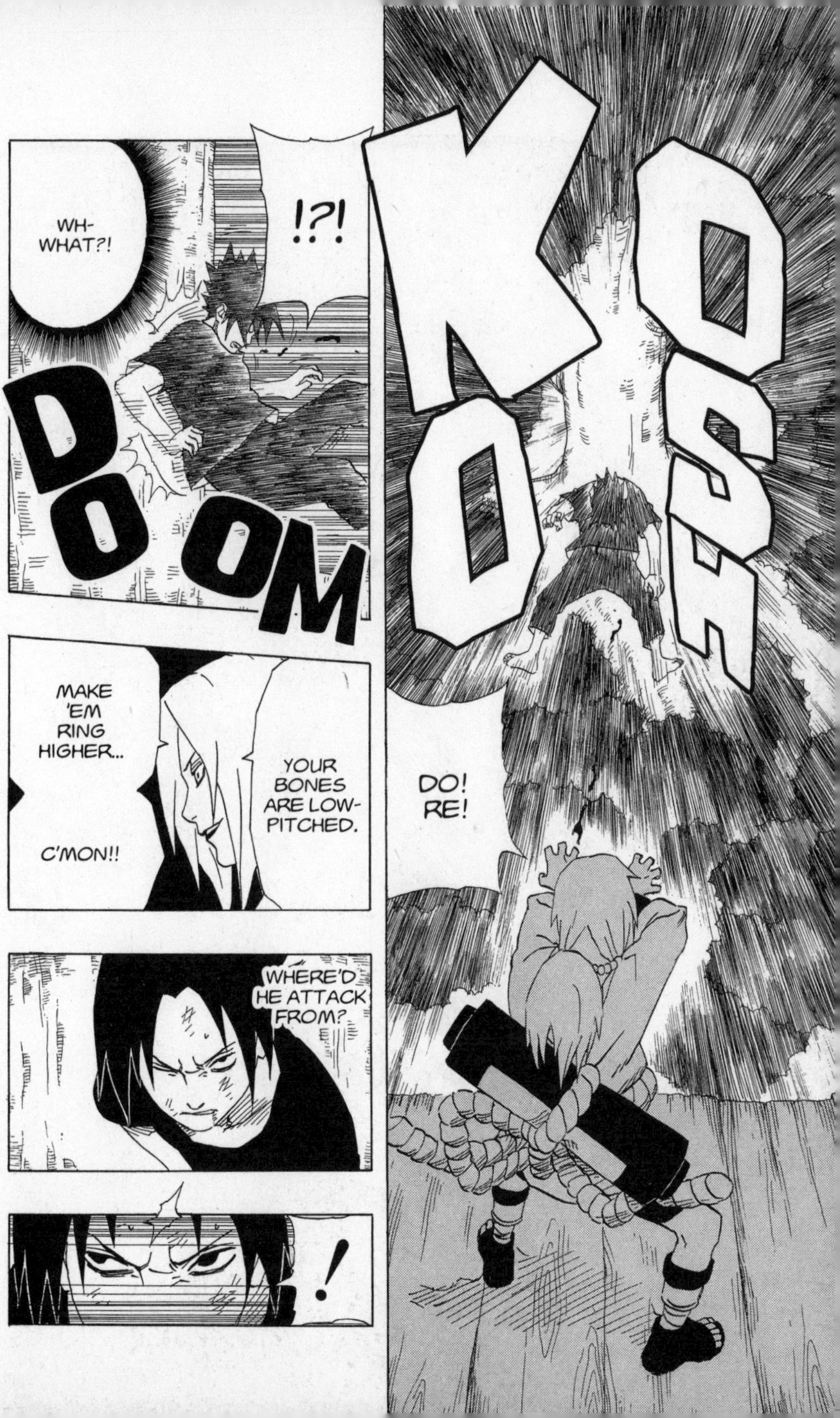
KOOSH
DO! RE!
!?!
WH-WHAT?!
DOOM
YOUR BONES ARE LOW-PITCHED.
MAKE 'EM RING HIGHER...
C'MON!!
WHERE'D HE ATTACK FROM?
!

READ THIS WAY

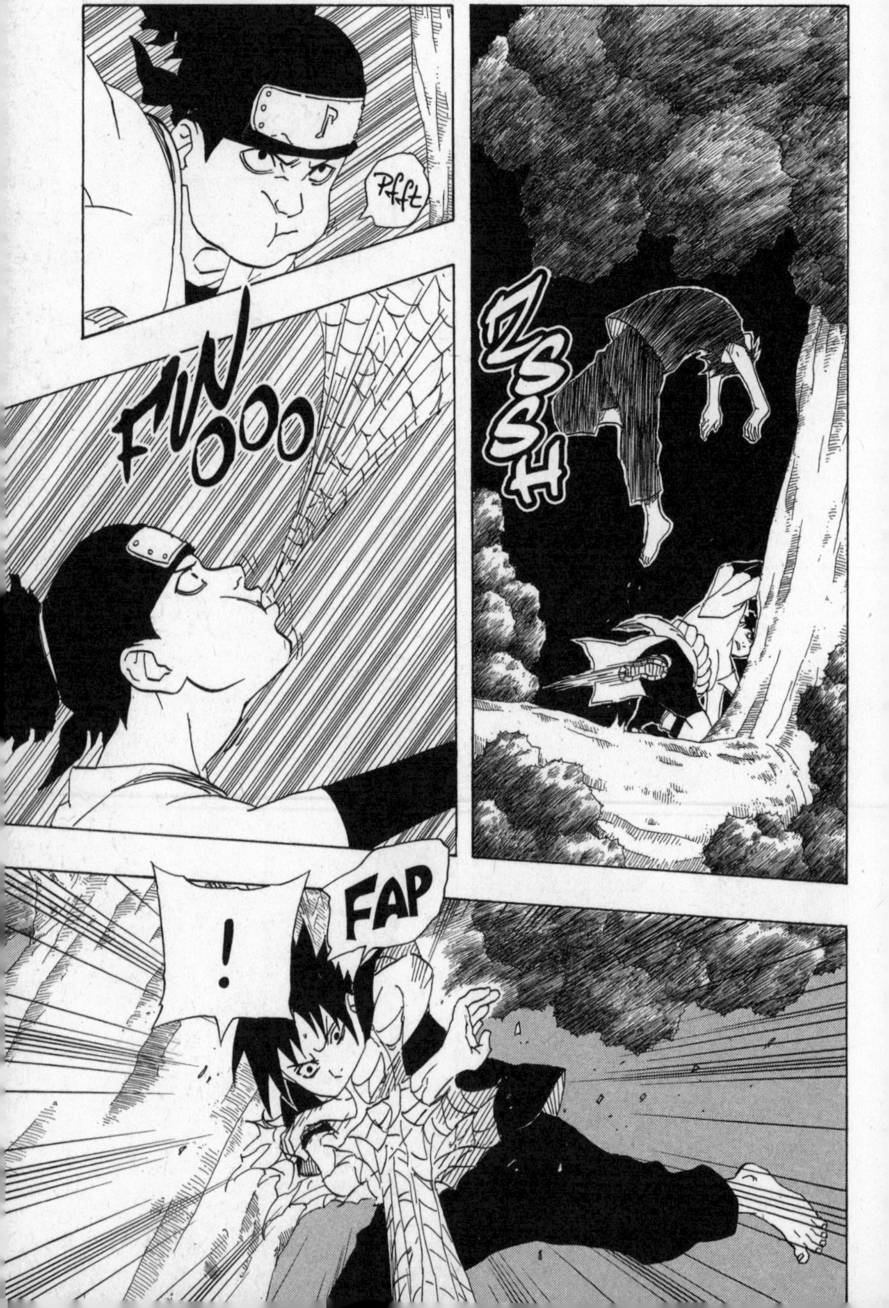

Pfft
FWOOO
FAP
!

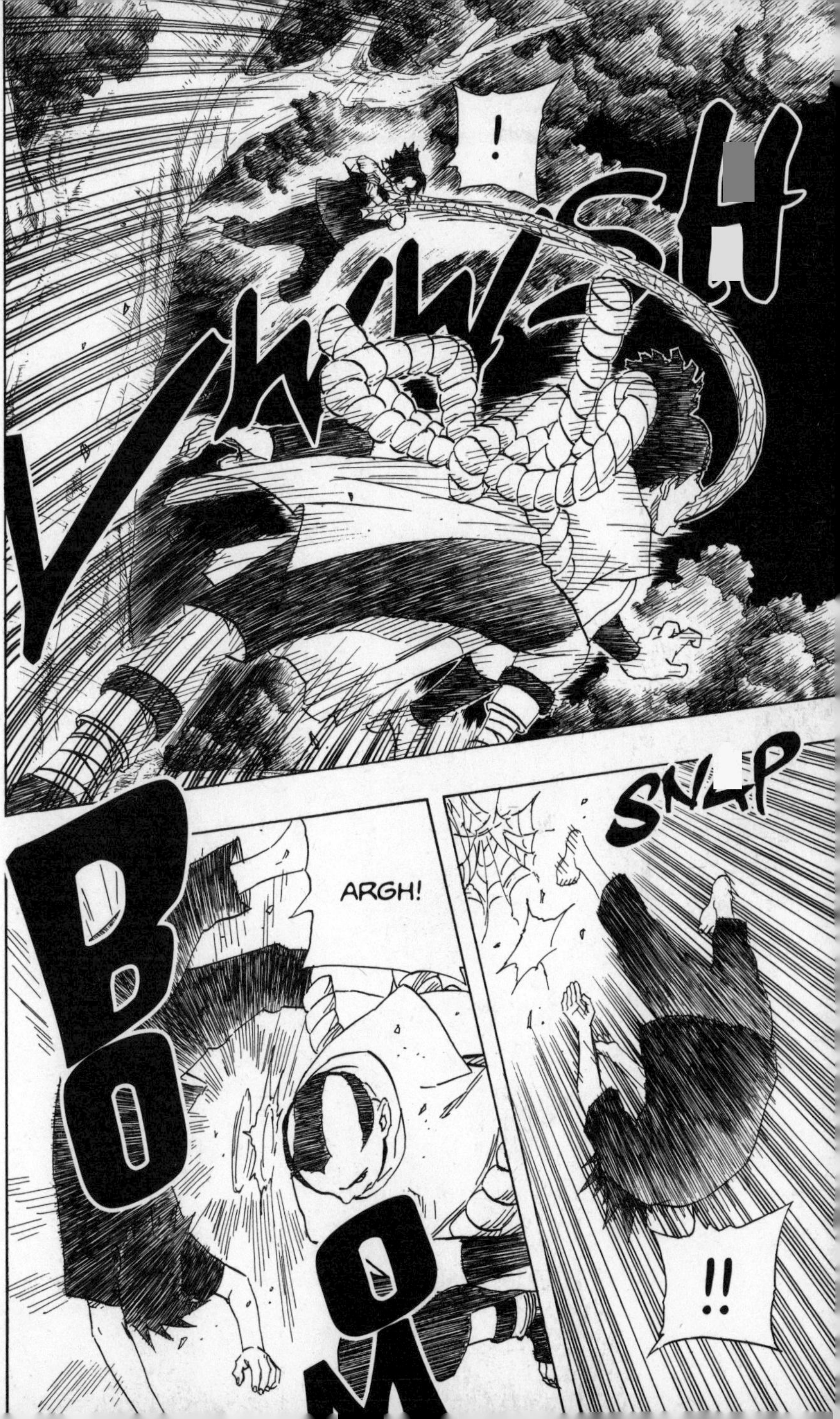
!
!!
ARGH!
BOOM

READ THIS WAY

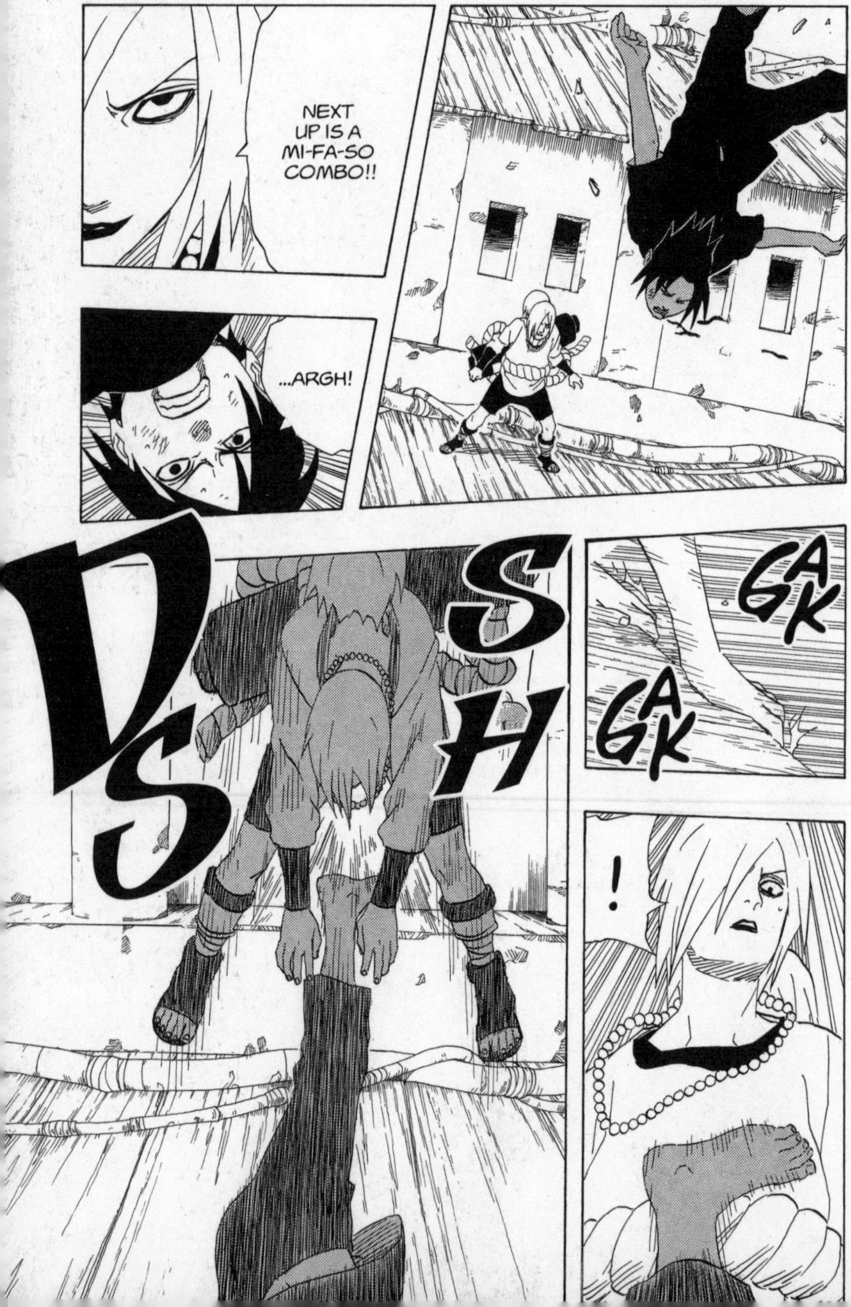
NEXT UP IS A MI-FA-SO COMBO!!
...ARGH!
GAK
GAK
!
DSSH

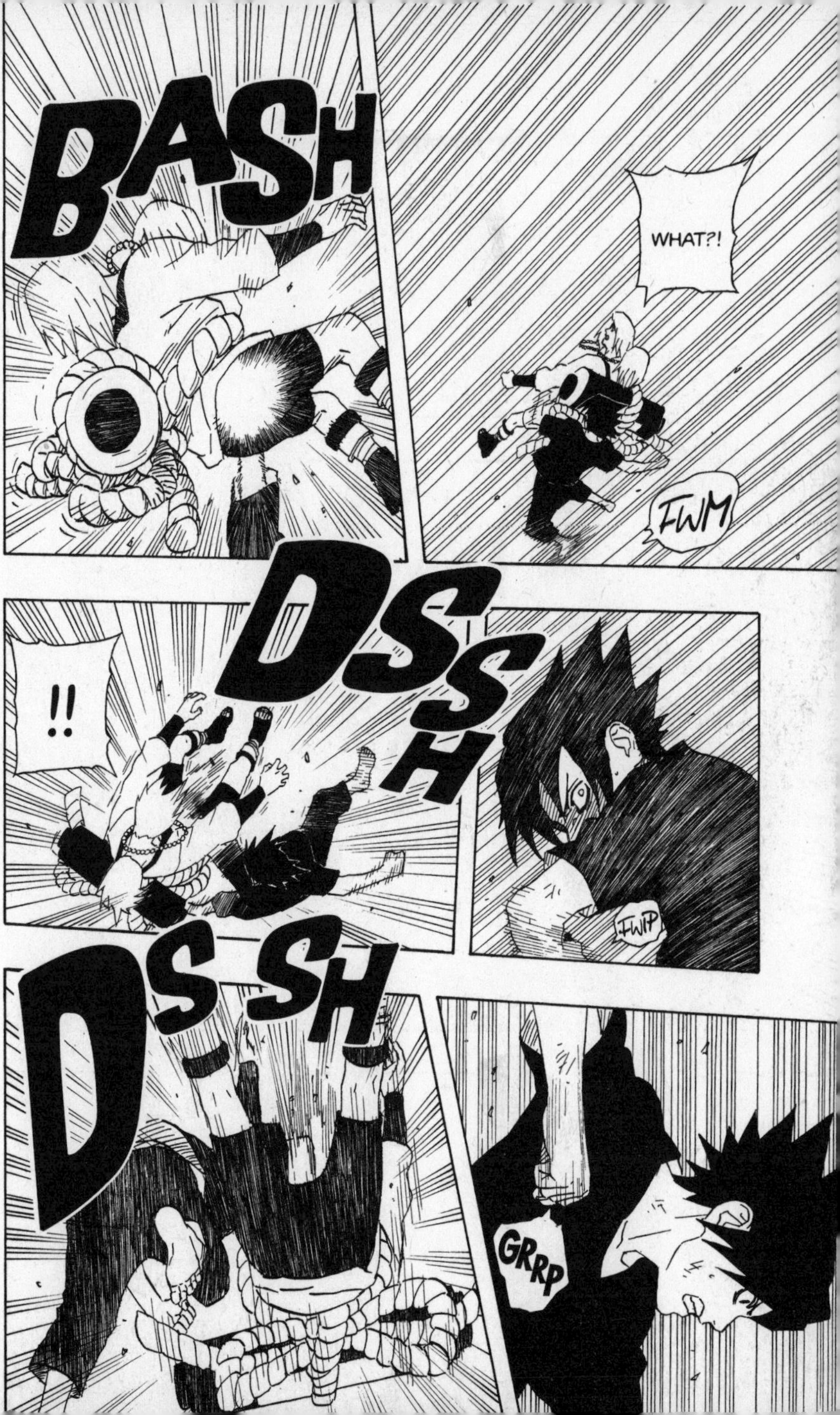
WHAT?!
FWM
BASH
DSSH
FWIP
!!
GRRP
DSSH

READ THIS WAY

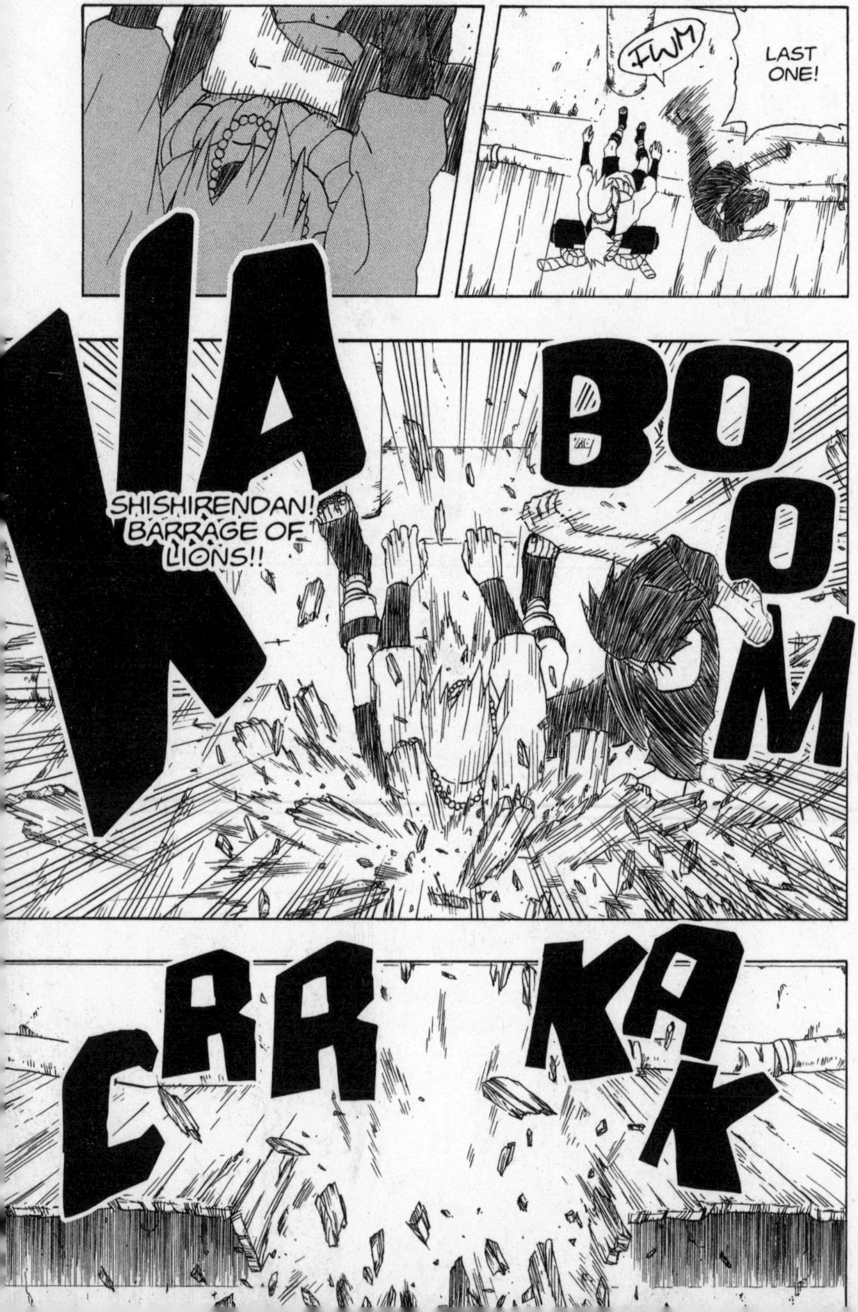
FWM
LAST ONE!
KA
BOOM
SHISHIRENDAN! BARRAGE OF LIONS!!
CRR
KAK

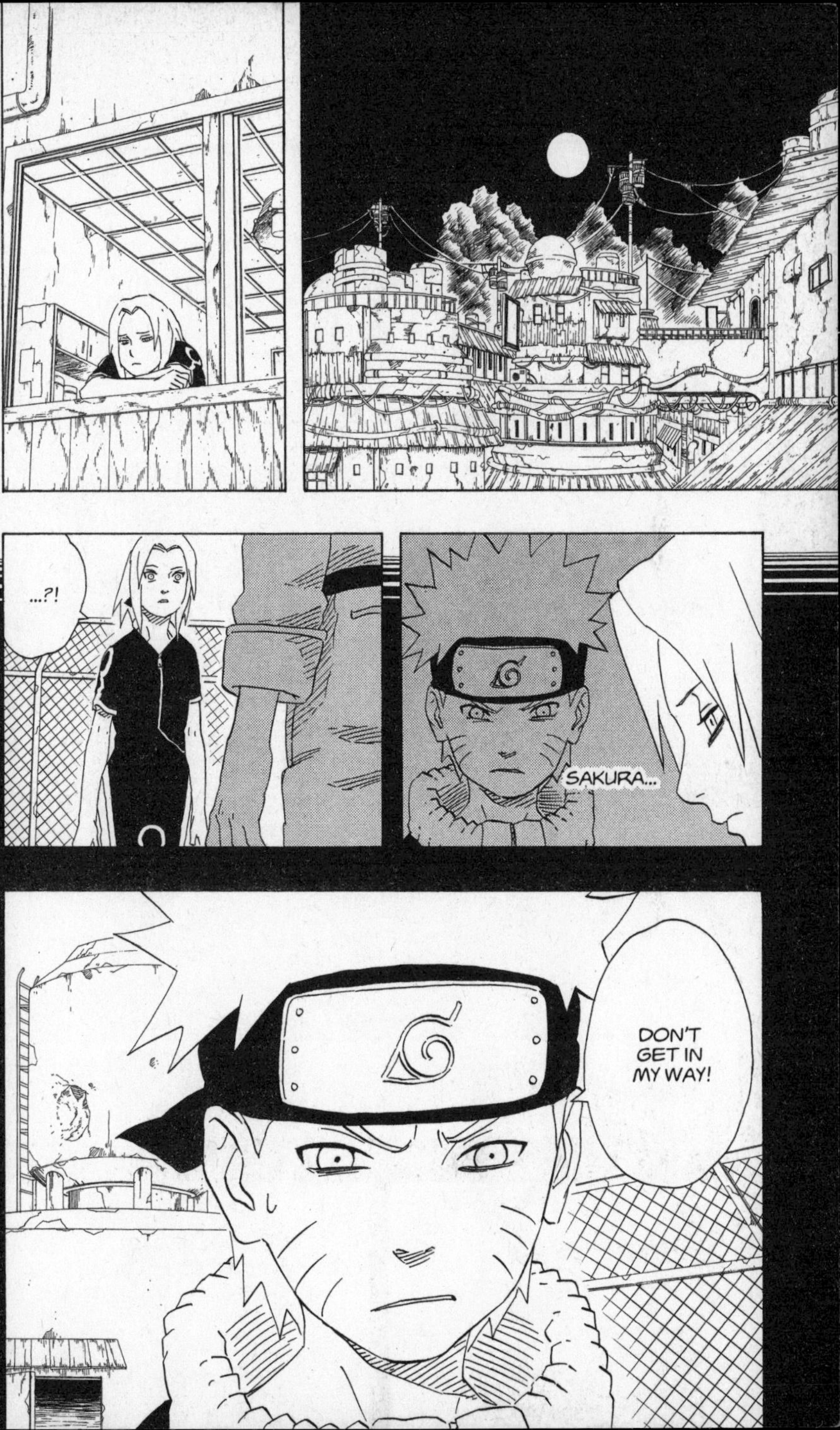
SAKURA...
...?!
DON'T GET IN MY WAY!

READ THIS WAY

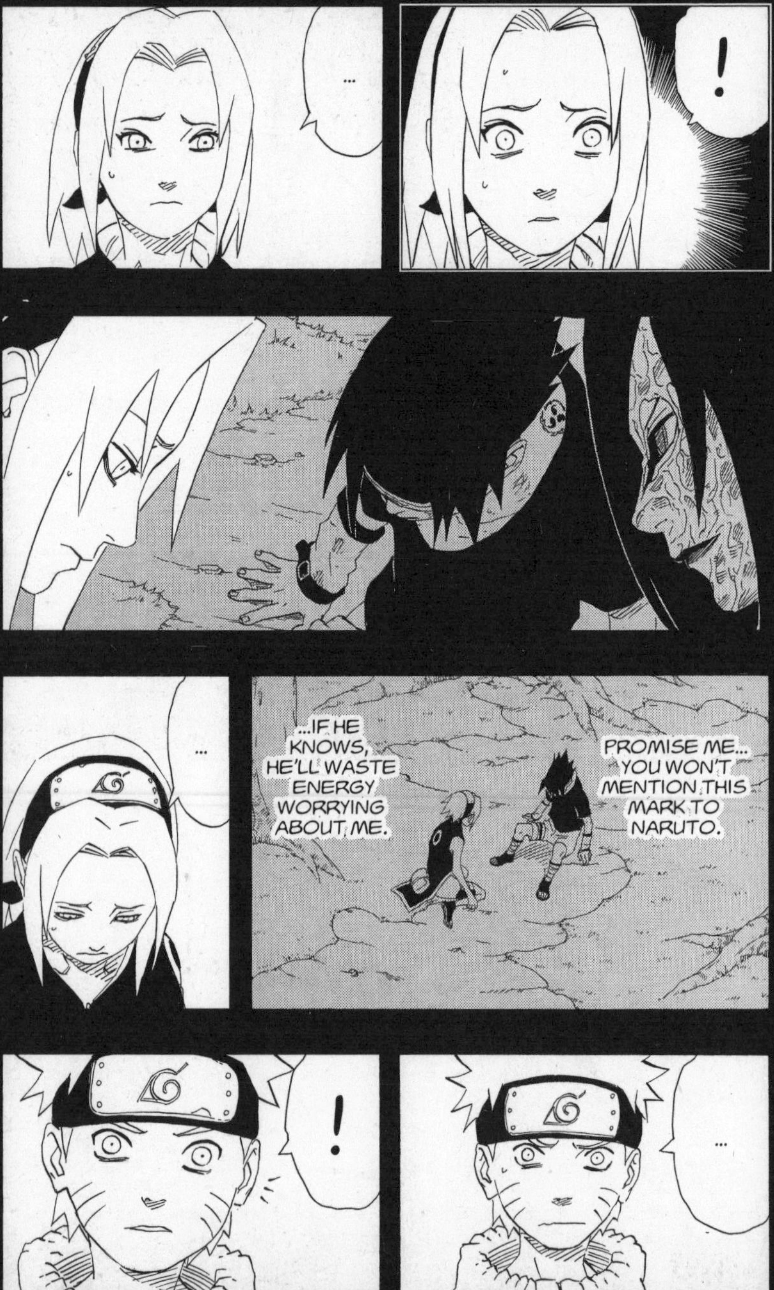
!
...
PROMISE ME... YOU WON'T MENTION THIS MARK TO NARUTO.
...IF HE KNOWS, HE'LL WASTE ENERGY WORRYING ABOUT ME.
...
...
!

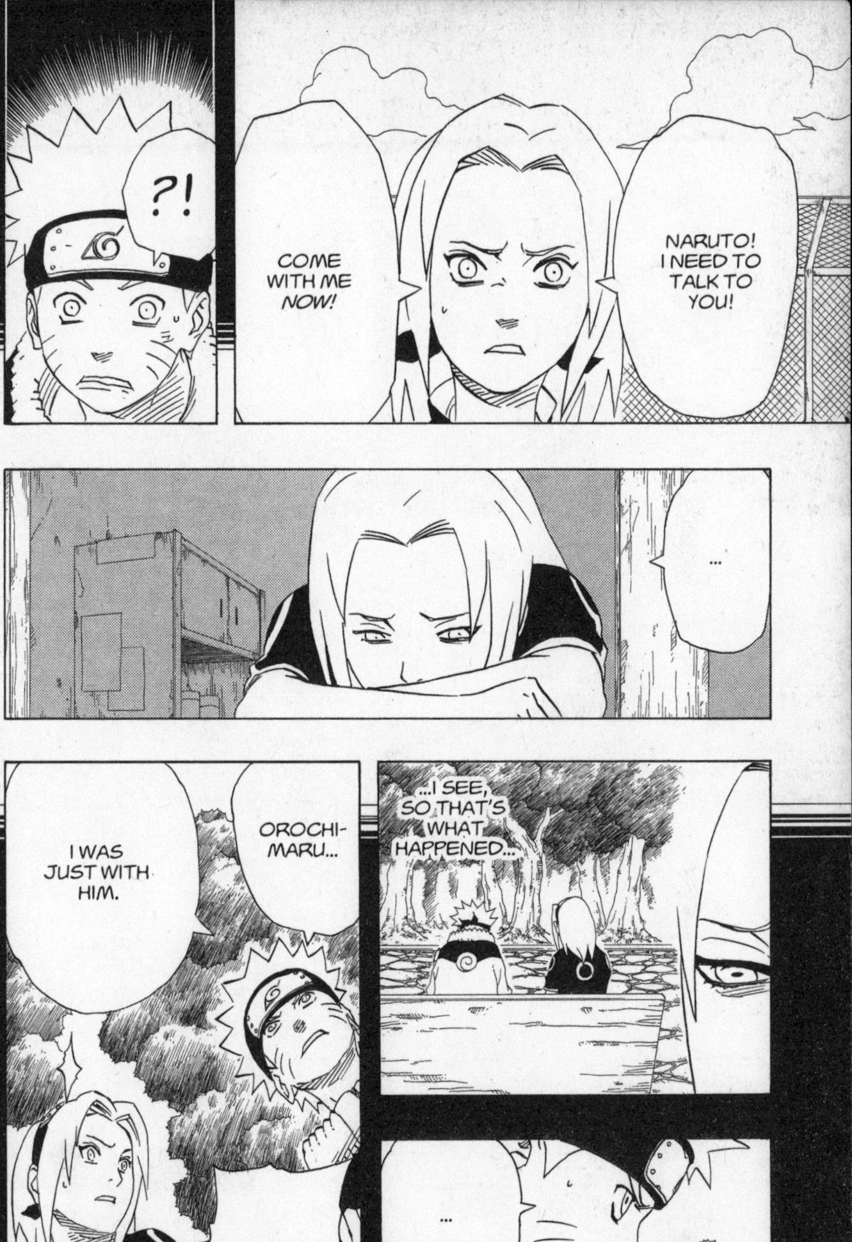
NARUTO! I NEED TO TALK TO YOU!
COME WITH ME NOW!
?!
...
...I SEE, SO THAT'S WHAT HAPPENED...
...
OROCHI-MARU...
I WAS JUST WITH HIM.
WHAT?!

READ THIS WAY

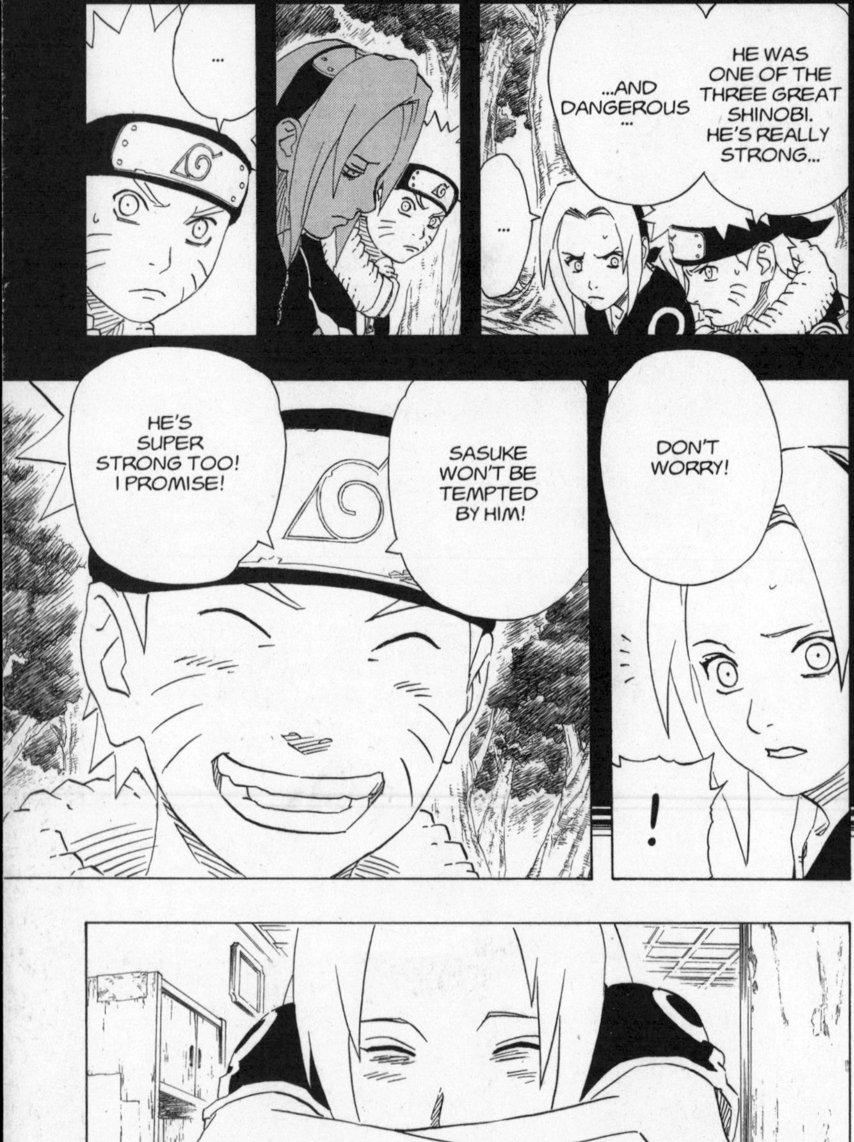

HE WAS ONE OF THE THREE GREAT SHINOBI. HE'S REALLY STRONG...
...AND DANGEROUS...
...
...
DON'T WORRY!
!
SASUKE WON'T BE TEMPTED BY HIM!
HE'S SUPER STRONG TOO! I PROMISE!

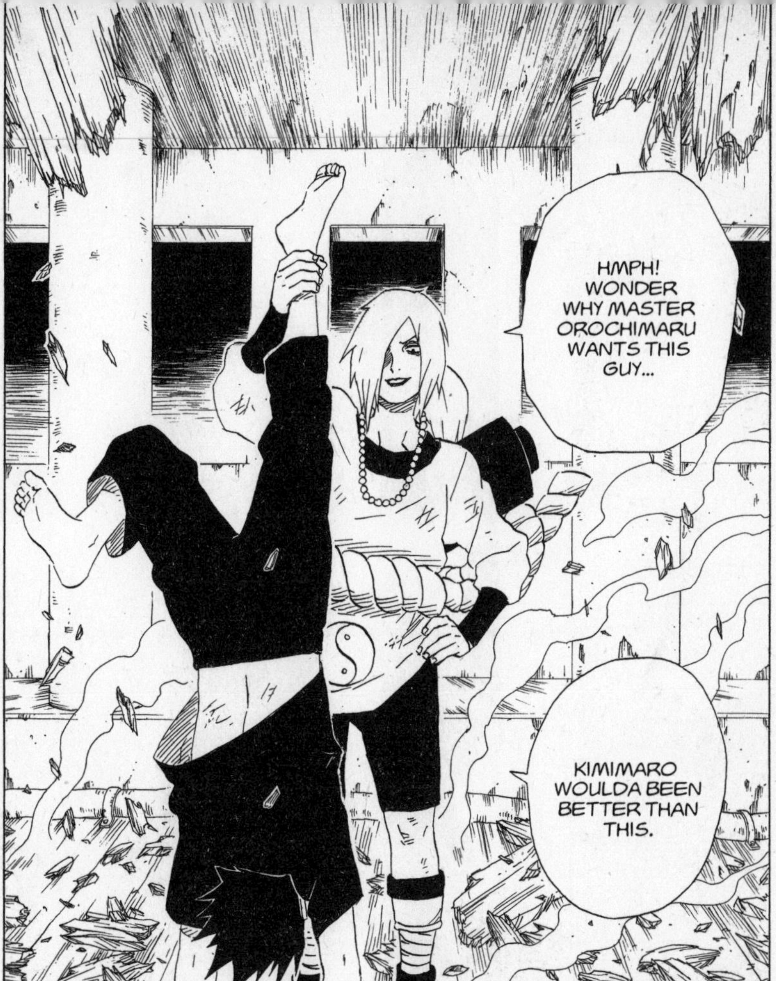
HMPH! WONDER WHY MASTER OROCHIMARU WANTS THIS GUY...
KIMIMARO WOULDA BEEN BETTER THAN THIS.

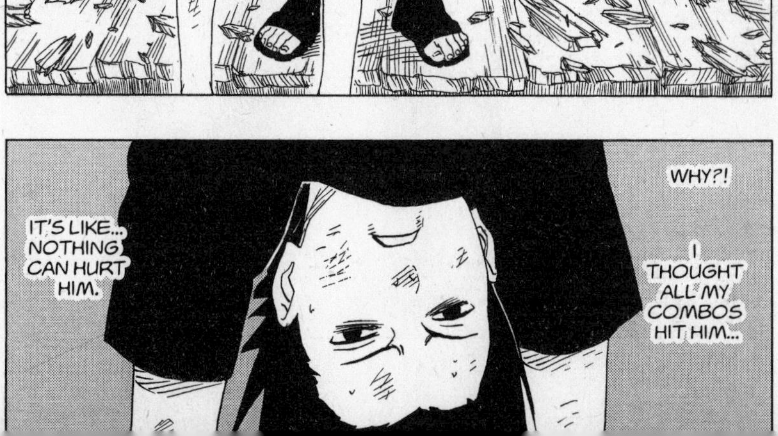
WHY?!
I THOUGHT ALL MY COMBOS HIT HIM...
IT'S LIKE... NOTHING CAN HURT HIM.

READ THIS WAY

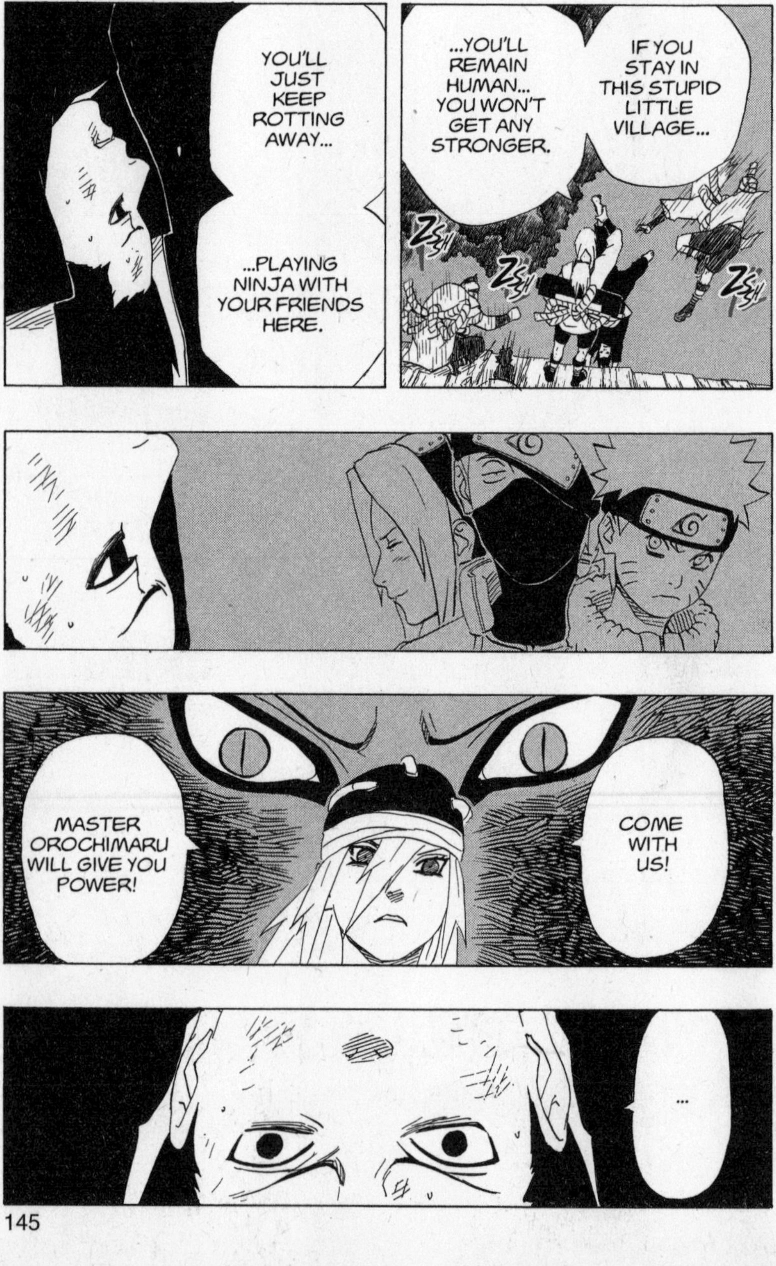
IF YOU STAY IN THIS STUPID LITTLE VILLAGE...
...YOU'LL REMAIN HUMAN... YOU WON'T GET ANY STRONGER.
ZSSH
ZSSH
ZSSH
YOU'LL JUST KEEP ROTTING AWAY...
...PLAYING NINJA WITH YOUR FRIENDS HERE.
COME WITH US!
MASTER OROCHIMARU WILL GIVE YOU POWER!
...

Mr. Kishimoto, Happy Birthday and congratulations on your marriage!! It's already Naruto's 4 year anniversary. I wonder how many more years it'll take to reach the end. Please take care of yourself and keep up the great work!!

And take care of your family too!!

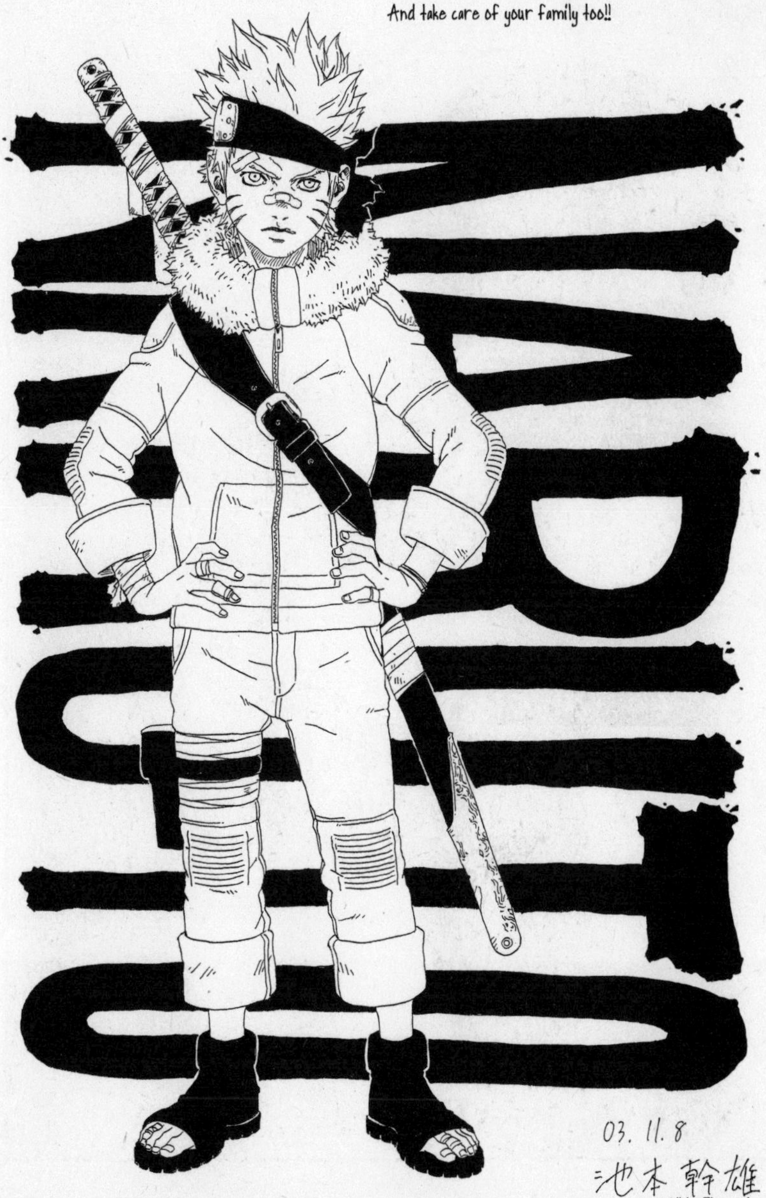

03. 11. 8

池本幹雄

Mikio Ikemoto

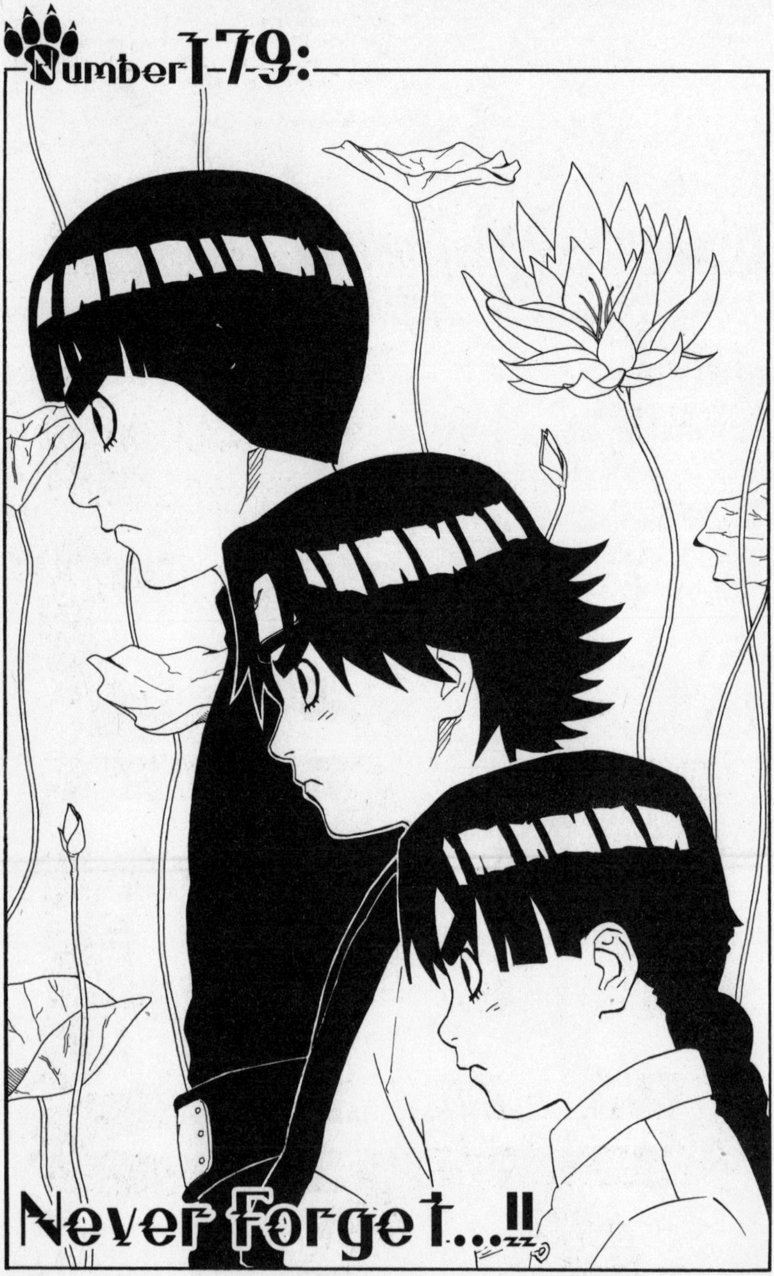
Number 179:
Never Forget...!!

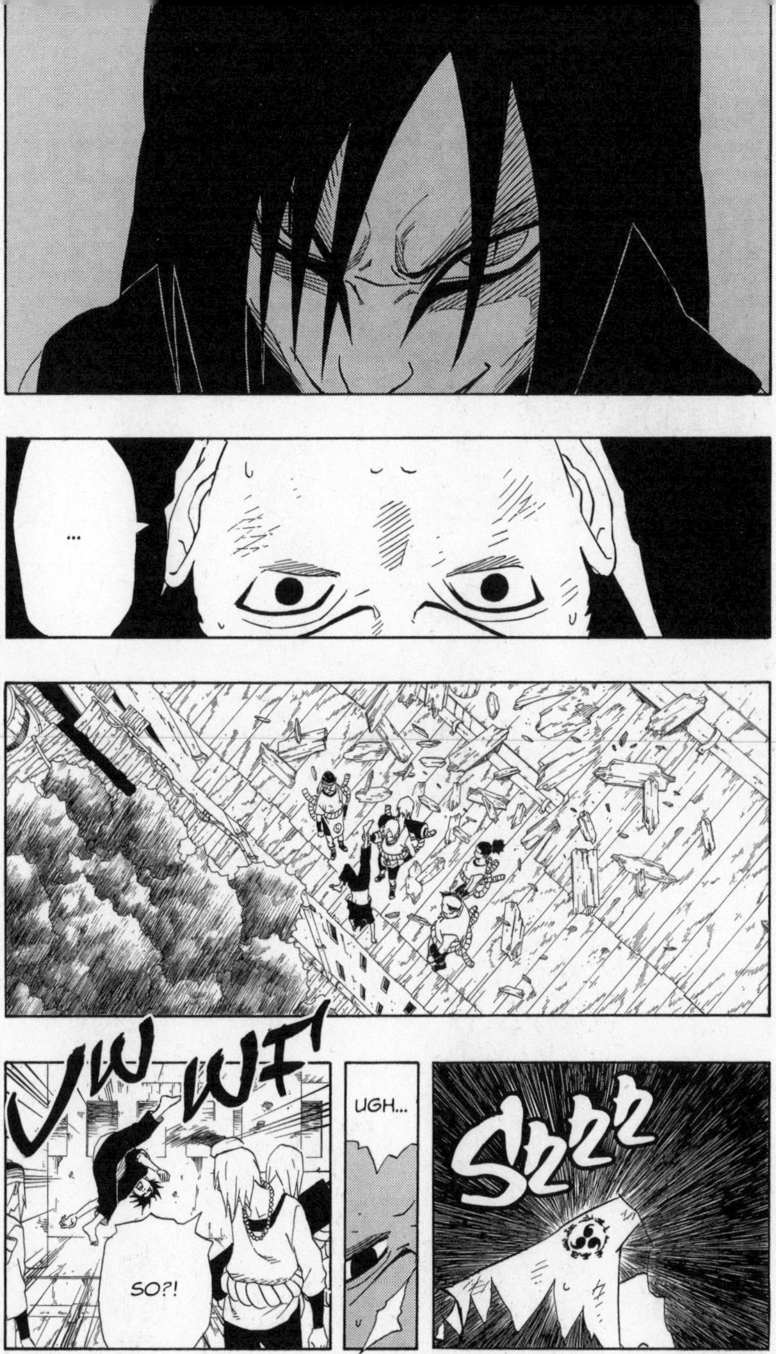
...
UGH...
VWWF!
SO?!

READ THIS WAY

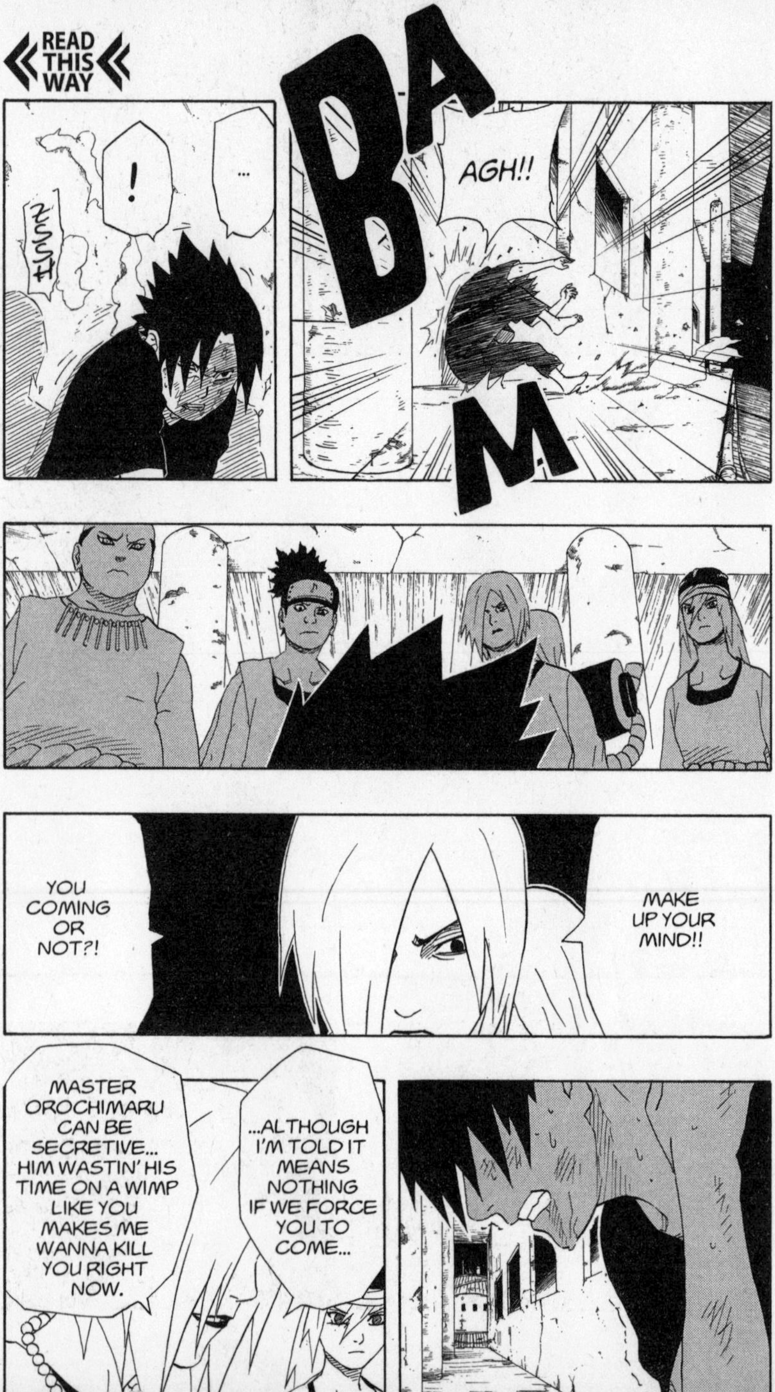
BADAM
AGH!!
ZSSH
...
!
MAKE UP YOUR MIND!!
YOU COMING OR NOT?!
...ALTHOUGH I'M TOLD IT MEANS NOTHING IF WE FORCE YOU TO COME...
MASTER OROCHIMARU CAN BE SECRETIVE... HIM WASTIN' HIS TIME ON A WIMP LIKE YOU MAKES ME WANNA KILL YOU RIGHT NOW.

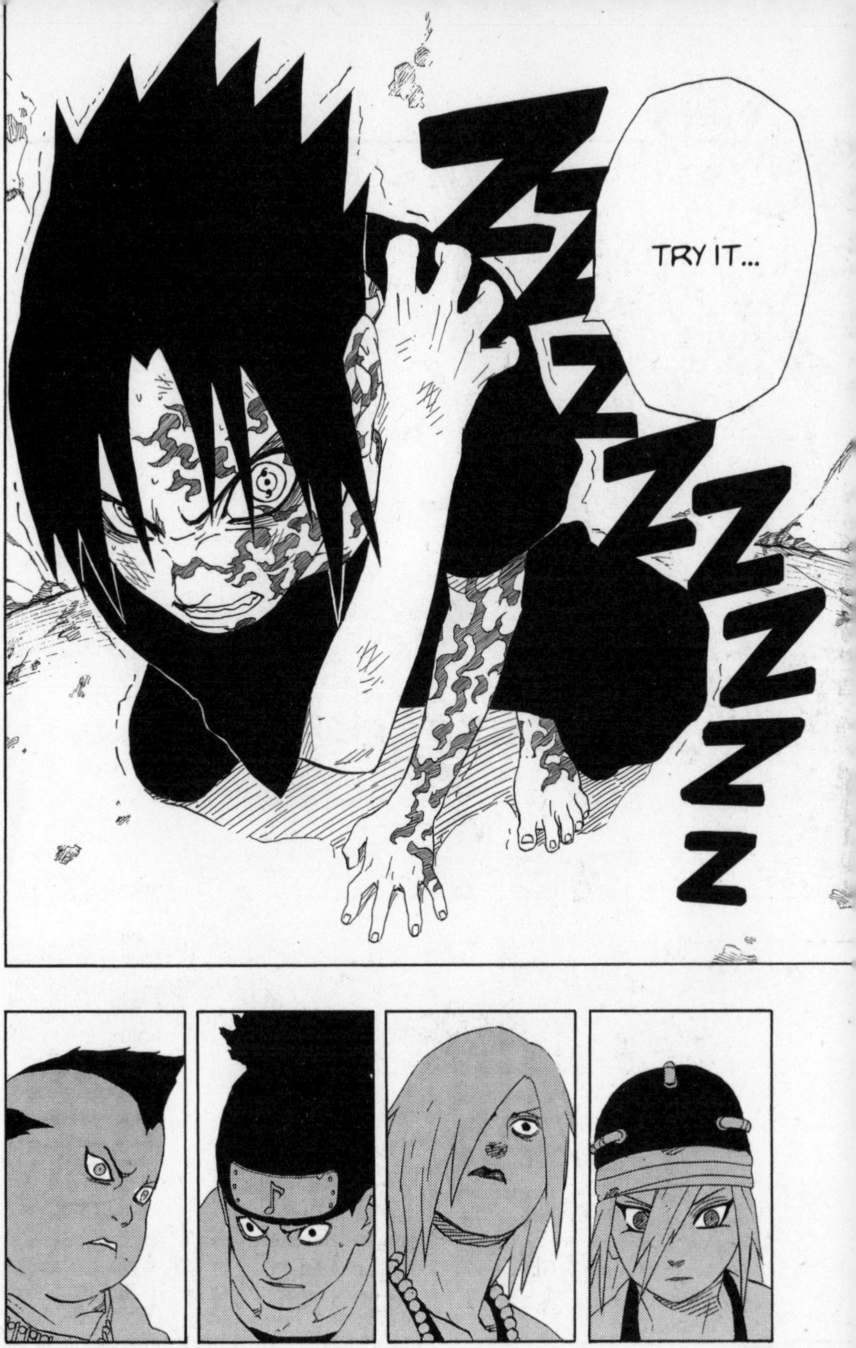
TRY IT...
ZZZZZZZZZ

READ THIS WAY

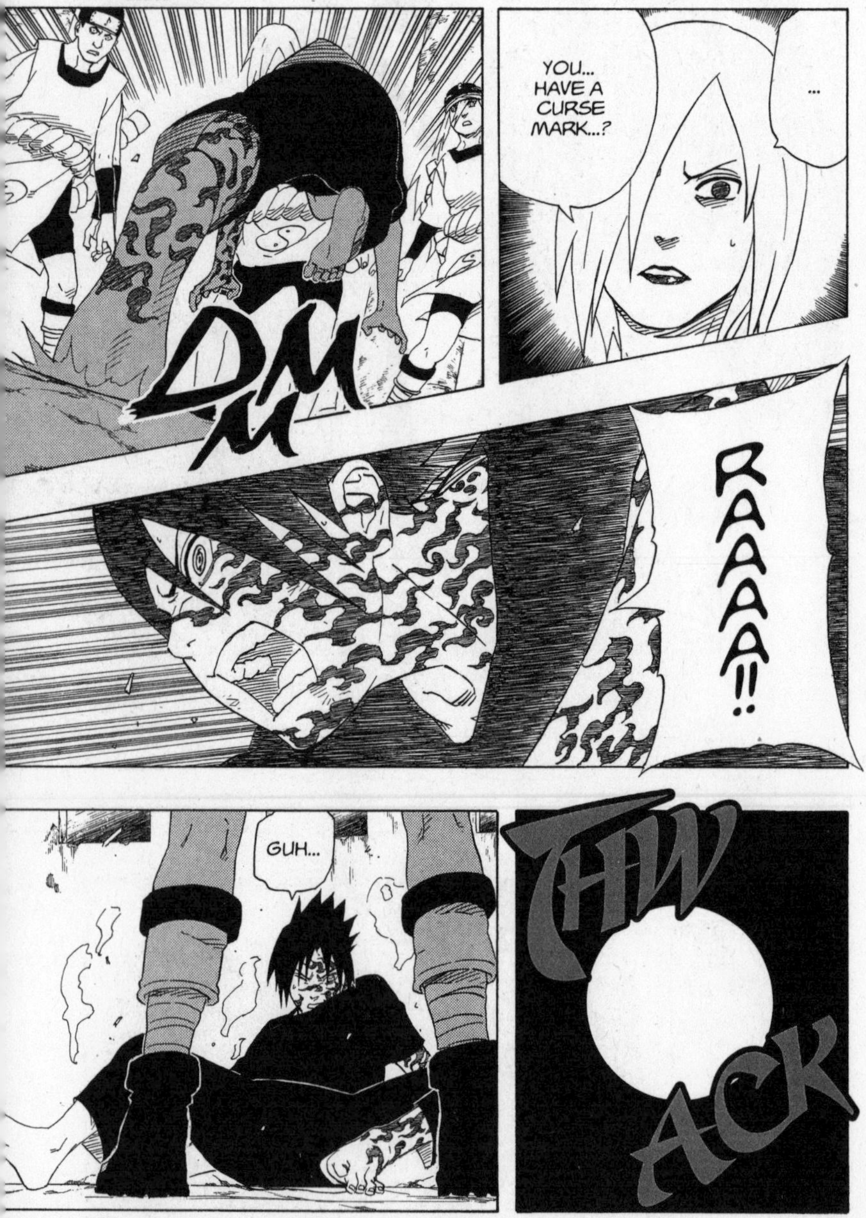
...
YOU... HAVE A CURSE MARK...?
DMM
RAAAA!!
THWACK
GUH...

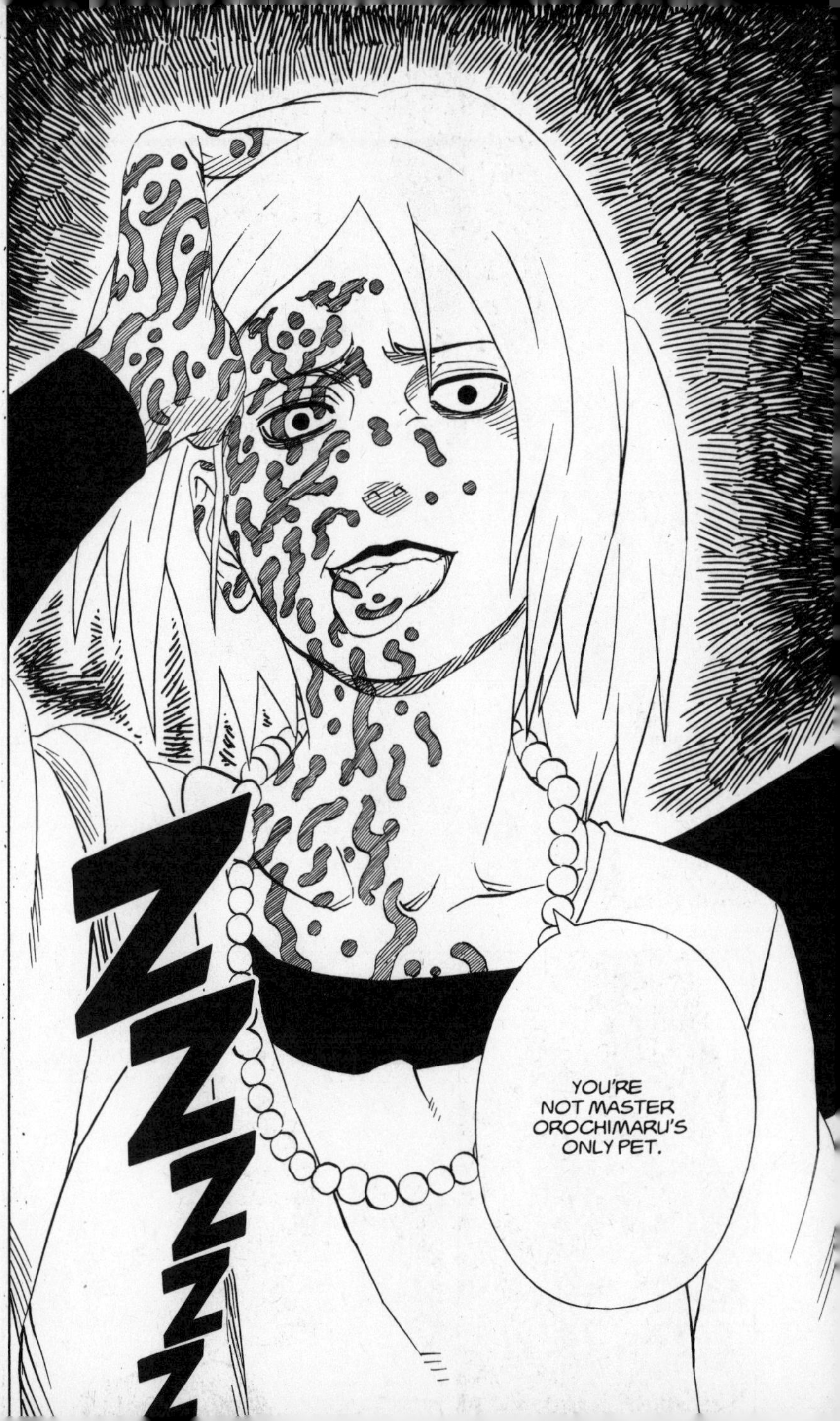
ZZZZZZ
YOU'RE NOT MASTER OROCHIMARU'S ONLY PET.

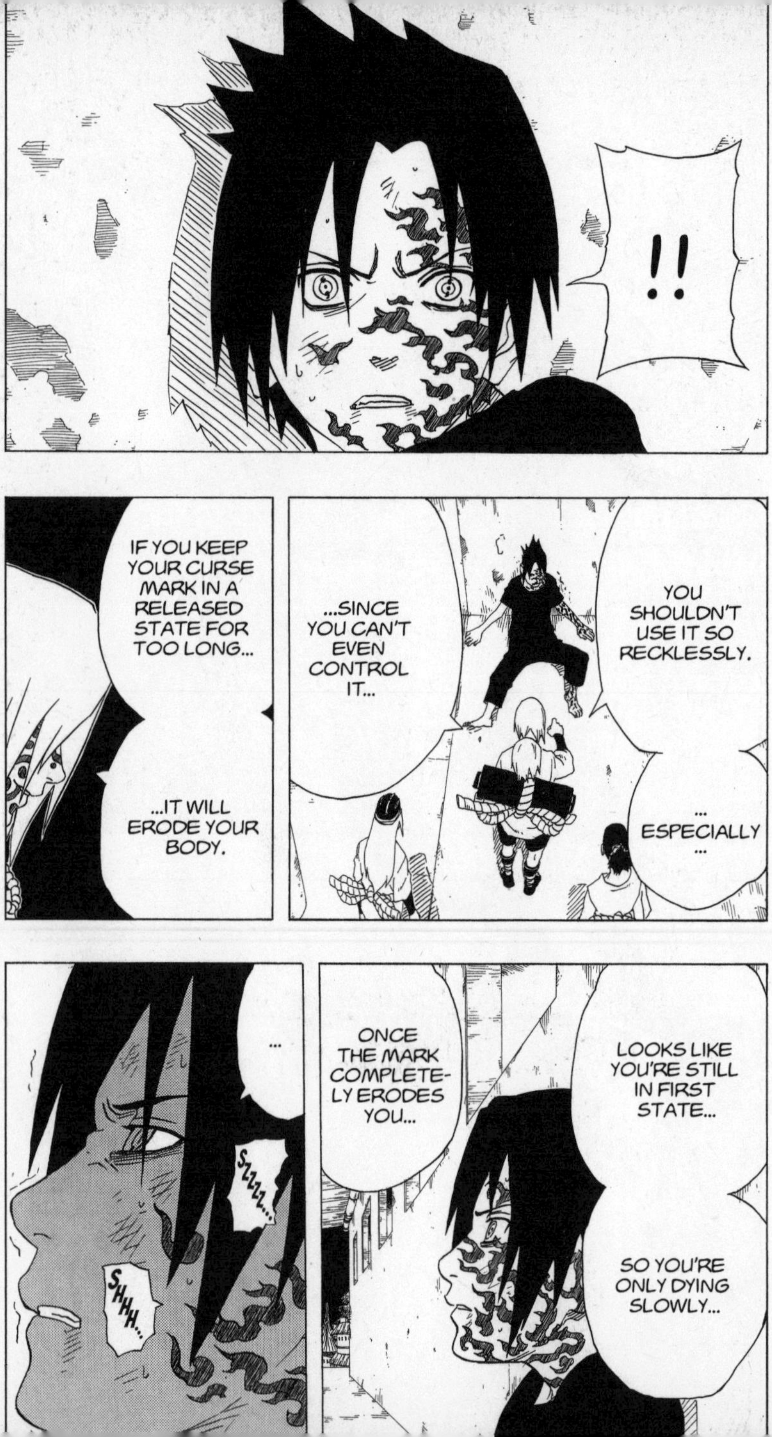
!!
YOU SHOULDN'T USE IT SO RECKLESSLY.
...ESPECIALLY...
...SINCE YOU CAN'T EVEN CONTROL IT...
IF YOU KEEP YOUR CURSE MARK IN A RELEASED STATE FOR TOO LONG...
...IT WILL ERODE YOUR BODY.
LOOKS LIKE YOU'RE STILL IN FIRST STATE...
SO YOU'RE ONLY DYING SLOWLY...
ONCE THE MARK COMPLETE-LY ERODES YOU...
...
SZZZZ...
SHHH...

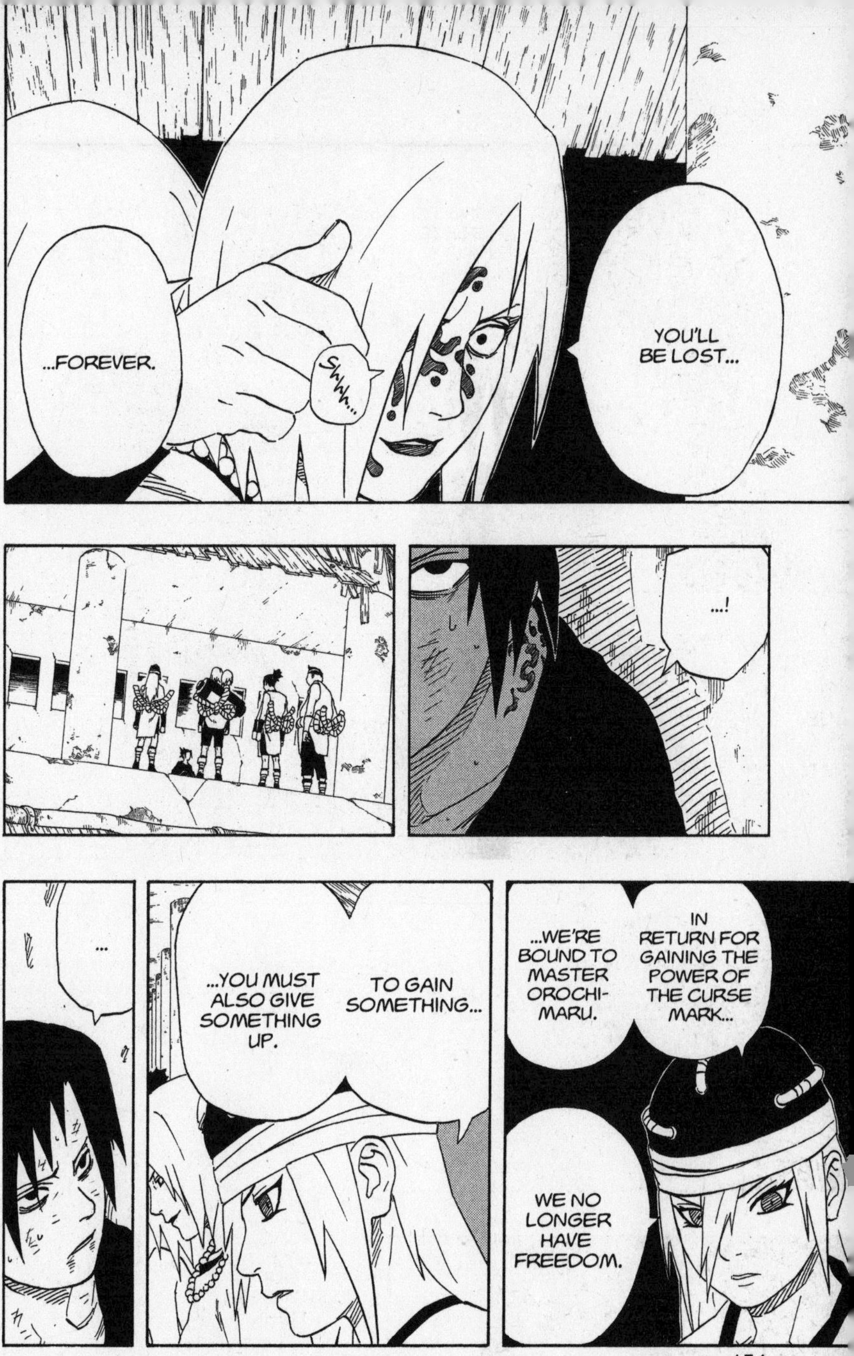
YOU'LL BE LOST...
Shhh...
...FOREVER.
...!
IN RETURN FOR GAINING THE POWER OF THE CURSE MARK...
...WE'RE BOUND TO MASTER OROCHI-MARU.
WE NO LONGER HAVE FREEDOM.
TO GAIN SOMETHING...
...YOU MUST ALSO GIVE SOMETHING UP.
...

READ THIS WAY

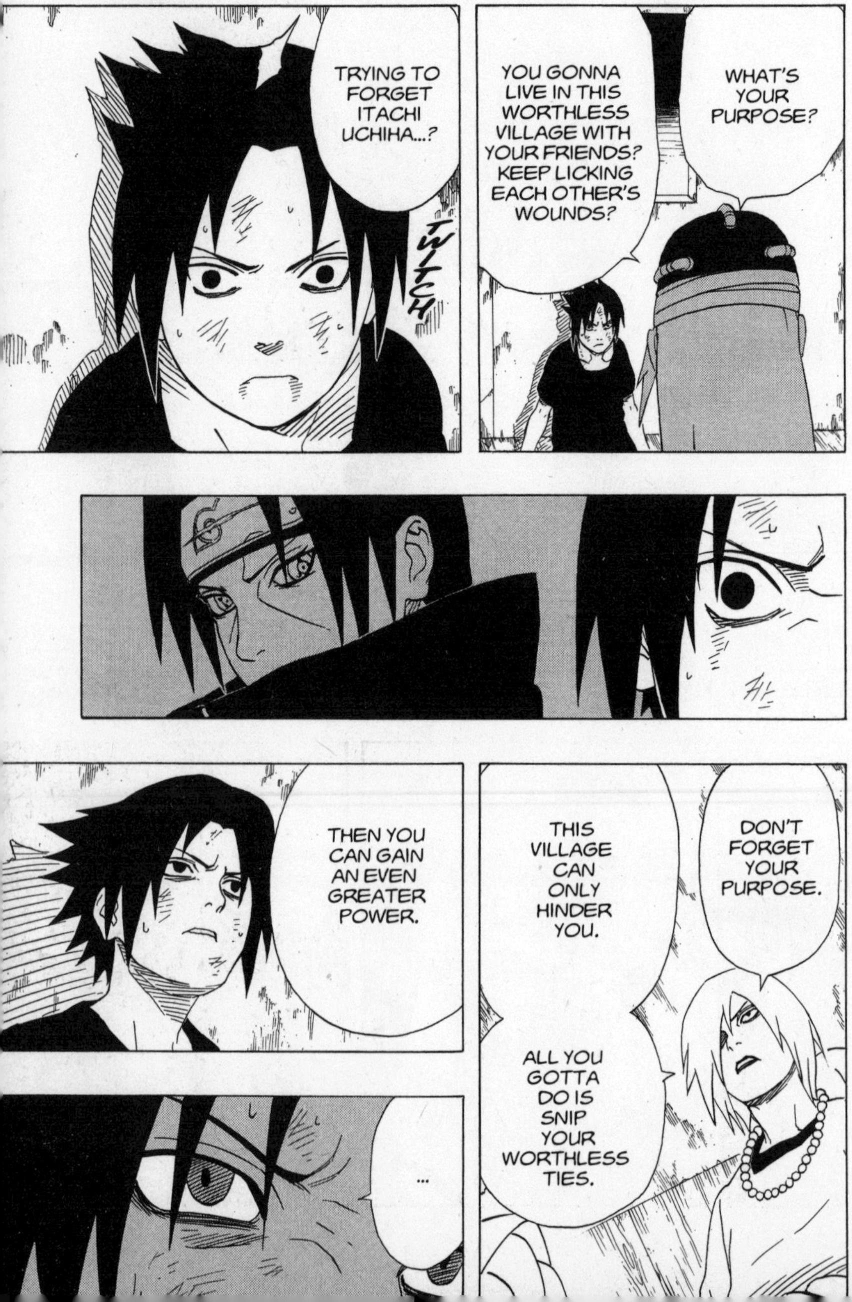

WHAT'S YOUR PURPOSE?
YOU GONNA LIVE IN THIS WORTHLESS VILLAGE WITH YOUR FRIENDS? KEEP LICKING EACH OTHER'S WOUNDS?
TRYING TO FORGET ITACHI UCHIHA...?
TWITCH
DON'T FORGET YOUR PURPOSE.
THIS VILLAGE CAN ONLY HINDER YOU.
ALL YOU GOTTA DO IS SNIP YOUR WORTHLESS TIES.
THEN YOU CAN GAIN AN EVEN GREATER POWER.
...

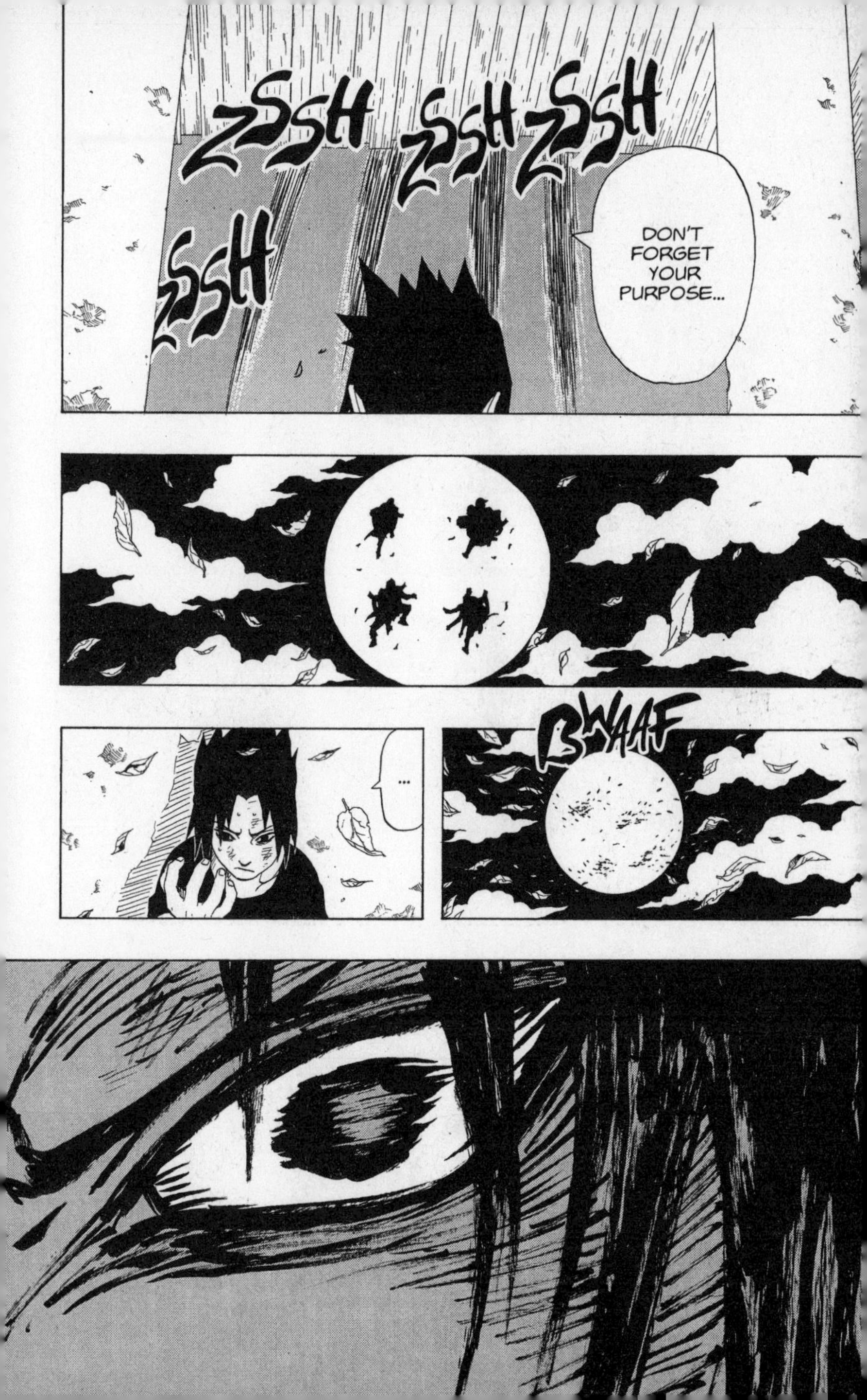
DON'T FORGET YOUR PURPOSE...
ZSSH ZSSH ZSSH
ZSSH
BWAAF
...

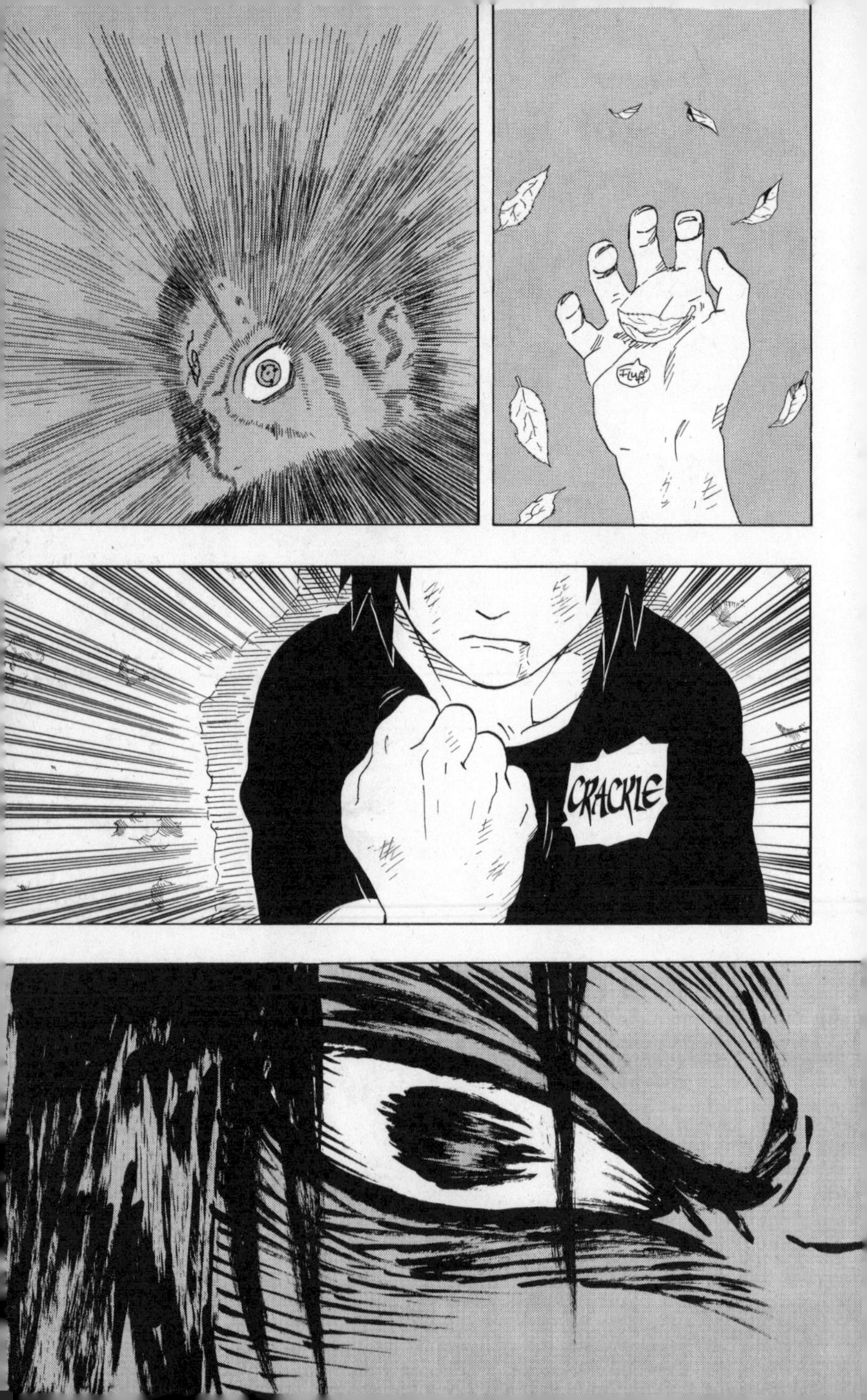
Fluff
CRACKLE

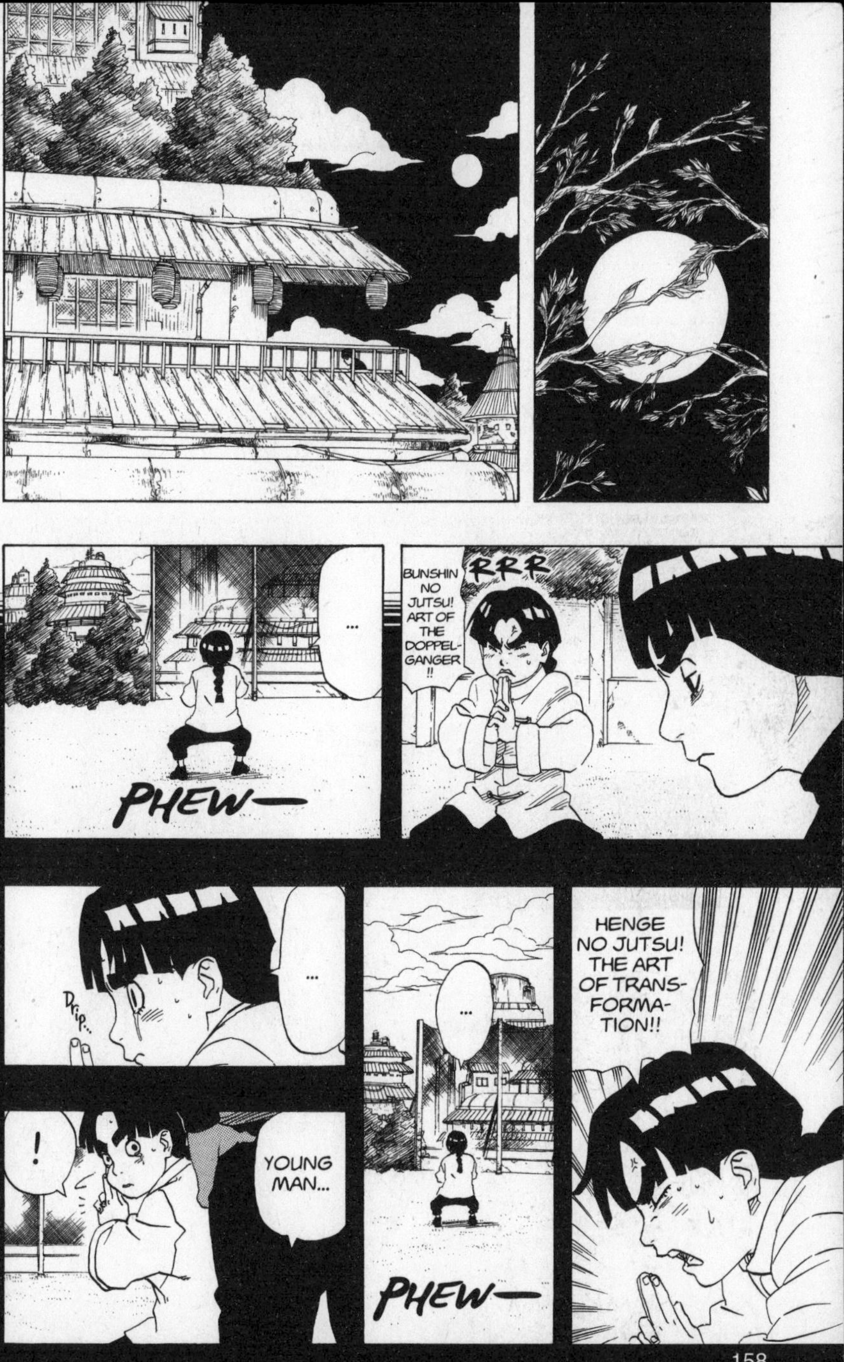
RRR
BUNSHIN NO JUTSU! ART OF THE DOPPEL-GANGER!!
...
PHEW—
HENGE NO JUTSU! THE ART OF TRANS-FORMA-TION!!
...
PHEW—
...
Drip...
YOUNG MAN...
!

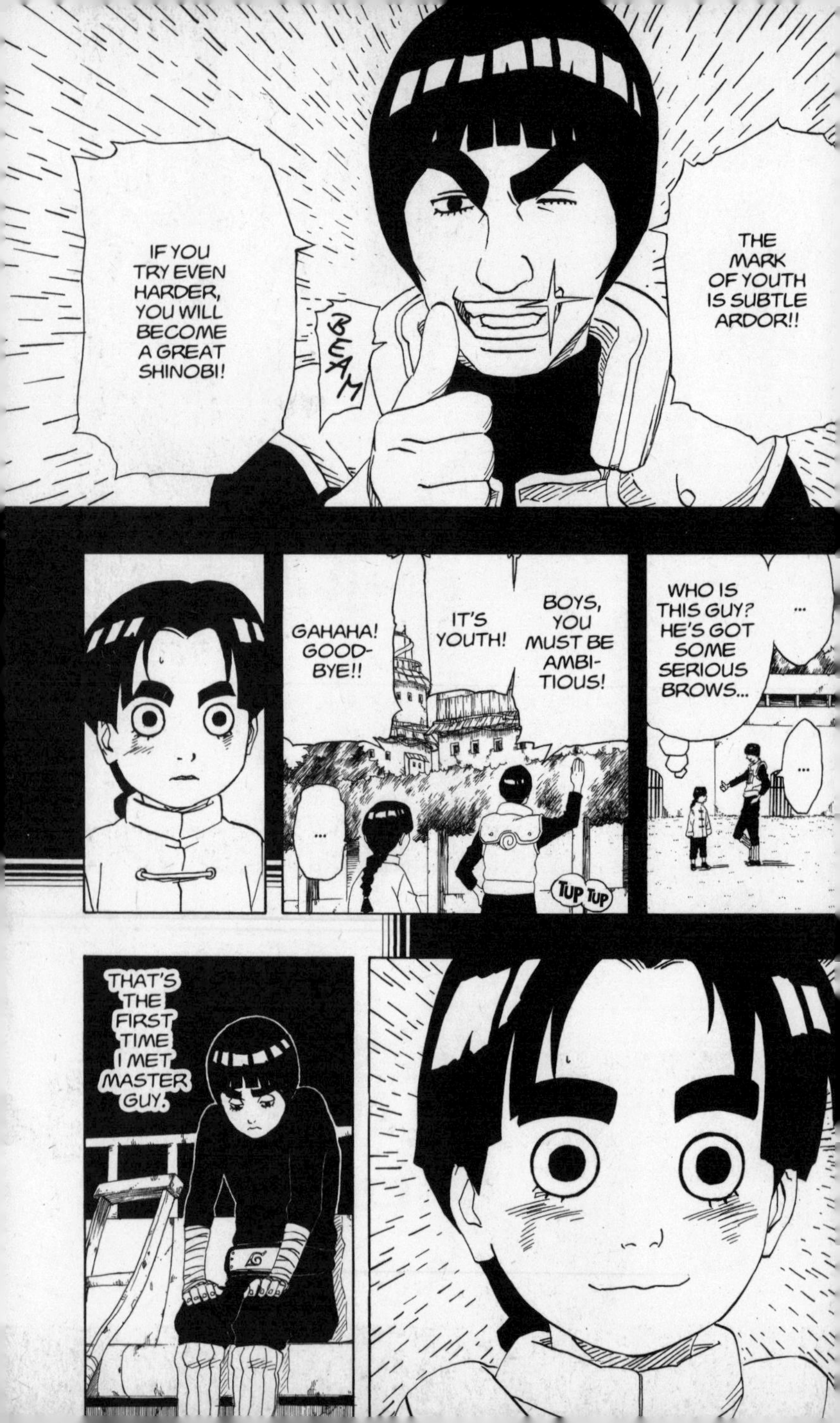
THE MARK OF YOUTH IS SUBTLE ARDOR!!
BEAM
IF YOU TRY EVEN HARDER, YOU WILL BECOME A GREAT SHINOBI!
...
WHO IS THIS GUY? HE'S GOT SOME SERIOUS BROWS...
...
BOYS, YOU MUST BE AMBITIOUS!
IT'S YOUTH!
GAHAHA! GOOD-BYE!!
...
TUP TUP
THAT'S THE FIRST TIME I MET MASTER GUY.

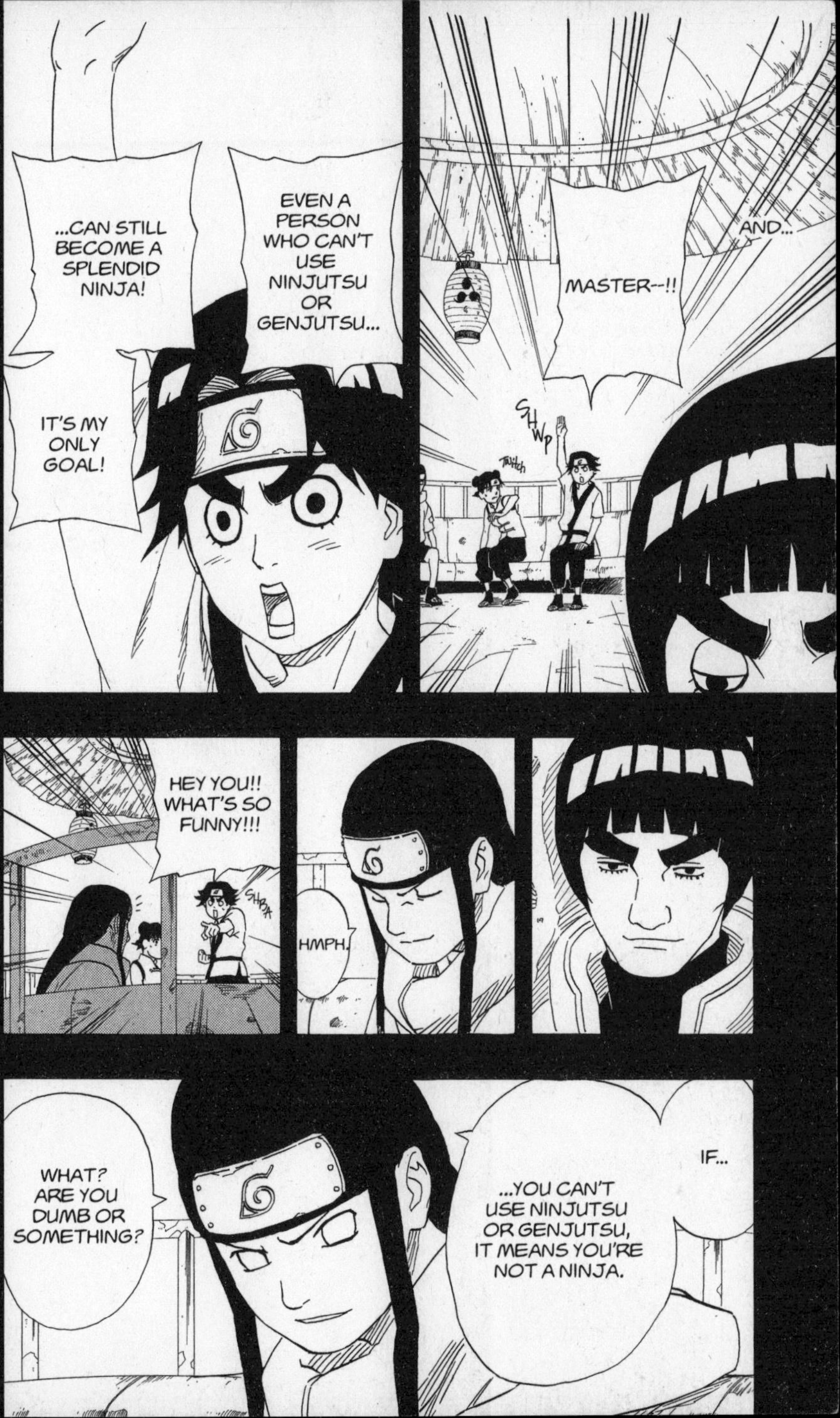
AND...
MASTER--!!
SHWP
TWITCH
EVEN A PERSON WHO CAN'T USE NINJUTSU OR GENJUTSU...
...CAN STILL BECOME A SPLENDID NINJA!
IT'S MY ONLY GOAL!
HMPH.
HEY YOU!! WHAT'S SO FUNNY!!!
SHBA
IF...
...YOU CAN'T USE NINJUTSU OR GENJUTSU, IT MEANS YOU'RE NOT A NINJA.
WHAT? ARE YOU DUMB OR SOMETHING?

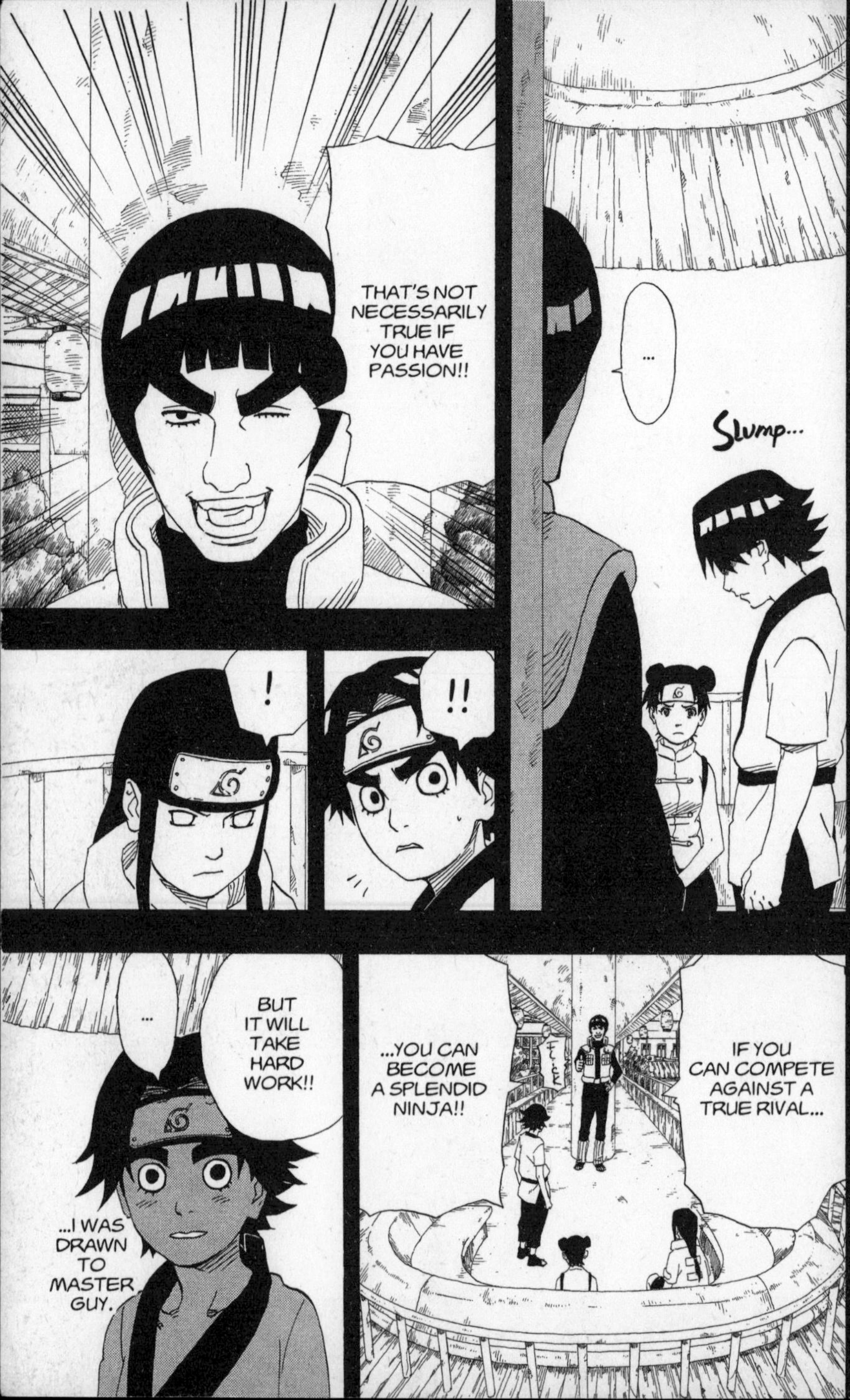
...
Slump...
THAT'S NOT NECESSARILY TRUE IF YOU HAVE PASSION!!
!!
!
IF YOU CAN COMPETE AGAINST A TRUE RIVAL...
...YOU CAN BECOME A SPLENDID NINJA!!
BUT IT WILL TAKE HARD WORK!!
...
...I WAS DRAWN TO MASTER GUY.

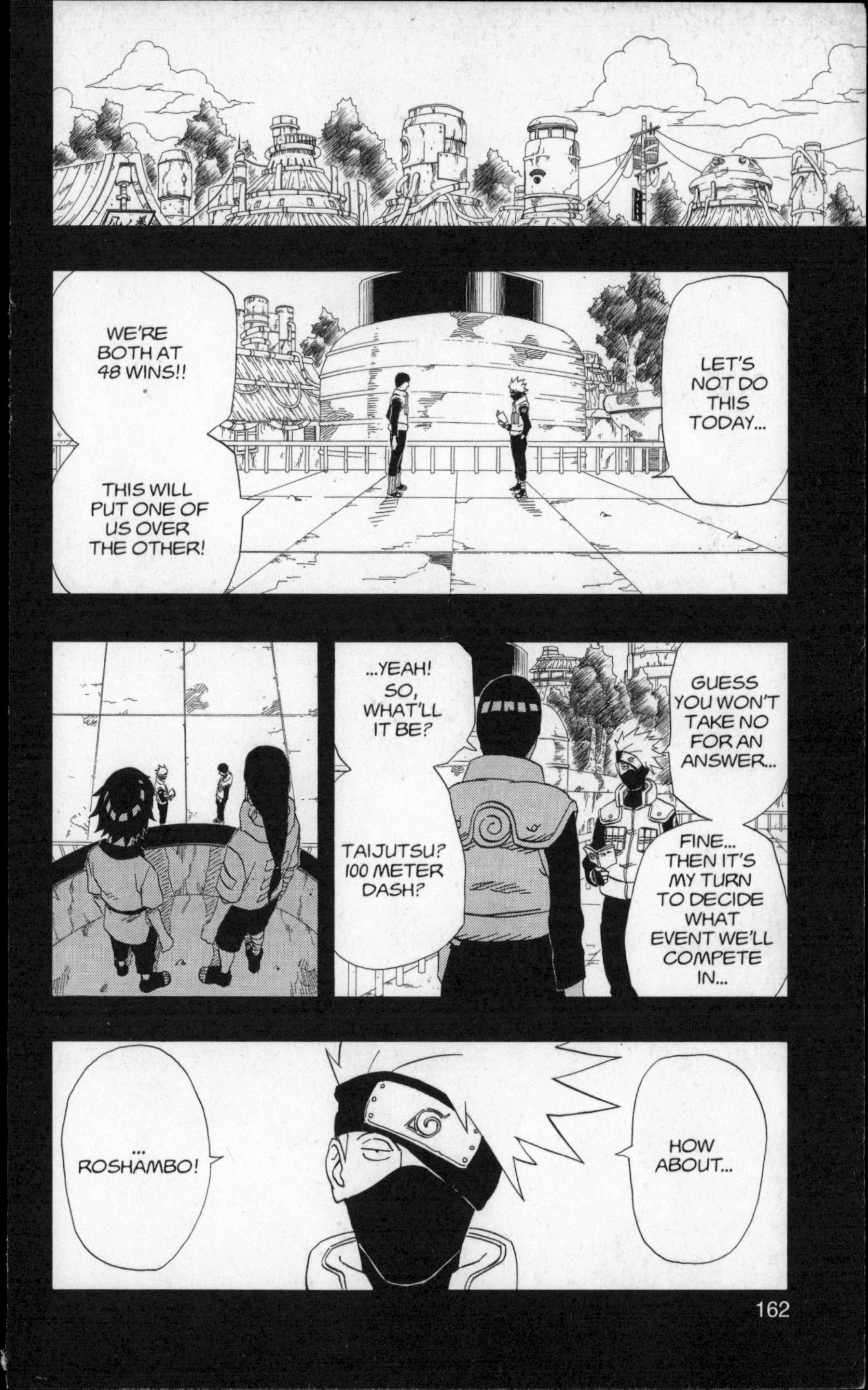
LET'S NOT DO THIS TODAY...
WE'RE BOTH AT 48 WINS!!
THIS WILL PUT ONE OF US OVER THE OTHER!
GUESS YOU WON'T TAKE NO FOR AN ANSWER...
...YEAH! SO, WHAT'LL IT BE?
TAIJUTSU? 100 METER DASH?
FINE... THEN IT'S MY TURN TO DECIDE WHAT EVENT WE'LL COMPETE IN...
HOW ABOUT...
...ROSHAMBO!

READ THIS WAY

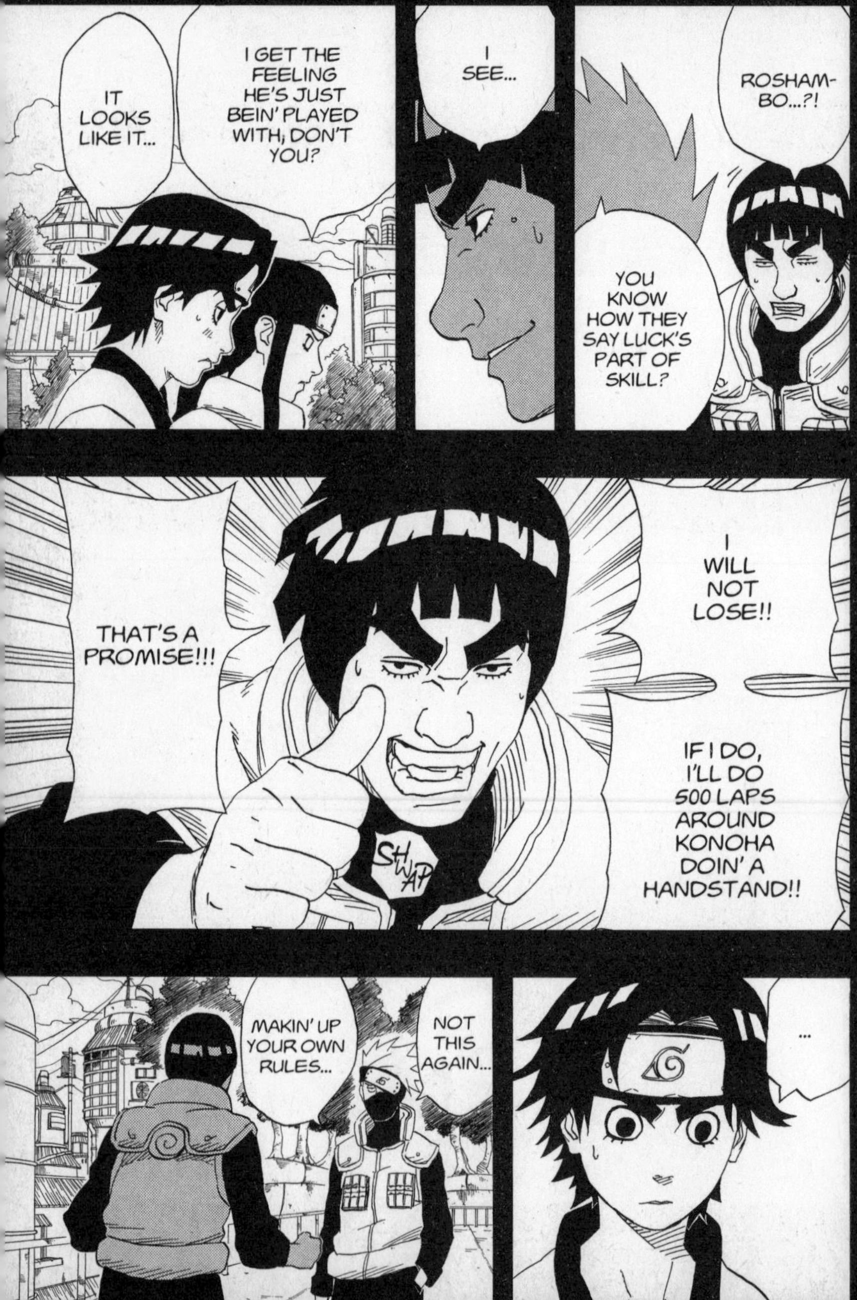
ROSHAM-BO...?!
YOU KNOW HOW THEY SAY LUCK'S PART OF SKILL?
I SEE...
I GET THE FEELING HE'S JUST BEIN' PLAYED WITH, DON'T YOU?
IT LOOKS LIKE IT...
I WILL NOT LOSE!!
IF I DO, I'LL DO 500 LAPS AROUND KONOHA DOIN' A HANDSTAND!!
SHWAP
THAT'S A PROMISE!!!
...
NOT THIS AGAIN...
MAKIN' UP YOUR OWN RULES...

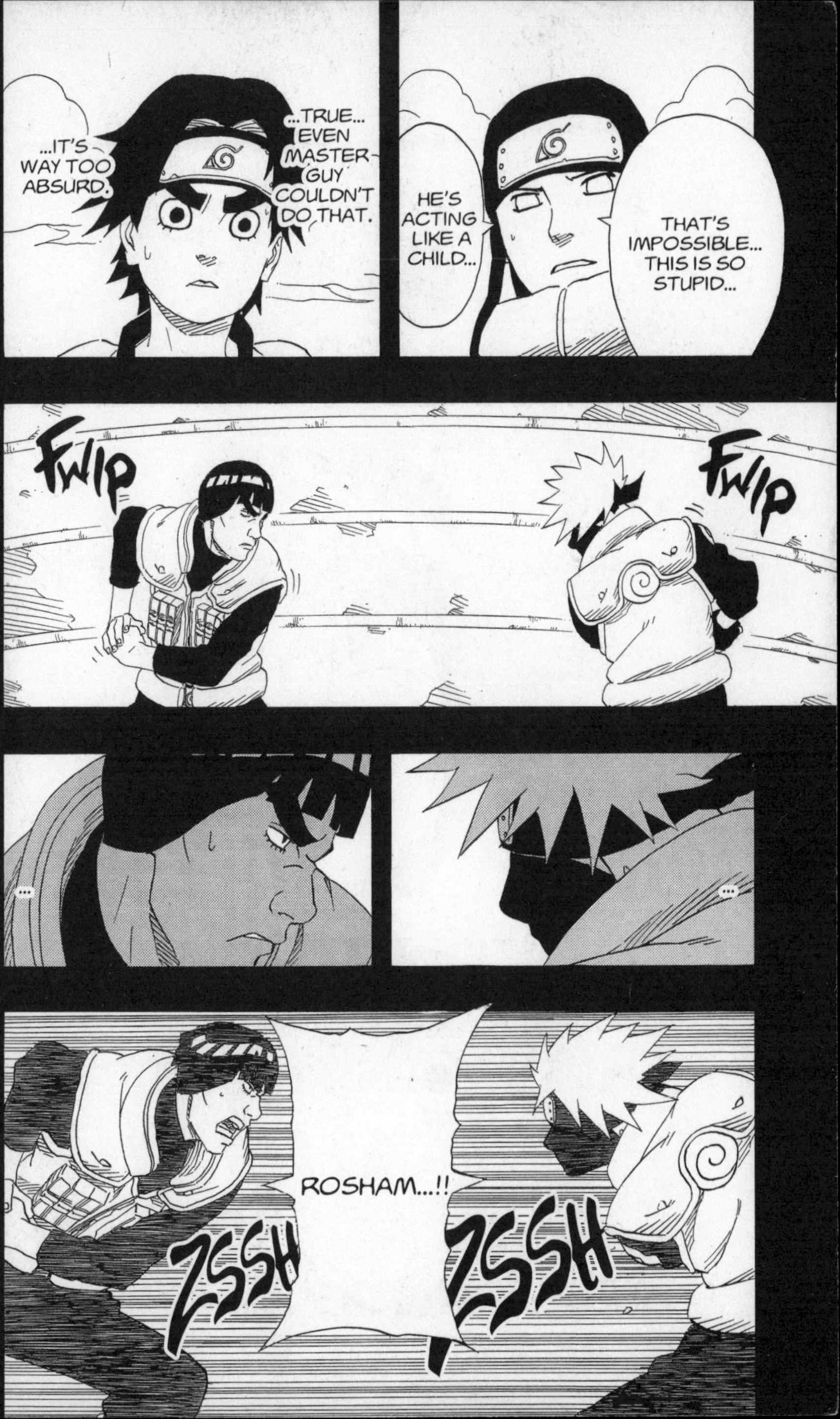

THAT'S IMPOSSIBLE... THIS IS SO STUPID...
HE'S ACTING LIKE A CHILD...
...TRUE... EVEN MASTER GUY COULDN'T DO THAT.
...IT'S WAY TOO ABSURD.
FWIP
FWIP
...
...
ROSHAM...!!
ZSSH
ZSSH

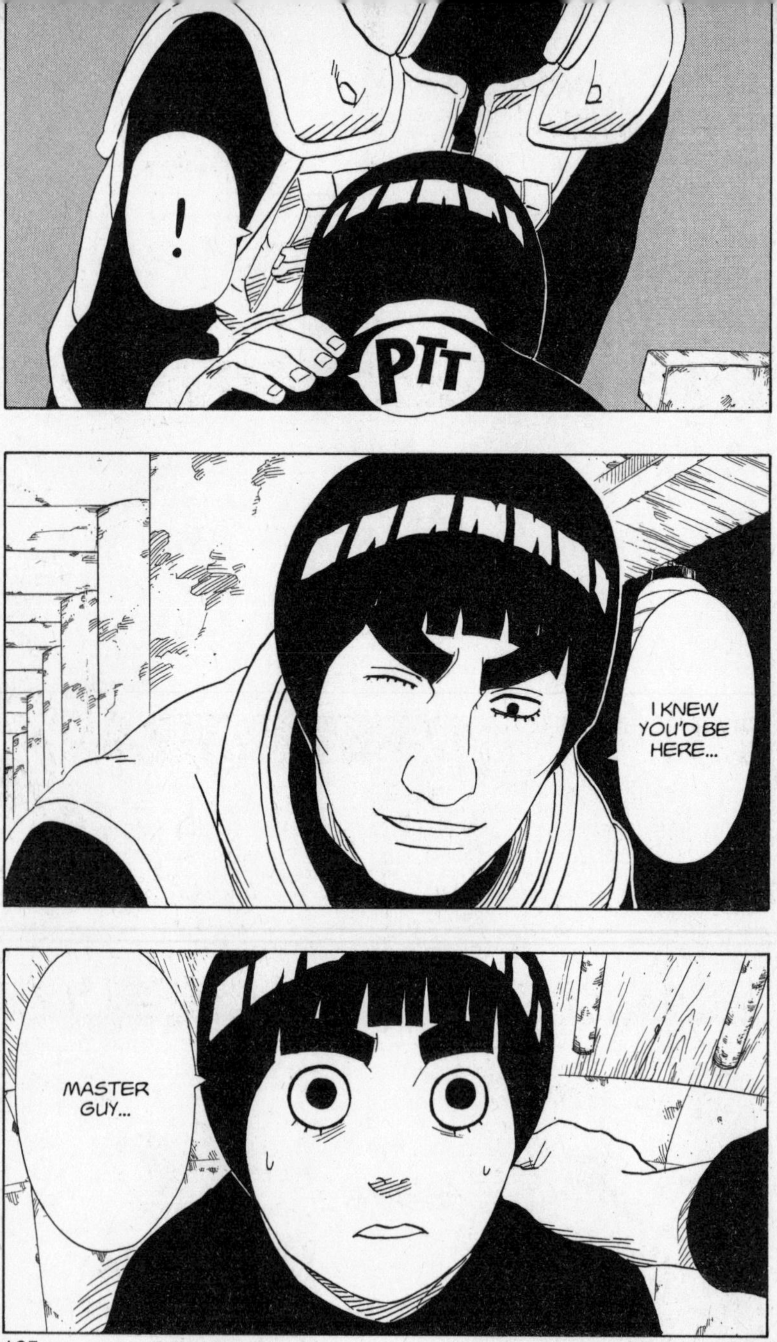
PTT
!
I KNEW YOU'D BE HERE...
MASTER GUY...

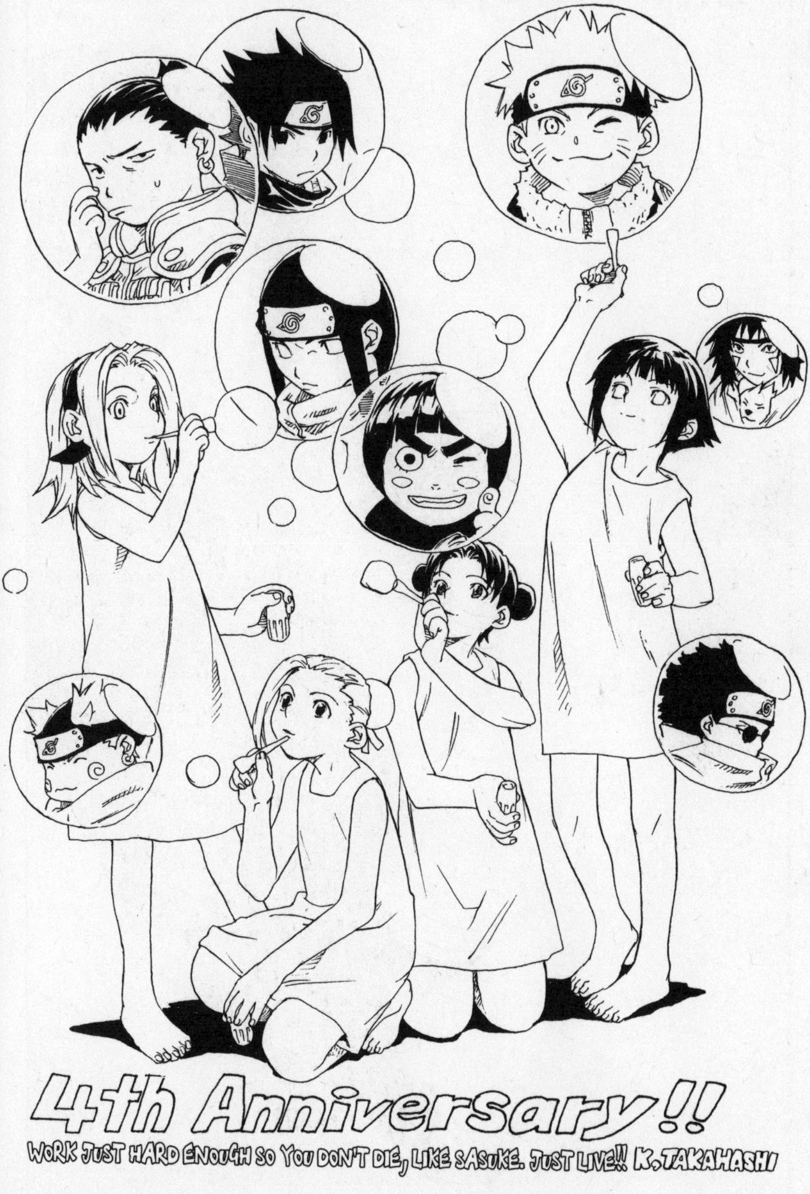

4th Anniversary!!

WORK JUST HARD ENOUGH SO YOU DON'T DIE, LIKE SASUKE. JUST LIVE!! K, TAKAHASHI

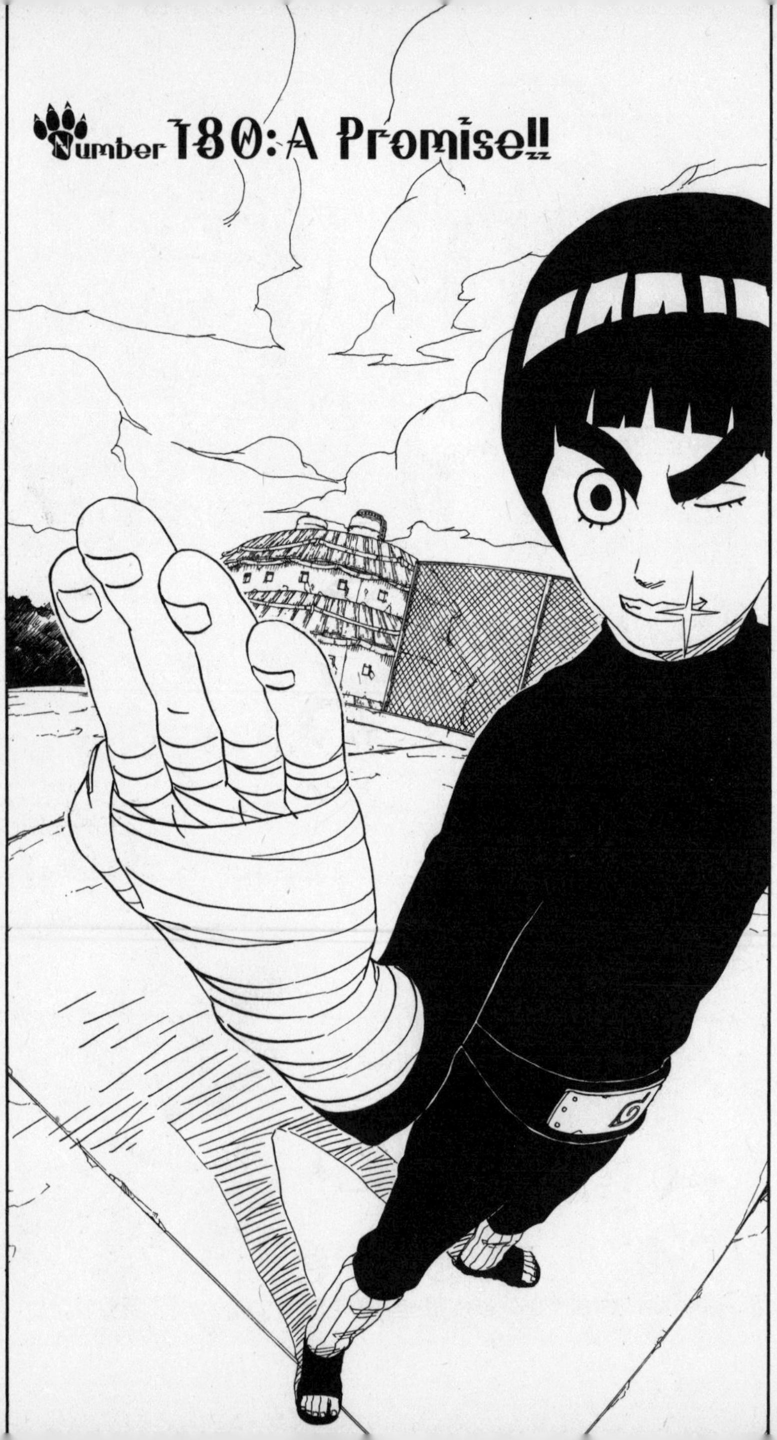
Number 180: A Promise!!

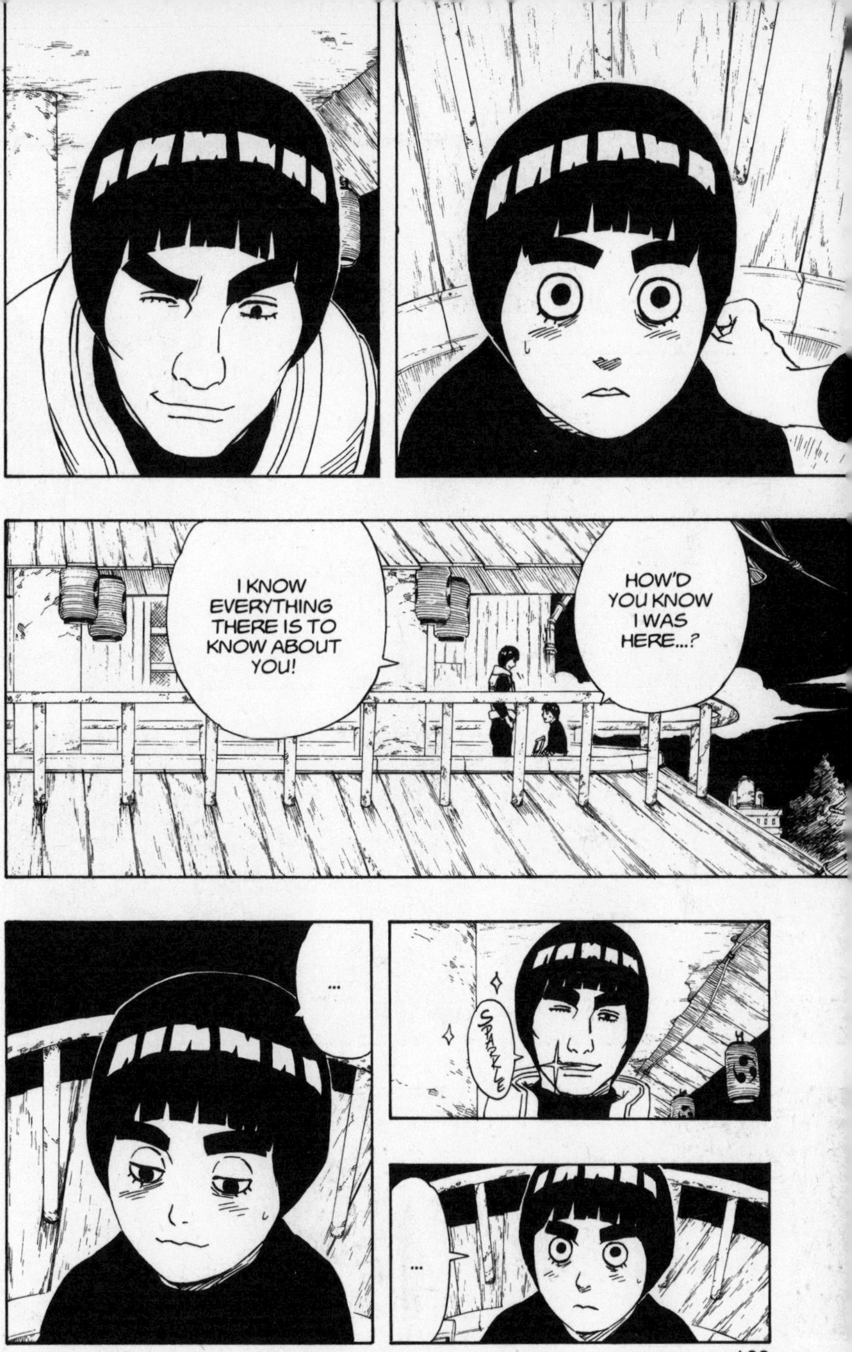
HOW'D YOU KNOW I WAS HERE...?
I KNOW EVERYTHING THERE IS TO KNOW ABOUT YOU!
SPARKLE
...
...

READ THIS WAY

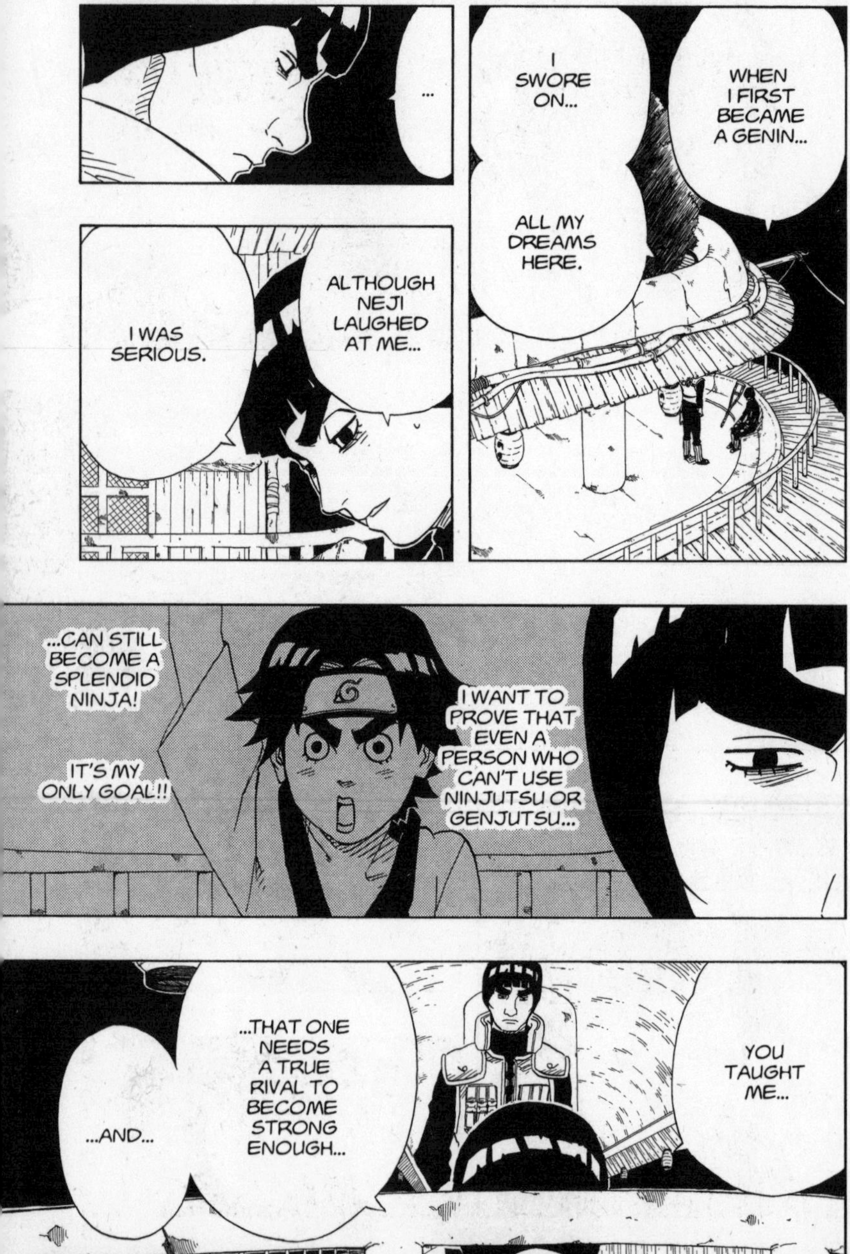
WHEN I FIRST BECAME A GENIN...
I SWORE ON...
ALL MY DREAMS HERE.
...
ALTHOUGH NEJI LAUGHED AT ME...
I WAS SERIOUS.
I WANT TO PROVE THAT EVEN A PERSON WHO CAN'T USE NINJUTSU OR GENJUTSU...
...CAN STILL BECOME A SPLENDID NINJA!
IT'S MY ONLY GOAL!!
YOU TAUGHT ME...
...THAT ONE NEEDS A TRUE RIVAL TO BECOME STRONG ENOUGH...
...AND...

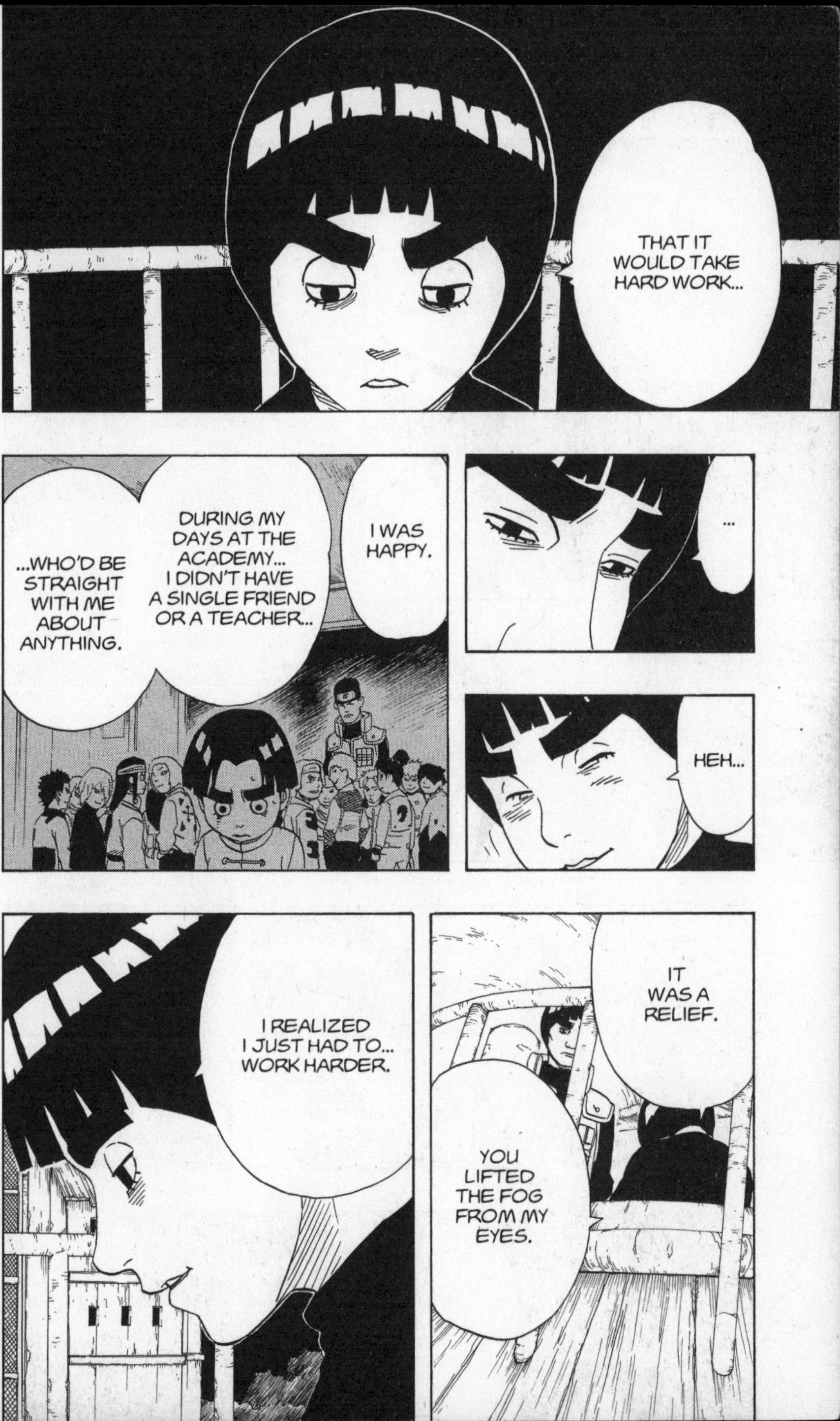
THAT IT WOULD TAKE HARD WORK...
...
HEH...
I WAS HAPPY.
DURING MY DAYS AT THE ACADEMY... I DIDN'T HAVE A SINGLE FRIEND OR A TEACHER...
...WHO'D BE STRAIGHT WITH ME ABOUT ANYTHING.
IT WAS A RELIEF.
YOU LIFTED THE FOG FROM MY EYES.
I REALIZED I JUST HAD TO... WORK HARDER.

READ THIS WAY

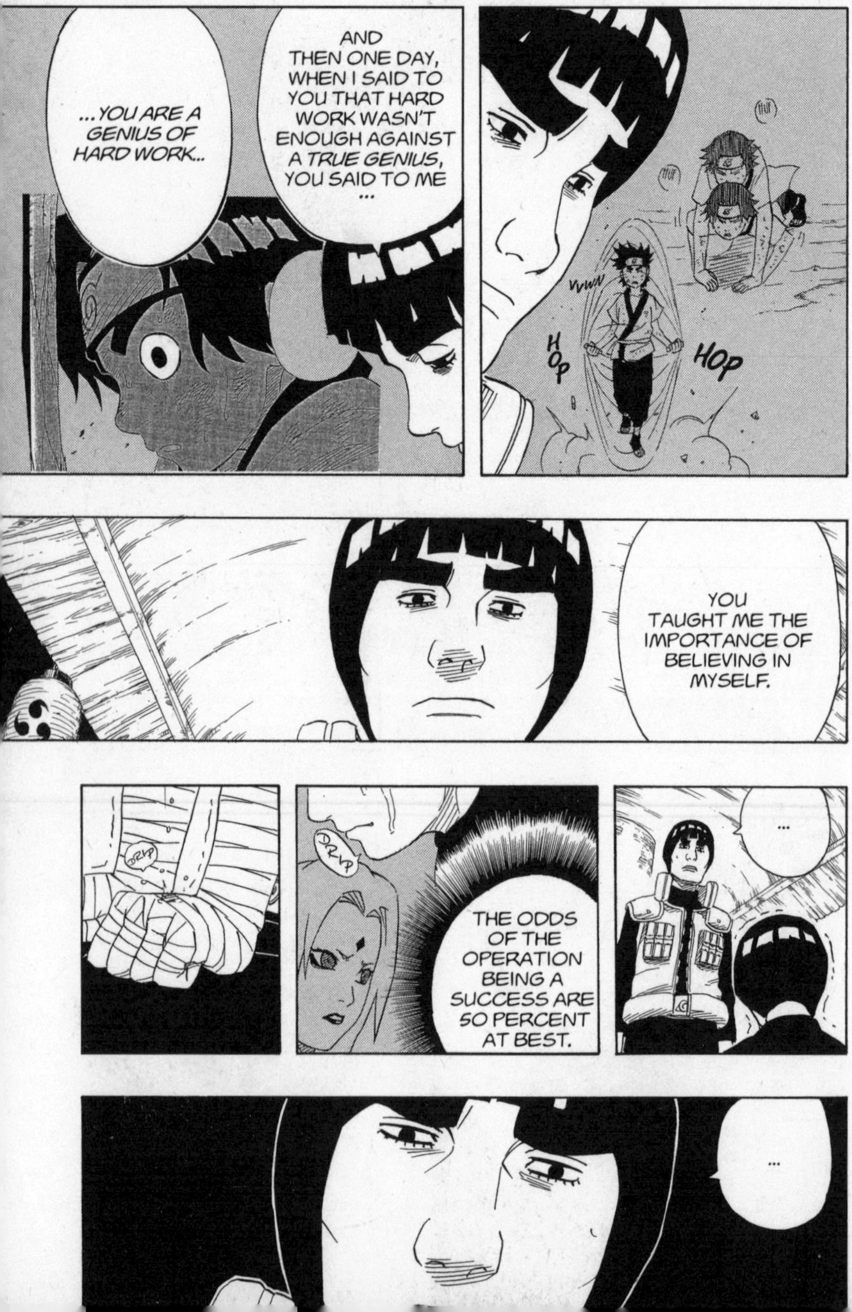
VVWN
HOP
HOP
AND THEN ONE DAY, WHEN I SAID TO YOU THAT HARD WORK WASN'T ENOUGH AGAINST A *TRUE GENIUS*, YOU SAID TO ME ...
...YOU ARE A GENIUS OF HARD WORK...
YOU TAUGHT ME THE IMPORTANCE OF BELIEVING IN MYSELF.
...
THE ODDS OF THE OPERATION BEING A SUCCESS ARE 50 PERCENT AT BEST.
DRIP
DRIP
...

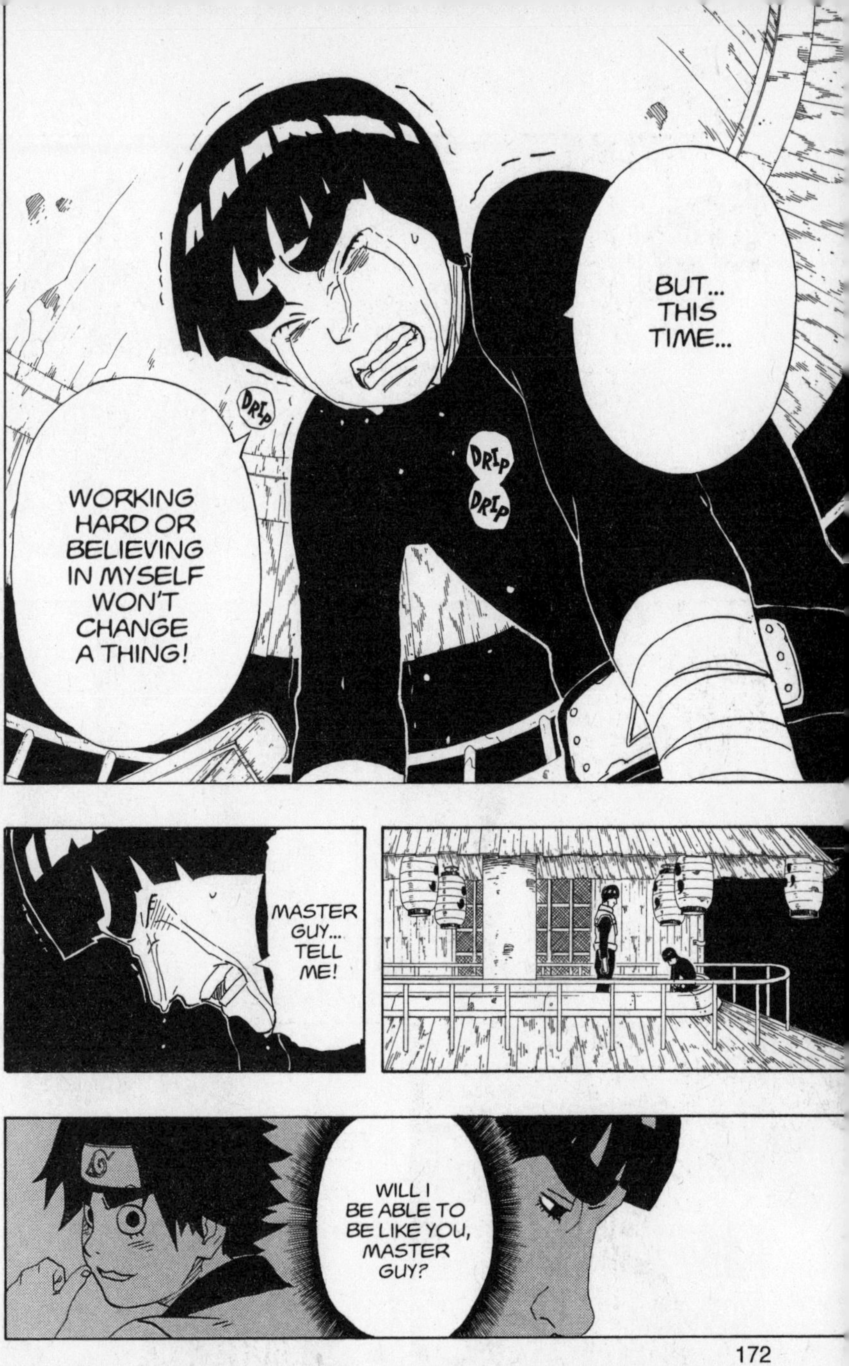
BUT... THIS TIME...
DRIP
DRIP
DRIP
WORKING HARD OR BELIEVING IN MYSELF WON'T CHANGE A THING!
MASTER GUY... TELL ME!
WILL I BE ABLE TO BE LIKE YOU, MASTER GUY?

READ THIS WAY

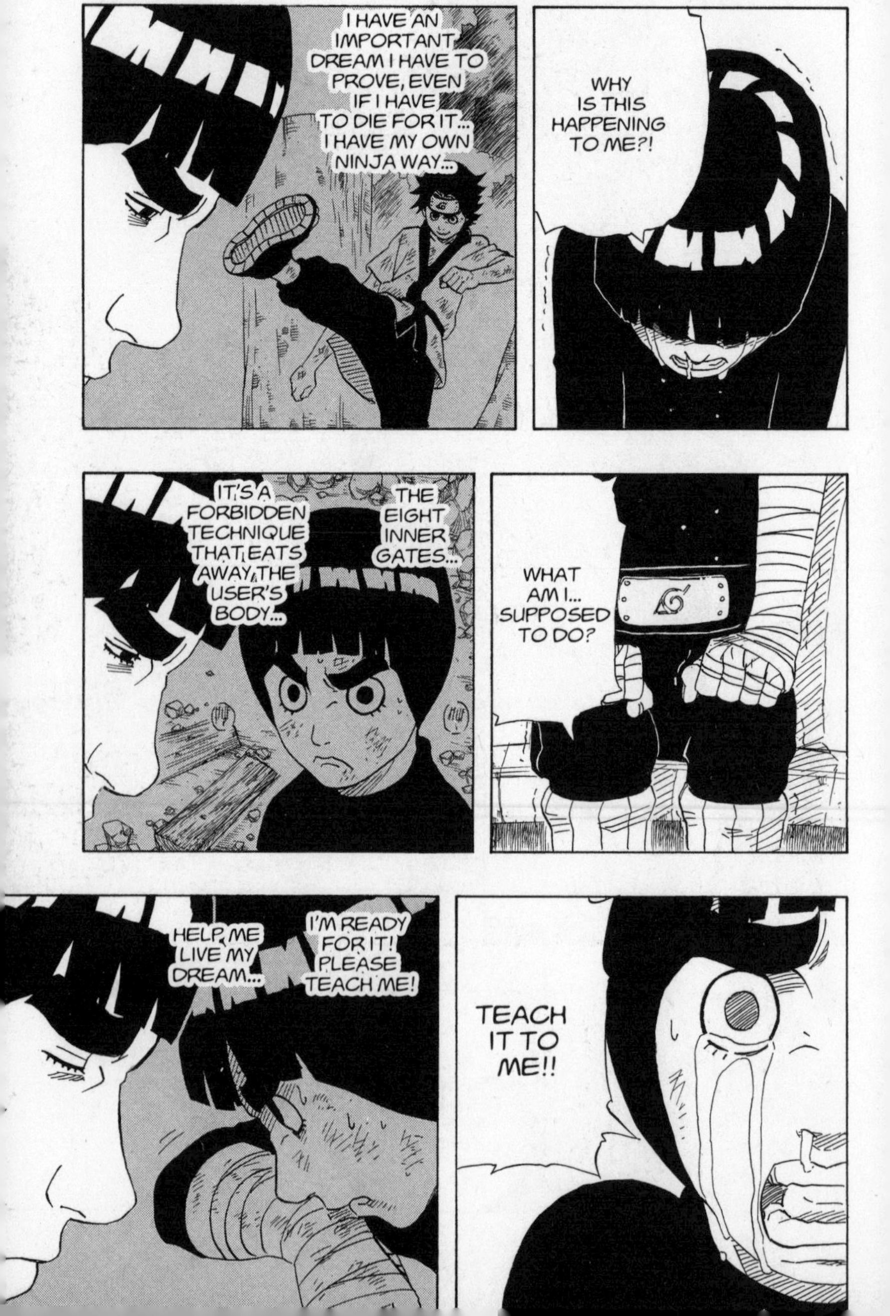

WHY IS THIS HAPPENING TO ME?!
I HAVE AN IMPORTANT DREAM I HAVE TO PROVE, EVEN IF I HAVE TO DIE FOR IT... I HAVE MY OWN NINJA WAY...
WHAT AM I... SUPPOSED TO DO?
THE EIGHT INNER GATES...
IT'S A FORBIDDEN TECHNIQUE THAT EATS AWAY THE USER'S BODY...
TEACH IT TO ME!!
I'M READY FOR IT! PLEASE TEACH ME!
HELP ME LIVE MY DREAM...

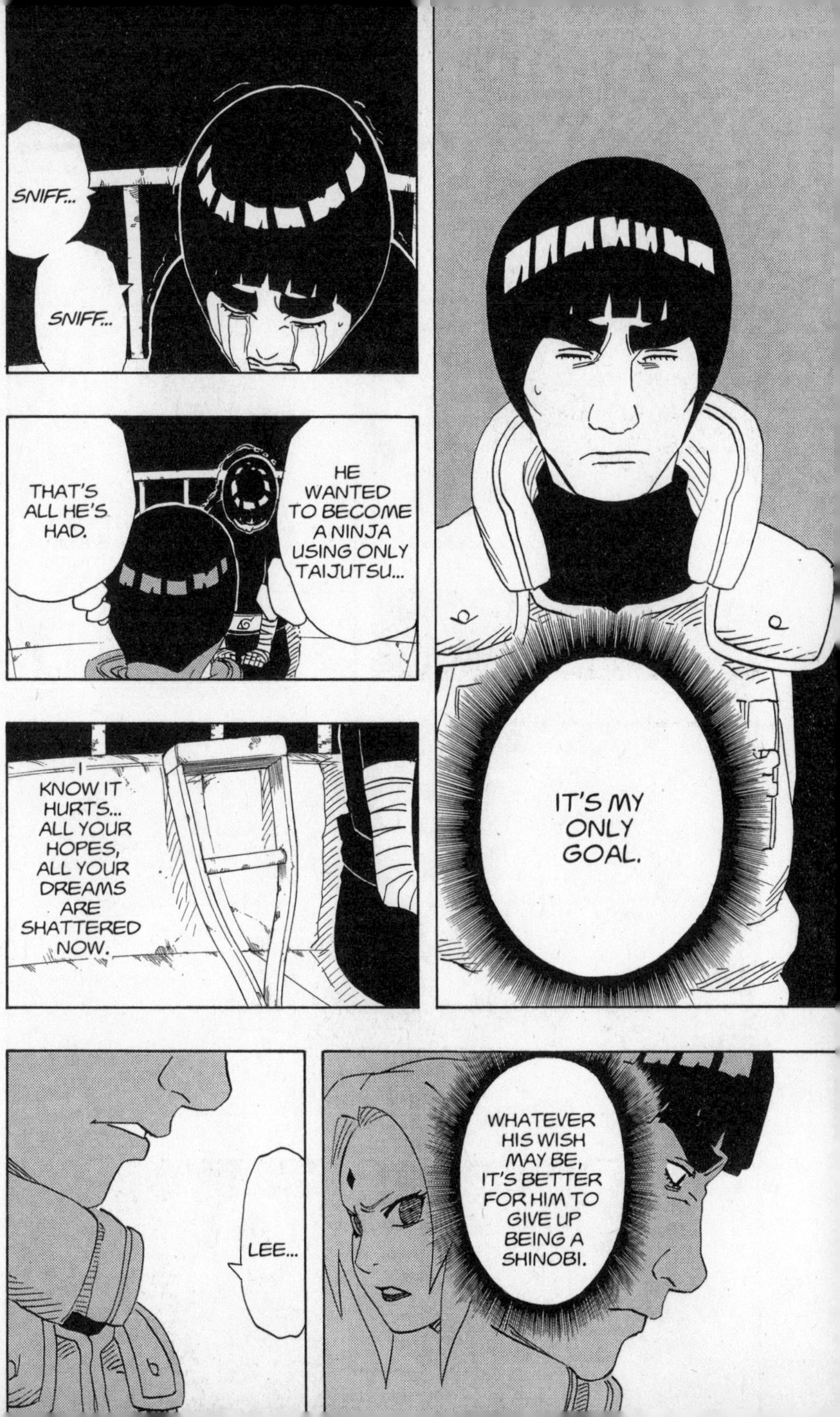
IT'S MY ONLY GOAL.
SNIFF...
SNIFF...
HE WANTED TO BECOME A NINJA USING ONLY TAIJUTSU...
THAT'S ALL HE'S HAD.
I KNOW IT HURTS... ALL YOUR HOPES, ALL YOUR DREAMS ARE SHATTERED NOW.
WHATEVER HIS WISH MAY BE, IT'S BETTER FOR HIM TO GIVE UP BEING A SHINOBI.
LEE...

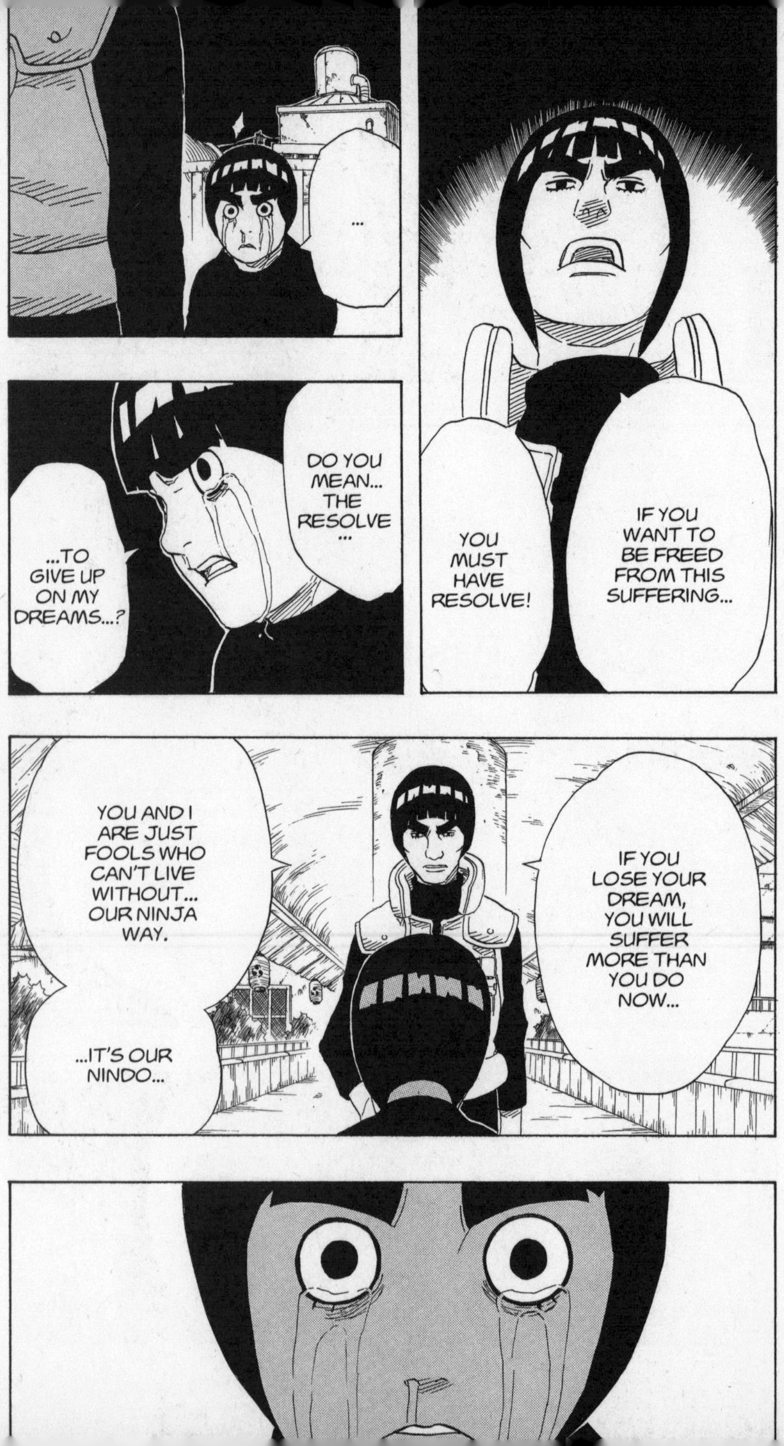
IF YOU WANT TO BE FREED FROM THIS SUFFERING...
YOU MUST HAVE RESOLVE!
...
DO YOU MEAN... THE RESOLVE ...
...TO GIVE UP ON MY DREAMS...?
IF YOU LOSE YOUR DREAM, YOU WILL SUFFER MORE THAN YOU DO NOW...
YOU AND I ARE JUST FOOLS WHO CAN'T LIVE WITHOUT... OUR NINJA WAY.
...IT'S OUR NINDO...

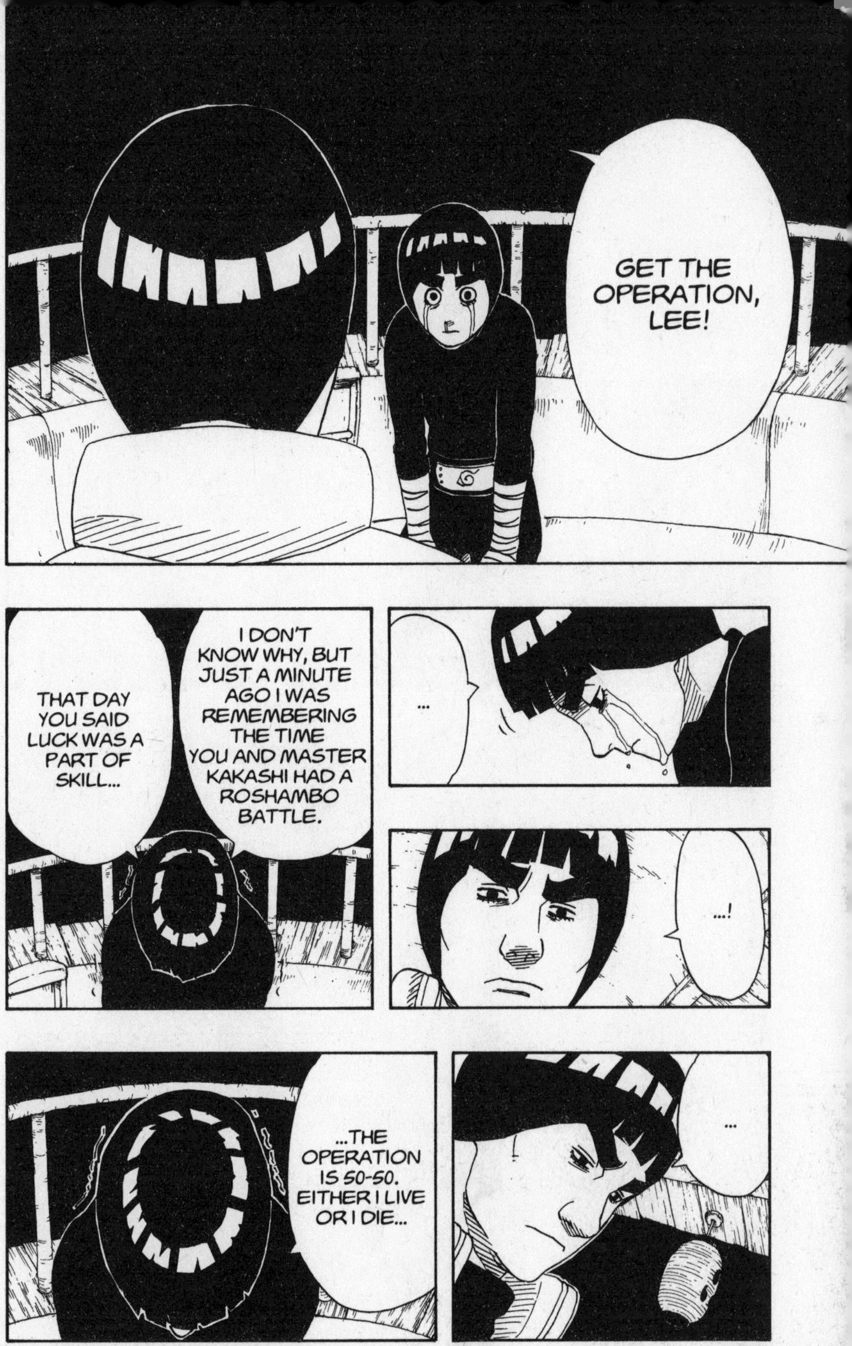

GET THE OPERATION, LEE!
...
...!
I DON'T KNOW WHY, BUT JUST A MINUTE AGO I WAS REMEMBERING THE TIME YOU AND MASTER KAKASHI HAD A ROSHAMBO BATTLE.
THAT DAY YOU SAID LUCK WAS A PART OF SKILL...
...
...THE OPERATION IS 50-50. EITHER I LIVE OR I DIE...

READ THIS WAY

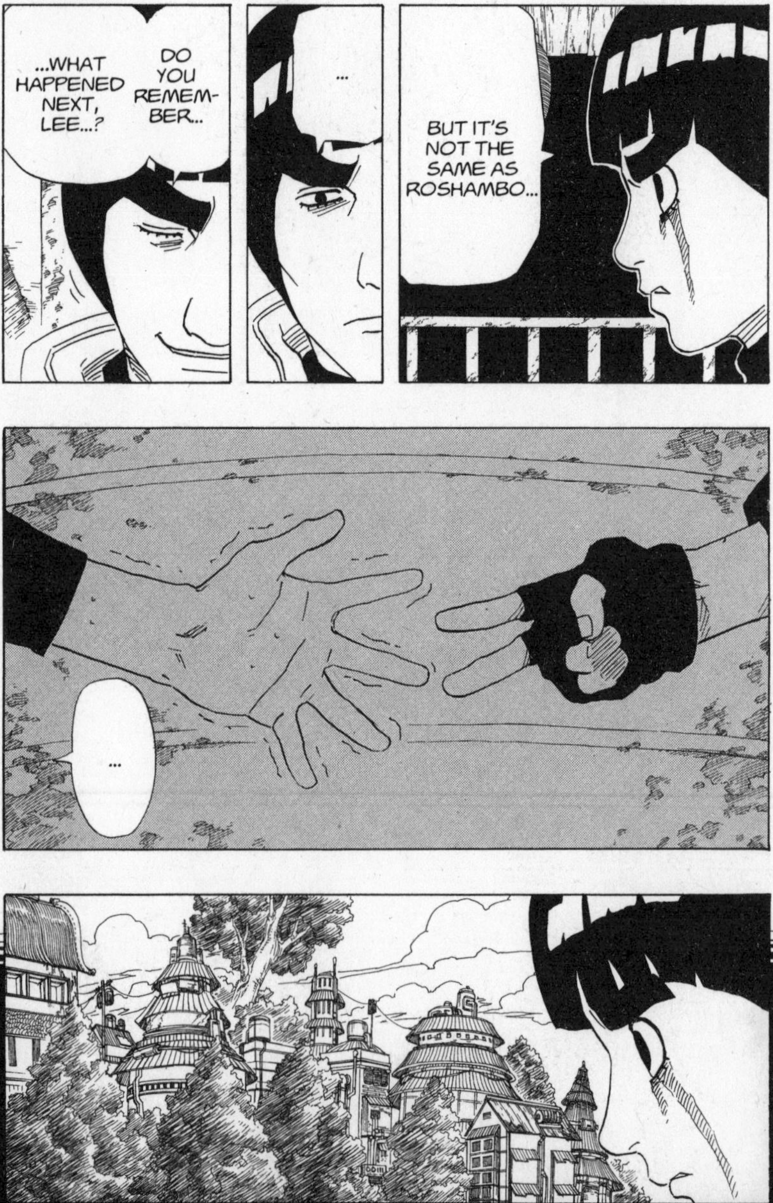
BUT IT'S NOT THE SAME AS ROSHAMBO...
...
DO YOU REMEMBER...
...WHAT HAPPENED NEXT, LEE...?
...

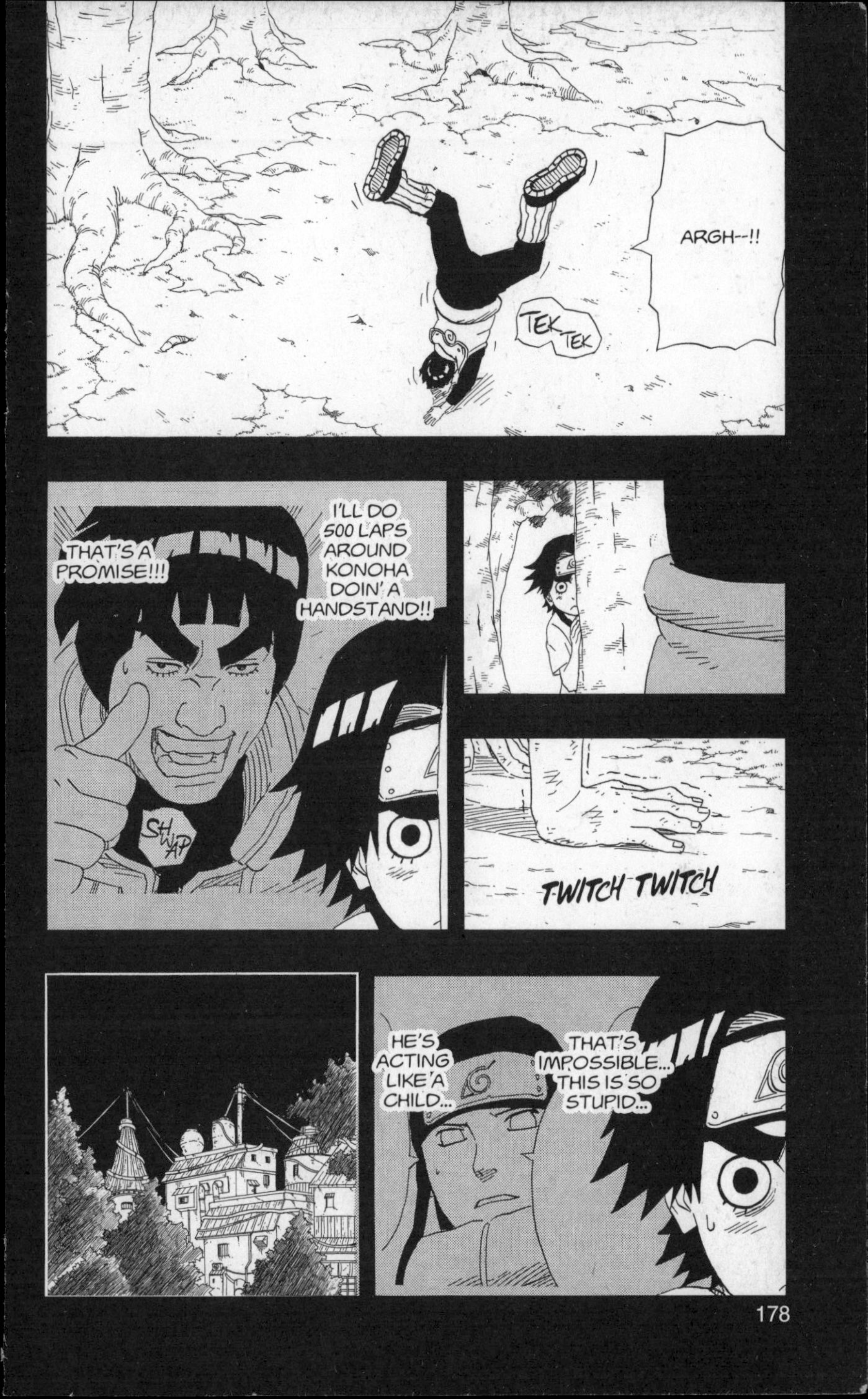
ARGH--!!
TEK TEK
TWITCH TWITCH
I'LL DO 500 LAPS AROUND KONOHA DOIN' A HANDSTAND!!
THAT'S A PROMISE!!!
SHWAP
THAT'S IMPOSSIBLE... THIS IS SO STUPID...
HE'S ACTING LIKE A CHILD...

READ THIS WAY

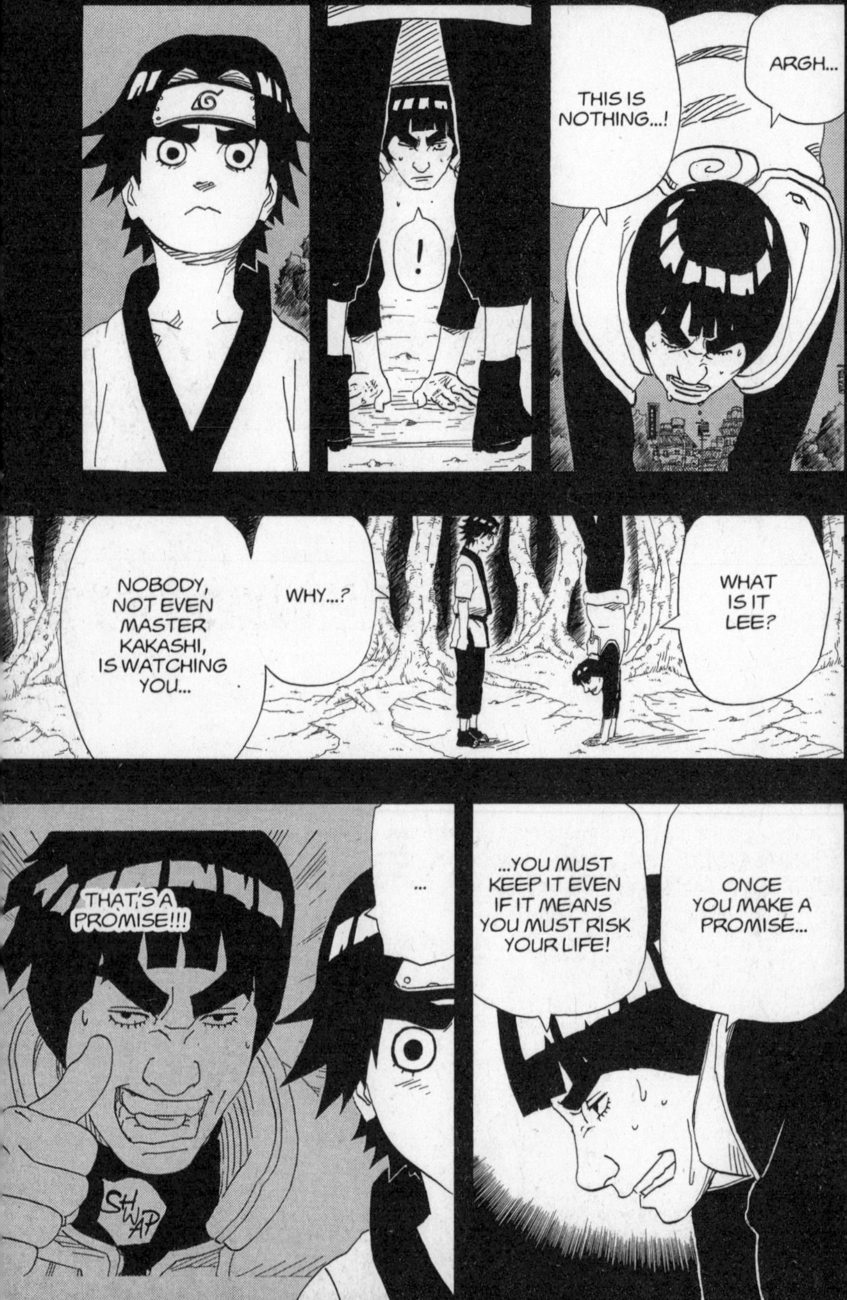
ARGH...
THIS IS NOTHING...!
!
WHAT IS IT LEE?
WHY...?
NOBODY, NOT EVEN MASTER KAKASHI, IS WATCHING YOU...
ONCE YOU MAKE A PROMISE...
...YOU MUST KEEP IT EVEN IF IT MEANS YOU MUST RISK YOUR LIFE!
...
THAT'S A PROMISE!!!
SHWAP

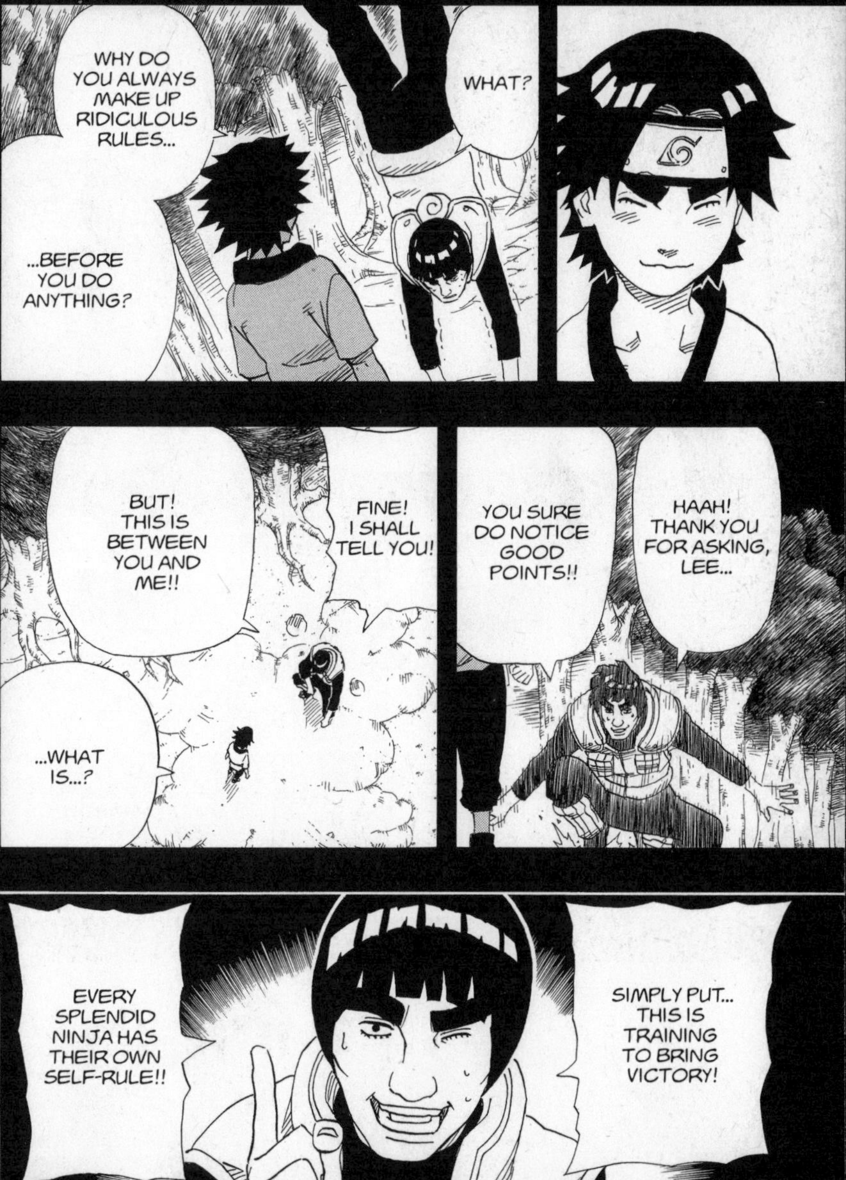
WHAT?
WHY DO YOU ALWAYS MAKE UP RIDICULOUS RULES...
...BEFORE YOU DO ANYTHING?
HAAH! THANK YOU FOR ASKING, LEE...
YOU SURE DO NOTICE GOOD POINTS!!
FINE! I SHALL TELL YOU!
BUT! THIS IS BETWEEN YOU AND ME!!
...WHAT IS...?
SIMPLY PUT... THIS IS TRAINING TO BRING VICTORY!
EVERY SPLENDID NINJA HAS THEIR OWN SELF-RULE!!

READ THIS WAY

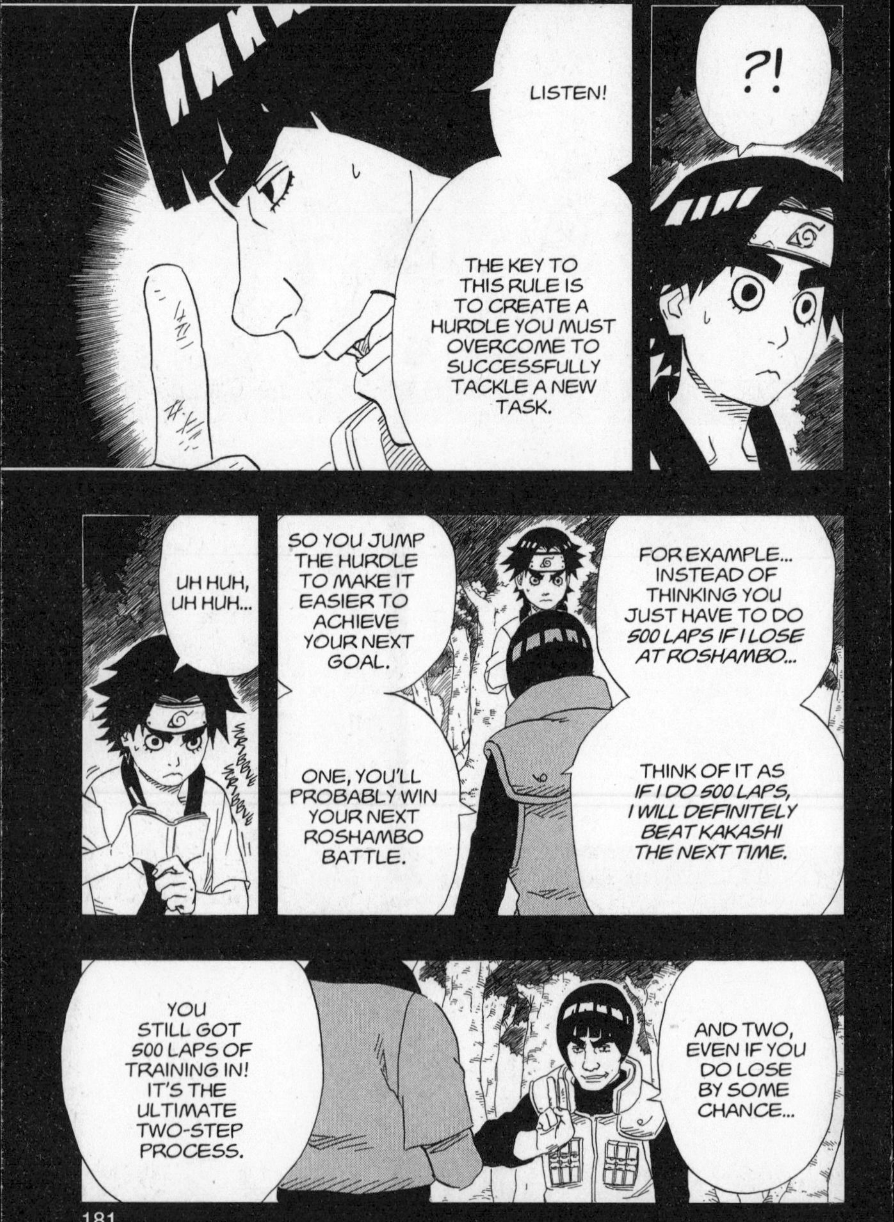

?!
LISTEN!
THE KEY TO THIS RULE IS TO CREATE A HURDLE YOU MUST OVERCOME TO SUCCESSFULLY TACKLE A NEW TASK.
FOR EXAMPLE... INSTEAD OF THINKING YOU JUST HAVE TO DO 500 LAPS IF I LOSE AT ROSHAMBO...
THINK OF IT AS IF I DO 500 LAPS, I WILL DEFINITELY BEAT KAKASHI THE NEXT TIME.
SO YOU JUMP THE HURDLE TO MAKE IT EASIER TO ACHIEVE YOUR NEXT GOAL.
ONE, YOU'LL PROBABLY WIN YOUR NEXT ROSHAMBO BATTLE.
UH HUH, UH HUH...
AND TWO, EVEN IF YOU DO LOSE BY SOME CHANCE...
YOU STILL GOT 500 LAPS OF TRAINING IN! IT'S THE ULTIMATE TWO-STEP PROCESS.

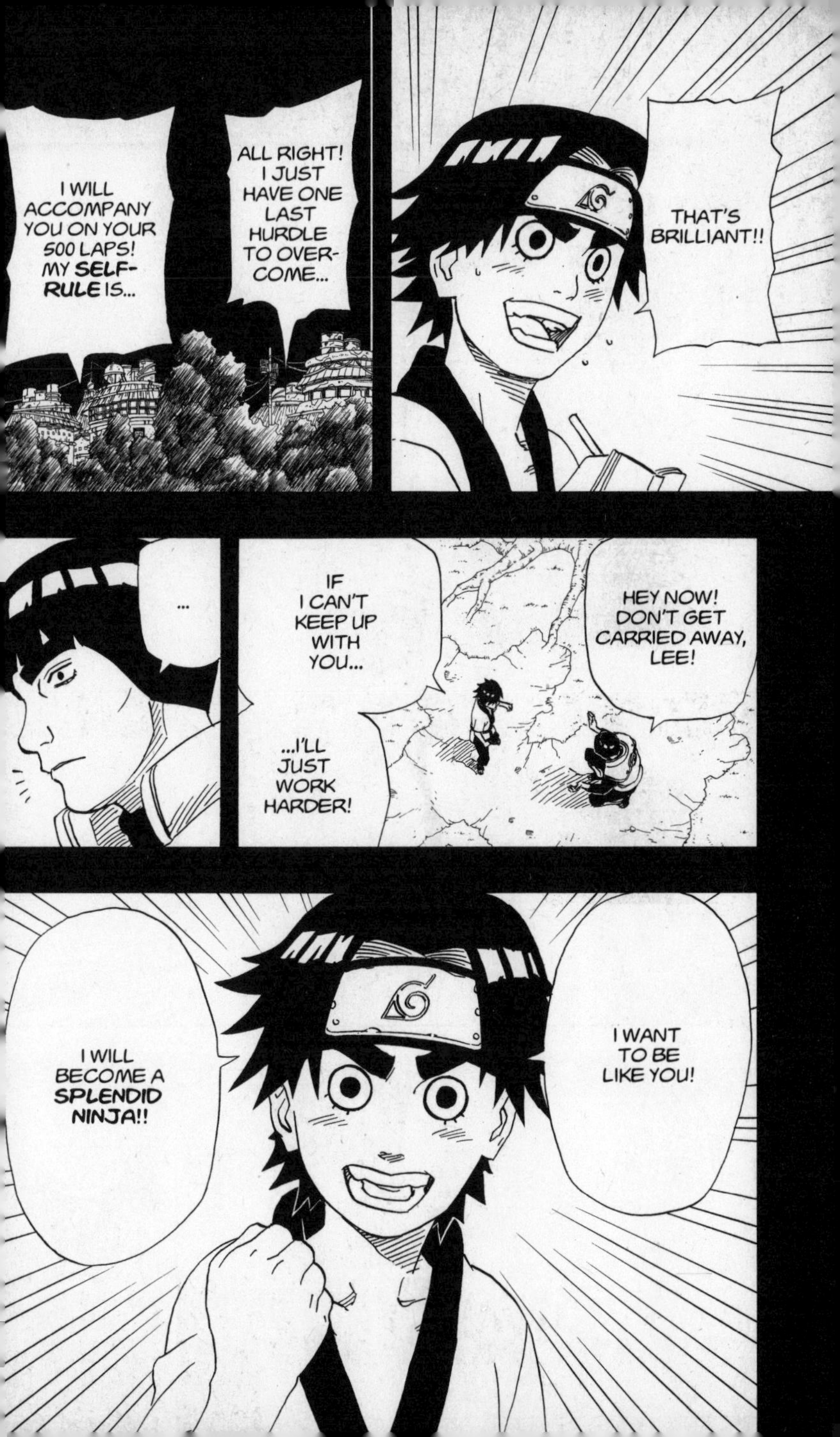
THAT'S BRILLIANT!!
ALL RIGHT! I JUST HAVE ONE LAST HURDLE TO OVER-COME...
I WILL ACCOMPANY YOU ON YOUR 500 LAPS! MY **SELF-RULE** IS...
HEY NOW! DON'T GET CARRIED AWAY, LEE!
IF I CAN'T KEEP UP WITH YOU...
...I'LL JUST WORK HARDER!
...
I WANT TO BE LIKE YOU!
I WILL BECOME A **SPLENDID** NINJA!!

READ THIS WAY

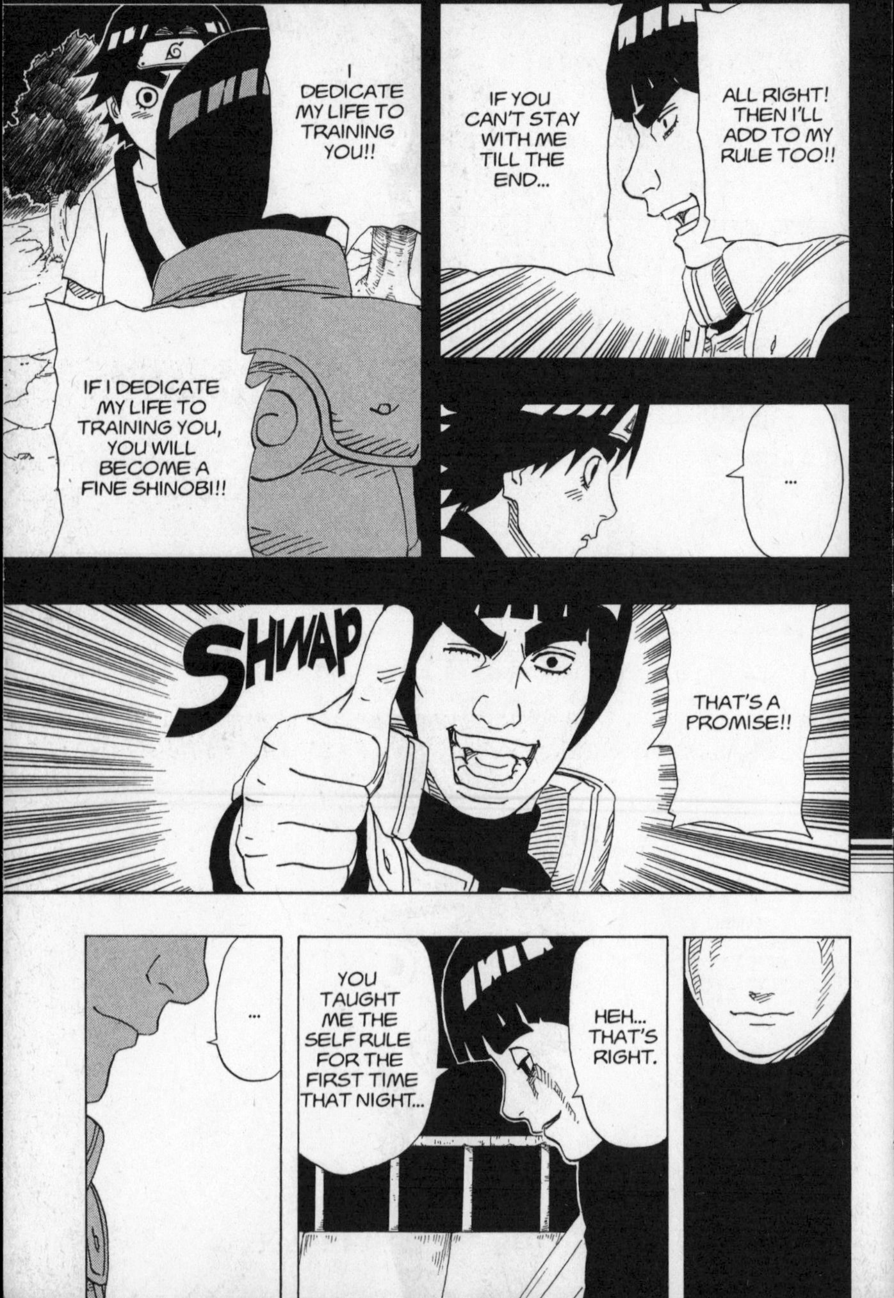
ALL RIGHT! THEN I'LL ADD TO MY RULE TOO!!
IF YOU CAN'T STAY WITH ME TILL THE END...
...
I DEDICATE MY LIFE TO TRAINING YOU!!
IF I DEDICATE MY LIFE TO TRAINING YOU, YOU WILL BECOME A FINE SHINOBI!!
...
THAT'S A PROMISE!!
SHWAP
HEH... THAT'S RIGHT.
YOU TAUGHT ME THE SELF RULE FOR THE FIRST TIME THAT NIGHT...
...

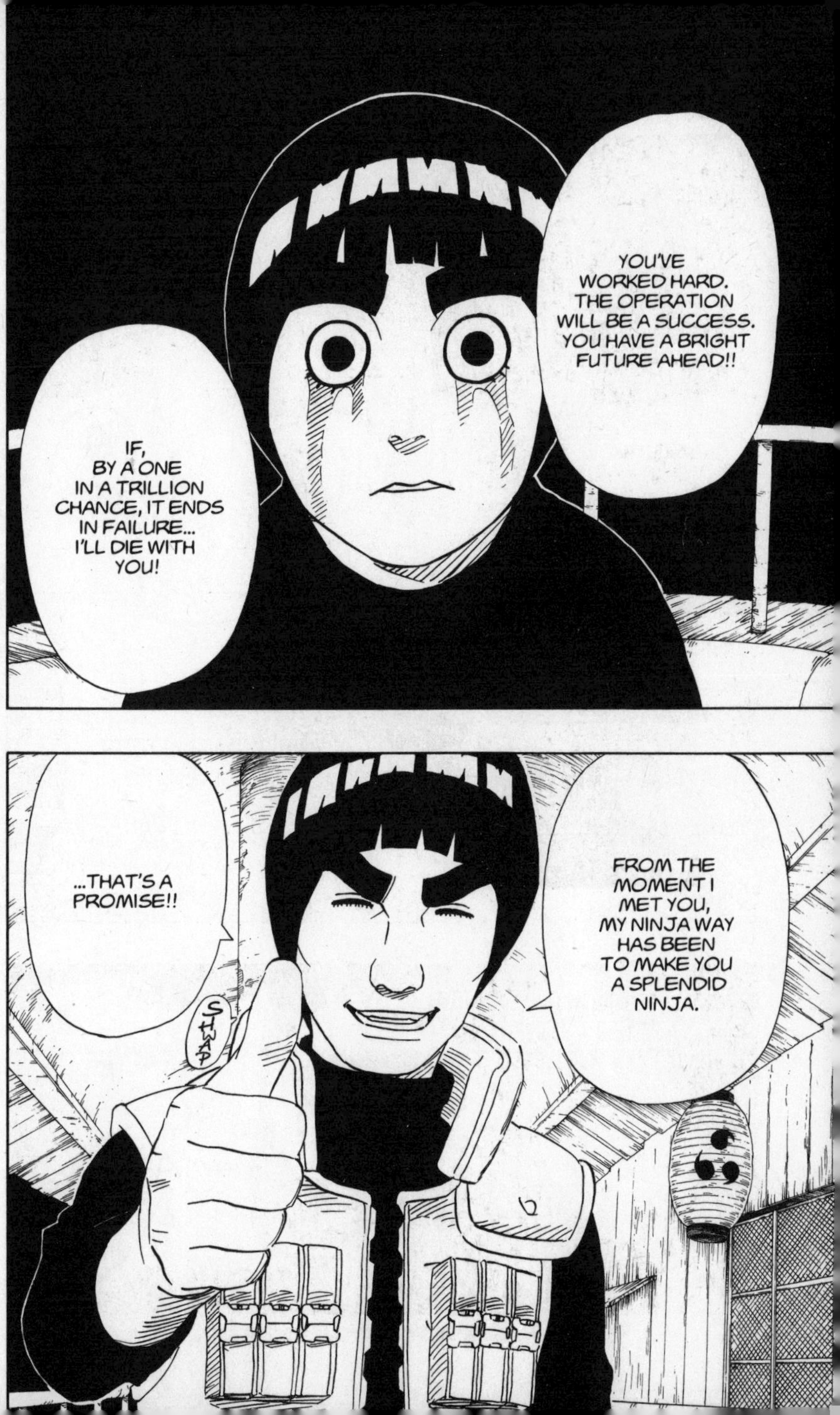
YOU'VE WORKED HARD. THE OPERATION WILL BE A SUCCESS. YOU HAVE A BRIGHT FUTURE AHEAD!!
IF, BY A ONE IN A TRILLION CHANCE, IT ENDS IN FAILURE... I'LL DIE WITH YOU!
FROM THE MOMENT I MET YOU, MY NINJA WAY HAS BEEN TO MAKE YOU A SPLENDID NINJA.
SHWAP
...THAT'S A PROMISE!!

READ THIS WAY

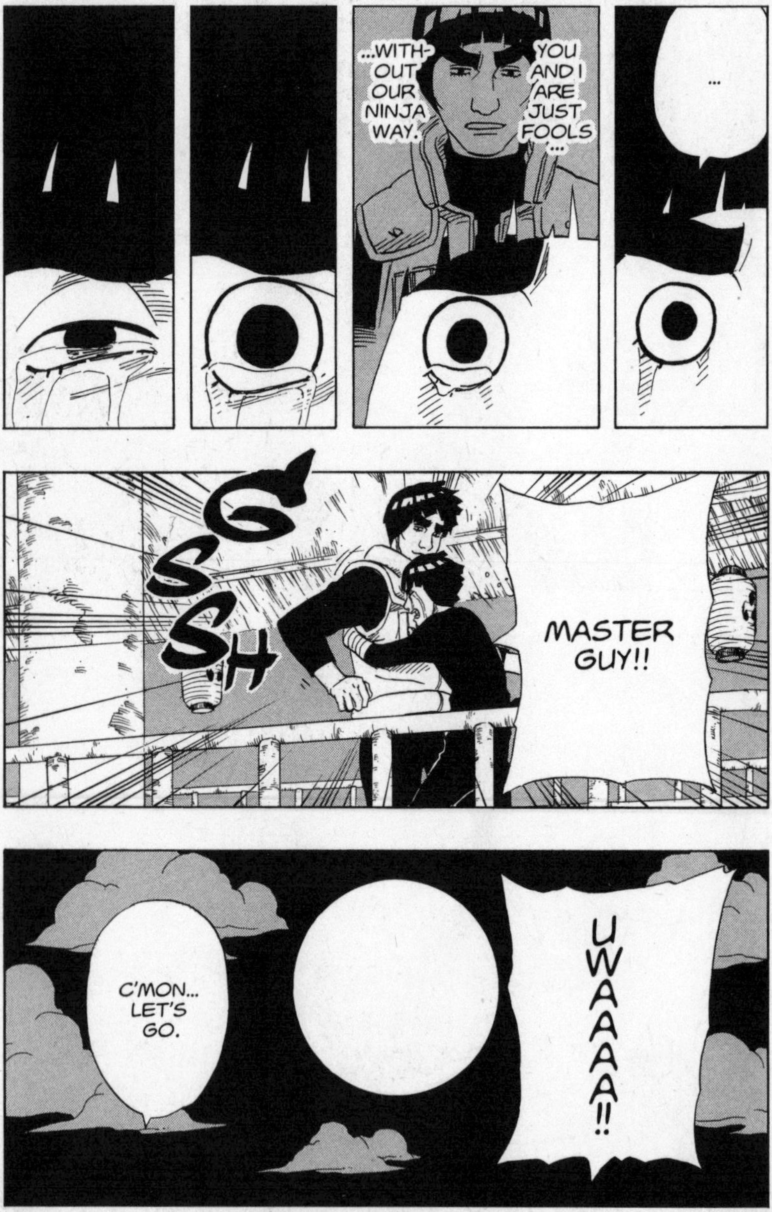
...
YOU AND I ARE JUST FOOLS...
...WITHOUT OUR NINJA WAY.
MASTER GUY!!
GSSSH
UWAAAAA!!
C'MON... LET'S GO.

TO BE CONTINUED IN *NARUTO* 21!

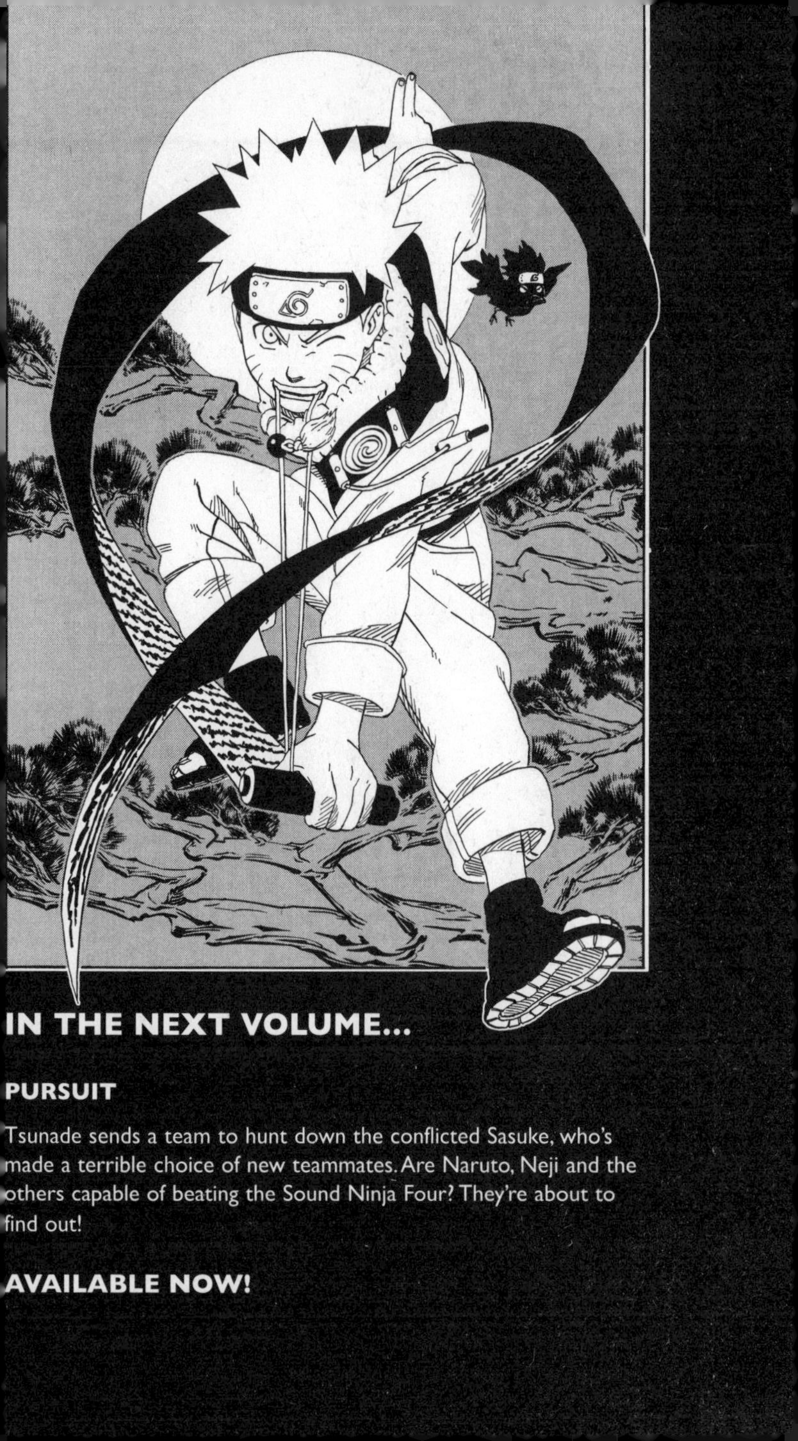

IN THE NEXT VOLUME...

PURSUIT

Tsunade sends a team to hunt down the conflicted Sasuke, who's made a terrible choice of new teammates. Are Naruto, Neji and the others capable of beating the Sound Ninja Four? They're about to find out!

AVAILABLE NOW!

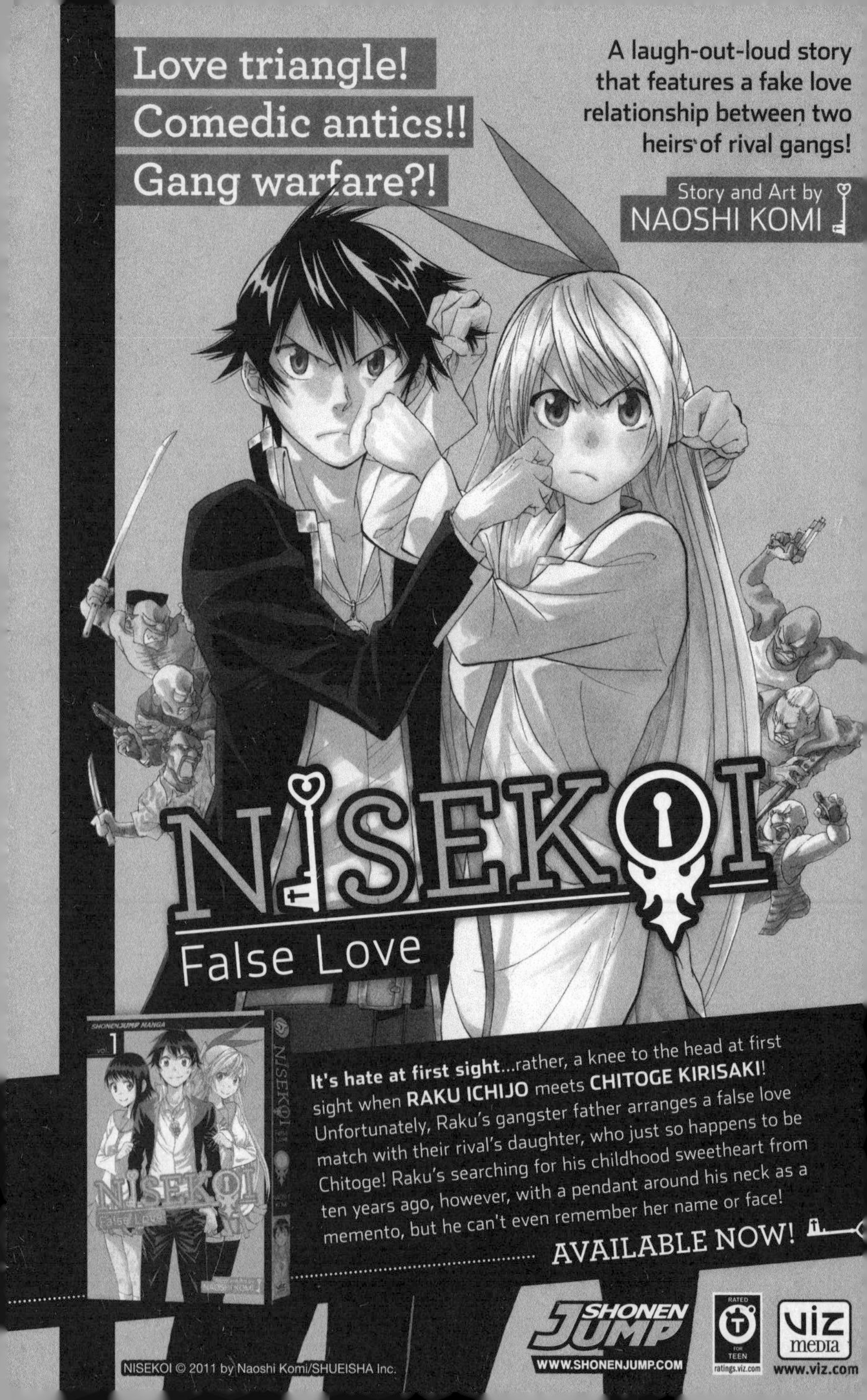
Love triangle!
Comedic antics!!
Gang warfare?!
A laugh-out-loud story that features a fake love relationship between two heirs of rival gangs!
Story and Art by
NAOSHI KOMI
NISEKOI
False Love
SHONENJUMP MANGA
vol. 1
It's hate at first sight...rather, a knee to the head at first sight when RAKU ICHIJO meets CHITOGE KIRISAKI! Unfortunately, Raku's gangster father arranges a false love match with their rival's daughter, who just so happens to be Chitoge! Raku's searching for his childhood sweetheart from ten years ago, however, with a pendant around his neck as a memento, but he can't even remember her name or face!
AVAILABLE NOW!
SHONEN JUMP
WWW.SHONENJUMP.COM
RATED T FOR TEEN
ratings.viz.com
viz media
www.viz.com
NISEKOI © 2011 by Naoshi Komi/SHUEISHA Inc.

A PREMIUM BOX SET OF THE FIRST TWO STORY ARCS OF ONE PIECE!

A PIRATE'S TREASURE FOR ANY MANGA FAN!

STORY AND ART BY EIICHIRO ODA

Comes with
EXCLUSIVE POSTER and the
ROMANCE DAWN
mini-comic!

As a child, Monkey D. Luffy dreamed of becoming King of the Pirates. But his life changed when he accidentally gained the power to stretch like rubber...at the cost of never being able to swim again! Years later, Luffy sets off in search of the "One Piece," said to be the greatest treasure in the world...

This box set includes VOLUMES 1-23, which comprise the EAST BLUE and BAROQUE WORKS story arcs.

EXCLUSIVE PREMIUMS and GREAT SAVINGS
over buying the individual volumes!

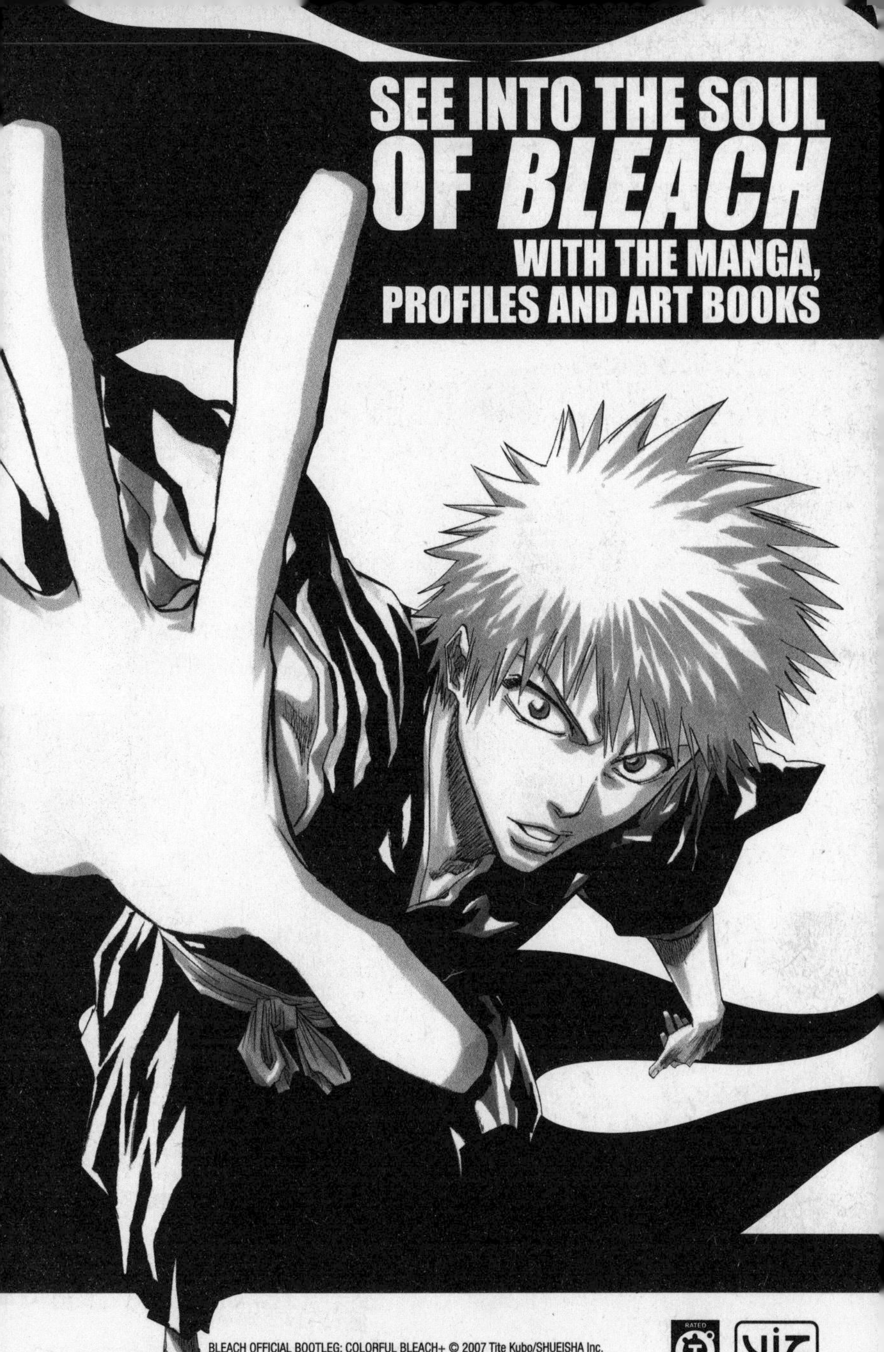
SEE INTO THE SOUL
OF *BLEACH*
WITH THE MANGA,
PROFILES AND ART BOOKS

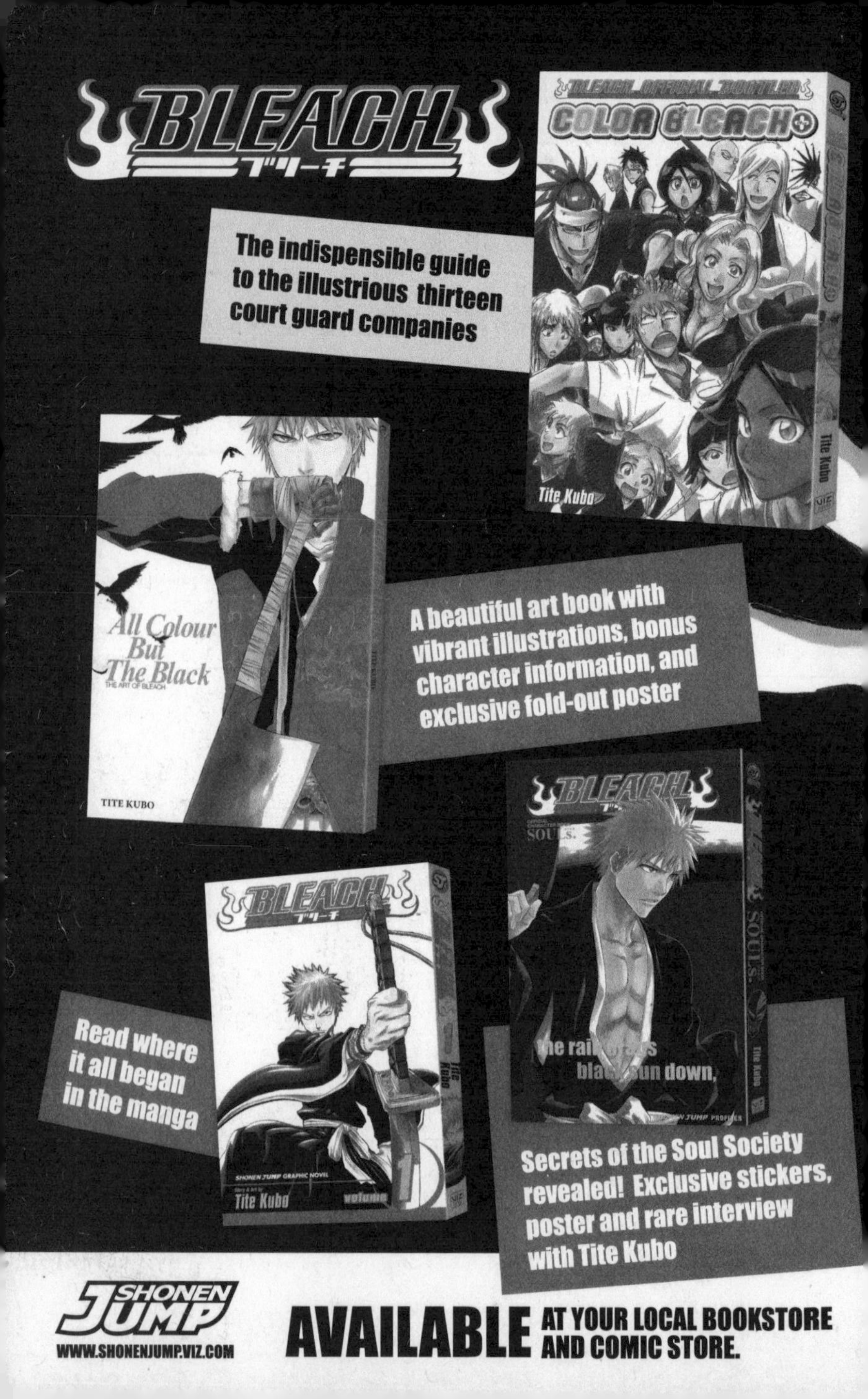

BLEACH
ブリーチ
The indispensible guide to the illustrious thirteen court guard companies
BLEACH OFFICIAL BOOTLEG
COLOR BLEACH+
Tite Kubo
All Colour But The Black
THE ART OF BLEACH
TITE KUBO
A beautiful art book with vibrant illustrations, bonus character information, and exclusive fold-out poster
BLEACH
SOULS.
Read where it all began in the manga
BLEACH
ブリーチ
SHONEN JUMP GRAPHIC NOVEL
Tite Kubo
Secrets of the Soul Society revealed! Exclusive stickers, poster and rare interview with Tite Kubo
SHONEN JUMP
WWW.SHONENJUMP.VIZ.COM
AVAILABLE AT YOUR LOCAL BOOKSTORE AND COMIC STORE.

You're Reading in the Wrong Direction!!

Whoops! Guess what? You're starting at the wrong end of the comic!

...It's true! In keeping with the original Japanese format, **Naruto** is meant to be read from right to left, starting in the upper-right corner.

Unlike English, which is read from left to right, Japanese is read from right to left, meaning that action, sound effects and word-balloon order are completely reversed...something which can make readers unfamiliar with Japanese feel pretty backwards themselves. For this reason, manga or Japanese comics published in the U.S. in English have sometimes been published "flopped"—that is, printed in exact reverse order, as though seen from the other side of a mirror.

By flopping pages, U.S. publishers can avoid confusing readers, but the compromise is not without its downside. For one thing, a character in a flopped manga series who once wore in the original Japanese version a T-shirt emblazoned with "M A Y" (as in "the merry month of") now wears one which reads "Y A M"! Additionally, many manga creators in Japan are themselves unhappy with the process, as some feel the mirror-imaging of their art alters their original intentions.

We are proud to bring you Masashi Kishimoto's **Naruto** in the original unflopped format. For now, though, turn to the other side of the book and let the ninjutsu begin...!

—Editor

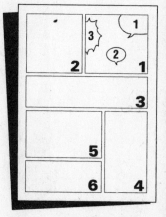

WORLD'S ~ULAR MANGA

SHONEN JUMP

NARUTO

volume **20**

Naruto is a ninja-in-training with an incorrigible knack for mischief. His wild antics amuse his teammates, but Naruto is completely serious about one thing: becoming the world's greatest ninja!

NARUTO VS. SASUKE

It's ninja vs. ninja! And Sakura is caught in the middle! With the Sound Four looming close and Lee in the hospital, all three friends hurl toward an uncertain future and find that growing up sometimes means growing apart.

www.shonenjump.com

9 USA $12.99 CAN   £6.99 UK

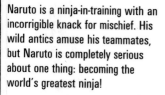

ook reads ight to left.

VIZ media

RATED
T
FOR TEEN
ratings.viz.com

ISBN-13: 978-1-4215-1655-4

50999

9 781421 516554